Computer Media and Communication
A Reader

Computer Media and Communication

A Reader

Edited by
Paul A. Mayer

OXFORD
UNIVERSITY PRESS

OXFORD
UNIVERSITY PRESS

Great Clarendon Street, Oxford ox2 6DP
Oxford University Press is a department of the University of Oxford.
It furthers the University's objective of excellence in research, scholarship,
and education by publishing worldwide in

Oxford New York

Athens Auckland Bangkok Bogotá Buenos Aires Calcutta
Cape Town Chennai Dar es Salaam Delhi Florence Hong Kong Istanbul
Karachi Kuala Lumpur Madrid Melbourne Mexico City Mumbai
Nairobi Paris São Paulo Singapore Taipei Tokyo Toronto Warsaw

and associated companies in Berlin Ibadan

Oxford is a registered trade mark of Oxford University Press
in the UK and certain other countries

Published in the United States
by Oxford University Press Inc., New York

British Library Cataloguing in Publication Data

Data available

Library of Congress Cataloging in Publication Data

Data available

ISBN 0–19–874257–6 (Pbk)

1 3 5 7 9 10 8 6 4 2

Typeset in Minion
by Jayvee, Trivandrum, India
Printed in Great Britain
on acid-free paper by
Biddles Ltd.,
Guildford & King's Lynn

Acknowledgements

FIRST AND FOREMOST, I owe a debt of gratitude to Klaus Bruhn Jensen, Associate Professor at the Department of Film and Media Studies at the University of Copenhagen, for his intellectual generosity and his keen interest in the systematic study of Computer Media. It is also a pleasure to thank Professor Brian Winston, Head of the School of Communication, Design, and Media at the University of Westminster, for his support of this volume and his many efforts to move it forward. Last but not least, I wish to extend thanks to both Fritz Saaby Pedersen, whose innumerable intellectual and philological insights are greatly appreciated, and Amelia E. Rogers, from whose enthusiasm for discussing mathematics, computing, and meaning, I have benefited greatly.

The Editor and Publisher gratefully acknowledge permission to reprint the following:

JAY DAVID BOLTER 'Topographic Writing: Hypertext and the Electronic Writing Space' from *Hypermedia and Literary Studies* edited by P. Delany and G. P. Landow (MIT Press, 1991), by permission of the author.

VANNEVAR BUSH 'As We May Think' from *Atlantic Monthly* 176 (1945), by permission of the publisher, The Atlantic Monthly.

DOUGLAS C. ENGELBART 'A Conceptual Framework for the Augmentation of Man's Intellect' from *Vistas in Information Handling* edited by Howerton and Weeks (Spartan Books, 1963), by permission of Bootstrap Institute.

NIELS OLE FINNEMANN 'Modernity Modernised: The Cultural Impact of Computerisation' from Report 50–97 *Center for Cultural Research,* Aarhus University (1997), by permission of the author.

SUSAN HERRING 'Posting in a Different Voice: Gender and Ethics in Computer-Mediated Communication' from *Philosophical Perspectives on Computer-Mediated Communication* edited by Charles Ess, © State University of New York, by permission of the State University of New York Press. All rights reserved.

JENS F. JENSEN 'Interactivity—tracking a new concept in Media and Communication Studies' newly revised and published in Danish as '"Interaktivitet": på sporet af et nyt begreb i medie- og kommunikationsvidenskaberne' from *MedieKultur* 26 (April 1997), by permission of *MedieKultur.*

KLAUS BRUHN JENSEN 'One Person, One Computer: The Social Construction of the Personal Computer' from *The Computer as Medium* edited by Peter Bøgh Andersen, Berit Holmqvist and Jens F. Jensen (Cambridge University Press, 1993), by permission of the author and the publisher.

STEVEN G. JONES 'Understanding Community in the Information Age' from *Cybersociety: Computer-Mediated Communication and Community* by Steven G. Jones (Sage Publications, 1995), by permission of the publisher.

ALAN KAY 'Computer Software', first published in *Scientific American*, 251: 3, September 1984, by permission of the publisher.

ALAN KAY AND ADELE GOLDBERG 'Personal Dynamic Media' first published in *Computer*, 10, March 1977, and amended by A. Goldberg (1988), by permission of the publisher, The Institute of Electrical and Electronic Engineers, Inc.

J. C. R. LICKLIDER 'Man-Computer Symbiosis' from *IRE Transactions on Human Factors in Electronics*, by permission of The Institute of Electrical and Electronic Engineers.

J. C. R. LICKLIDER AND ROBERT W. TAYLOR 'The Computer as a Communication Device' from *International Science and Technology* (April 1968).

DAVID MILES 'The CD-ROM Novel *Myst* and McLuhan's Fourth Law of Media: *Myst* and Its "Retrievals"' from *Journal of Communication* 46: 2 (1996), by permission of the publisher, Oxford University Press.

TED NELSON 'A New Home for the Mind' from *Datamation* (March 1982).

ALLUCQUERE ROSANNE STONE 'Will the Real Body Please Stand Up?: Boundary Stories about Virtual Cultures' from *Cyberspace: First Steps*, edited by M. Benedikt (MIT Press, 1991), by permission of the publisher.

A. M. TURING 'Computing Machinery and Intelligence' from *Mind* 59: 236 (1950), by permission of the publisher, Oxford University Press.

LANGDON WINNER 'Who Will We Be in Cyberspace?' from *The Information Society: An International Journal* 12(1) (Taylor & Francis, 1996), (*http://www.tandf.co.uk/JNLS/TIS.HTM*), by permission of the Information Society and the publisher.

Despite every effort to trace and contact copyright holders before publication this has not been possible in a few cases. If notified, the publisher will be pleased to rectify any errors or omissions at the earliest opportunity.

Contents

List of Authors   ix

Preface   xiii

Part 1: History   **1**

Introduction
From Logic Machines to the Dynabook: An Overview
of the Conceptual Development of Computer Media   3
PAUL A. MAYER

1. As We May Think   23
   VANNEVAR BUSH

2. Computing Machinery and Intelligence   37
   A. M. TURING

3. Man-Computer Symbiosis   59
   J. C. R. LICKLIDER

4. A Conceptual Framework for the Augmentation of Man's Intellect   72
   DOUGLAS C. ENGELBART

5. The Computer as a Communication Device   97
   J. C. R. LICKLIDER AND ROBERT W. TAYLOR

6. Personal Dynamic Media   111
   ALAN KAY AND ADELE GOLDBERG

7. A New Home for the Mind   120
   TED NELSON

8. Computer Software   129
   ALAN KAY

Part 2: Systematic Studies   **139**

9. Modernity Modernised—The Cultural Impact of Computerisation   141
   NIELS OLE FINNEMANN

10. 'Interactivity'—Tracking a New Concept in Media and
    Communication Studies   160
    JENS F. JENSEN

11. One Person, One Computer: The Social Construction of the
    Personal Computer   188
    KLAUS BRUHN JENSEN

12. Who Will We Be in Cyberspace?   207
    LANGDON WINNER

13. Understanding Community in the Information Age   219
    STEVEN G. JONES

14. Posting in a Different Voice: Gender and Ethics in Computer-
    Mediated Communication   241
    SUSAN HERRING

15. Will the Real Body Please Stand Up? Boundary Stories about Virtual
   Cultures   266
   ALLUCQUERE ROSANNE STONE

16. Topographic Writing: Hypertext and the Electronic Writing Space   294
   JAY DAVID BOLTER

17. The CD-ROM Novel *Myst* and McLuhan's Fourth Law of Media:
   Myst and It's 'Retrievals'   307
   DAVID MILES

18. Epilogue
   Computer Media Studies: An Emerging Field   320
   PAUL A. MAYER

   Index   337

List of Authors

JAY DAVID BOLTER, Ph.D, is Professor at the School of Literature, Communication, and Culture at the Georgia Institute of Technology. He is author of *Writing Space: The Computer, Hypertext, and the History of Writing* (Hillsdale, NJ: Lawrence Erlbaum, 1991) and *Turing's Man: Western Culture in the Computer Age* (Chapel Hill: University of North Carolina Press, 1984), as well as numerous publications on computer-related and literary topics.

VANNEVAR BUSH (1890–1974) was one of the foremost engineers in American science during the middle of the twentieth century. First as professor of Electrical Power Transmission at MIT, and later as Vice-President at MIT and Dean of the School of Engineering, he developed the Differential Analyser in the 1930s. In the 1940s Bush served as a leading scientific advisor to President Roosevelt, via a series of directorships and committee chairmanships. In this period Bush was a central figure in the development of nuclear fission and the Manhattan Project. Also in this period Bush began to lay the groundwork for the American National Science Foundation, which was formed in 1950. Bush became chairman of the MIT Corporation in 1957, a post he held until 1959.

DOUGLAS C. ENGELBART received his Ph.D in Electrical Engineering from the University of California at Berkeley. In 1957 he took a research position at the Stanford Research Institute, and in 1963 he received a grant from ARPA-IPTO to found the Augmentation Research Center (ARC). From 1977 to 1989 he was Senior Scientist at Tymeshare, Inc., and continued after McDonnell Douglas's purchase of the firm in 1984. In 1989 Engelbart founded the Bootstrap Institute. Engelbart is author of numerous articles and scientific papers, of which many are related to systems development.

NIELS OLE FINNEMANN, Dr.Phil., is Associate Professor at the Department of Information and Media Science, University of Aarhus, Aarhus, Denmark. At present he is the Director of the Centre for Cultural Research at the University of Aarhus. He has published volumes in Danish on the symbolic properties of the computer (1994), the concept of nature in literature and science (1987), the cultural influence of Social Democracy in Denmark in the twentieth century (1985), and literary modernism (1972).

ADELE GOLDBERG received her Ph.D in Information Science from the University of Chicago. She joined Xerox PARC in 1973 as a laboratory and research scientist. In 1988 she founded PARCPlace, Inc., where she was President and CEO. She left PARCPlace in 1996 and has recently founded Neometron, Inc. She is author and co-editor of volumes on SmallTalk-80 and object-oriented techniques, and editor of *A History of Personal Workstations* (New York: ACM Press, 1988).

SUSAN HERRING, Ph.D, is Associate Professor of Linguistics at the Program in Linguistics, University of Texas at Arlington. She is editor of *Computer-Mediated Communication: Linguistic, Social, and Cross-Cultural Perspectives* (Amsterdam: John Benjamins, 1996) and widely published in the area of computer mediated communication as well as topics related to discourse, grammar, and the history of Dravidian languages.

JENS F. JENSEN, Cand.Mag., is Associate Professor at the Department of Communication at Aalborg University, Aalborg, Denmark. In addition to being editor of numerous volumes in Danish concerning topics related to computer media, he is co-editor of *The Computer as Medium* (Cambridge: Cambridge University Press, 1993), and author of diverse articles treating themes related to computer media.

KLAUS BRUHN JENSEN, Ph.D, is Associate Professor at the Department for Film and Media Studies, University of Copenhagen, Copenhagen, Denmark. He is author of *The Social Semiotics of Mass Communication* (London: Routledge, 1995), editor of *News of the World: World Cultures Look at Television News* (London: Routledge, 1998), and co-editor of *A Handbook of Qualitative Methodologies For Mass Communications Research* (London: Routledge, 1991). In addition, Jensen is co-author of volumes on Danish media history and media education, as well as author of a number of articles treating themes related to audience and mass communication research.

STEVEN G. JONES, Ph.D, is Professor and Department Head of the Department of Communications at the University of Illinois at Chicago. He is editor of *Cybersociety 2.0: Revisiting Computer-Mediated Communication and Technology* (London: Sage, 1998), *Virtual Culture: Identity & Communication in Cybersociety* (London: Sage Publications, 1997), *Cybersociety: Computer Mediated Communication and Community* (London: Sage, 1995), and author of *Rock Formation: Music, Technology, and Mass Communication* (London: Sage, 1992).

ALAN KAY received his Ph.D in Computer Science from the University of Utah. After a period at the Artificial Intelligence Project at Stanford, he joined Xerox PARC as a founding principal in 1970, where he led research that resulted in a number of central developments, including the SmallTalk object-oriented development environment and the overlapping window interface. In 1980 he left PARC and was later Chief Scientist at Atari before becoming an Apple Fellow in 1984. Alan Kay is Vice-President and Disney Fellow at Walt Disney Imageering. Kay has written and lectured extensively on user-oriented computing.

J. C. R. LICKLIDER (1915–90) received his Ph.D in Psychology from the University of Rochester in 1942. Following research and lecturing positions at Swarthmore, Harvard, and MIT, in 1957 he joined Bolt, Beranek, and Newman (BBN), where among other projects he championed the idea of time-sharing. In 1962 he started the Information Processing Techniques Office (IPTO) of the American Department of Defense's Advanced Research Projects Agency (ARPA); he returned as director of IPTO in 1974. In 1967 Licklider became the director of Project MAC at MIT; now the

Laboratory for Computer Science at MIT. He remained at MIT until he retired in 1986.

PAUL A. MAYER is an Assistant Professor at the Department of Film and Media Studies at the University of Copenhagen. His research is concerned with the social semiotic analysis of computer media. His dissertation, entitled 'A Social Semiotic Analysis of Computer Media', elaborates a theoretical framework for research concerning computer media and the empirical study of their reception. He has published and lectured on themes related to the study of computer media.

DAVID MILES, Ph.D, has taught at the Department of Communication at Seton Hall University in the areas of television production, digital technologies, and multimedia design and production.

TED NELSON is Professor of Environmental Information, Keio University Shonan Fujisawa Campus, Fujisawa, Japan. He is best known for coining the terms 'hypertext' and 'hypermedia' (1965), and for the proposal of a global publishing system called Xanadu. His publications include *Computer Lib/Dream Machines* (self-published, 1974) and *Literary Machines* (self-published, 1981/1987). He has also served as editor of *Creative Computing* magazine.

ALLUCQUERE ROSANNE STONE is Associate Professor in the department of Radio-TV-Film at the University of Texas at Austin, where she studies issues related to interface, interaction, and desire. She is Director of the Advanced Communication Technologies Laboratory. She is author of *The War of Desire and Technology at the Close of the Mechanical Age* (Cambridge, Mass.: MIT Press, 1995), and is widely published in the areas of computer mediated communication, cyberspace, and on-line embodiment.

ROBERT W. TAYLOR has a Ph.D in psychology. In 1963 he joined Douglas Engelbart's Augmentation Research Center (ARC) at the Stanford Research Institute (SRI) as a programmer on the On-Line System (NLS). From 1966 to 1968 he was Director of the Information Processing Techniques Office (IPTO) of the American Department of Defense's Advanced Research Projects Agency (ARPA). In 1970, after a year at the University of Utah, he joined Xerox's Palo Alto Research Center (PARC) as Associate Manager of the Computer Science Laboratory. In 1983 he became the Director of Digital Equipment Corporation's Systems Research Center, also in Palo Alto, where he remained until he retired.

A. M. TURING FRS, OBE (1912–54) was the English mathematician who founded computer science. In 1936 he published an article in which he described an abstract device for performing all possible computations using a finite set of procedures. During World War II he developed means to break the German 'Enigma' codes, by which he is credited with helping win the Battle of the Atlantic. In the late 1940s Turing contributed to the development of leading computer designs at the National Physics Laboratory in London, and later at the University of Manchester. Also in this period Turing concerned himself with programming, neural networks, and the possibility of artificial intelligence.

LANGDON WINNER, Ph.D, is Professor of Political Science at Rensselaer Polytechnic Institute. He is a political theorist whose work focuses upon social and political issues that surround modern technological change. He is the author of *Autonomous Technology* (Cambridge, Mass.: MIT Press, 1977), a study of the idea of 'technology-out-of-control' in modern social thought, *The Whale and The Reactor: A Search for Limits in an Age of High Technology* (Chicago: University of Chicago Press, 1988), editor of *Democracy in a Technological Society* (London: Kluwer Academic Publishers, 1992), and has published more than one hundred scholarly articles.

Preface

I
N THE PAST fifty or so years the power of electronic digital computers has extended from prestigious centres of research, to government, industry, and business, and beyond to an ever-expanding range of digital consumer technologies. In the form of personal computers, appliances, consumer electronics, and large-scale infrastructure, computing plays an increasingly important, if not critical, role in many domains of everyday life. Though individual access to personal computing technology is far from uniform on a global plane, in many regions of the world computers are ordinary features in business, educational, and domestic settings. Where at one time an interest in computers and computing was considered an unusual technical pursuit, or a necessity of certain kinds of specialized work, now a basic understanding of certain computer functions and applications is compulsory for many kinds of everyday tasks. Indeed, in many parts of the world it is difficult to imagine a major organization in which computers are not employed in regular operations. In education the computer is a product of intense research that has contributed to dramatic change in the possibilities for the further creation, navigation, storage, and spread of knowledge in all fields. In domestic settings personal computers are used for entertainment, interpersonal communication, self-expression, and access to information of many kinds. Most significantly, in each of these settings computers are used not as calculating machines, but as communication technologies. Computers are being used *as media*.

The social significance of computers as media is further underscored as more and more computers are connected to local networks and the global Internet. Exemplary popular forms of computer media applications include the World Wide Web, computer games, CD-ROM reference works, e-mail, and a diverse range of applications for displaying and manipulating text, images, graphics, music, databases, and the like. The ever-increasing popularity of these and other computer media applications have manifold consequences for communication in everyday life.

Computer Media and Communication: A Reader is a collection of historical texts that trace the conceptual origins of present forms of computer media, as well as contemporary articles that demonstrate approaches to their study and analysis. Though the expression 'computer media' embraces diverse applications and hardware configurations, forms of communication in which computers play a central role share unique characteristics and a common conceptual heritage. In part, this is due to the generality of modern personal computers, which have the capacity to replicate many of the functions of other media forms, while extending significant new possibilities for expression and interaction. Seen from this perspective, the personal computer is a powerful 'metamedium'.[1] Preceding the formulation of computer as media, there is a particularly rich and fascinating history of conceptual development

---

1 Kay and Goldberg (1988), reproduced in this volume as Ch. 6.

that spans the past forty or so years. By collecting writings of early visionaries whose ideas contributed to the development of thought about computers and communication, this volume is intended to help the reader appreciate how contemporary forms of computer media evolved. Furthermore, in response to the rapid growth in the communication-related use of personal computers, contemporary scholars from diverse fields have turned attention to the description and analysis of these new media forms. Their analyses help us to understand the forms, uses, and implications of computer media. By collecting contemporary analyses, the volume is further intended to acquaint the reader with central issues surrounding current forms of computer media and their relation to meaning, communication, and culture.

Reflecting the significance of historical development and contemporary studies, the volume is organized in two Parts. The articles in Part One are illuminating, highly regarded, historically relevant texts. Many of these helped inspire the development of the computer media forms we know today; all of them offer insight into the nature of computer media and the thinking that fuelled early development. These texts are discussed in a chronology of conceptual developments that provided the foundation for contemporary understandings of computers as media. These texts are recommended for the reader who would like to understand how visionary thinkers conceived of the uses of computers that we take for granted. They help the reader gain a better sense of the trains of thought and contexts that helped shape everyday interactions with and via computers.

The articles in Part Two describe contemporary computer media while offering important analyses of their implications for culture and society. Each of these articles contributes insights concerning a specific theme related to computer media while illustrating an approach to their study. Some of these texts take their point of departure in a specific application; others discuss the social and cultural impact of computer media. Through reading these articles the reader will come to understand better the significance of these media for communication, culture, and the form of modern society.

With its emphasis on conceptual developments as well as the diversity in contemporary research, this volume is intended to offer an accessible introduction to historic highlights and central themes for the study of computer media.

PART ONE

History

Introduction
From Logic Machines to the Dynabook: An Overview of the Conceptual Development of Computer Media

Paul A. Mayer

THOUGH POPULAR USE of digital computers is a relatively new phenomenon, thought about the social uses of computing technology has a long and interesting history. As with other media forms, innovations in technology and pivotal conceptual insights have, over a long period, led to the development and social integration of computer media. One of the premises of this review is that the study of computer media requires not only systematic analyses of concepts and phenomena related to these media forms and their usage, but also an understanding of the chronology of seminal ideas and technical developments that have factored in their realization. The chronology presented here is divided into two periods of development. The first, beginning with the German philosopher Gottfried Wilhelm von Leibniz in the late seventeenth century, runs up until the middle part of the twentieth century. This period is one dominated by the development of computing technology, primarily as mechanical machines and later as electromechanical devices. Also in this period, fundamental concepts for automated computing begin to evolve, particularly in the nineteenth century. Furthermore, we see a measure of thought about the social relevance of automated computation as early as Leibniz, and again as the need for automated computing becomes more pressing during the Industrial Revolution. The period around World War II marks the transition to the second period of conceptual development. This period is characterized by increasingly interactive forms of computing. The articles collected in Part One are hallmarks of this development in that they have either been definitional for development or have explanatory value in hindsight. Many of them elaborate central ideas that contributed to the eventual realization of personal computing, the global networks, and the variety of applications and interfaces with which we are familiar today. Thus, looking back over a fascinating history, the present overview is intended to refresh the knowledge of readers who may have already encountered the material, while providing an introduction for readers to whom it is new.[1]

---

1 For further reading on the history of computers and computer media, see Bolter (1991), Goldberg (1988), Goldstine (1972), Levy (1984), Metropolis (1980/85), Nyce and Kahn (1991), Quarterman (1990), Rheingold (1985, 1991), Vallee (1982), Williams (1985), Winston (1989), Woolley (1992).

From Leibniz to the Electric Behemoths

The German philosopher Baron Gottfried Wilhelm von Leibniz (1646–1716) is credited with formulating the first comprehensive vision of the power of mechanical calculation in modern times.[2] Regarded as a universal genius, he made significant contributions as a philosopher, jurist, mathematician, logician, and diplomat. Leibniz is also known for significant improvements he made in the calculating technology of his day. He designed a device that could add and subtract accurately—overcoming the problems of previous devices.[3] For the current discussion, Leibniz is significant because he also elaborated a vision of the 'calculation' of logical propositions and other forms of reasoning.[4] Among the thinkers who advanced comprehensive philosophical systems during the Age of Reason, Leibniz envisioned a 'universal logic machine'—a logical system that would implement 'a general method in which all truths of the reason would be reduced to a kind of calculation'.[5] Discussing the significance of this system of logic, Leibniz wrote: 'Once the characteristic numbers are established for most concepts, mankind will then possess a new instrument which will enhance the capabilities of the mind to a far greater extent than optical instruments strengthen the eyes, and will supersede the microscope and telescope to the same extent that reason is superior to eyesight'.[6]

There are two significant dimensions to Leibniz's vision. The first is a universal symbolic language, a *characteristica universalis*, into which the assertions of logical and scientific discourse could be expressed. This special language of logic would accomplish two ends: first, it would be common and thereby break down language barriers, 'achieving community of thought and accelerating the circulation of new scientific ideas'.[7] Secondly, by the substitution of ideograms for phonograms of ordinary language, this system of expression would further the process of logical analysis and synthesis. The second significant dimension of Leibniz's vision is a set of rules for manipulating these systems of symbols representing assertions such that true conclusions would be drawn. This would constitute a mathematics of reasoning, or *calculus ratiocinator*. Leibniz hoped that the disputes of science, law, and logic could be settled with the help of such calculation. Speaking of Leibniz and his *characteristica universalis* in *A History of Western Philosophy*, Bertrand Russell writes:

> 'If we had it,' he says, 'we should be able to reason in metaphysics and morals in much the same way as in geometry and analysis. If controversies were to arise, there would be no more need of disputation between two philosophers than between two accountants. For it would

2   Heim (1993), 93–5.

3   Leibniz designed a device he called a stepped drum to solve partially the problem of carrying decimal places by mechanical means.

4   See Leibniz (1987).

5   Gottfried Wilhelm Leibniz, *De Arte Combinatoria* (1666). Cited in Goldstine (1972), 9.

6   Leibniz (1951), 23. Cited in Dreyfus (1972/1992), 71.

7   Lewis and Langford (1951), 5.

suffice to take their pencils in their hands, to sit down to their slates, and to say to each other . . . "Let us calculate".[8]

The relevance of Leibniz's vision lies in his desire to adapt the repetitive, rule-driven nature of a logical method to the task of simulating the human capacity of reasoning in the social world. Leibniz saw nothing sinister in this, in fact he thought it would further the progress of knowledge and the state of human affairs. As we will see below, history has witnessed many refinements and adaptations to this basic interest in uniting logic, machines, and intelligence. Though the universal machine for reasoning envisioned by Leibniz has not yet been created, one result of his thought in this area is the foundation he provided for the field of symbolic logic. George Boole (1815–64), who developed Boolean algebra, a seminal theoretical advance in this field of study, was greatly inspired by Leibniz in this regard.[9] Boole's work established the mathematics of binary logic, which is integral to the structure and operation of computers.

The nineteenth century brought a number of technical and conceptual advances in both mathematics and mechanics. Among these, the English mathematician and inventor Charles Babbage's[10] designs for the Difference and Analytic Engines are particularly relevant. The first was to become the most complex digital calculating machinery hitherto seen; the second was the first comprehensive design for a general, programmable, digital computation device, which foreshadowed the universality of modern computers. Babbage has the dubious honour of launching the first government-funded project to develop a digital, mechanical calculating machine. The Difference Engine, which was eventually subsidized by the English government, was designed to produce accurate mathematical tables of constant values. In the midst of the Industrial Revolution such tables were crucial for calculations in navigation, engineering, astronomy, and physics, as well as other scientific and non-scientific purposes. These tables were otherwise produced by hand by people called 'computers', and accuracy suffered dramatically. One of the particular promises the Difference Engine offered was to eliminate sources of inaccuracy. Designed to mechanize the method of differences,[11] the Difference Engine could calculate polynomial values and deliver the results of its calculations on a plate for printing.[12] Thus, by doing the calculation and producing the ready-to-print table, two sources of human error would be eliminated.[13] Babbage never finished this machine. However, a device built by the Swedish engineer Pehr Georg Scheutz (1785–1873) and his son Edvard, based on Babbage's design, was completed with Babbage's help and

---

[8] Bertrand Russell, *A History of Western Philosophy* (New York: Simon and Schuster, 1952), 592. Cited in Winograd (1991), 200.

[9] Goldstine (1972), 9.

[10] There is uncertainty as to Babbage's birthplace and date of birth. He was born in 1791 or 1792 and died in 1871.

[11] The method of differences is a means of using the addition and subtraction of constant differences to do more complex operations like multiplication and division.

[12] Babbage's Difference Engine was designed to calculate polynomials of degree six $a + bN + cN^2 + dN^3 + eN^4 + fN^5 + gN^6$. Goldstine (1972), 19.

[13] Williams (1985), 166 f.

displayed in London in 1854.[14] One of the reasons Babbage never built the Difference Engine himself was that an even more compelling device distracted him.

This new device, the Analytical Engine, was intended to harvest the benefits of accurate and fast calculation, without the Difference Engine's limitation of a fixed configuration. The ability to alter the configuration of the machine such that it could calculate any one of a wide range of functions on variable data is now regarded as a seminal step toward the modern conception of computing. Babbage's design illustrates two central concepts. The first of these is generality of purpose. Generality is achieved via programmability, which is the second significant concept illustrated by Babbage's design for the Analytic Engine.[15] This is also a feature of Leibniz's scheme for a system of universal logic, but Babbage found a means to implement this feature in a system for mechanical computation. As such, this design is now regarded as a conceptual predecessor of the modern computer. The design of the machine called for two sets of punched cards. The first set described the operations for completing a particular mathematical calculation. The second described the constants to which these operations were to be applied. In use, the machine would first be set up using instruction cards from a 'library' of operation cards. After this configuration phase, the machine would then be ready to calculate tables based on input values. Though the mechanics for the Analytical Engine were not possible in his time,[16] Babbage devoted great effort to working out the operation set for his machine. It was not until the early 1940s that a fully operational machine with all of the functions of Babbage's Analytical Engine was actually built.[17] Again, the critical distinctions between the Difference and Analytical Engines are generality and programmability.

The latter half of the nineteenth century brought a number of other advances in the history of computing. Many of these are technical in nature and generally changed the face of calculator technology. Most of these advances lie outside the scope of this overview; however, there is an event that deserves elaboration, primarily because of its relevance to the social significance of computing. This is the American census of 1890, the first in which an electromechanical tabulating machine was used to tabulate results and statistics. After a concept suggested by John Shaw Billings (1839–1913), Herman Hollerith (1860–1929) built the device used in 1890.[18] This machine not only expedited the census tally, but was also used to derive statistical information about a large population on a hitherto inaccessible scale. The system used a form of coding where holes representing answers to the census questionnaire were punched into cards. The cards could then be sorted and run through the tallying machine in batches. Thereby it became dramatically

14 Goldstine (1972), 15.

15 Babbage encountered the mechanics of this kind of programmability at a viewing of the Jacquard Loom (1805), which could be configured to weave different patterns via a set of cards.

16 Components of the Analytical Engine ordered by Babbage's son were delivered in 1906 and demonstrated that the design was workable. Williams (1985), 190.

17 This was a machine known as the IBM-Harvard Mark I.

18 There is significant dispute over attribution of the idea for this machine. Goldstine (1972), 67.

easier to answer aggregate questions like, 'How many people have character-istics X, Y, and Z, and what portion of the population do they represent?' The 1890 census was tallied in one month—a record time. The anticipation of this new capacity to process demographic data contributed to an expanded set of questions. Though the device employed under this census was a rela-tively simple counter, the use of the cards imparted an unparalleled power to manipulate demographic data that contributed to the new, modern image of society. The way in which these cards could be queried represents a primitive form of database analysis that provided a glimpse at the power of data-handling techniques of the future. Hollerith's tabulating machine was so successful that it provided the foundation of a commercial enterprise which became the International Business Machines Corporation in 1924.

Though Leibniz, Boole, and Babbage, among others, explored the signifi-cant conceptual groundwork for modern computers, it is in the late 1930s that development begins in earnest. Conceptual breakthroughs in math-ematical logic, the development of electromechanical and electronic tech-nologies suitable for providing the speed, reliability, and flexibility these new machines required, and the imperative necessities of war established the con-ditions for significant advances. Many individuals contributed in a myriad of ways to the trajectory of development which resulted in the first automatic, general-purpose computers. In deference to the seminal nature of the theor-etical concepts they furthered, two of these figures will discussed here.[19] The first of these is the English mathematician Alan M. Turing (1912–54); the second is the Hungarian-born polymath John von Neumann (1903–57). In overlapping efforts, Turing and von Neumann formulated concepts signifi-cant for understanding the logical nature of computers. In addition, both worked out solutions for mathematical and practical problems related to such machines, and both contributed important visions concerning the practical use and social significance of these devices. In a paper on the nature of computable numbers from 1936–7,[20] Turing demonstrated the logical possibility of an imaginary machine now known as the Universal Turing Machine, inspired in part by comments made by von Neumann.[21] As we shall see, Turing's universal machine is the first complete description of a device that has capacities similar to those which Leibniz envisioned. In his paper, Turing was addressing a theoretical problem in the area of 'undecidable propositions' that troubled mathematicians in the early part of this century. But his importance for the present discussion lies in the consequences of how he addressed this problem. To illustrate his argument Turing described a unique machine that carries out the stepwise procedures of calculation. Based on an analogy with the capacities of a human doing a calculation, Tur-ing demonstrated that certain classes of numbers are computable by an abstract automatic machine, which he called a 'computing machine'.

For the present purposes, a computing machine in Turing's sense can be seen as a device for calculating a specific value, like the value of π (to a given precision), much like Babbage's Difference Engine. The components of

---

19 Readers interested in a broader overview should see Goldstine (1972) and Williams (1985).

20 Turing (1936–7).

21 Hodges (1983/1992), 96.

Turing's computing machine include: (1) a tape (like an infinitely long scratch pad), divided into fields which can contain a symbol; (2) a means to scan and write upon the tape, one field at a time; (3) an internal 'configuration', like a small memory; and (4) a table of rules, to be followed so as to accomplish a particular sequence of operations. The action of the machine proceeds by sequentially scanning the tape for a symbol and automatically updating the internal configuration according to provided rules. In accordance with the value of the current configuration and the symbol (or lack of a symbol) on the tape, the machine continues in one of the following ways: it may write a new symbol on the current field; it may erase the symbol on the current field; it may shift the tape one field to the left or to right; it may change its configuration; or, it may stop if there is no applicable rule available.

This machine illustrates a number of significant new abstractions that have proved important for the development of electronic computers. Among these was Turing's insight that his machine represented an algorithmic process of a general nature. It would be able to work upon any form of symbolic expression that could be represented in the machine's notational system—as long as the procedure for doing so could be described in a predetermined table of rules. Thus, given this notational system, an ability to maintain an internal state, and the limited set of operations listed above, Turing concluded that, 'these operations include all those which are used in the computation of a number'.[22] The significance of this can be made clearer if one recalls that values like π are *infinite* decimals. Turing's basic machine provides a *finite* means for calculating these, given a table of rules and an infinite tape upon which to note its intermediary steps and the digits of the result. The fact that the calculation of such numbers could be expressed as a set of rules was crucial for Turing's mathematical problem.[23] However, it is the next device Turing described which is most significant.

As described, Turing's computing machine was confined to showing that one particular number was calculable given a specific set of rules, as defined by the table of rules being operated upon. However, in a conceptual leap similar to Babbage's transition from the specificity of the Difference Engine to the generality of the Analytical Engine, Turing continued in this paper to describe the nature of an even more general abstract machine. This machine, which is now know as the Universal Turing Machine, but which he called the 'the universal machine', should do not just one kind of calculation, but any computation or symbolic transformation that his computing machine could perform. This device carries out *any* formal procedure that can be carried out by a specific computing machine. Of decisive importance is the fact that such a machine is first and foremost conceived as a *logic machine* and not a calculator—it should also process symbols other than numbers. Though it can be used to do calculations, its primary characteristic is to interpret, follow, and store *symbolic* values in a systematic, consistent, and predictable manner. In certain respects Turing's universal machine has the characteristics and

---

22 Turing (1936–7), 118.

23 Hodges (1983/1992), 100 ff.

powers that Leibniz sought. And, though today this sounds quite basic, in 1936 Turing's conception of a universal machine was recognized as a significant way to think about human processes of computation, algorithmic procedures, and an automatic machine. Modern computers, with their capacity to operate on any kind of digitized information, are a realization of Turing's universal machine. Indeed, it was at this time that the right combination of concepts, technology and political will colluded to launch the construction of machines recognizable today as computers in the modern sense.

Beginning in 1936, Turing was a graduate student at Princeton University, and von Neumann was a professor at the Institute for Advanced Study. Von Neumann took an interest in Turing's universal machine,[24] and offered him an assistantship at the Institute. Turing turned this offer down to resume the fellowship he held at Cambridge, in 1938. They met again in the course of World War II, when both were working on projects related to computers and the war effort. Through a series of chance events, John von Neumann came to take Turing's universal machine a step further by providing the refinements necessary to realize Turing's vision in an actual device. Von Neumann is known as an extraordinarily colourful figure and is often referred to as 'the father of the computer'. His contributions in the areas of mathematical physics and computing played a pivotal role in the American effort during World War II. In the present context, von Neumann's improvements to the ENIAC[25] are most significant. A truly enormous machine, the ENIAC is the first electronic, digital, general-purpose, scientific computer.[26] It was built by a team lead by John Presper Eckert, Jr. and John William Mauchly at the Moore School of Electrical Engineering, at the University of Pennsylvania. The device, which was operational in the autumn of 1945, was closely followed by a series of more flexible computers. These, including the British EDSAC[27] (May 1949),[28] the EDVAC[29] (1952),[30] and the IAS[31] machine (June 1952), all share characteristics with a new type of machine design von Neumann described in a report from earlier that year.[32] These were the first computers that included a memory store capable of containing running programs and the data upon which they operated. The computer described by von Neumann is the first programmable, stored-memory, general-purpose computer—the manifestation of Turing's Universal Machine. This design defined the nature of large-scale computing well into the 1960s in what is known as 'the von Neumann architecture'. The technical details are beyond the scope of this discussion; however, the realization of a machine that can automatically process symbolic expressions is a crucial step toward

---

24 It should be noted that, unbeknownst to Turing or von Neumann, Emil L. Post published a paper describing a similar automaton in 1936. Goldstine (1972), 174.

25 Electronic Numeric Integrator and Calculator.

26 Burks (1980/1985).

27 Electronic Delay Storage Automatic Computer, Cambridge University.

28 Williams (1985), 413.

29 Electronic Discrete Variable Computer, successor to the ENIAC.

30 Williams (1985), 413.

31 Institute for Advanced Study, Princeton.

32 von Neumann (1945).

the realization of the computers and applications which are now increasingly central to modern society.

___

From Tool to Medium

While these developments were taking place in the realm of hardware, Turing, in an article from 1950, effectively inaugurated a new phase of the history of computing; a phase in which the relation between humans and computers is a driving force for development. In 'Computing Machinery and Intelligence',[33] the famous Turing Test is first described. Turing used this article to ask two thoughtful and provocative questions, namely 'Can machines think?' and 'How can we test for this?' As in his paper from 1937, a singular part of his contribution is the very manner in which he answered these questions. Sidestepping the nasty problem of defining what it means 'to think', Turing took his point of departure in an entertainment called 'the imitation game'. This game is a contest involving three people: One person, the questioner, is isolated from the other two. It is the questioner's task to guess which of the other two is a man and which is a woman. Of the two respondents, one is chosen to answer such that the questioner is led astray and makes a false identification. In Turing's adaptation, the deceiving respondent is replaced with a digital computer, and the focal question changes from discerning sex, to discerning which of the respondents is a machine. Thus, this game, which in its original form challenges the resourcefulness of three people in their abilities of detection and deception, provides a suitably complex test for the capacities of a machine to simulate human intelligence and a person's capacity to detect the machine.[34]

While repeatedly emphasizing the theoretical nature of his position, Turing went to great pains to respond to a range of possible objections to his argument—that a suitable machine could be built to play this game. And though he spoke from experience with actual computers, describing the nature of digital computation and the mathematical circumstances of the task, he was careful to point out that his answer was preliminary. Turing concluded his discussion by advancing the idea of an intelligent machine programmed to learn. This 'programme-child' should benefit from a form of education, and demonstrate its abilities by playing chess at a suitable level. The set-up of the Turing Test proved captivating, setting the agenda for research in Artificial Intelligence, and stimulating a great deal of discussion in a number of other fields, including philosophy and psychology. Chess also became a central contest for research.[35] One of the considerable products of the research that followed upon Turing's article is a deepened understanding of just how complex the mind and human intellectual capacities actually are, and how complicated programming Turing's 'child-programme' really is. Turing concluded his article by saying: 'We can only see a short distance

___

33 Turing (1950); reproduced in this volume as Ch. 2.

34 The man-machine nexus has stimulated numerous excellent treatments in science fiction. Consider Arthur C. Clarke's and Stanley Kubrick's classic *2001: A Space Odyssey*, the *Terminator* series, and Ridley Scott's *Blade Runner* to name but a few contemporary examples which illustrate the implications of worlds which also include intelligent machines.

35 A profile of research in AI is offered in the Epilogue, pp. 328–30.

ahead, but we can see plenty there that needs to be done.' Almost fifty years on, it is still fair to say that in the domain of programmed intelligence this continues to hold true.

As described above, Turing's focus with respect to this man–machine nexus is one of extensive simulation. Turing discusses a machine that thinks and learns, or at least appears to do so. In the early 1950s the advent of computers captured the popular imagination as well as the interest of the scientific community, which reacted immediately to the implications of thinking machines. This new technology seemed to promise radically new horizons for expectations about the replication of intelligence in a mechanical form. This is one of the reasons why Turing's article was so captivating, and why it provided an inspiration for early research in Artificial Intelligence (AI). AI has pursued the idea of extensive simulation of the human capabilities of logic and reason, as well as of error and irrationality. However, AI is only one way to approach the relationship between man and machine. The field of Human Computer Interaction (HCI) provides others. HCI gained strength in the 1960s as a form of development research, which applies studies in cognitive ergonomics and human factors to the design of application interfaces. One historical development effort that continues to provide inspiration for HCI is Augmentation Research.[36] This research focused on the extension of human capacities via computing technology. Instead of attempting to replicate human intelligence in a machine, or design a machine for impersonation, this research focused on applications that extend people's capacities to create, think, and communicate. This approach is very much in tune with the awareness of technologies as extensions of man's capacities which Marshall McLuhan promoted in the early 1960s.[37]

It was the description of an 'association machine' by Vannevar Bush (1890–1974) which has proven to be a particularly fertile idea for Augmentation Research, as well as for the conception of computers as media. Bush is among the engineers in early computer science to see far beyond the arithmetic applications of computational devices. Rather, Bush pursued the potential of technology for the creation, storage, and propagation of knowledge. In an article entitled 'As We May Think',[38] published in the midst of science's moral and ethical quandary after World War II, Bush argued that technologically assisted knowledge production was a humane, redemptive application of science's virtues. 'As We May Think' is relevant because of Bush's concepts for an apparatus designed to assist human thought. From his point of view, as a leading scientist of his day,[39] information overload was already overwhelming in 1945: 'There is a growing mountain of research. But there is increased evidence that we are being bogged down today as specialization extends. The investigator is staggered by the findings and conclusions

---

36 A profile of research related to HCI and Augmentation Research is offered in the Epilogue. See pp. 330–2.

37 McLuhan (1962 and 1964).

38 Bush (1945); reproduced in this volume as Chapter 1.

39 In the course of his career, Bush served in some of the highest American government positions in research and development policy, and in the period from 1941 to 1947 he was the Director of the Office of Scientific Research and Development for the Roosevelt Administration. See also Bush's entry in the List of Authors.

of thousands of other workers—conclusions that he cannot find time to grasp, much less to remember, as they appear'.[40]

The immediate impetus driving Bush's concern was the realization that the means at hand for accessing and synthesizing useful knowledge were hopelessly inadequate. He describes the situation in terms of practices a century out of date: 'The summation of human experience is being expanded at a prodigious rate, and the means we use for threading through the consequent maze to the momentarily important item is the same as was used in the days of square-rigged ships'.[41] In response to this situation Bush called for a technological intervention, and exemplifies it by describing a tool for managing knowledge. Though this description of his device is fascinating, the vital focus provided by Bush is the question of how to augment the human capacity of thought in the face of a deluge of information. Bush anticipated that such a device would do the repetitive and the mnemonic work, for which people are not so well adapted. He accepted that mental processes could not be fully duplicated by technology, and instead considered what could be learned from how we think. Thus, he sought to extend and supplement human capacities with a personal tool for working with knowledge. In pursuing this programme, Bush observed that thought is a matter of selection and combination, and that the classic, hierarchical, methods of indexing knowledge are artificial and are indeed a hindrance to this process. Rather, he advocated the idea that human thought is primarily 'associative', stating that, 'Selection by association, rather than by indexing, may yet be mechanized'. Bush's conception of association was not precisely defined in his article. Nevertheless he offers this description of the action of thought: 'With one item in its grasp, it snaps instantly to the next that is suggested by the association of thoughts, in accordance with some intricate web of trails carried by the cells of the brain.'[42] Weight is placed on immediacy, non-linear progression, and a trail of associations. The apparatus Bush envisioned would therefore be correlational in nature, able to take in vast amounts of information, process it both indexically and symbolically, and present it for viewing and further extension. On the one hand, the device would be able to deliver up the volumes in a person's library, on the other, it could be used to record and recall the user's chosen associative trail through the archive and his commentaries. As such, the device was intended as a tool for an individual user; however, there is attention given to being able to copy content from one machine into another. Originally describing this technology in terms of microfilm, dry photography, multiple projection-positions, and telautography (remote stylus control), Bush named his fantastic device the 'Memex':[43] 'It affords an immediate step . . . to associative indexing, the basic idea of which is a provision whereby any item may be caused at will to select immediately and automatically another.

---

40 This volume, Ch. 1, p. 24.

41 Ibid.

42 Ibid. 33.

43 Bush's thinking about such a device dates from the early 1930s. He updated his vision in a series of unpublished revisions to an article entitled 'Memex II' from 1959, in which he responds to various developments in technology. Discussion of the history of the Memex concept as well as a version of this later article is published in Nyce and Kahn (1991).

This is the essential feature of the memex. The process of tying two items together is the important thing.'[44]

The Memex was never built as such, but Bush's programme of research on the union of technology and human thought, and the quest for associative indexing tools, inspired a number of application development efforts which began to take shape in the 1960s. Today, we can trace the origins of concepts like hypertext and hypermedia, and the linked structure of the World Wide Web, to Bush's conception of the Memex and his vision of a combinatory and associational epistemology, implemented in a personal device designed to complement human intellectual capacities.[45]

By 1960 advances in technology and the climate of applications development had some visionaries thinking that it was conceivable that Bush's Memex might actually be implemented. At that time IBM was selling transistorized computers, and the PDP-1, the first in a series of famous Digital Equipment computers, was available. In the same year J. C. R. Licklider (1915–90), an MIT psychologist, had just published an article entitled 'Man-computer symbiosis',[46] Douglas Engelbart was seeking a home for his brand of Augmentation Research, and Theodore Holm Nelson was considering a new world of electronic publishing. First we will focus on Licklider's ideas and the work he set in motion by funding Engelbart's research. Licklider's hypothesis was that, given an effective introduction into the thought process, computing technology could be used to 'improve and facilitate thinking and problem solving in an important way'. He anticipated what he called the 'cooperative interaction between men and electronic computers', based on a division of activity where 'men will set the goals, formulate the hypotheses, determine the criteria, and perform the evaluations. Computing machines will do the routinizable work that must be done to prepare the way for insights and decisions in technical and scientific thinking.'[47]

Licklider's focus was on systems where computers and men interact in a dynamic partnership in real time. At the time he wrote, the prevailing paradigm of computer use was characterized by predetermined calculation, where a programmer composed a program, which was then compiled, and run afterwards. Responding to trends in AI research, Licklider anticipated what he considered a *symbiotic* relationship between men and computers, where the capacities of each part would contribute to deriving solutions to significant problems. As he put it, the question one may ask a computer in the future may not be 'What's the answer?', but rather, 'What's the question?' There are clear lines of comparison between Bush's and Licklider's visions; however, there are some significant differences as well. Both speak about the relationship between technology and knowledge, though they skew the relationship very differently. Bush's train of thought springs from a question concerning how we think, and progresses to an analysis of the process of human thought. The imagery of Licklider's conceptualization assumes that thought is a process that can be actively *shared* with machines: 'The hope is

44 This volume, Ch. 1, p. 34.

45 Bolter (1991), 23; Woolley (1992), 158.

46 Licklider (1960); reproduced in this volume as Ch. 3.

47 Ibid. 59.

that, in not too many years, human brains and computing machines will be coupled together very tightly, and that the resulting partnership will think as no human brain has ever thought and process data in a way not approached by the information-handling machines we know today.'[48] In Licklider's conception, the co-operative interaction of man and machine would yield a process of thought that neither could sustain alone.

Licklider provided a sketch of some of the mechanics of how this relationship should be implemented, though he acknowledged that the technology required for realizing this symbiosis was not yet at hand. Nevertheless, he elaborated upon a number of sophisticated technological requirements, most notably a visionary combination of interface systems. A 'Desk-Surface Display and Control' should provide a means whereby the user and system could 'draw graphs and pictures and . . . write notes and equations to each other on the same display surface'.[49] A 'Computer-Posted Wall Display' should be a shared viewing system for information created and posted by individual users in the same location. And finally, the system should include 'Automatic Speech Production and Recognition', such that users could interact verbally with the computer. Despite the technological barriers, Licklider pointed out: 'A multidisciplinary study group, examining future research and development problems of the Air Force, estimated that it would be 1980 before developments in artificial intelligence make it possible for machines alone to do much thinking or problem solving of military significance.' His argument was that the symbiotic system, which could be ready in five years, would be easier to build that a thinking machine, and would contribute to a period which would 'be intellectually the most creative and exciting in the history of mankind'.[50] Licklider's appraisal of the general result of real-time computing and the integration of computing in processes of thought are, with a doubt, prescient. Indeed, Licklider was given a prime opportunity to stimulate crucial advances towards fulfilling this vision via his appointment to the post of Director of the Information Processing Techniques Office (IPTO), of the American Advanced Research Projects Agency (ARPA) in 1962. In that capacity, Licklider organized funding for pioneering work done by a number of inspired researchers, including Ivan Sutherland, who invented *Sketchpad*, a landmark graphics program, and Douglas Engelbart, who established a comprehensive conceptual framework for a range of augmentation-oriented software and hardware advances.

In another article from 1968, Licklider and Robert Taylor offer an inspiring insight into the far-reaching implications of one of the early generations of Engelbart's workstation system. In 'The Computer as a Communication Device', Licklider and Taylor provide a key analysis of the conceptual terrain surrounding this new use of a computing device.[51] They begin with a dramatic statement: 'In a few years, men will be able to communicate more effectively through a machine than face to face.' This prophecy is based on a progress review meeting hosted by Engelbart and attended by Licklider and

---

48 Ibid. 60.

49 Ibid. 68.

50 Ibid. 61.

51 Licklider and Taylor (1968); reproduced in this volume as Ch. 5.

Taylor.[52] The element of the meeting that drew such enthusiastic response from the authors was a unique, new, multi-user workstation system designed to facilitate communication and interaction between a group of people. The authors concluded that they accomplished more in two days via computer than otherwise could be done in a week. From their perspective, the computer provided a superior means of externalizing what they call 'mental models'. In their words, mental models are 'the conceptual structures of abstractions formulated initially in the mind of one of the persons who would communicate'.[53] Accordingly, Licklider and Taylor explain that communication is the process of externalizing these models. In this meeting, the computer provided a means of sharing and discussing particular pieces of information. Speakers at the meeting provided materials in advance, which were displayed on multiple screens in front of which participants sat. Participants could use novel devices, 'mice', to point at items being referenced in the discussion, so all could identify the item to which a comment referred.

In addition to documenting this version of what we now call 'groupware', Licklider and Taylor go on to describe the state of on-line communities in the days of fledgling computer networks. Speaking of distributed intellectual resources, the authors identify significant contours of communities composed of geographically distant members, connected via computer, where association is based on common interests. Speaking somewhat euphorically about the nature of on-line communities, they identify four characteristics:

> First, life will be happier for the on-line individual because the people with whom one interacts most strongly will be selected more by commonality of interests and goals than by accidents of proximity. Second, communication will be more effective and productive, and therefore more enjoyable. Third, much communication and interaction will be with programs and programming models, which will be (a) highly responsive, (b) supplementary to one's own capabilities, rather than competitive, and (c) capable of representing progressively more complex ideas without necessarily displaying all the levels of their structure at the same time—and which will therefore be both challenging and rewarding. And, fourth, there will be plenty of opportunity for everyone (who can afford a console) to find his calling, for the whole world of information, with all its fields and disciplines, will be open to him, with programs ready to guide him or to help him explore.[54]

Though utopian in some regards, their prognosis is refreshing for its candid and considered optimism. The authors also identify and describe a unique 'regenerative' ethos of on-line interaction, which they attribute to the co-operative exchange of information and the extensive mutual support required for implementing and using the new computer communication links. In the wake of the popularization of the global Internet, a number of authors in the 1980s and 1990s returned to themes concerning the principles of cohesion in on-line community, the epistemological implications of new

52 Ibid. 97.
53 Ibid. 98.
54 Ibid. 110.

resources for sharing knowledge, the augmentation effect of on-line systems, and the ethics of social equality inspired by access to diverse forms of information, already identified by Licklider and Taylor in this article.[55]

In addition to these insights, there are two further elements worthy of note. The first is the authors' very focus on the computer as a communications technology, as a medium, with unique capacities for facilitating new forms of representation, new forms of communication between people, and new forms of community and culture. This theme is cogently developed in this oft-cited article, that circulated much farther than the limited distribution of conference proceedings via which much professional work in computer-related fields was communicated in the 1960s. The second significant element is that here we begin to see how visions of the uses of computer technology as comprehensive communication-related applications come into being. It is fair to say that Licklider and Taylor were enthusiasts of contemporary computer media on the eve of their realization. They were both involved in funding and working on pioneering projects which provided the first 'demos', the first evidence of the computer's vast potential as a technology for working with knowledge and extending communication. In sum, this far-reaching article elaborates a powerful set of ideas about computer-based communication and the social implications of computer networking in this period of their development.

As mentioned previously, Douglas Engelbart is a central figure in the history of augmentation research. Whereas many of those who have been discussed so far have been primarily conceptual innovators, Engelbart not only furthered a complete program for augmentation research, he also developed a number of hardware and software innovations which we still employ today. Working at the Stanford Research Institute (SRI), in 1962 Engelbart consolidated his thinking in a report entitled 'Augmenting Human Intellect: A Conceptual Framework'.[56] This document, which won him funding from Licklider shortly after its publication, sets out Engelbart's vision for how to develop computer systems to extend the human intellect: 'I had this immensely intuitive feeling that humans were going to be able to derive a great deal of capability from computer systems. I had very real images in my mind of sitting at a display console, interacting with a computer, seeing all sorts of strange symbology coming up that we could invent and develop to facilitate our thinking.'[57]

Recall that this was in a period in the development of computing technology where input and output still took place via paper tape and other asynchronous means of communication. Real-time computing was in its infancy, graphic display consoles were rare, and the dominant use of computing power was for serial calculation, not synchronous presentation, or interaction. In a remarkably short time Engelbart did much to change this. Driven by his vision of a form of personal computing, he thought of a workstation as '. . . the portal into a person's "augmented knowledge workshop"—the place in which he finds the data and tools with which he does his knowledge work,

55 For example, see Bolter, (1984); Hiltz (1984); Jones (1995), reproduced in this volume as Ch. 13; Rheingold (1985, 1991, and 1994); Winner (1996), reproduced in this volume as Ch. 12; and Woolley (1992).

56 Engelbart (1963); reproduced in this volume as Chapter 4.

57 Engelbart (1988), 214.

and through which he collaborates with similarly equipped workers'.[58] Engelbart described his idea of augmentation in terms of four domains, namely artefacts, language, methods, and training. His thesis was that change in any one of these implied change in the system as a whole, and that by concentrating the effect of the system, the result would be augmenting human intellect: 'By "augmenting human intellect" we mean increasing the capability of a man to approach a complex problem situation, to gain comprehension to suit his particular needs, and to derive solutions to problems.'[59]

Working at what became known as The Augmentation Research Center (ARC), by 1964 Engelbart and his team had a personal workstation system complete with separate graphic display, a detached keyboard, and supplementary pointing devices. This system was based on a central computer, where the user sat at a remote workstation. In attempting to cater to the needs of a user, ergonomics and ease-of-use were top priorities in the design and development of this assemblage. Realizing that navigation of a graphic screen via a keyboard was very impractical, Engelbart's team was particularly concerned with additional forms of input to supplement the keyboard. This pursuit led to the invention of the mouse as a pointing device, which is among the first examples of the concept of direct manipulation in HCI. The impressive multi-user system described by Licklider and Taylor was ready in 1967. Feeling that more attention was due to the capacities of the On-Line System, or NLS as it was called, Engelbart decided to do a live presentation at the ACM/IEEE[60] Fall Joint Computer Conference in 1968. This demonstration was a nascent multimedia extravaganza involving remote communication links and large screen projection of overlays of live video images showing screen output and operator actions. There, Engelbart's team demonstrated the system's capabilities for working with text and graphics on a precursor to the personal computer.[61] They demonstrated synchronous user input via the mouse, and most importantly, various means of structuring ideas, as in lists, as well as the direct manipulation of items displayed on screen, and interactive work with diagrams. In the period from 1969 until ARC was sold to Tymeshare, Inc. in 1977, the NLS project implemented a number of concepts and technologies that we now take for granted as obvious elements of interactive personal computing. These include windowing, mail software, networking support, an administrative software package, a document management system, an integrated help system, multi-user collaboration, modem support, a document oriented file system, remote access, printing support, and enhanced graphics support. Thus, in 1975 Engelbart's team had a prototype system for what we now take to be normal elements of computer media. In sum, Engelbart elaborated and pursued a contemporary programme for the integration of computing power and human intelligence. In so doing, he made Licklider's vision of man-computer symbiosis concrete and inspired a number of innovators who went on to participate in designing the products

---

58 Ibid. 187.

59 This volume, p. 72.

60 These are the acronyms of two prominent professional organizations in computing and engineering: The Association for Computing Machinery and The Institute of Electrical and Electronics Engineers.

61 Engelbart (1988).

of the personal computer revolution which really got under way in the late 1970s.

In addition to the sites of prestigious, government-funded projects, the 1960s also gave rise to visionaries from other quarters. Ted Nelson, and his approach to the computer as a device of radical cultural change, comparable to the Gutenberg press, is noteworthy among these. As engineers, Licklider and Engelbart strove to work with the limits of the technologies available to them. Ted Nelson was less pragmatic. In 1960 Nelson announced the end of the book by 1962, and claimed that the software to accomplish this feat could be written in six months.[62] His vision of a universal, egalitarian, 'pay-as-you-go', electronic document publishing system,[63] known by the fortuitous name of Xanadu, has not been fully realized.[64] Nevertheless, in his prodigious efforts to promote an idea perhaps before its time, Nelson is credited with inventing the expressions 'hypertext' and 'hypermedia'.[65] Were it built, the Xanadu system would represent an advanced, multi-user, network-based version of Bush's Memex. Like Memex, Xanadu was designed to be a kind of content repository and authoring system. However, the Xanadu concept supported multiple users who could access and create links between information in the archive. Information in the Xanadu system was not limited to the page or file level, but reached down to word and paragraph level. Xanadu would serve document elements and provide a means for the creation of new ones. And therewith, the idea is that by linking information new meaning would be made: 'These links are the key to the Xanadu concept, since it is through links, through the creation of structures within a vast, shapeless mass of information, that Xanadu creates new meanings and interpretations that would be inaccessible using conventional methods of information storage.'[66] Nelson foresaw that the nature of representation would change in an on-line Xanadu information and knowledge system. Authors and readers would have much greater freedom in terms of access to information, as well as more flexible means for clarifying and elaborating their ideas. Furthermore, such a system would require new models for information economics and ownership of intellectual rights. The significant historical point is that Bush's concept of linked paths of information yielded fruit, and, with the evangelical help of Nelson, among others, it inspired a new way of organizing information and meaning in a highly flexible manner. Though there have been many popular hypermedia authoring systems, the World Wide Web is the premier global implementation of this dynamic media form. Though the Web utilizes structural principles that differ significantly from those of Xanadu, it nevertheless displays interactive elements and a fertile form of non-linearity. This is an epic achievement: 'With the development of interactive computing, [the] classic author/reader distinction is looking less and less valid. Nicholas Negroponte's prediction that "Prime time will become my time" expresses the hope that technology can

62 Woolley (1992), 158.

63 See Nelson (1982); reproduced in this volume as Ch. 7.

64 Wolf (1995).

65 Bolter (1991), 23.

66 Woolley (1992), 159.

destroy the tyranny of Biblical authority.'[67] Though oft berated by Xanadu die-hards as coarse and clumsy, the World Wide Web is the most extensive implementation of a global-scale, dynamic, hyper-linked database to date.

By the beginning of the 1970s there were a number of other pioneering efforts that contributed to the development of personal computer media. The Xerox Palo Alto Research Center (PARC) is particularly important in this regard. The famous Alto (1972–80) and Star 8010 (1979–81) personal workstations were products of the commercial development research done at PARC. These systems eventually inspired a host of hardware and software products which came to the market in the 1980s, including the Apple Lisa (1983) and Macintosh (1984) consumer computers, and their operating systems which featured a graphic user interface (GUI). The Alto was based on a concept for a small computer system called the 'reactive engine' described by Alan Kay in his Ph.D dissertation from 1969. Alto was intended to be a system that would 'provide a complete work environment for its user, including text and graphics manipulation, computing and communications capability'.[68] It is particularly significant that the user is seen as entering into a communication environment in relation to his personal computer. This device is one that creates a context for communicative action. The user enters into communication with the device, and expresses him- or herself via the device. Furthermore, there was the idea that the device should be a powerful, inexpensive system that would fuel a revolution in the spread of programming: 'millions of people will write nontrivial programs, and hundreds of thousands will try to sell them . . . Almost everyone who uses a pencil will use a computer, and although most people will not do any serious programming, almost everyone will be a potential customer for serious programs of some kind.'[69] The Alto's designers anticipated that this type of device would have a consequential cultural impact. It would change the way we get things done, enhance our freedom of expression, generally increase effectiveness, and improve our access to knowledge and information. This was to be accomplished by implementing 'personal distributed computing' via a combination of hardware and software that provided features for editing, managing, and sharing a variety of types of common resources. The Alto system, which included a windowed, graphical operating system, mouse support, and other interface enhancements, eventually implemented a distributed computing model based on servers to manage shared resources. These resources included printers, shared files, and means of communication between users. Major innovations came from the Alto project: advanced GUI windowing systems, the Ethernet[70] local area networking (LAN) standard, laser printers, and significant concepts for programming, editing, and illustration software.[71]

Beyond being a testbed for research and development, the Alto was a component in a larger conceptual development called the Dynabook.[72] Kay,

67 Ibid. 153.

68 Thacker (1988), 270.

69 Lampson (1972). Cited in Thacker (1988), 271.

70 Ethernet is one of the major networking standards in use today.

71 Lampson (1988).

72 The Alto is also referred to as 'the interim Dynabook'.

who was hired by PARC and worked on the development of the Alto, was interested in a further set of refinements to the concept of personal computing. The Dynabook was conceived as a 'personal dynamic medium the size of a notebook . . . which could be owned by everyone and could have the power to handle virtually all of its owner's information-related needs'.[73] The Alto served as a temporary hardware base for exploring and programming the Dynabook's functionality. In conjunction with this project, a prototype object-oriented programming system, called Smalltalk, was developed by Kay to support dynamic text, graphics, music, and simulation applications, which were the core of the Dynabook concept of personal media. In a description of the conceptual significance of the Dynabook system from 1977, Alan Kay and Adele Goldberg explain that the system is based on the metaphor of a musical instrument, which provides flexibility, resolution, and response. The system is described as a

> self-contained knowledge manipulator in a portable package the size and shape of an ordinary notebook . . . [with] enough power to outrace your sense of sight and hearing, enough capacity to store for later retrieval thousands of page-equivalents of reference materials, poems, letters, recipes, records, drawings, animations, musical scores, waveforms, dynamic simulations, and anything else you would like to remember and change.[74]

Goldberg and Kay, working at the PARC Learning Research Group, chose to develop the Dynabook system with children as a focal user community. They found that children were capable of serious programming and that representation of programming abstractions and the means to manipulate these visually provided significant inspiration. Goldberg and Kay report that their user group loved their work with the system:

> The interactive nature of the dialogue, the fact that *they* are in control, the feeling that they are doing *real* things rather than playing with toys or working out 'assigned' problems, the pictorial and auditory nature of their results, all contribute a tremendous sense of accomplishment to their existence. Their attention spans are measured in hours rather than minutes.[75]

Goldberg and Kay also found that children were demanding. They required more from the system in terms of immediacy, which translated into the need for more computational power and higher communication bandwidth. Goldberg and Kay's choice of children as a user group only reflected a portion of vision for the Dynabook. In their description they conceive of the Dynabook as a *metamedium*, or a technology with the broadest capabilities to simulate and expand upon the functionality and power of other forms of mediated expression. The Dynabook was designed to be flexible in the sense of supporting a wide range of expression, as well as in the sense that one

---

73 Kay and Goldberg (1988); reproduced in this volume as Ch. 6, p. 111.

74 Ibid. 112.

75 Ibid. 113.

would be able to develop tools and patterns of use which would suit one's own needs. Thus, for example, a musician and an accountant might have needs of significantly different types, which would result in the use of different programs and data types. The Dynabook should be able to accommodate this, as a general, open, flexible personal medium.

In the Dynabook concept we see a culmination of many generations of thinking about computational machines and human intellect. The Dynabook represents an inspiring realization of Leibniz's generality of symbolic representation, Babbage and Turing's functional universality, Bush's individuality of representation, as well as Licklider and Engelbart's integration of intellect and communication. Furthermore, the Dynabook design, with its explicit focus on the computer as a medium for personal expression, reference, and communication, defined a number of important standards for education, personal computing, as well as hardware and software functionality, many of which have only been partially implemented today.

References   JAY DAVID BOLTER, *Writing Space: The Computer, Hypertext, and the History of Writing* (Hillsdale, NJ: Lawrence Erlbaum, 1991).

—— *Turing's Man: Western Culture in the Computer Age* (Chapel Hill: University of North Carolina Press, 1984).

ARTHUR W. BURKS, 'From ENIAC to the Stored-Program Computer: Two Revolutions in Computers', in *A History of Computing in the Twentieth Century: A Collection of Essays with Introductory Essay and Indexes*, eds. N. Metropolis, J. Howlett, and Gian-Carlo Rota (London: Academic Press, 1980/1985), 311–44.

VANNEVAR BUSH, 'As We May Think,' *Atlantic Monthly*, 176 (1945), 101–8.

HUBERT L. DREYFUS, *What Computers Still Can't Do: A Critique of Artificial Reason* (Cambridge, Mass.: MIT Press, 1979/1992).

DOUGLAS C. ENGELBART, 'A Conceptual Framework for the Augmentation of Man's Intellect', in *The Augmentation of Man's Intellect by Machine*, eds. Howerton and Weeks. Vistas in Information, Vol. 1 Handling (Washington, DC: Spartan Books, 1963), pp. 1–27.

—— 'The Augmented Knowledge Workshop', in *A History of Personal Workstations*, ed. Adele Goldberg, *ACM Press History Series* (New York: ACM Press, 1988), 187–232.

HERMAN H. GOLDSTINE, *The Computer from Pascal to von Neumann* (Princeton, NJ: Princeton University Press, 1972).

MICHAEL HEIM, *The Metaphysics of Virtual Reality* (New York and Oxford: Oxford University Press, 1993).

STARR ROXANNE HILTZ, *Online Communities: A Case Study of the Office of the Future* (Norwood, NJ: Ablex Publishing Corporation, 1984).

ANDREW HODGES, *Alan Turing: The Enigma* (London: Vintage, 1983/1992).

STEVEN G. JONES, 'Understanding Community in the Information Age', in *Cybersociety: Computer Mediated Communication and Community*, ed. Steven G. Jones (London: Sage, 1995), pp. 10–35.

ALAN KAY and ADELE GOLDBERG, 'Personal Dynamic Media', in *A History of Personal Workstations*, ed. Adele Goldberg, *ACM Press History Series* (New York: ACM Press, 1988), 254–63.

BUTLER W. LAMPSON, 'Guest Editorial', *Software—Practice and Experience*, 2 (1972), 195–6.

BUTLER W. LAMPSON, 'Personal Distributed Computing: The Alto and Ethernet Software', in *A History of Personal Workstations*, ed. Adele Goldberg, *ACM Press History Series* (New York: ACM Press, 1988), 293–335.

STEVEN LEVY, *Hackers: Heroes of the Computer Revolution* (Harmondsworth: Penguin Books, 1984).

GOTTFRIED WILHELM LEIBNIZ, *Selections*, ed. Philip Weiner (New York: Scribner, 1951).

—— 'Thought, Signs and the Foundations of Logic,' in *Leibniz. Language, Signs and Thought*, ed. Marcelo Dascal, *Foundations of Semiotics* (Amsterdam: John Benjamins Publishing Company, 1987), 10, pp. 181–8.

CLARENCE IRVING LEWIS and HAROLD LANGFORD COOPER, Symbolic Logic (New York: Dover Publications, Inc., 1951).

JOHN C. R. LICKLIDER, 'Man-Computer Symbiosis', *IRE Transactions on Human Factors in Electronics*, HFE-1, March (1960), 4–11.

—— and ROBERT W. TAYLOR, 'The Computer as a Communication Device', *International Science and Technology* (April 1968), 21–31.

MARSHALL MCLUHAN, *The Gutenberg Galaxy* (Toronto: University of Toronto Press, 1962).

—— *Understanding Media: The Extensions of Man*, 2nd edn. (New York: New American Library, 1964).

TED NELSON, 'A New Home for the Mind', *Datamation* (28 March 1982), 169, 171, 174, 178, 180.

JAMES M. NYCE and PAUL KAHN, eds., *From Memex to Hypertext: Vannevar Bush and the Mind's Machine* (London: Academic Press, Inc., 1991).

JOHN S. QUARTERMAN, *The Matrix: Computer Networks and Conferencing Systems Worldwide* (Bedford, Mass.: Digital Press, 1990).

HOWARD RHEINGOLD, *Tools For Thought: The People and Ideas behind the Next Computer Revolution* (New York: Simon & Schuster, 1985).

—— *Virtual Reality* (New York: Simon & Schuster, 1991).

—— *The Virtual Community: Surfing the Internet* (London: Minerva, 1994).

CHARLES P. THACKER, 'Personal Distributed Computing: The Alto and Ethernet Hardware,' in *A History of Personal Workstations*, ed. Adele Goldberg, *ACM Press History Series* (New York: ACM Press, 1988), 267–89.

ALAN M. TURING, 'On Computable Numbers—With an Application to the Entscheidungs Problem', in *The Undecidable: Basic Papers On Undecidable Propositions, Unsolvable Problems and Computable Functions*, ed. Martin Davis (New York: Raven Press, 1965), 116–51.

—— 'Computing Machinery and Intelligence', *Mind*, 59, 236 (1950), 433–60.

JACQUES VALLEE, *The Network Revolution: Confessions of a Computer Scientist* (Berkeley: And/Or Press, 1982).

JOHN L. VON NEUMANN, 'First Draft of a Report on the EDVAC', Moore School of Engineering, University of Pennsylvania, Philadelphia, Pa., 30 June 1945.

TERRY WINOGRAD, 'Thinking Machines: Can There Be? Are We?', in *The Boundaries of Humanity: Humans, Animals, Machines*, eds. James J. Sheenan and Morton Sosna (Berkeley: University of California Press, 1991), 198–223.

MICHAEL R. WILLIAMS, *A History of Computing Technology*, Prentice-Hall Series in Computational Mathematics (Englewood Cliffs, NJ: Prentice-Hall, Inc., 1985).

LANGDON WINNER, 'Who Will We Be in Cyberspace?', *The Information Society*, 12 (1996), 63–72.

GARY WOLF, 'The Curse of Xanadu', *Wired Magazine*, 3.06 (June 1995).

BRIAN WINSTON, *Media Technology and Society: A History: From the Telegraph to the Internet* (London: Routledge, 1998).

BENJAMIN WOOLLEY, *Virtual Worlds: A Journey in Hype and Hyperreality* (Harmondsworth: Penguin Books, 1992).

1

As We May Think

Vannevar Bush

In this article from 1945 Vannevar Bush describes his conception of a personal machine for the navigation of vast quantities of information. Responding to what Bush identifies as the associational nature of human thought, this device, called the Memex, should provide a means for viewing texts, linking information, and attaching annotations. As described in this article, Bush's idea of this machine for augmenting human intellectual capacities was a significant source of inspiration in the development of personal computing and hypertext.

THIS HAS NOT been a scientist's war; it has been a war in which all have had a part. The scientists, burying their old professional competition in the demand of a common cause, have shared greatly and learned much. It has been exhilarating to work in effective partnership. Now, for many, this appears to be approaching an end. What are the scientists to do next?

For the biologists, and particularly for the medical scientists, there can be little indecision, for their war work has hardly required them to leave the old paths. Many indeed have been able to carry on their war research in their familiar peacetime laboratories. Their objectives remain much the same.

It is the physicists who have been thrown most violently off stride, who have left academic pursuits for the making of strange destructive gadgets, who have had to devise new methods for their unanticipated assignments. They have done their part on the devices that made it possible to turn back the enemy. They have worked in combined effort with the physicists of our allies. They have felt within themselves the stir of achievement. They have been part of a great team. Now, as peace approaches, one asks where they will find objectives worthy of their best.

1   Of what lasting benefit has been man's use of science and of the new instruments which his research brought into existence? First, they have increased his control of his material environment. They have improved his food, his clothing, his shelter; they have increased his security and released him partly from the bondage of bare existence. They have given him increased knowledge of his own biological processes so that he has had a progressive freedom

from disease and an increased span of life. They are illuminating the interactions of his physiological and psychological functions, giving the promise of an improved mental health.

Science has provided the swiftest communication between individuals; it has provided a record of ideas and has enabled man to manipulate and to make extracts from that record so that knowledge evolves and endures throughout the life of a race rather than that of an individual.

There is a growing mountain of research. But there is increased evidence that we are being bogged down today as specialization extends. The investigator is staggered by the findings and conclusions of thousands of other workers—conclusions which he cannot find time to grasp, much less to remember, as they appear. Yet specialization becomes increasingly necessary for progress, and the effort to bridge between disciplines is correspondingly superficial.

Professionally our methods of transmitting and reviewing the results of research are generations old and by now are totally inadequate for their purpose. If the aggregate time spent in writing scholarly works and in reading them could be evaluated, the ratio between these amounts of time might well be startling. Those who conscientiously attempt to keep abreast of current thought, even in restricted fields, by close and continuous reading might well shy away from an examination calculated to show how much of the previous month's efforts could be produced on call. Mendel's concept of the laws of genetics was lost to the world for a generation because his publication did not reach the few who were capable of grasping and extending it; and this sort of catastrophe is undoubtedly being repeated all about us, as truly significant attainments become lost in the mass of the inconsequential.

The difficulty seems to be, not so much that we publish unduly in view of the extent and variety of present-day interests, but rather that publication has been extended far beyond our present ability to make real use of the record. The summation of human experience is being expanded at a prodigious rate, and the means we use for threading through the consequent maze to the momentarily important item is the same as was used in the days of square-rigged ships.

But there are signs of a change as new and powerful instrumentalities come into use. Photocells capable of seeing things in a physical sense, advanced photography which can record what is seen or even what is not, thermionic tubes capable of controlling potent forces under the guidance of less power than a mosquito uses to vibrate his wings, cathode ray tubes rendering visible an occurrence so brief that by comparison a microsecond is a long time, relay combinations which will carry out involved sequences of movements more reliably than any human operator and thousands of times as fast—there are plenty of mechanical aids with which to effect a transformation in scientific records.

Two centuries ago Leibnitz invented a calculating machine which embodied most of the essential features of recent keyboard devices, but it could not then come into use. The economics of the situation were against it: the labor involved in constructing it, before the days of mass production, exceeded the labor to be saved by its use, since all it could accomplish could be duplicated by sufficient use of pencil and paper. Moreover, it would have been subject to frequent breakdown, so that it could not have been depended upon; for at that time and long after, complexity and unreliability were synonymous.

Babbage, even with remarkably generous support for his time, could not produce his great arithmetical machine. His idea was sound enough, but construction and maintenance costs were then too heavy. Had a Pharaoh been given detailed and explicit designs of an automobile, and had he understood them completely, it would have taxed the resources of his kingdom to have fashioned the thousands of parts for a single car, and that car would have broken down on the first trip to Giza.

Machines with interchangeable parts can now be constructed with great economy of effort. In spite of much complexity, they perform reliably. Witness the humble typewriter, or the movie camera, or the automobile. Electrical contacts have ceased to stick when thoroughly understood. Note the automatic telephone exchange, which has hundreds of thousands of such contacts, and yet is reliable. A spider web of metal, sealed in a thin glass container, a wire heated to brilliant glow, in short, the thermionic tube of radio sets, is made by the hundred million, tossed about in packages, plugged into sockets—and it works! Its gossamer parts, the precise location and alignment involved in its construction, would have occupied a master craftsman of the guild for months; now it is built for thirty cents. The world has arrived at an age of cheap complex devices of great reliability; and something is bound to come of it.

2 A record, if it is to be useful to science, must be continuously extended, it must be stored, and above all it must be consulted. Today we make the record conventionally by writing and photography, followed by printing; but we also record on film, on wax disks, and on magnetic wires. Even if utterly new recording procedures do not appear, these present ones are certainly in the process of modification and extension.

Certainly progress in photography is not going to stop. Faster material and lenses, more automatic cameras, finer-grained sensitive compounds to allow an extension of the mini-camera idea, are all imminent. Let us project this trend ahead to a logical, if not inevitable, outcome. The camera hound of the future wears on his forehead a lump a little larger than a walnut. It takes pictures 3 millimeters square, later to be projected or enlarged, which after all involves only a factor of 10 beyond present practice. The lens is of universal focus, down to any distance accommodated by the unaided eye, simply because it is of short focal length. There is a built-in photocell on the walnut such as we now have on at least one camera, which automatically adjusts exposure for a wide range of illumination. There is film in the walnut for a hundred exposures, and the spring for operating its shutter and shifting its film is wound once for all when the film clip is inserted. It produces its result in full color. It may well be stereoscopic, and record with two spaced glass eyes, for striking improvements in stereoscopic technique are just around the corner.

The cord which trips its shutter may reach down a man's sleeve within easy reach of his fingers. A quick squeeze, and the picture is taken. On a pair of ordinary glasses is a square of fine lines near the top of one lens, where it is out of the way of ordinary vision. When an object appears in that square, it is lined up for its picture. As the scientist of the future moves about the laboratory or the field, every time he looks at something worthy of the record, he trips the shutter and in it goes, without even an audible click. Is this all fantastic? The only fantastic thing about it is the idea of making as many pictures as would result from its use.

Will there be dry photography? It is already here in two forms. When Brady made his Civil War pictures, the plate had to be wet at the time of exposure. Now it has to be wet during development instead. In the future perhaps it need not be wetted at all. There have long been films impregnated with diazo dyes which form a picture without development, so that it is already there as soon as the camera has been operated. An exposure to ammonia gas destroys the unexposed dye, and the picture can then be taken out into the light and examined. The process is now slow, but someone may speed it up, and it has no grain difficulties such as now keep photographic researchers busy. Often it would be advantageous to be able to snap the camera and to look at the picture immediately.

Another process now in use is also slow, and more or less clumsy. For fifty years impregnated papers have been used which turn dark at every point where an electrical contact touches them, by reason of the chemical change thus produced in an iodine compound included in the paper. They have been used to make records, for a pointer moving across them can leave a trail behind. If the electrical potential on the pointer is varied as it moves, the line becomes light or dark in accordance with the potential.

This scheme is now used in facsimile transmission. The pointer draws a set of closely spaced lines across the paper one after another. As it moves, its potential is varied in accordance with a varying current received over wires from a distant station, where these variations are produced by a photocell which is similarly scanning a picture. At every instant the darkness of the line being drawn is made equal to the darkness of the point on the picture being observed by the photocell. Thus, when the whole picture has been covered, a replica appears at the receiving end.

A scene itself can be just as well looked over line by line by the photocell in this way as can a photograph of the scene. This whole apparatus constitutes a camera, with the added feature, which can be dispensed with if desired, of making its picture at a distance. It is slow, and the picture is poor in detail. Still, it does give another process of dry photography, in which the picture is finished as soon as it is taken.

It would be a brave man who would predict that such a process will always remain clumsy, slow, and faulty in detail. Television equipment today transmits sixteen reasonably good pictures a second, and it involves only two essential differences from the process described above. For one, the record is made by a moving beam of electrons rather than a moving pointer, for the reason that an electron beam can sweep across the picture very rapidly indeed. The other difference involves merely the use of a screen which glows momentarily when the electrons hit, rather than a chemically treated paper or film which is permanently altered. This speed is necessary in television, for motion pictures rather than stills are the object.

Use chemically treated film in place of the glowing screen, allow the apparatus to transmit one picture only rather than a succession, and a rapid camera for dry photography results. The treated film needs to be far faster in action than present examples, but it probably could be. More serious is the objection that this scheme would involve putting the film inside a vacuum chamber, for electron beams behave normally only in such a rarefied environment. This difficulty could be avoided by allowing the electron beam to play on one side of a partition, and by pressing the film against the other side, if this partition were such as to allow the electrons to go through perpendicular to its surface, and to prevent them from spreading out sideways. Such partitions, in crude form, could certainly be constructed, and they will hardly hold up the general development.

Like dry photography, microphotography still has a long way to go. The basic scheme of reducing the size of the record, and examining it by projection rather than directly, has possibilities too great to be ignored. The combination of optical projection and photographic reduction is already producing some results in microfilm for scholarly purposes, and the potentialities are highly suggestive. Today, with microfilm, reductions by a linear factor of 20 can be employed and still produce full clarity when the material is re-enlarged for examination. The limits are set by the graininess of the film, the excellence of the optical system, and the efficiency of the light sources employed. All of these are rapidly improving.

Assume a linear ration of 100 for future use. Consider film of the same thickness as paper, although thinner film will certainly be usable. Even under these conditions there would be a total factor of 10,000 between the bulk of the ordinary record on books, and its microfilm replica. The *Encyclopedia Britannica* could be reduced to the volume of a matchbox. A library of a million volumes could be compressed into one end of a desk. If the human race has produced since the invention of movable type a total record, in the form of magazines, newspapers, books, tracts, advertising blurbs, correspondence, having a volume corresponding to a billion books, the whole affair, assembled and compressed, could be lugged off in a moving van. Mere compression, of course, is not enough; one needs not only to make and store a record but also be able to consult it, and this aspect of the matter comes later. Even the modern great library is not generally consulted; it is nibbled at by a few.

Compression is important, however, when it comes to costs. The material for the microfilm *Britannica* would cost a nickel, and it could be mailed anywhere for a cent. What would it cost to print a million copies? To print a sheet of newspaper, in a large edition, costs a small fraction of a cent. The entire material of the *Britannica* in reduced microfilm form would go on a sheet eight and one-half by eleven inches. Once it is available, with the photographic reproduction methods of the future, duplicates in large quantities could probably be turned out for a cent apiece beyond the cost of materials. The preparation of the original copy? That introduces the next aspect of the subject.

3   To make the record, we now push a pencil or tap a typewriter. Then comes the process of digestion and correction, followed by an intricate process of typesetting, printing, and distribution. To consider the first stage of the

procedure, will the author of the future cease writing by hand or typewriter and talk directly to the record? He does so indirectly, by talking to a stenographer or a wax cylinder; but the elements are all present if he wishes to have his talk directly produce a typed record. All he needs to do is to take advantage of existing mechanisms and to alter his language.

At a recent World Fair a machine called a Voder was shown. A girl stroked its keys and it emitted recognizable speech. No human vocal chords entered into the procedure at any point; the keys simply combined some electrically produced vibrations and passed these on to a loudspeaker. In the Bell Laboratories there is the converse of this machine, called a Vocoder. The loud-speaker is replaced by a microphone, which picks up sound. Speak to it, and the corresponding keys move. This may be one element of the postulated system.

The other element is found in the stenotype, that somewhat disconcerting device encountered usually at public meetings. A girl strokes its keys languidly and looks about the room and sometimes at the speaker with a disquieting gaze. From it emerges a typed strip which records in a phonetically simplified language a record of what the speaker is supposed to have said. Later this strip is retyped into ordinary language, for in its nascent form it is intelligible only to the initiated. Combine these two elements, let the Vocoder run the stenotype, and the result is a machine which types when talked to.

Our present languages are not especially adapted to this sort of mechanization, it is true. It is strange that the inventors of universal languages have not seized upon the idea of producing one which better fitted the technique for transmitting and recording speech. Mechanization may yet force the issue, especially in the scientific field; whereupon scientific jargon would become still less intelligible to the layman.

One can now picture a future investigator in his laboratory. His hands are free, and he is not anchored. As he moves about and observes, he photographs and comments. Time is automatically recorded to tie the two records together. If he goes into the field, he may be connected by radio to his recorder. As he ponders over his notes in the evening, he again talks his comments into the record. His typed record, as well as his photographs, may both be in miniature, so that he projects them for examination.

Much needs to occur, however, between the collection of data and observations, the extraction of parallel material from the existing record, and the final insertion of new material into the general body of the common record. For mature thought there is no mechanical substitute. But creative thought and essentially repetitive thought are very different things. For the latter there are, and may be, powerful mechanical aids.

Adding a column of figures is a repetitive thought process, and it was long ago properly relegated to the machine. True, the machine is sometimes controlled by a keyboard, and thought of a sort enters in reading the figures and poking the corresponding keys, but even this is avoidable. Machines have been made which will read typed figures by photocells and then depress the corresponding keys; these are combinations of photocells for scanning the type, electric circuits for sorting the consequent variations, and relay circuits for interpreting the result into the action of solenoids to pull the keys down.

All this complication is needed because of the clumsy way in which we have learned to write figures. If we recorded them positionally, simply by the configuration of a set of dots on a card, the automatic reading mechanism would become comparatively simple. In fact, if the dots are holes, we have the punched-card machine long ago produced by Hollorith for the purposes of the census, and now used throughout business. Some types of complex businesses could hardly operate without these machines.

Adding is only one operation. To perform arithmetical computation involves also subtraction, multiplication, and division, and in addition some method for temporary storage of results, removal from storage for further manipulation, and recording of final results by printing. Machines for these purposes are now of two types: keyboard machines for accounting and the like, manually controlled for the insertion of data, and usually automatically controlled as far as the sequence of operations is concerned; and punched-card machines in which separate operations are usually delegated to a series of machines, and the cards then transferred bodily from one to another. Both forms are very useful; but as far as complex computations are concerned, both are still in embryo.

Rapid electrical counting appeared soon after the physicists found it desirable to count cosmic rays. For their own purposes the physicists promptly constructed thermionic-tube equipment capable of counting electrical impulses at the rate of 100,000 a second. The advanced arithmetical machines of the future will be electrical in nature, and they will perform at 100 times present speeds, or more.

Moreover, they will be far more versatile than present commercial machines, so that they may readily be adapted for a wide variety of operations. They will be controlled by a control card or film, they will select their own data and manipulate it in accordance with the instructions thus inserted, they will perform complex arithmetical computations at exceedingly high speeds, and they will record results in such form as to be readily available for distribution or for later further manipulation. Such machines will have enormous appetites. One of them will take instructions and data from a whole roomful of girls armed with simple keyboard punches, and will deliver sheets of computed results every few minutes. There will always be plenty of things to compute in the detailed affairs of millions of people doing complicated things.

4   The repetitive processes of thought are not confined, however, to matters of arithmetic and statistics. In fact, every time one combines and records facts in accordance with established logical processes, the creative aspect of thinking is concerned only with the selection of the data and the process to be employed, and the manipulation thereafter is repetitive in nature and hence a fit matter to be relegated to the machines. Not so much has been done along these lines, beyond the bounds of arithmetic, as might be done, primarily because of the economics of the situation. The needs of business, and the extensive market obviously waiting, assured the advent of mass-produced arithmetical machines just as soon as production methods were sufficiently advanced.

With machines for advanced analysis no such situation existed; for there was and is no extensive market; the users of advanced methods of manipulating data are a very small part of the population. There are, however, machines for solving differential equations—and functional and integral equations, for that matter. There are many special machines, such as the harmonic synthesizer which predicts the tides. There will be many more, appearing certainly first in the hands of the scientist and in small numbers.

If scientific reasoning were limited to the logical processes of arithmetic, we should not get far in our understanding of the physical world. One might as well attempt to grasp the game of poker entirely by the use of the mathematics of probability. The abacus, with its beads strung on parallel wires, led the Arabs to positional numeration and the concept of zero many centuries before the rest of the world; and it was a useful tool—so useful that it still exists.

It is a far cry from the abacus to the modern keyboard accounting machine. It will be an equal step to the arithmetical machine of the future. But even this new machine will not take the scientist where he needs to go. Relief must be secured from laborious detailed manipulation of higher mathematics as well, if the users of it are to free their brains for something more than repetitive detailed transformations in accordance with established rules. A mathematician is not a man who can readily manipulate figures; often he cannot. He is not even a man who can readily perform the transformations of equations by the use of calculus. He is primarily an individual who is skilled in the use of symbolic logic on a high plane, and especially he is a man of intuitive judgment in the choice of the manipulative processes he employs.

All else he should be able to turn over to his mechanism, just as confidently as he turns over the propelling of his car to the intricate mechanism under the hood. Only then will mathematics be practically effective in bringing the growing knowledge of atomistics to the useful solution of the advanced problems of chemistry, metallurgy, and biology. For this reason there will come more machines to handle advanced mathematics for the scientist. Some of them will be sufficiently bizarre to suit the most fastidious connoisseur of the present artifacts of civilization.

---

5   The scientist, however, is not the only person who manipulates data and examines the world about him by the use of logical processes, although he sometimes preserves this appearance by adopting into the fold anyone who becomes logical, much in the manner in which a British labor leader is elevated to knighthood. Whenever logical processes of thought are employed—that is, whenever thought for a time runs along an accepted groove—there is an opportunity for the machine. Formal logic used to be a keen instrument in the hands of the teacher in his trying of students' souls. It is readily possible to construct a machine which will manipulate premises in accordance with formal logic, simply by the clever use of relay circuits. Put a set of premises into such a device and turn the crank, and it will readily pass out conclusion after conclusion, all in accordance with logical law, and with no more slips than would be expected of a keyboard adding machine.

Logic can become enormously difficult, and it would undoubtedly be well to produce more assurance in its use. The machines for higher analysis have usually been equation solvers. Ideas are beginning to appear for equation transformers, which will rearrange the relationship expressed by an equation in accordance with strict and rather advanced logic. Progress is inhibited by the exceedingly crude way in which mathematicians express their relationships. They employ a symbolism which grew like Topsy and has little consistency; a strange fact in that most logical field.

A new symbolism, probably positional, must apparently precede the reduction of mathematical transformations to machine processes. Then, on beyond the strict logic of the mathematician, lies the application of logic in everyday affairs. We may some day click off arguments on a machine with the same assurance that we now enter sales on a cash register. But the machine of logic will not look like a cash register, even of the streamlined model.

So much for the manipulation of ideas and their insertion into the record. Thus far we seem to be worse off than before—for we can enormously extend the record; yet even in its present bulk we can hardly consult it. This is a much larger matter than merely the extraction of data for the purposes of scientific research; it involves the entire process by which man profits by his inheritance of acquired knowledge. The prime action of use is selection, and here we are halting indeed. There may be millions of fine thoughts, and the account of the experience on which they are based, all encased within stone walls of acceptable architectural form; but if the scholar can get at only one a week by diligent search, his syntheses are not likely to keep up with the current scene.

Selection, in this broad sense, is a stone adze in the hands of a cabinetmaker. Yet, in a narrow sense and in other areas, something has already been done mechanically on selection. The personnel officer of a factory drops a stack of a few thousand employee cards into a selecting machine, sets a code in accordance with an established convention, and produces in a short time a list of all employees who live in Trenton and know Spanish. Even such devices are much too slow when it comes, for example, to matching a set of fingerprints with one of five million on file. Selection devices of this sort will soon be speeded up from their present rate of reviewing data at a few hundred a minute. By the use of photocells and microfilm they will survey items at the rate of a thousand a second, and will print out duplicates of those selected.

This process, however, is simple selection: it proceeds by examining in turn every one of a large set of items, and by picking out those which have certain specified characteristics. There is another form of selection best illustrated by the automatic telephone exchange. You dial a number and the machine selects and connects just one of a million possible stations. It does not run over them all. It pays attention only to a class given by a first digit, then only to a subclass of this given by the second digit, and so on; and thus proceeds rapidly and almost unerringly to the selected station. It requires a few seconds to make the selection, although the process could be speeded up if increased speed were economically warranted. If necessary, it could be made extremely fast by substituting thermionic-tube switching for mechanical switching, so that the full selection could be made in one-hundredth of a second. No one would wish to spend the money necessary to make this change in the telephone system, but the general idea is applicable elsewhere.

Take the prosaic problem of the great department store. Every time a charge sale is made, there are a number of things to be done. The inventory needs to be revised, the salesman needs to be given credit for the sale, the general accounts need an entry, and, most important, the customer needs to be charged. A central records device has been developed in which much of this work is done conveniently. The salesman places on a stand the customer's identification card, his own card, and the card taken from the article sold—all punched cards. When he pulls a lever, contacts are made through the holes, machinery at a central point makes the necessary computations and entries, and the proper receipt is printed for the salesman to pass to the customer.

But there may be ten thousand charge customers doing business with the store, and before the full operation can be completed someone has to select the right card and insert it at the central office. Now rapid selection can slide just the proper card into position in an instant or two, and return it afterward. Another difficulty occurs, however. Someone must read a total on the card, so that the machine can add its computed item to it. Conceivably the cards might be of the dry photography type I have described. Existing totals could then be read by photocell, and the new total entered by an electron beam.

The cards may be in miniature, so that they occupy little space. They must move quickly. They need not be transferred far, but merely into position so that the photocell and recorder can operate on them. Positional dots can enter the data. At the end of the month a machine can readily be made to read these and to print an ordinary bill. With tube selection, in which no mechanical parts are involved in the switches, little time need be occupied in bringing the correct card into use—a second should suffice for the entire operation. The whole record on the card may be made by magnetic dots on a steel sheet if desired, instead of dots to be observed optically, following the scheme by which Poulsen long ago put speech on a magnetic wire. This method has the advantage of simplicity and ease of erasure. By using photography, however, one can arrange to project the record in enlarged form, and at a distance by using the process common in television equipment.

One can consider rapid selection of this form, and distant projection for other purposes. To be able to key one sheet of a million before an operator in a second or two, with the possibility of then adding notes thereto, is suggestive in many ways. It might even be of use in libraries, but that is another story. At any rate, there are now some interesting combinations possible. One might, for example, speak to a microphone, in the manner described in connection with the speech-controlled typewriter, and thus make his selections. It would certainly beat the usual file clerk.

---

6   The real heart of the matter of selection, however, goes deeper than a lag in the adoption of mechanisms by libraries, or a lack of development of devices for their use. Our ineptitude in getting at the record is largely caused by the artificiality of systems of indexing. When data of any sort are placed in storage, they are filed alphabetically or numerically, and information is found (when it is) by tracing it down from subclass to subclass. It can be in only one place, unless duplicates are used; one has to have rules as to which

path will locate it, and the rules are cumbersome. Having found one item, moreover, one has to emerge from the system and re-enter on a new path.

The human mind does not work that way. It operates by association. With one item in its grasp, it snaps instantly to the next that is suggested by the association of thoughts, in accordance with some intricate web of trails carried by the cells of the brain. It has other characteristics, of course; trails that are not frequently followed are prone to fade, items are not fully permanent, memory is transitory. Yet the speed of action, the intricacy of trails, the detail of mental pictures, is awe-inspiring beyond all else in nature.

Man cannot hope fully to duplicate this mental process artificially, but he certainly ought to be able to learn from it. In minor ways he may even improve, for his records have relative permanency. The first idea, however, to be drawn from the analogy concerns selection. Selection by association, rather than by indexing, may yet be mechanized. One cannot hope thus to equal the speed and flexibility with which the mind follows an associative trail, but it should be possible to beat the mind decisively in regard to the permanence and clarity of the items resurrected from storage.

Consider a future device for individual use, which is a sort of mechanized private file and library. It needs a name, and, to coin one at random, 'memex' will do. A memex is a device in which an individual stores all his books, records, and communications, and which is mechanized so that it may be consulted with exceeding speed and flexibility. It is an enlarged intimate supplement to his memory.

It consists of a desk, and while it can presumably be operated from a distance, it is primarily the piece of furniture at which he works. On the top are slanting translucent screens, on which material can be projected for convenient reading. There is a keyboard, and sets of buttons and levers. Otherwise it looks like an ordinary desk.

In one end is the stored material. The matter of bulk is well taken care of by improved microfilm. Only a small part of the interior of the memex is devoted to storage, the rest to mechanism. Yet if the user inserted 5000 pages of material a day it would take him hundreds of years to fill the repository, so he can be profligate and enter material freely.

Most of the memex contents are purchased on microfilm ready for insertion. Books of all sorts, pictures, current periodicals, newspapers, are thus obtained and dropped into place. Business correspondence takes the same path. And there is provision for direct entry. On the top of the memex is a transparent platen. On this are placed longhand notes, photographs, memoranda, all sorts of things. When one is in place, the depression of a lever causes it to be photographed onto the next blank space in a section of the memex film, dry photography being employed.

There is, of course, provision for consultation of the record by the usual scheme of indexing. If the user wishes to consult a certain book, he taps its code on the keyboard, and the title page of the book promptly appears before him, projected onto one of his viewing positions. Frequently-used codes are mnemonic, so that he seldom consults his code book; but when he does, a single tap of a key projects it for his use. Moreover, he has supplemental levers. On deflecting one of these levers to the right he runs through the book before him, each page in turn being projected at a speed which just allows a recognizing glance at each. If he deflects it further to the right, he steps through the book 10 pages at a time; still further at 100 pages at a time. Deflection to the left gives him the same control backwards.

A special button transfers him immediately to the first page of the index. Any given book of his library can thus be called up and consulted with far greater facility than if it were taken from a shelf. As he has several projection positions, he can leave one item in position while he calls up another. He can add marginal notes and comments, taking advantage of one possible type of dry photography, and it could even be arranged so that he can do this by a stylus scheme, such as is now employed in the telautograph seen in railroad waiting rooms, just as though he had the physical page before him.

7   All this is conventional, except for the projection forward of present-day mechanisms and gadgetry. It affords an immediate step, however, to associative indexing, the basic idea of which is a provision whereby any item may be caused at will to select immediately and automatically another. This is the essential feature of the memex. The process of tying two items together is the important thing.

When the user is building a trail, he names it, inserts the name in his code book, and taps it out on his keyboard. Before him are the two items to be joined, projected onto adjacent viewing positions. At the bottom of each there are a number of blank code spaces, and a pointer is set to indicate one of these on each item. The user taps a single key, and the items are permanently joined. In each code space appears the code word. Out of view, but also in the code space, is inserted a set of dots for photocell viewing; and on each item these dots by their positions designate the index number of the other item.

Thereafter, at any time, when one of these items is in view, the other can be instantly recalled merely by tapping a button below the corresponding code space. Moreover, when numerous items have been thus joined together to form a trail, they can be reviewed in turn, rapidly or slowly, by deflecting a lever like that used for turning the pages of a book. It is exactly as though the physical items had been gathered together from widely separated sources and bound together to form a new book. It is more than this, for any item can be joined into numerous trails.

The owner of the memex, let us say, is interested in the origin and properties of the bow and arrow. Specifically he is studying why the short Turkish bow was apparently superior to the English long bow in the skirmishes of the Crusades. He has dozens of possibly pertinent books and articles in his memex. First he runs through an encyclopedia, finds an interesting but sketchy article, leaves it projected. Next, in a history, he finds another pertinent item, and ties the two together. Thus he goes, building a trail of many items. Occasionally he inserts a comment of his own, either linking it into the main trail or joining it by a side trail to a particular item. When it becomes evident that the elastic properties of available materials had a great deal to do with the bow, he branches off on a side trail which takes him through textbooks on elasticity and tables of physical constants. He inserts a page of longhand analysis of his own. Thus he builds a trail of his interest through the maze of materials available to him.

And his trails do not fade. Several years later, his talk with a friend turns to the queer ways in which a people resist innovations, even of vital interest. He has an example, in the fact that the outranged Europeans still failed to adopt the Turkish bow. In fact he has a trail on it. A touch brings up the code book. Tapping a few keys projects the head of the trail. A lever runs through it at will, stopping at interesting items, going off on side excursions. It is an interesting trail, pertinent to the discussion. So he sets a reproducer in action, photographs the whole trail out, and passes it to his friend for insertion in his own memex, there to be linked into the more general trail.

---

8 Wholly new forms of encyclopedias will appear, ready-made with a mesh of associative trails running through them, ready to be dropped into the memex and there amplified. The lawyer has at his touch the associated opinions and decisions of his whole experience, and of the experience of friends and authorities. The patent attorney has on call the millions of issued patents, with familiar trails to every point of his client's interest. The physician, puzzled by a patient's reactions, strikes the trail established in studying an earlier similar case, and runs rapidly through analogous case histories, with side references to the classics for the pertinent anatomy and histology. The chemist, struggling with the synthesis of an organic compound, has all the chemical literature before him in his laboratory, with trails following the analogies of compounds, and side trails to their physical and chemical behavior.

The historian, with a vast chronological account of a people, parallels it with a skip trail which stops only on the salient items, and can follow at any time contemporary trails which lead him all over civilization at a particular epoch. There is a new profession of trail blazers, those who find delight in the task of establishing useful trails through the enormous mass of the common record. The inheritance from the master becomes, not only his additions to the world's record, but for his disciples the entire scaffolding by which they were erected.

Thus science may implement the ways in which man produces, stores, and consults the record of the race. It might be striking to outline the instrumentalities of the future more spectacularly, rather than to stick closely to methods and elements now known and undergoing rapid development, as has been done here. Technical difficulties of all sorts have been ignored, certainly, but also ignored are means as yet unknown which may come any day to accelerate technical progress as violently as did the advent of the thermionic tube. In order that the picture may not be too commonplace, by reason of sticking to present-day patterns, it may be well to mention one such possibility, not to prophesy but merely to suggest, for prophecy based on extension of the known has substance, while prophecy founded on the unknown is only a doubly involved guess.

All our steps in creating or absorbing material of the record proceed through one of the senses—the tactile when we touch keys, the oral when we speak or listen, the visual when we read. Is it not possible that some day the path may be established more directly?

We know that when the eye sees, all the consequent information is transmitted to the brain by means of electrical vibrations in the channel of the optic nerve. This is an exact analogy with the electrical vibrations which occur in the cable of a television set: they convey the picture from the photocells which see it to the radio transmitter from which it is broadcast. We know further that if we can approach that cable with the proper instruments, we do not need to touch it; we can pick up those vibrations by electrical induction and thus discover and reproduce the scene which is being transmitted, just as a telephone wire may be tapped for its message.

The impulses which flow in the arm nerves of a typist convey to her fingers the translated information which reaches her eye or ear, in order that the fingers may be caused to strike the proper keys. Might not these currents be intercepted, either in the original form in which information is conveyed to the brain, or in the marvelously metamorphosed form in which they then proceed to the hand?

By bone conduction we already introduce sounds into the nerve channels of the deaf in order that they may hear. Is it not possible that we may learn to introduce them without the present cumbersomeness of first transforming electrical vibrations to mechanical ones, which the human mechanism promptly transforms back to the electrical form? With a couple of electrodes on the skull the encephalograph now produces pen-and-ink traces which bear some relation to the electrical phenomena going on in the brain itself. True, the record is unintelligible, except as it points out certain gross misfunctioning of the cerebral mechanism; but who would now place bounds on where such a thing may lead?

In the outside world, all forms of intelligence, whether of sound or sight, have been reduced to the form of varying currents in an electric circuit in order that they may be transmitted. Inside the human frame exactly the same sort of process occurs. Must we always transform to mechanical movements in order to proceed from one electrical phenomenon to another? It is a suggestive thought, but it hardly warrants prediction without losing touch with reality and immediateness.

Presumably man's spirit should be elevated if he can better review his shady past and analyze more completely and objectively his present problems. He has built a civilization so complex that he needs to mechanize his records more fully if he is to push his experiment to its logical conclusion and not merely become bogged down part way there by overtaxing his limited memory. His excursions may be more enjoyable if he can reacquire the privilege of forgetting the manifold things he does not need to have immediately at hand, with some assurance that he can find them again if they prove important.

The applications of science have built man a well-supplied house, and are teaching him to live healthily therein. They have enabled him to throw masses of people against one another with cruel weapons. They may yet allow him truly to encompass the great record and to grow in the wisdom of race experience. He may perish in conflict before he learns to wield that record for his true good. Yet, in the application of science to the needs and desires of man, it would seem to be a singularly unfortunate stage at which to terminate the process, or to lose hope as to the outcome.

2

Computing Machinery and Intelligence

A. M. Turing

In this article from 1950 Alan Turing establishes an initial programme for research in Artificial Intelligence. In his discussion he elaborates upon the feasibility of an intelligent machine, while proposing a test by which to evaluate the intelligence of such a device. Though he addresses a number of objections to the development of intelligent machines, he nevertheless proceeds to speculate upon the idea of learning machines.

1. The Imitation Game

I PROPOSE TO consider the question, 'Can machines think?' This should begin with definitions of the meaning of the terms 'machine' and 'think'. The definitions might be framed so as to reflect so far as possible the normal use of the words, but this attitude is dangerous. If the meaning of the words 'machine' and 'think' are to be found by examining how they are commonly used it is difficult to escape the conclusion that the meaning and the answer to the question, 'Can machines think?' is to be sought in a statistical survey such as a Gallup poll. But this is absurd. Instead of attempting such a definition I shall replace the question by another, which is closely related to it and is expressed in relatively unambiguous words.

The new form of the problem can be described in terms of a game which we call the 'imitation game'. It is played with three people, a man (A), a woman (B), and an interrogator (C) who may be of either sex. The interrogator stays in a room apart from the other two. The object of the game for the interrogator is to determine which of the other two is the man and which is the woman. He knows them by labels X and Y, and at the end of the game he says either 'X is A and Y is B' or 'X is B and Y is A'. The interrogator is allowed to put questions to A and B thus:

C: Will X please tell me the length of his or her hair?

Now suppose X is actually A, then A must answer. It is A's object in the game to try and cause C to make the wrong identification. His answer might therefore be:

'My hair is shingled, and the longest strands are about nine inches long.'

In order that tones of voice may not help the interrogator the answers should be written, or better still, typewritten. The ideal arrangement is to

From *Mind*, 59: 236 (Oct. 1950).

have a teleprinter communicating between the two rooms. Alternatively the question and answers can be repeated by an intermediary. The object of the game for the third player (B) is to help the interrogator. The best strategy for her is probably to give truthful answers. She can add such things as 'I am the woman, don't listen to him!' to her answers, but it will avail nothing as the man can make similar remarks.

We now ask the question, 'What will happen when a machine takes the part of A in this game?' Will the interrogator decide wrongly as often when the game is played like this as he does when the game is played between a man and a woman? These questions replace our original, 'Can machines think?'

2. Critique of the New Problem

As well as asking, 'What is the answer to this new form of the question', one may ask, 'Is this new question a worthy one to investigate?' This latter question we investigate without further ado, thereby cutting short an infinite regress.

The new problem has the advantage of drawing a fairly sharp line between the physical and the intellectual capacities of a man. No engineer or chemist claims to be able to produce a material which is indistinguishable from the human skin. It is possible that at some time this might be done, but even supposing this invention available we should feel there was little point in trying to make a 'thinking machine' more human by dressing it up in such artificial flesh. The form in which we have set the problem reflects this fact in the condition which prevents the interrogator from seeing or touching the other competitors, or hearing their voices. Some other advantages of the proposed criterion may be shown up by specimen questions and answers. Thus:

Q: Please write me a sonnet on the subject of the Forth Bridge.
A: Count me out on this one. I never could write poetry.
Q: Add 34957 to 70764
A: (Pause about 30 seconds and then give as answer) 105621.
Q: Do you play chess?
A: Yes.
Q: I have K at my K1, and no other pieces. You have only K at K6 and R at R1. It is your move. What do you play?
A: (After a pause of 15 seconds) R-R8 mate.

The question and answer method seems to be suitable for introducing almost any one of the fields of human endeavour that we wish to include. We do not wish to penalise the machine for its inability to shine in beauty competitions, nor to penalise a man for losing in a race against an aeroplane. The conditions of our game make these disabilities irrelevant. The 'witnesses' can brag, if they consider it advisable, as much as they please about their charms, strength or heroism, but the interrogator cannot demand practical demonstrations.

The game may perhaps be criticised on the ground that the odds are weighted too heavily against the machine. If the man were to try and pretend to be the machine he would clearly make a very poor showing. He would be given away at once by slowness and inaccuracy in arithmetic. May not machines carry out something which ought to be described as thinking but which is very different from what a man does? This objection is a very strong one, but at least we can say that if, nevertheless, a machine can be constructed to play the imitation game satisfactorily, we need not be troubled by this objection.

It might be urged that when playing the 'imitation game' the best strategy for the machine may possibly be something other than imitation of the behaviour of a man. This may be, but I think it is unlikely that there is any great effect of this kind. In any case there is no intention to investigate here the theory of the game, and it will be assumed that the best strategy is to try to provide answers that would naturally be given by a man.

3. The Machines Concerned in the Game

The question which we put in §1 will not be quite definite until we have specified what we mean by the word 'machine'. It is natural that we should wish to permit every kind of engineering technique to be used in our machines. We also wish to allow the possibility than an engineer or team of engineers may construct a machine which works, but whose manner of operation cannot be satisfactorily described by its constructors because they have applied a method which is largely experimental. Finally, we wish to exclude from the machines men born in the usual manner. It is difficult to frame the definitions so as to satisfy these three conditions. One might for instance insist that the team of engineers should be all of one sex, but this would not really be satisfactory, for it is probably possible to rear a complete individual from a single cell of the skin (say) of a man. To do so would be a feat of biological technique deserving of the very highest praise, but we would not be inclined to regard it as a case of 'constructing a thinking machine'. This prompts us to abandon the requirement that every kind of technique should be permitted. We are the more ready to do so in view of the fact that the present interest in 'thinking machines' has been aroused by a particular kind of machine, usually called an 'electronic computer' or 'digital computer'. Following this suggestion we only permit digital computers to take part in our game.

This restriction appears at first sight to be a very drastic one. I shall attempt to show that it is not so in reality. To do this necessitates a short account of the nature and properties of these computers.

It may also be said that this identification of machines with digital computers, like our criterion for 'thinking', will only be unsatisfactory if (contrary to my belief), it turns out that digital computers are unable to give a good showing in the game.

There are already a number of digital computers in working order, and it may be asked, 'Why not try the experiment straight away? It would be easy to satisfy the conditions of the game. A number of interrogators could be used, and statistics compiled to show how often the right identification was given.' The short answer is that we are not asking whether all digital computers would do well in the game nor whether the computers at present available would do well, but whether there are imaginable computers which would do well. But this is only the short answer. We shall see this question in a different light later.

---

4. Digital Computers

The idea behind digital computers may be explained by saying that these machines are intended to carry out any operations which could be done by a human computer. The human computer is supposed to be following fixed rules; he has no authority to deviate from them in any detail. We may suppose that these rules are supplied in a book, which is altered whenever he is put on to a new job. He has also an unlimited supply of paper on which he does his calculations. He may also do his multiplications and additions on a 'desk machine', but this is not important.

If we use the above explanation as a definition we shall be in danger of circularity of argument. We avoid this by giving an outline of the means by which the desired effect is achieved. A digital computer can usually be regarded as consisting of three parts:

(i) Store.
(ii) Executive unit.
(iii) Control.

The store is a store of information, and corresponds to the human computer's paper, whether this is the paper on which he does his calculations or that on which his book of rules is printed. In so far as the human computer does calculations in his head a part of the store will correspond to his memory.

The executive unit is the part which carries out the various individual operations involved in a calculation. What these individual operations are will vary from machine to machine. Usually fairly lengthy operations can be done such as 'Multiply 3540675445 by 7076345687' but in some machines only very simple ones such as 'Write down 0' are possible.

We have mentioned that the 'book of rules' supplied to the computer is replaced in the machine by a part of the store. It is then called the 'table of instructions'. It is the duty of the control to see that these instructions are obeyed correctly and in the right order. The control is so constructed that this necessarily happens.

The information in the store is usually broken up into packets of moderately small size. In one machine, for instance, a packet might consist of ten decimal digits. Numbers are assigned to the parts of the store in which the various packets of information are stored, in some systematic manner. A typical instruction might say—

'Add the number stored in position 6809 to that in 4302 and put the result back into the latter storage position'.

Needless to say it would not occur in the machine expressed in English. It would more likely be coded in a form such as 6809430217. Here 17 says which of various possible operations is to be performed on the two numbers. In this case the operation is that described above, viz. 'Add the number. . . .' It will be noticed that the instruction takes up 10 digits and so forms one packet of information, very conveniently. The control will normally take the instructions to be obeyed in the order of the positions in which they are stored, but occasionally an instruction such as

'Now obey the instruction stored in position 5606, and continue from there'
may be encountered, or again

'If position 4505 contains 0 obey next the instruction stored in 6707, otherwise continue straight on.'

Instructions of these latter types are very important because they make it possible for a sequence of operations to be repeated over and over again until some condition is fulfilled, but in doing so to obey, not fresh instructions on each repetition, but the same ones over and over again. To take a domestic analogy. Suppose Mother wants Tommy to call at the cobbler's every morning on his way to school to see if her shoes are done, she can ask him afresh every morning. Alternatively she can stick up a notice once and for all in the hall which he will see when he leaves for school and which tells him to call for the shoes, and also to destroy the notice when he comes back if he has the shoes with him.

The reader must accept it as a fact that digital computers can be constructed, and indeed have been constructed, according to the principles we have described, and that they can in fact mimic the actions of a human computer very closely.

The book of rules which we have described our human computer as using is of course a convenient fiction. Actual human computers really remember what they have got to do. If one wants to make a machine mimic the behaviour of the human computer in some complex operation one has to ask him how it is done, and then translate the answer into the form of an instruction table. Constructing instruction tables is usually described as 'programming'. To 'programme a machine to carry out the operation A' means to put the appropriate instruction table into the machine so that it will do A.

An interesting variant on the idea of a digital computer is a 'digital computer with a random element'. These have instructions involving the throwing of a die or some equivalent electronic process; one such instruction might for instance be, 'Throw the die and put the resulting number into store 1000'. Sometimes such a machine is described as having free will (though I would not use this phrase myself). It is not normally possible to determine from observing a machine whether it has a random element, for a similar effect can be produced by such devices as making the choices depend on the digits of the decimal for π.

Most actual digital computers have only a finite store. There is no theoretical difficulty in the idea of a computer with an unlimited store. Of course only a finite part can have been used at any one time. Likewise only a finite amount can have been constructed, but we can imagine more and more being added as required. Such computers have special theoretical interest and will be called infinitive capacity computers.

The idea of a digital computer is an old one. Charles Babbage, Lucasian Professor of Mathematics at Cambridge from 1828 to 1839, planned such a machine, called the Analytical Engine, but it was never completed. Although Babbage had all the essential ideas, his machine was not at that time such a very attractive prospect. The speed which would have been available would be definitely faster than a human computer but something like 100 times slower than the Manchester machine, itself one of the slower of the modern machines. The storage was to be purely mechanical, using wheels and cards.

The fact that Babbage's Analytical Engine was to be entirely mechanical will help us to rid ourselves of a superstition. Importance is often attached to the fact that modern digital computers are electrical, and that the nervous system also is electrical. Since Babbage's machine was not electrical, and since all digital computers are in a sense equivalent, we see that this use of electricity cannot be of theoretical importance. Of course electricity usually comes in where fast signalling is concerned, so that it is not surprising that we find it in both these connections. In the nervous system chemical phenomena are at least as important as electrical. In certain computers the storage system is mainly acoustic. The feature of using electricity is thus seen to be only a very superficial similarity. If we wish to find such similarities we should look rather for mathematical analogies of function.

5. Universality of Digital Computers

The digital computers considered in the last section may be classified amongst the 'discrete state machines'. These are the machines which move by sudden jumps or clicks from one quite definite state to another. These states are sufficiently different for the possibility of confusion between them to be ignored. Strictly speaking there are no such machines. Everything really moves continuously. But there are many kinds of machine which can profitably be *thought of* as being discrete state machines. For instance in considering the switches for a lighting system it is a convenient fiction that each switch must be definitely on or definitely off. There must be intermediate positions, but for most purposes we can forget about them. As an example of a discrete state machine we might consider a wheel which clicks round through 120° once a second, but may be stopped by a lever which can be operated from outside; in addition a lamp is to light in one of the positions of the wheel. This machine could be described abstractly as follows. The internal state of the machine (which is described by the position of the wheel) may be q_1, q_2 or q_3. There is an input signal i_0 or i_1 (position of lever). The internal state at any moment is determined by the last state and input signal according to the table

		Last State		
		q_1	q_2	q_3
Input	i_0	q_2	q_3	q_1
	i_1	q_1	q_2	q_3

The output signals, the only externally visible indication of the internal state (the light) are described by the table

State	q_1	q_2	q_3
Output	o_0	o_0	o_1

This example is typical of discrete state machines. They can be described by such tables provided they have only a finite number of possible states.

It will seem that given the initial state of the machine and the input signals it is always possible to predict all future states. This is reminiscent of Laplace's view that from the complete state of the universe at one moment of time, as described by the positions and velocities of all particles, it should be possible to predict all future states. The prediction which we are considering is, however, rather nearer to practicability than that considered by Laplace. The system of the 'universe as a whole' is such that quite small errors in the initial conditions can have an overwhelming effect at a later time. The displacement of a single electron by a billionth of a centimetre at one moment might make the difference between a man being killed by an avalanche a year later, or escaping. It is an essential property of the mechanical systems which we have called 'discrete state machines' that this phenomenon does not occur. Even when we consider the actual physical machines instead of the idealised machines, reasonably accurate knowledge of the state at one moment yields reasonably accurate knowledge any number of steps later.

As we have mentioned, digital computers fall within the class of discrete state machines. But the number of states of which such a machine is capable is usually enormously large. For instance, the number for the machine now working at Manchester is about $2^{165,000}$, *i.e.* about $10^{50,000}$. Compare this with our example of the clicking wheel described above, which had three states. It is not difficult to see why the number of states should be so immense. The computer includes a store corresponding to the paper used by a human computer. It must be possible to write into the store any one of the combinations of symbols which might have been written on the paper. For simplicity suppose that only digits from 0 to 9 are used as symbols. Variations in handwriting are ignored. Suppose the computer is allowed 100 sheets of paper each containing 50 lines each with room for 30 digits. Then the number of states is $10^{100 \times 50 \times 30}$, *i.e.* $10^{150,000}$. This is about the number of states of three Manchester machines put together. The logarithm to the base two of the number of states is usually called the 'storage capacity' of the machine. Thus the Manchester machine has a storage capacity of about 165,000 and the wheel machine of our example about 1.6. If two machines are put together their capacities must be added to obtain the capacity of the resultant machine. This leads to the possibility of statements such as 'The Manchester machine contains 64 magnetic tracks each with a capacity of 2560, eight electronic tubes with a capacity of 1280. Miscellaneous storage amounts to about 300 making a total of 174,380.'

Given the table corresponding to a discrete state machine it is possible to predict what it will do. There is no reason why this calculation should not be carried out by means of a digital computer. Provided it could be carried out sufficiently quickly the digital computer could mimic the behaviour of any discrete state machine. The imitation game could then be played with the machine in question (as B) and the mimicking digital computer (as A) and the interrogator would be unable to distinguish them. Of course the digital computer must have an adequate storage capacity as well as working sufficiently fast. Moreover, it must be programmed afresh for each new machine which it is desired to mimic.

This special property of digital computers, that they can mimic any discrete state machine, is described by saying that they are *universal* machines. The existence of machines with this property has the important consequence that, considerations of speed apart, it is unnecessary to design various new machines to do various computing processes. They can all be done with one digital computer, suitably programmed for each case. It will be seen that as a consequence of this all digital computers are in a sense equivalent.

We may now consider again the point raised at the end of §3. It was suggested tentatively that the question, 'Can machines think?' should be replaced by 'Are there imaginable digital computers which would do well in the imitation game?' If we wish we can make this superficially more general and ask 'Are there discrete state machines which would do well?' But in view of the universality property we see that either of these questions is equivalent to this, 'Let us fix our attention on one particular digital computer C. Is it true that by modifying this computer to have an adequate storage, suitably increasing its speed of action, and providing it with an appropriate programme, C can be made to play satisfactorily the part of A in the imitation game, the part of B being taken by a man?'

6. Contrary Views on the Main Question

We may now consider the ground to have been cleared and we are ready to proceed to the debate on our question, 'Can machines think?' and the variant of it quoted at the end of the last section. We cannot altogether abandon the original form of the problem, for opinions will differ as to the appropriateness of the substitution and we must at least listen to what has to be said in this connexion.

It will simplify matters for the reader if I explain first my own beliefs in the matter. Consider first the more accurate form of the question. I believe that in about fifty years' time it will be possible to programme computers, with a storage capacity of about 10^9, to make them play the imitation game so well that an average interrogator will not have more than 70 per cent chance of making the right identification after five minutes of questioning. The original question, 'Can machines think?' I believe to be too meaningless to deserve discussion. Nevertheless I believe that at the end of the century the use of words and general educated opinion will have altered so much that one will be able to speak of machines thinking without expecting to be contradicted. I believe further that no useful purpose is served by concealing these beliefs. The popular view that scientists proceed inexorably from well-established fact to well-established fact, never being influenced by any unproved conjecture, is quite mistaken. Provided it is made clear which are proved facts and which are conjectures, no harm can result. Conjectures are of great importance since they suggest useful lines of research.

I now proceed to consider opinions opposed to my own.

1. The Theological
Objection

Thinking is a function of man's immortal soul. God has given an immortal soul to every man and woman, but not to any other animal or to machines. Hence no animal or machine can think.

I am unable to accept any part of this, but will attempt to reply in theological terms. I should find the argument more convincing if animals were classed with men, for there is a greater difference, to my mind, between the typical animate and the inanimate than there is between man and the other animals. The arbitrary character of the orthodox view becomes clearer if we consider how it might appear to a member of some other religious community. How do Christians regard the Moslem view that women have no souls? But let us leave this point aside and return to the main argument. It appears to me that the argument quoted above implies a serious restriction of the omnipotence of the Almighty. It is admitted that there are certain things that He cannot do such as making one equal to two, but should we not believe that He has freedom to confer a soul on an elephant if He sees fit? We might expect that He would only exercise this power in conjunction with a mutation which provided the elephant with an appropriately improved brain to minister to the needs of this soul. An argument of exactly similar form may be made for the case of machines. It may seem different because it is more difficult to 'swallow'. But this really only means that we think it would be less likely that He would consider the circumstances suitable for conferring a soul. The circumstances in question are discussed in the rest of this paper. In attempting to construct such machines we should not be irreverently usurping His power of creating souls, any more than we are in the procreation of children: rather we are, in either case, instruments of His will providing mansions for the souls that He creates.[1]

However, this is mere speculation. I am not very impressed with theological arguments whatever they may be used to support. Such arguments have often been found unsatisfactory in the past. In the time of Galileo it was argued that the texts, 'And the sun stood still . . . and hasted not to go down about a whole day' (Joshua x. 13) and 'He laid the foundations of the earth, that it should not move at any time' (Psalm cv. 5) were an adequate refutation of the Copernican theory. With our present knowledge such an argument appears futile. When that knowledge was not available it made a quite different impression.

2. The 'Heads in the
Sand' Objection

'The consequences of machines thinking would be too dreadful. Let us hope and believe that they cannot do so.'

This argument is seldom expressed quite so openly as in the form above. But it affects most of us who think about it at all. We like to believe that Man is in some subtle way superior to the rest of creation. It is best if he can be shown to be *necessarily* superior, for then there is no danger of him losing his commanding position. The popularity of the theological argument is clearly connected with this feeling. It is likely to be quite strong in intellectual people, since they value the power of thinking more highly than others, and are more inclined to base their belief in the superiority of Man on this power.

---

1 Possibly this view is heretical. St Thomas Aquinas (*Summa Theologica*. quoted by Bertrand Russell, p. 480) states that God cannot make a man to have no soul. But this may not be a real restriction on His powers, but only a result of the fact that men's souls are immortal, and therefore indestructible.

I do not think that this argument is sufficiently substantial to require refutation. Consolation would be more appropriate: perhaps this should be sought in the transmigration of souls.

3. The Mathematical
Objection

There are a number of results of mathematical logic which can be used to show that there are limitations to the powers of discrete-state machines. The best known of these results is known as Gödel's theorem,[2] and shows that in any sufficiently powerful logical system statements can be formulated which can neither be proved nor disproved within the system, unless possibly the system itself is inconsistent. There are other, in some respects similar, results due to *Church, Kleene, Rosser,* and *Turing.* The latter result is the most convenient to consider, since it refers directly to machines, whereas the others can only be used in a comparatively indirect argument: for instance if Gödel's theorem is to be used we need in addition to have some means of describing logical systems in terms of machines, and machines in terms of logical systems. The result in question refers to a type of machine which is essentially a digital computer with an infinite capacity. It states that there are certain things that such a machine cannot do. If it is rigged up to give answers to questions as in the imitation game, there will be some questions to which it will either give a wrong answer, or fail to give an answer at all however much time is allowed for a reply. There may, of course, be many such questions, and questions which cannot be answered by one machine may be satisfactorily answered by another. We are of course supposing for the present that the questions are of the kind to which an answer 'Yes' or 'No' is appropriate, rather than questions such as 'What do you think of Picasso?' The questions that we know the machines must fail on are of this type, 'Consider the machine specified as follows. . . . Will this machine ever answer "Yes" to any question?' The dots are to be replaced by a description of some machine in a standard form, which could be something like that used in §5. When the machine described bears a certain comparatively simple relation to the machine which is under interrogation, it can be shown that the answer is either wrong or not forthcoming. This is the mathematical result: it is argued that it proves a disability of machines to which the human intellect is not subject.

The short answer to this argument is that although it is established that there are limitations to the powers of any particular machine, it has only been stated, without any sort of proof, that no such limitations apply to the human intellect. But I do not think this view can be dismissed quite so lightly. Whenever one of these machines is asked the appropriate critical question, and gives a definite answer, we know that this answer must be wrong, and this gives us a certain feeling of superiority. Is this feeling illusory? It is no doubt quite genuine, but I do not think too much importance should be attached to it. We too often give wrong answers to questions ourselves to be justified in being very pleased at such evidence of fallibility on the part of the machines. Further, our superiority can only be felt on such an occasion in relation to the one machine over which we have scored our petty triumph. There would be no question of triumphing simultaneously over *all* machines. In short, then,

2 Author's names in italics refer to the References.

there might be men cleverer than any given machine, but then again there might be other machines cleverer again, and so on.

Those who hold to the mathematical argument would, I think, mostly be willing to accept the imitation game as a basis for discussion. Those who believe in the two previous objections would probably not be interested in any criteria.

4. The Argument from Consciousness

This argument is very well expressed in *Professor Jefferson's* Lister Oration for 1949, from which I quote. 'Not until a machine can write a sonnet or compose a concerto because of thoughts and emotions felt, and not by the chance fall of symbols, could we agree that machine equals brain—that is, not only write it but know that it had written it. No mechanism could feel (and not merely artificially signal, an easy contrivance) pleasure at its successes, grief when its valves fuse, be warmed by flattery, be made miserable by its mistakes, be charmed by sex, be angry or depressed when it cannot get what it wants.'

This argument appears to be a denial of the validity of our test. According to the most extreme form of this view the only way by which one could be sure that a machine thinks is to *be* the machine and to feel oneself thinking. One could then describe these feelings to the world, but of course no one would be justified in taking any notice. Likewise according to this view the only way to know that a *man* thinks is to be that particular man. It is in fact the solipsist point of view. It may be the most logical view to hold but it makes communication of ideas difficult. A is liable to believe 'A thinks but B does not' whilst B believes 'B thinks but A does not'. Instead of arguing continually over this point it is usual to have the polite convention that everyone thinks.

I am sure that Professor Jefferson does not wish to adopt the extreme and solipsist point of view. Probably he would be quite willing to accept the imitation game as a test. The game (with the player B omitted) is frequently used in practice under the name of *viva voce* to discover whether some one really understands something or has 'learnt it parrot fashion'. Let us listen in to a part of such a *viva voce:*

Interrogator: In the first line of your sonnet which reads 'Shall I compare thee to a summer's day', would not 'a spring day' do as well or better?

Witness: It wouldn't scan.

Interrogator: How about 'a winter's day' That would scan all right.

Witness: Yes, but nobody wants to be compared to a winter's day.

Interrogator: Would you say Mr Pickwick reminded you of Christmas?

Witness: In a way.

Interrogator: Yet Christmas is a winter's day, and I do not think Mr Pickwick would mind the comparison.

Witness: I don't think you're serious. By a winter's day one means a typical winter's day, rather than a special one like Christmas.

And so on. What would Professor Jefferson say if the sonnet-writing machine was able to answer like this in the *viva voce?* I do not know whether he would regard the machine as 'merely artificially signalling' these answers, but if the answers were as satisfactory and sustained as in the above passage I do not think he would describe it as 'an easy contrivance'. This phrase is, I think, intended to cover such devices as the inclusion in the machine of a record of someone reading a sonnet, with appropriate switching to turn it on from time to time.

In short then, I think that most of those who support the argument from consciousness could be persuaded to abandon it rather than be forced into the solipsist position. They will then probably be willing to accept our test.

I do not wish to give the impression that I think there is no mystery about consciousness. There is, for instance, something of a paradox connected with any attempt to localise it. But I do not think these mysteries necessarily need to be solved before we can answer the question with which we are concerned in this paper.

5. Arguments from Various Disabilities

These arguments take the form, 'I grant you that you can make machines do all the things you have mentioned but you will never be able to make one to do X'. Numerous features X are suggested in this connexion. I offer a selection:

> Be kind, resourceful, beautiful, friendly (p. 49), have initiative, have a sense of humour, tell right from wrong, make mistakes (p. 49), fall in love, enjoy strawberries and cream (p. 49), make some one fall in love with it, learn from experience (p. 55), use words properly, be the subject of its own thought (p. 49), have as much diversity of behaviour as a man, do something really new (p. 50). (Some of these disabilities are given special consideration as indicated by the page numbers.)

No support is usually offered for these statements. I believe they are mostly founded on the principle of scientific induction. A man has seen thousands of machines in his lifetime. From what he sees of them he draws a number of general conclusions. They are ugly, each is designed for a very limited purpose, when required for a minutely different purpose they are useless, the variety of behaviour of any one of them is very small, etc., etc. Naturally he concludes that these are necessary properties of machines in general. Many of these limitations are associated with the very small storage capacity of most machines. (I am assuming that the idea of storage capacity is extended in some way to cover machines other than discrete-state machines. The exact definition does not matter as no mathematical accuracy is claimed in the present discussion.) A few years ago, when very little had been heard of digital computers, it was possible to elicit much incredulity concerning them, if one mentioned their properties without describing their construction. That was presumably due to a similar application of the principle of scientific induction. These applications of the principle are of course largely unconscious. When a burnt child fears the fire and shows that he fears it by avoiding it, I should say that he was applying scientific induction. (I could of course also describe his behaviour in many other ways.) The works and customs of mankind do not seem to be very suitable material to which to apply scientific induction. A very large part of space-time must be investigated, if reliable results are to be obtained. Otherwise we may (as most English children do) decide that everybody speaks English, and that it is silly to learn French.

There are, however, special remarks to be made about many of the disabilities that have been mentioned. The inability to enjoy strawberries and cream may have struck the reader as frivolous. Possibly a machine might be made to enjoy this delicious dish, but any attempt to make one do so would be idiotic. What is important about this disability is that it contributes to some of the other disabilities, e.g. to the difficulty of the same kind of friendliness occurring between man and machine as between white man and white man, or between black man and black man.

The claim that 'machines cannot make mistakes' seems a curious one. One is tempted to retort, 'Are they any the worse for that?' But let us adopt a more sympathetic attitude, and try to see what is really meant. I think this criticism can be explained in terms of the imitation game. It is claimed that the interrogator could distinguish the machine from the man simply by setting them a number of problems in arithmetic. The machine would be unmasked because of its deadly accuracy. The reply to this is simple. The machine (programmed for playing the game) would not attempt to give the *right* answers to the arithmetic problems. It would deliberately introduce mistakes in a manner calculated to confuse the interrogator. A mechanical fault would probably show itself through an unsuitable decision as to what sort of a mistake to make in the arithmetic. Even this interpretation of the criticism is not sufficiently sympathetic. But we cannot afford the space to go into it much further. It seems to me that this criticism depends on a confusion between two kinds of mistake. We may call them 'errors of functioning' and 'errors of conclusion'. Errors of functioning are due to some mechanical or electrical fault which causes the machine to behave otherwise than it was designed to do. In philosophical discussions one likes to ignore the possibility of such errors; one is therefore discussing 'abstract machines'. These abstract machines are mathematical fictions rather than physical objects. By definition they are incapable of errors of functioning. In this sense we can truly say that 'machines can never make mistakes'. Errors of conclusion can only arise when some meaning is attached to the output signals from the machine. The machine might, for instance, type out mathematical equations, or sentences in English. When a false proposition is typed we say that the machine has committed an error of conclusion. There is clearly no reason at all for saying that a machine cannot make this kind of mistake. It might do nothing but type out repeatedly '0 = 1'. To take a less perverse example, it might have some method for drawing conclusions by scientific induction. We must expect such a method to lead occasionally to erroneous results.

The claim that a machine cannot be the subject of its own thought can of course only be answered if it can be shown that the machine has *some* thought with *some* subject matter. Nevertheless, 'the subject matter of a machine's operations' does seem to mean something, at least to the people who deal with it. If, for instance, the machine was trying to find a solution of the equation $x^2 - 40x - 11 = 0$ one would be tempted to describe this equation as part of the machine's subject matter at that moment. In this sort of sense a machine undoubtedly can be its own subject matter. It may be used to help in making up its own programmes, or to predict the effect of alterations in its own structure. By observing the results of its own behaviour it can modify its own programmes so as to achieve some purpose more effectively. These are possibilities of the near future, rather than Utopian dreams.

The criticism that a machine cannot have much diversity of behaviour is just a way of saying that it cannot have much storage capacity. Until fairly recently a storage capacity of even a thousand digits was very rare.

The criticisms that we are considering here are often disguised forms of the argument from consciousness. Usually if one maintains that a machine *can* do one of these things, and describes the kind of method that the machine could use, one will not make much of an impression. It is thought that the method (whatever it may be, for it must be mechanical) is really rather base. Compare the parenthesis in Jefferson's statement quoted above.

6. Lady Lovelace's Objection

Our most detailed information of Babbage's Analytical Engine comes from a memoir by *Lady Lovelace*. In it she states, 'The Analytical Engine has no pretensions to *originate* anything. It can do *whatever we know how to order it* to perform' (her italics). This statement is quoted by *Hartree* (p. 70) who adds: 'This does not imply that it may not be possible to construct electronic equipment which will "think for itself", or in which, in biological terms, one could set up a conditioned reflex, which would serve as a basis for "learning". Whether this is possible in principle or not is a stimulating and exciting question, suggested by some of these recent developments. But it did not seem that the machines constructed or projected at the time had this property'.

I am in thorough agreement with Hartree over this. It will be noticed that he does not assert that the machines in question had not got the property, but rather that the evidence available to Lady Lovelace did not encourage her to believe that they had it. It is quite possible that the machines in question had in a sense got this property. For suppose that some discrete-state machine has the property. The Analytical Engine was a universal digital computer, so that, if its storage capacity and speed were adequate, it could by suitable programming be made to mimic the machine in question. Probably this argument did not occur to the Countess or to Babbage. In any case there was no obligation on them to claim all that could be claimed.

This whole question will be considered again under the heading of learning machines.

A variant of Lady Lovelace's objection states that a machine can 'never do anything really new'. This may be parried for a moment with the saw, 'There is nothing new under the sun'. Who can be certain that 'original work' that he has done was not simply the growth of the seed planted in him by teaching, or the effect of following well-known general principles. A better variant of the objection says that a machine can never 'take us by surprise'. This statement is a more direct challenge and can be met directly. Machines take me by surprise with great frequency. This is largely because I do not do sufficient calculation to decide what to expect them to do, or rather because, although I do a calculation, I do it in a hurried, slipshod fashion, taking risks. Perhaps I say to myself, 'I suppose the voltage here ought to be the same as there: anyway let's assume it is.' Naturally I am often wrong, and the result is a surprise for me for by the time the experiment is done these assumptions have been forgotten. These admissions lay me open to lectures on the subject of my vicious ways, but do not throw any doubt on my credibility when I testify to the surprises I experience.

I do not expect this reply to silence my critic. He will probably say that such surprises are due to some creative mental act on my part, and reflect no credit on the machine. This leads us back to the argument from consciousness, and far from the idea of surprise. It is a line of argument we must consider closed, but it is perhaps worth remarking that the appreciation of something as surprising requires as much of a 'creative mental act' whether the surprising event originates from a man, a book, a machine or anything else.

The view that machines cannot give rise to surprises is due, I believe, to a fallacy to which philosophers and mathematicians are particularly subject. This is the assumption that as soon as a fact is presented to a mind all consequences of that fact spring into the mind simultaneously with it. It is a very useful assumption under many circumstances, but one too easily forgets that it is false. A natural consequence of doing so is that one then assumes that there is no virtue in the mere working out of consequences from data and general principles.

7. Argument from Continuity in the Nervous System

The nervous system is certainly not a discrete-state machine. A small error in the information about the size of a nervous impulse impinging on a neuron, may make a large difference to the size of the outgoing impulse. It may be argued that, this being so, one cannot expect to be able to mimic the behaviour of the nervous system with a discrete-state system.

It is true that a discrete-state machine must be different from a continuous machine. But if we adhere to the conditions of the imitation game, the interrogator will not be able to take any advantage of this difference. The situation can be made clearer if we consider some other simpler continuous machine. A differential analyser will do very well. (A differential analyser is a certain kind of machine not of the discrete-state type used for some kinds of calculation.) Some of these provide their answers in a typed form, and so are suitable for taking part in the game. It would not be possible for a digital computer to predict exactly what answers the differential analyser would give to a problem, but it would be quite capable of giving the right sort of answer. For instance, if asked to give the value of π (actually about 3.1416) it would be reasonable to choose at random between the values 3.12, 3.13, 3.14, 3.15, 3.16 with the probabilities of 0.05, 0.15, 0.55, 0.19, 0.06 (say). Under these circumstances it would be very difficult for the interrogator to distinguish the differential analyser from the digital computer.

8. The Argument from Informality of Behaviour

It is not possible to produce a set of rules purporting to describe what a man should do in every conceivable set of circumstances. One might for instance have a rule that one is to stop when one sees a red traffic light, and to go if one sees a green one, but what if by some fault both appear together? One may perhaps decide that it is safest to stop. But some further difficulty may well arise from this decision later. To attempt to provide rules of conduct to cover every eventuality, even those arising from traffic lights, appears to be impossible. With all this I agree.

From this it is argued that we cannot be machines. I shall try to reproduce the argument, but I fear I shall hardly do it justice. It seems to run something like this. 'If each man had a definite set of rules of conduct by which he regulated his life he would be no better than a machine. But there are no such rules, so men cannot be machines.' The undistributed middle is glaring. I do not think the argument is ever put quite like this, but I believe this is the argument used nevertheless. There may however be a certain confusion between 'rules of conduct' and 'laws of behaviour' to cloud the issue. By 'rules of conduct' I mean precepts such as 'Stop if you see red lights', on which one can act, and of which one can be conscious. By 'laws of behaviour' I mean laws of nature as applied to a man's body such as 'if you pinch him he will squeak'. If we substitute 'laws of behaviour which regulate his life' for 'laws of conduct by which he regulates his life' in the argument quoted the undistributed middle is no longer insuperable. For we believe that it is not only true that being regulated by laws of behaviour implies being some sort of machine (though not necessarily a discrete-state machine), but that conversely being such a machine implies being regulated by such laws. However, we cannot so easily convince ourselves of the absence of complete laws of behaviour as of complete rules of conduct. The only way we know of for finding such laws is scientific observation, and we certainly know of no circumstances under which we could say, 'We have searched enough. There are no such laws.'

We can demonstrate more forcibly that any such statement would be unjustified. For suppose we could be sure of finding such laws if they existed. Then given a discrete-state machine it should certainly be possible to discover by observation sufficient about it to predict its future behaviour, and this within a reasonable time, say a thousand years. But this does not seem to be the case. I have set up on the Manchester computer a small programme using only 1000 units of storage, whereby the machine supplied with one sixteen figure number replies with another within two seconds. I would defy anyone to learn from these replies sufficient about the programme to be able to predict any replies to untried values.

9. The Argument from Extra-Sensory Perception

I assume that the reader is familiar with the idea of extra-sensory perception, and the meaning of the four items of it, *viz.* telepathy, clairvoyance, precognition and psycho-kinesis. These disturbing phenomena seem to deny all our usual scientific ideas. How we should like to discredit them! Unfortunately the statistical evidence, at least for telepathy, is overwhelming. It is very difficult to rearrange one's ideas so as to fit these new facts in. Once one has accepted them it does not seem a very big step to believe in ghosts and bogies. The idea that our bodies move simply according to the known laws of physics, together with some others not yet discovered but somewhat similar, would be one of the first to go.

This argument is to my mind quite a strong one. One can say in reply that many scientific theories seem to remain workable in practice, in spite of clashing with ESP; that in fact one can get along very nicely if one forgets about it. This is rather cold comfort, and one fears that thinking is just the kind of phenomenon where ESP may be especially relevant.

A more specific argument based on ESP might run as follows: 'Let us play the imitation game, using as witnesses a man who is good as a telepathic receiver, and a digital computer. The interrogator can ask such questions as

"What suit does the card in my right hand belong to?" The man by telepathy or clairvoyance gives the right answer 130 times out of 400 cards. The machine can only guess at random, and perhaps gets 104 right, so the interrogator makes the right identification.' There is an interesting possibility which opens here. Suppose the digital computer contains a random number generator. Then it will be natural to use this to decide what answer to give. But then the random number generator will be subject to the psycho-kinetic powers of the interrogator. Perhaps this psycho-kinesis might cause the machine to guess right more often than would be expected on a probability calculation, so that the interrogator might still be unable to make the right identification. On the other hand, he might be able to guess right without any questioning, by clairvoyance. With ESP anything may happen.

If telepathy is admitted it will be necessary to tighten our test up. The situation could be regarded as analogous to that which would occur if the interrogator were talking to himself and one of the competitors was listening with his ear to the wall. To put the competitors into a 'telepathy-proof room' would satisfy all requirements.

7. Learning Machines

The reader will have anticipated that I have no very convincing arguments of a positive nature to support my views. If I had I should not have taken such pains to point out the fallacies in contrary views. Such evidence as I have I shall now give.

Let us return for a moment to Lady Lovelace's objection, which stated that the machine can only do what we tell it to do. One could say that a man can 'inject' an idea into the machine, and that it will respond to a certain extent and then drop into quiescence, like a piano string struck by a hammer. Another simile would be an atomic pile of less than critical size: an injected idea is to correspond to a neutron entering the pile from without. Each such neutron will cause a certain disturbance which eventually dies away. If, however, the size of the pile is sufficiently increased, the disturbance caused by such an incoming neutron will very likely go on and on increasing until the whole pile is destroyed. Is there a corresponding phenomenon for minds, and is there one for machines? There does seem to be one for the human mind. The majority of them seem to be 'sub-critical', i.e. to correspond in this analogy to piles of subcritical size. An idea presented to such a mind will on average give rise to less than one idea in reply. A smallish proportion are super-critical. An idea presented to such a mind may give rise to a whole 'theory' consisting of secondary, tertiary and more remote ideas. Animals minds seem to be very definitely sub-critical. Adhering to this analogy we ask, 'Can a machine be made to be super-critical?'

The 'skin of an onion' analogy is also helpful. In considering the functions of the mind or the brain we find certain operations which we can explain in purely mechanical terms. This we say does not correspond to the real mind: it is a sort of skin which we must strip off if we are to find the real mind. But then in what remains we find a further skin to be stripped off, and so on. Proceeding in this way do we ever come to the 'real' mind, or do we eventually come to the skin which has nothing in it? In the latter case the whole mind is mechanical. (It would not be a discrete-state machine however. We have discussed this.)

These last two paragraphs do not claim to be convincing arguments. They should rather be described as 'recitations tending to produce belief'.

The only really satisfactory support that can be given for the view expressed at the beginning of §6, will be that provided by waiting for the end of the century and then doing the experiment described. But what can we say in the meantime? What steps should be taken now if the experiment is to be successful?

As I have explained, the problem is mainly one of programming. Advances in engineering will have to be made too, but it seems unlikely that these will not be adequate for the requirements. Estimates of the storage capacity of the brain vary from 10^{10} to 10^{15} binary digits. I incline to the lower values and believe that only a very small fraction is used for the higher types of thinking. Most of it is probably used for the retention of visual impressions. I should be surprised if more than 10^9 was required for satisfactory playing of the imitation game, at any rate against a blind man. (Note—The capacity of the *Encyclopaedia Britannica*, 11th edition, is 2×10^9.) A storage capacity of 10^7 would be a very practicable possibility even by present techniques. It is probably not necessary to increase the speed of operations of the machines at all. Parts of modern machines which can be regarded as analogues of nerve cells work about a thousand times faster than the latter. This should provide a 'margin of safety' which could cover losses of speed arising in many ways. Our problem then is to find out how to programme these machines to play the game. At my present rate of working I produce about a thousand digits of programme a day, so that about sixty workers, working steadily through the fifty years might accomplish the job, if nothing went into the waste-paper basket. Some more expeditious method seems desirable.

In the process of trying to imitate an adult human mind we are bound to think a good deal about the process which has brought it to the state that it is in. We may notice three components,

    (*a*) The initial state of the mind, say at birth,
    (*b*) The education to which it has been subjected,
    (*c*) Other experience, not to be described as education, to which it has been subjected.

Instead of trying to produce a programme to simulate the adult mind, why not rather try to produce one which simulates the child's? If this were then subjected to an appropriate course of education one would obtain the adult brain. Presumably the child-brain is something like a note-book as one buys it from the stationers. Rather little mechanism, and lots of blank sheets. (Mechanism and writing are from our point of view almost synonymous.) Our hope is that there is so little mechanism in the child-brain that something like it can be easily programmed. The amount of work in the education we can assume, as a first approximation, to be much the same as for the human child.

We have thus divided our problem into two parts. The child-programme and the education process. These two remain very closely connected. We cannot expect to find a good child-machine at the first attempt. One must experiment with teaching one such machine and see how well it learns. One can then try another and see if it is better or worse. There is an obvious connection between this process and evolution, by the identifications

Structure of the child machine = Hereditary material
Changes of the child machine   = Mutations
Natural selection   = Judgment of the experimenter

One may hope, however, that this process will be more expeditious than evolution. The survival of the fittest is a slow method for measuring advantages. The experimenter, by the exercise of intelligence, should be able to speed it up. Equally important is the fact that he is not restricted to random mutations. If he can trace a cause for some weakness he can probably think of the kind of mutation which will improve it.

It will not be possible to apply exactly the same teaching process to the machine as to a normal child. It will not, for instance, be provided with legs, so that it could not be asked to go out and fill the coal scuttle. Possibly it might not have eyes. But however well these deficiencies might be overcome by clever engineering, one could not send the creature to school without the other children making excessive fun of it. It must be given some tuition. We need not be too concerned about the legs, eyes, etc. The example of Miss *Helen Keller* shows that education can take place provided that communication in both directions between teacher and pupil can take place by some means or other.

We normally associate punishments and rewards with the teaching process. Some simple child-machines can be constructed or programmed on this sort of principle. The machine has to be so constructed that events which shortly preceded the occurrence of a punishment-signal are unlikely to be repeated, whereas a reward-signal increased the probability of repetition of the events which led up to it. These definitions do not pre-suppose any feelings on the part of the machine. I have done some experiments with one such child-machine, and succeeded in teaching it a few things, but the teaching method was too unorthodox for the experiment to be considered really successful.

The use of punishments and rewards can at best be a part of the teaching process. Roughly speaking, if the teacher has no other means of communicating to the pupil, the amount of information which can reach him does not exceed the total number of rewards and punishments applied. By the time a child has learnt to repeat 'Casabianca' he would probably feel very sore indeed, if the text could only be discovered by a 'Twenty Questions' technique, every 'NO' taking the form of a blow. It is necessary therefore to have some other 'unemotional' channels of communication. If these are available it is possible to teach a machine by punishments and rewards to obey orders given in some language, *e.g.* a symbolic language. These orders are to be transmitted through the 'unemotional' channels. The use of this language will diminish greatly the number of punishments and rewards required.

Opinions may vary as to the complexity which is suitable in the child machine. One might try to make it as simple as possible consistently with the general principles. Alternatively one might have a complete system of logical inference 'built in'.[3] In the latter case the store would be largely occupied with

---

3 Or rather 'programmed in' for our child-machine will be programmed in a digital computer. But the logical system will not have to be learnt.

definitions and propositions. The propositions would have various kinds of status, *e.g.* well-established facts, conjectures, mathematically proved theorems, statements given by an authority, expressions having the logical form of proposition but not belief-value. Certain propositions may be described as 'imperatives'. The machine should be so constructed that as soon as an imperative is classed as 'well-established' the appropriate action automatically takes place. To illustrate this, suppose the teacher says to the machine, 'Do your homework now'. This may cause 'Teacher says "Do your homework now"' to be included amongst the well-established facts. Another such fact might be, 'Everything that teacher says is true'. Combining these may eventually lead to the imperative, 'Do your homework now', being included amongst the well-established facts, and this, by the construction of the machine, will mean that the homework actually gets started, but the effect is very satisfactory. The processes of inference used by the machine need not be such as would satisfy the most exacting logicians. There might for instance be no hierarchy of types. But this need not mean that type fallacies will occur, any more than we are bound to fall over unfenced cliffs. Suitable imperatives (expressed *within* the systems, not forming part of the rules *of* the system) such as 'Do not use a class unless it is a subclass of one which has been mentioned by teacher' can have a similar effect to 'Do not go too near the edge'.

The imperatives that can be obeyed by a machine that has no limbs are bound to be of a rather intellectual character, as in the example (doing homework) given above. Important amongst such imperatives will be ones which regulate the order in which the rules of the logical system concerned are to be applied. For at each stage when one is using a logical system, there is a very large number of alternative steps, any of which one is permitted to apply, so far as obedience to the rules of the logical system is concerned. These choices make the difference between a brilliant and a footling reasoner, not the difference between a sound and a fallacious one. Propositions leading to imperatives of this kind might be 'When Socrates is mentioned, use the syllogism in Barbara' or 'If one method has been proved to be quicker than another, do not use the slower method'. Some of these may be 'given by authority', but others may be produced by the machine itself, e.g. by scientific induction.

The idea of a learning machine may appear paradoxical to some readers. How can the rules of operation of the machine change? They should describe completely how the machine will react whatever its history might be, whatever changes it might undergo. The rules are thus quite time-invariant. This is quite true. The explanation of the paradox is that the rules which get changed in the learning process are of a rather less pretentious kind, claiming only an ephemeral validity. The reader may draw a parallel with the Constitution of the United States.

An important feature of a learning machine is that its teacher will often be very largely ignorant of quite what is going on inside, although he may still be able to some extent to predict his pupil's behaviour. This should apply most strongly to the later education of a machine arising from a child-machine of well-tried design (or programme). This is in clear contrast with normal procedure when using a machine to do computations: one's object is then to have a clear mental picture of the state of the machine at each moment in the computation. This object can only be achieved with a struggle. The view that 'the machine can only do what we know how to order it to do',[4] appears strange in face of this. Most of the programmes which we can put into the machine will result in its doing something that we cannot make sense of at all, or which we regard as completely random behaviour. Intelligent behaviour presumably consists in a departure from the completely disciplined behaviour involved in computation, but a rather slight one, which does not give rise to random behaviour, or to pointless repetitive loops. Another important result of preparing our machine for its part in the imitation game by a process of teaching and learning is that 'human fallibility' is likely to be omitted in a rather natural way, *i.e.* without special 'coaching'. Processes that are learnt do not produce a hundred per cent certainty of result; if they did they could not be unlearnt.

It is probably wise to include a random element in a learning machine (see p. 41). A random element is rather useful when we are searching for a solution of some problem. Suppose for instance we wanted to find a number between 50 and 200 which was equal to the square of the sum of its digits, we might start at 51 then try 52 and go on until we got a number that worked. Alternatively we might choose numbers at random until we got a good one. This method has the advantage that it is unnecessary to keep track of the values that have been tried, but the disadvantage that one may try the same one twice, but this is not very important if there are several solutions. The systematic method has the disadvantage that there may be an enormous block without any solutions in the region which has to be investigated first. Now the learning process may be regarded as a search for a form of behaviour which will satisfy the teacher (or some other criterion). Since there is probably a very large number of satisfactory solutions the random method seems to be better than the systematic. It should be noticed that it is used in the analogous process of evolution. But there the systematic method is not possible. How could one keep track of the different genetical combinations that had been tried, so as to avoid trying them again?

We may hope that machines will eventually compete with men in all purely intellectual fields. But which are the best ones to start with? Even this is a difficult decision. Many people think that a very abstract activity, like the playing of chess, would be best. It can also be maintained that it is best to provide the machine with the best sense organs that money can buy, and then teach it to understand and speak English. This process could follow the normal teaching of a child. Things would be pointed out and named, etc. Again I do not know what the right answer is, but I think both approaches should be tried.

We can only see a short distance ahead, but we can see plenty there that needs to be done.

References   SAMUEL BUTLER *Erewhon* (London, 1865). Chapters 23, 24, 25, 'The Book of the Machines'.

ALONZO CHURCH, 'An Unsolvable Problem of Elementary Number Theory', *American J. of Math.*, 58 (1936), 345–63.

4 Compare Lady Lovelace's statement (p. 50), which does not contain the word 'only'.

K. Gödel, 'Über formal unentscheidbare Sätze der Principia Mathematica und verwandter Systeme, I', *Monatshefte für Math. und Phys.* (1931), 173–89.

D. R. Hartree, *Calculating Instruments and Machines* (New York, 1949).

S. C. Kleene, 'General Recursive Functions of Natural Numbers', *American J. of Math.*, 57 (1935), 153–73 and 219–44.

G. Jefferson, 'The Mind of Mechanical Man'. Lister Oration for 1949. *British Medical Journal*, vol. i (1949), 1105–21.

Countess of Lovelace, 'Translator's Notes' to an Article on Babbage's Analytical Engine', *Scientific Memoirs* (ed. by R. Taylor), vol. 3 (1842), 691–731.

Bertrand Russell, *History of Western Philosophy* (London, 1940).

A. M. Turing, 'On Computable Numbers, with an Application to the Entscheidungsproblem', *Proc. London Math. Soc.* (2), 42 (1937), 230–65.

3

Man-Computer Symbiosis

J. C. R. Licklider

In this article from 1960 J. C. R. Licklider describes a form of co-operation in which phases and process of thought are distributed between man and computer. In his discussion, Licklider proposed that real-time interaction between men and computers could lead to new processes of thought, in which computers would not only perform calculations, but also enter into the formulative phases of thinking. In addition, he describes a sophisticated set of interfaces to support this man–computer symbiosis. Licklider, in his role as director of ARPA-IPTO, funded development research by Douglas Engelbart, whose work contributed to the realization of some of the ideas described in this article.

Original Summary—Man-computer symbiosis is an expected development in cooperative interaction between men and electronic computers. It will involve very close coupling between the human and the electronic members of the partnership. The main aims are 1) to let computers facilitate formulative thinking as they now facilitate the solution of formulated problems, and 2) to enable men and computers to cooperate in making decisions and controlling complex situations without inflexible dependence on predetermined programs. In the anticipated symbiotic partnership, men will set the goals, formulate the hypotheses, determine the criteria, and perform the evaluations. Computing machines will do the routinizable work that must be done to prepare the way for insights and decisions in technical and scientific thinking. Preliminary analyses indicate that the symbiotic partnership will perform intellectual operations much more effectively than man alone can perform them. Prerequisites for the achievement of the effective, cooperative association include developments in computer time sharing, in memory components, in memory organization, in programming languages, and in input and output equipment.

I. Introduction

A. Symbiosis

THE FIG TREE is pollinated only by the insect *Blastophaga grossorum*. The larva of the insect lives in the ovary of the fig tree, and there it gets its food. The tree and the insect are thus heavily interdependent: the tree cannot reproduce without the insect; the insect cannot eat without the tree; together, they constitute not only a viable but a productive and thriving partnership. This cooperative 'living together in intimate association, or even close union, of two dissimilar organisms' is called symbiosis.[1]

'Man-computer symbiosis' is a subclass of man-machine systems. There are many man-machine systems. At present, however, there are no

From *IRE Transactions on Human Factors in Electronics* (March 1960).

1 'Webster's New International Dictionary,' 2nd ed., G. and C. Merriam Co., Springfield, Mass., p. 2555; 1958.

man-computer symbioses. The purposes of this paper are to present the concept and, hopefully, to foster the development of man-computer symbiosis by analyzing some problems of interaction between men and computing machines, calling attention to applicable principles of man-machine engineering, and pointing out a few questions to which research answers are needed. The hope is that, in not too many years, human brains and computing machines will be coupled together very tightly, and that the resulting partnership will think as no human brain has ever thought and process data in a way not approached by the information-handling machines we know today.

B. Between 'Mechanically Extended Man' and 'Artificial Intelligence'

As a concept, man-computer symbiosis is different in an important way from what North[2] has called 'mechanically extended man.' In the man-machine systems of the past, the human operator supplied the initiative, the direction, the integration, and the criterion. The mechanical parts of the systems were mere extensions, first of the human arm, then of the human eye. These systems certainly did not consist of 'dissimilar organisms living together . . .' There was only one kind of organism—man—and the rest was there only to help him.

In one sense of course, any man-made system is intended to help man, to help a man or men outside the system. If we focus upon the human operator(s) within the system, however, we see that, in some areas of technology, a fantastic change has taken place during the last few years. 'Mechanical extension' has given way to replacement of men, to automation, and the men who remain are there more to help than to be helped. In some instances, particularly in large computer-centered information and control systems, the human operators are responsible mainly for functions that it proved infeasible to automate. Such systems ('humanly extended machines,' North might call them) are not symbiotic systems. They are 'semi-automatic' systems, systems that started out to be fully automatic but fell short of the goal.

Man-computer symbiosis is probably not the ultimate paradigm for complex technological systems. It seems entirely possible that, in due course, electronic or chemical 'machines' will outdo the human brain in most of the functions we now consider exclusively within its province. Even now, Gelernter's IBM-704 program for proving theorems in plane geometry proceeds at about the same pace as Brooklyn high school students, and makes similar errors.[3] There are, in fact, several theorem-proving, problem-solving, chess-playing, and pattern-recognizing programs (too many for complete reference[4] capable of rivaling human intellectual performance in

2 J. D. North, 'The rational behavior of mechanically extended man,' Boulton Paul Aircraft Ltd., Wolverhampton, Eng.; September, 1954.

3 H. Gelernter, 'Realization of a Geometry Theorem Proving Machine,' Unesco, NS, ICIP, 1.6.6, Internatl. Conf. on Information Processing, Paris, France; June, 1959.

4 A. Newell and J. C. Shaw, 'Programming the logic theory machine,' *Proc. WJCC*, pp. 230–240; March, 1957. P. C. Gilmore, 'A Program for the Production of Proofs for Theorems Derivable Within the First Order Predicate Calculus from Axioms,' Unesco, NS, ICIP, 1.6.14, Internatl. Conf. on Information Processing, Paris, France; June, 1959. B. G. Farley and W. A. Clark, 'Simulation of self-organizing systems by digital computers,' IRE TRANS. ON INFORMATION THEORY, vol. IT–4, pp. 76–84; September, 1954. R. M. Friedberg, 'A learning machine: Part I,' *IBM J. Res. & Dev.*, vol. 2, pp. 2–13; January, 1958. O. G. Selfridge, 'Pandemonium, a paradigm for learning,' *Proc. Symp. Mechanisation of Thought Processes, Natl. Physical Lab.*, Teddington, Eng.; November, 1958. W. W. Bledsoe and

restricted areas; and Newell, Simon, and Shaw's[5] 'general problem solver' may remove some of the restrictions. In short, it seems worthwhile to avoid argument with (other) enthusiasts for artificial intelligence by conceding dominance in the distant future of cerebration to machines alone. There will nevertheless be a fairly long interim during which the main intellectual advances will be made by men and computers working together in intimate association. A multidisciplinary study group, examining future research and development problems of the Air Force, estimated that it would be 1980 before developments in artificial intelligence make it possible for machines alone to do much thinking or problem solving of military significance. That would leave, say, five years to develop man-computer symbiosis and 15 years to use it. The 15 may be 10 or 500, but those years should be intellectually the most creative and exciting in the history of mankind.

II. Aims of Man-Computer Symbiosis

Present-day computers are designed primarily to solve preformulated problems or to process data according to predetermined procedures. The course of the computation may be conditional upon results obtained during the computation, but all the alternatives must be foreseen in advance. (If an unforeseen alternative arises, the whole process comes to a halt and awaits the necessary extension of the program.) The requirement for preformulation or predetermination is sometimes no great disadvantage. It is often said that programming for a computing machine forces one to think clearly, that it disciplines the thought process. If the user can think his problem through in advance, symbiotic association with a computing machine is not necessary.

However, many problems that can be thought through in advance are very difficult to think through in advance. They would be easier to solve, and they could be solved faster, through an intuitively guided trial-and-error procedure in which the computer cooperated, turning up flaws in the reasoning or revealing unexpected turns in the solution. Other problems simply cannot be formulated without computing-machine aid. Poinearé anticipated the frustration of an important group of would-be computer users when he said, 'The question is not, "What is the answer?" The question is, "What is the question?" ' One of the main aims of man-computer symbiosis is to bring the computing machine effectively into the formulative parts of technical problems.

I. Browning, 'Pattern Recognition and Reading by Machine,' presented at the Eastern Joint Computer Conf., Boston, Mass., December, 1959. C. E. Shannon, 'Programming a computer for playing chess,' *Phil. Mag.*, vol. 41, pp. 256–75; March, 1950. A. Newell, 'The chess machine: an example of dealing with a complex task by adaptation,' *Proc. WJCC*, pp. 101–108; March, 1955. A. Bernstein and M. deV. Roberts, 'Computer versus chess-player,' *Scientific American*, vol. 198, pp. 96–98; June, 1958. A. Newell, J. C. Shaw, and H. A. Simon, 'Chess-playing programs and the problem of complexity,' *IBM J. Res. & Dev.*, vol. 2, pp. 320–335; October, 1958. H. Sherman, 'A Quasi-Topological Method for Recognition of Line Patterns,' Unesco, NS, ICIP, H.L.5, Internatl. Conf. on Information Processing, Paris, France; June, 1959. G. P. Dinncen, 'Programming pattern recognition,' *Proc. WJCC*, pp. 94–100; March, 1955.

5 A. Newell, H. A. Simon, and J. C. Shaw, 'Report on a general problem-solving program,' Unesco, NS, ICIP, 1.6.8, Internatl. Conf. on Information Processing, Paris, France; June, 1959.

62   J. C. R. LICKLIDER

The other main aim is closely related. It is to bring computing machines effectively into processes of thinking that must go on in 'real time,' time that moves too fast to permit using computers in conventional ways. Imagine trying, for example, to direct a battle with the aid of a computer on such a schedule as this. You formulate your problem today. Tomorrow you spend with a programmer. Next week the computer devotes 5 minutes to assembling your program and 47 seconds to calculating the answer to your problem. You get a sheet of paper 20 feet long, full of numbers that, instead of providing a final solution, only suggest a tactic that should be explored by simulation. Obviously, the battle would be over before the second step in its planning was begun. To think in interaction with a computer in the same way that you think with a colleague whose competence supplements your own will require much tighter coupling between man and machine than is suggested by the example and than is possible today.

III. Need for Computer Participation in Formulative and Real-Time Thinking

The preceding paragraphs tacitly made the assumption that, if they could be introduced effectively into the thought process, the functions that can be performed by data-processing machines would improve or facilitate thinking and problem solving in an important way. That assumption may require justification.

A. A Preliminary and Informal Time-and-Motion Analysis of Technical Thinking

Despite the fact that there is a voluminous literature on thinking and problem solving, including intensive case-history studies of the process of invention, I could find nothing comparable to a time-and-motion-study analysis of the mental work of a person engaged in a scientific or technical enterprise. In the spring and summer of 1957, therefore, I tried to keep track of what one moderately technical person actually did during the hours he regarded as devoted to work. Although I was aware of the inadequacy of the sampling, I served as my own subject.

It soon became apparent that the main thing I did was to keep records, and the project would have become an infinite regress if the keeping of records had been carried through in the detail envisaged in the initial plan. It was not. Nevertheless, I obtained a picture of my activities that gave me pause. Perhaps my spectrum is not typical—I hope it is not, but I fear it is.

About 85 per cent of my 'thinking' time was spent getting into a position to think, to make a decision, to learn something I needed to know. Much more time went into finding or obtaining information than into digesting it. Hours went into the plotting of graphs, and other hours into instructing an assistant how to plot. When the graphs were finished, the relations were obvious at once, but the plotting had to be done in order to make them so. At one point, it was necessary to compare six experimental determinations of a function relating speech-intelligibility to speech-to-noise ratio. No two experimenters had used the same definition or measure of speech-to-noise ratio. Several hours of calculating were required to get the data into comparable form. When they were in comparable form, it took only a few seconds to determine what I needed to know.

Throughout the period I examined, in short, my 'thinking' time was devoted mainly to activities that were essentially clerical or mechanical: searching, calculating, plotting, transforming, determining the logical or dynamic consequences of a set of assumptions or hypotheses, preparing the way for a decision or an insight. Moreover, my choices of what to attempt and what not to attempt were determined to an embarrassingly great extent by considerations of clerical feasibility, not intellectual capability.

The main suggestion conveyed by the findings just described is that the operations that fill most of the time allegedly devoted to technical thinking are operations that can be performed more effectively by machines than by men. Severe problems are posed by the fact that these operations have to be performed upon diverse variables and in unforeseen and continually changing sequences. If those problems can be solved in such a way as to create a symbiotic relation between a man and a fast information-retrieval and data-processing machine, however, it seems evident that the cooperative interaction would greatly improve the thinking process.

B. Comparative Capabilities of Men and Computers

It may be appropriate to acknowledge, at this point, that we are using the term 'computer' to cover a wide class of calculating, data-processing, and information-storage-and-retrieval machines. The capabilities of machines in this class are increasing almost daily. It is therefore hazardous to make general statements about capabilities of the class. Perhaps it is equally hazardous to make general statements about the capabilities of men. Nevertheless, certain genotypic differences in capability between men and computers do stand out, and they have a bearing on the nature of possible man-computer symbiosis and the potential value of achieving it.

As has been said in various ways, men are noisy, narrow-band devices, but their nervous systems have very many parallel and simultaneously active channels. Relative to men, computing machines are very fast and very accurate, but they are constrained to perform only one or a few elementary operations at a time. Men are flexible, capable of 'programming themselves contingently' on the basis of newly received information. Computing machines are single-minded, constrained by their 'pre-programming.' Men naturally speak redundant languages organized around unitary objects and coherent actions and employing 20 to 60 elementary symbols. Computers 'naturally' speak nonredundant languages, usually with only two elementary symbols and no inherent appreciation either of unitary objects or of coherent actions.

To be rigorously correct, those characterizations would have to include many qualifiers. Nevertheless, the picture of dissimilarity (and therefore potential supplementation) that they present is essentially valid. Computing machines can do readily, well, and rapidly many things that are difficult or impossible for man, and men can do readily and well, though not rapidly, many things that are difficult or impossible for computers. That suggests that a symbiotic cooperation, if successful in integrating the positive characteristics of men and computers, would be of great value. The differences in speed and in language, of course, pose difficulties that must be overcome.

IV. Separable Functions of Men and Computers in the Anticipated Symbiotic Association

It seems likely that the contributions of human operators and equipment will blend together so completely in many operations that it will be difficult to separate them neatly in analysis. That would be the case if, in gathering data on which to base a decision, for example, both the man and the computer came up with relevant precedents from experience and if the computer then suggested a course of action that agreed with the man's intuitive judgment. (In theorem-proving programs, computers find precedents in experience, and in the SAGE System, they suggest courses of action. The foregoing is not a far-fetched example.) In other operations, however, the contributions of men and equipment will be to some extent separable.

Men will set the goals and supply the motivations, of course, at least in the early years. They will formulate hypotheses. They will ask questions. They will think of mechanisms, procedures, and models. They will remember that such-and-such a person did some possibly relevant work on a topic of interest back in 1947, or at any rate shortly after World War II, and they will have an idea in what journals it might have been published. In general, they will make approximate and fallible, but leading, contributions, and they will define criteria and serve as evaluators, judging the contributions of the equipment and guiding the general line of thought.

In addition, men will handle the very-low-probability situations when such situations do actually arise. (In current man-machine systems, that is one of the human operator's most important functions. The sum of the probabilities of very-low-probability alternatives is often much too large to neglect.) Men will fill in the gaps, either in the problem solution or in the computer program, when the computer has no mode or routine that is applicable in a particular circumstance.

The information-processing equipment, for its part, will convert hypotheses into testable models and then test the models against data (which the human operator may designate roughly and identify as relevant when the computer presents them for his approval). The equipment will answer questions. It will simulate the mechanisms and models, carry out the procedures, and display the results to the operator. It will transform data, plot graphs ('cutting the cake' in whatever way the human operator specifies, or in several alternative ways if the human operator is not sure what he wants). The equipment will interpolate, extrapolate, and transform. It will convert static equations or logical statements into dynamic models so the human operator can examine their behavior. In general, it will carry out the routinizable, clerical operations that fill the intervals between decisions.

In addition, the computer will serve as a statistical-inference, decision-theory, or game-theory machine to make elementary evaluations of suggested courses of action whenever there is enough basis to support a formal statistical analysis. Finally, it will do as much diagnosis, pattern matching, and relevance recognizing as it profitably can, but it will accept a clearly secondary status in those areas.

V. Prerequisites for Realization of Man-Computer Symbiosis

The data-processing equipment tacitly postulated in the preceding section is not available. The computer programs have not been written. There are in fact several hurdles that stand between the nonsymbiotic present and the anticipated symbiotic future. Let us examine some of them to see more clearly what is needed and what the chances are of achieving it.

A. Speed Mismatch Between Men and Computers

Any present-day large-scale computer is too fast and too costly for real-time cooperative thinking with one man. Clearly, for the sake of efficiency and economy, the computer must divide its time among many users. Time-sharing systems are currently under active development. There are even arrangements to keep users from 'clobbering' anything but their own personal programs.

It seems reasonable to envision, for a time 10 or 15 years hence, a 'thinking center' that will incorporate the functions of present-day libraries together with anticipated advances in information storage and retrieval and the symbiotic functions suggested earlier in this paper. The picture readily enlarges itself into a network of such centers, connected to one another by wide-band communication lines and to individual users by leased-wire services. In such a system, the speed of the computers would be balanced, and the cost of the gigantic memories and the sophisticated programs would be divided by the number of users.

B. Memory Hardware Requirements

When we start to think of storing any appreciable fraction of a technical literature in computer memory, we run into billions of bits and, unless things change markedly, billions of dollars.

The first thing to face is that we shall not store all the technical and scientific papers in computer memory. We may store the parts that can be summarized most succinctly—the quantitative parts and the reference citations—but not the whole. Books are among the most beautifully engineered, and human-engineered, components in existence, and they will continue to be functionally important within the context of man-computer symbiosis. (Hopefully, the computer will expedite the finding, delivering, and returning of books.)

The second point is that a very important section of memory will be permanent: part *indelible memory* and part *published memory*. The computer will be able to write once into indelible memory, and then read back indefinitely, but the computer will not be able to erase indelible memory. (It may also over-write, turning all the 0's into 1's, as though marking over what was written earlier.) Published memory will be 'read-only' memory. It will be introduced into the computer already structured. The computer will be able to refer to it repeatedly, but not to change it. These types of memory will become more and more important as computers grow larger. They can be made more compact than core, thin-film, or even tape memory, and they will be much less expensive. The main engineering problems will concern selection circuitry.

In so far as other aspects of memory requirement are concerned, we may count upon the continuing development of ordinary scientific and business computing machines. There is some prospect that memory elements will become as fast as processing (logic) elements. That development would have a revolutionary effect upon the design of computers.

C. Memory Organization Requirements

Implicit in the idea of man-computer symbiosis are the requirements that information be retrievable both by name and by pattern and that it be accessible through procedure much faster than serial search. At least half of the problem of memory organization appears to reside in the storage procedure. Most of the remainder seems to be wrapped up in the problem of pattern recognition within the storage mechanism or medium. Detailed discussion of these problems is beyond the present scope. However, a brief outline of one promising idea, 'trie memory,' may serve to indicate the general nature of anticipated developments.

Trie memory is so called by its originator, Fredkin,[6] because it is designed to facilitate re*trie*val of information and because the branching storage structure, when developed, resembles a tree. Most common memory systems store functions of arguments at locations designated by the arguments. (In one sense, they do not store the arguments at all. In another and more realistic sense, they store all the possible arguments in the framework structure of the memory.) The trie memory system, on the other hand, stores both the functions and the arguments. The argument is introduced into the memory first, one character at a time, starting at a standard initial register. Each argument register has one cell for each character of the ensemble (e.g., two for information encoded in binary form) and each character cell has within it storage space for the address of the next register. The argument is stored by writing a series of addresses, each one of which tells where to find the next. At the end of the argument is a special 'end-of-argument' marker. Then follow directions to the function, which is stored in one or another of several ways, either further trie structure or 'list structure' often being most effective.

The trie memory scheme is inefficient for small memories, but it becomes increasingly efficient in using available storage space as memory size increases. The attractive features of the scheme are these: 1) The retrieval process is extremely simple. Given the argument, enter the standard initial register with the first character, and pick up the address of the second. Then go to the second register, and pick up the address of the third, etc. 2) If two arguments have initial characters in common, they use the same storage space for those characters. 3) The lengths of the arguments need not be the same, and need not be specified in advance. 4) No room in storage is reserved for or used by any argument until it is actually stored. The trie structure is created as the items are introduced into the memory. 5) A function can be used as an argument for another function, and that function as an argument for the next. Thus, for example, by entering with the argument, 'matrix multiplication,' one might retrieve the entire program for performing a matrix multiplication on the computer. 6) By examining the storage at a given level, one can determine what thus-far similar items have been stored. For example, if there is no citation for Egan, J. P., it is but a step or two backward to pick up the trail of Egan, James. . . .

6 Fredkin, Edward (1960), 'Trie Memory', *Communications of the ACM* v.3 no. 8 (August) pp. 490–9.

The properties just described do not include all the desired ones, but they bring computer storage into resonance with human operators and their predilection to designate things by naming or pointing.

D. The Language Problem
The basic dissimiliarity between human languages and computer languages may be the most serious obstacle to true symbiosis. It is reassuring, however, to note what great strides have already been made, through interpretive programs and particularly through assembly or compiling programs such as FORTRAN, to adapt computers to human language forms. The 'Information Processing Language' of Shaw, Newell, Simon, and Ellis[7] represents another line of rapprochement. And, in ALGOL and related systems, men are proving their flexibility by adopting standard formulas of representation and expression that are readily translatable into machine language.

For the purposes of real-time cooperation between men and computers, it will be necessary, however, to make use of an additional and rather different principle of communication and control. The idea may be highlighted by comparing instructions ordinarily addressed to intelligent human beings with instructions ordinarily used with computers. The latter specify precisely the individual steps to take and the sequence in which to take them. The former present or imply something about incentive or motivation, and they supply a criterion by which the human executor of the instructions will know when he has accomplished his task. In short: instructions directed to computers specify courses; instructions directed to human beings specify goals.

Men appear to think more naturally and easily in terms of goals than in terms of courses. True, they usually know something about directions in which to travel or lines along which to work, but few start out with precisely formulated itineraries. Who, for example, would depart from Boston for Los Angeles with a detailed specification of the route? Instead, to paraphrase Wiener, men bound for Los Angeles try continually to decrease the amount by which they are not yet in the smog.

Computer instruction through specification of goals is being approached along two paths. The first involves problem-solving, hill-climbing, self-organizing programs. The second involves real-time concatenation of preprogrammed segments and closed subroutines which the human operator can designate and call into action simply by name.

Along the first of these paths, there has been promising exploratory work. It is clear that, working within the loose constraints of predetermined strategies, computers will in due course be able to devise and simplify their own procedures for achieving stated goals. Thus far, the achievements have not been substantively important; they have constituted only 'demonstration in principle.' Nevertheless, the implications are far-reaching.

Although the second path is simpler and apparently capable of earlier realization, it has been relatively neglected. Fredkin's trie memory provides a promising paradigm. We may in due course see a serious effort to develop computer programs that can be connected together like the words and phrases of speech to do whatever computation or control is required at the

---

7 J. C. Shaw, A. Newell, H. A. Simon, and T. O. Ellis, 'A command structure for complex information processing,' *Proc. WJCC*, pp. 119–128; May, 1958.

moment. The consideration that holds back such an effort, apparently, is that the effort would produce nothing that would be of great value in the context of existing computers. It would be unrewarding to develop the language before there are any computing machines capable of responding meaningfully to it.

E. Input and Output Equipment

The department of data processing that seems least advanced, in so far as the requirements of man-computer symbiosis are concerned, is the one that deals with input and output equipment or, as it is seen from the human operator's point of view, displays and controls. Immediately after saying that, it is essential to make qualifying comments, because the engineering of equipment for high-speed introduction and extraction of information has been excellent, and because some very sophisticated display and control techniques have been developed in such research laboratories as the Lincoln Laboratory. By and large, in generally available computers, however, there is almost no provision for any more effective, immediate man-machine communication than can be achieved with an electric typewriter.

Displays seem to be in a somewhat better state than controls. Many computers plot graphs on oscilloscope screens, and a few take advantage of the remarkable capabilities, graphical and symbolic, of the charactron display tube. Nowhere, to my knowledge, however, is there anything approaching the flexibility and convenience of the pencil and doodle pad or the chalk and blackboard used by men in technical discussion.

1. Desk-Surface Display and Control

Certainly, for effective man-computer interaction, it will be necessary for the man and the computer to draw graphs and pictures and to write notes and equations to each other on the same display surface. The man should be able to present a function to the computer, in a rough but rapid fashion, by drawing a graph. The computer should read the man's writing, perhaps on the condition that it be in clear block capitals, and it should immediately post, at the location of each hand-drawn symbol, the corresponding character as interpreted and put into precise typeface. With such an input-output device, the operator would quickly learn to write or print in a manner legible to the machine. He could compose instructions and sub-routines, set them into proper format, and check them over before introducing them finally into the computer's main memory. He could even define new symbols, as Gilmore and Savell[8] have done at the Lincoln Laboratory, and present them directly to the computer. He could sketch out the format of a table roughly and let the computer shape it up with precision. He could correct the computer's data, instruct the machine via flow diagrams, and in general interact with it very much as he would with another engineer, except that the 'other engineer' would be a precise draftsman, a lightning calculator, a mnemonic wizard, and many other valuable partners all in one.

2. Computer-Posted Wall Display

In some technological systems, several men share responsibility for controlling vehicles whose behaviors interact. Some information must be presented

8 J. T. Gilmore and R. E. Savell, 'The Lincoln Writer,' Lincoln Laboratory, M.I.T., Lexington, Mass., Rept. 51–8; October, 1959.

simultaneously to all the men, preferably on a common grid, to coordinate their actions. Other information is of relevance only to one or two operators. There would be only a confusion of uninterpretable clutter if all the information were presented on one display to all of them. The information must be posted by a computer, since manual plotting is too slow to keep it up to date.

The problem just outlined is even now a critical one, and it seems certain to become more and more critical as time goes by. Several designers are convinced that displays with the desired characteristics can be constructed with the aid of flashing lights and time-sharing viewing screens based on the light-valve principle.

The large display should be supplemented, according to most of those who have thought about the problem, by individual display-control units. The latter would permit the operators to modify the wall display without leaving their locations. For some purposes, it would be desirable for the operators to be able to communicate with the computer through the supplementary displays and perhaps even through the wall display. At least one scheme for providing such communication seems feasible.

The large wall display and its associated system are relevant, of course, to symbiotic cooperation between a computer and a team of men. Laboratory experiments have indicated repeatedly that informal, parallel arrangements of operators, coordinating their activities through reference to a large situation display, have important advantages over the arrangement, more widely used, that locates the operators at individual consoles and attempts to correlate their actions through the agency of a computer. This is one of several operator-team problems in need of careful study.

3. Automatic Speech Production and Recognition

How desirable and how feasible is speech communication between human operators and computing machines? That compound question is asked whenever sophisticated data-processing systems are discussed. Engineers who work and live with computers take a conservative attitude toward the desirability. Engineers who have had experience in the field of automatic speech recognition take a conservative attitude toward the feasibility. Yet there is continuing interest in the idea of talking with computing machines. In large part, the interest stems from realization that one can hardly take a military commander or a corporation president away from his work to teach him to type. If computing machines are ever to be used directly by top-level decision makers, it may be worth-while to provide communication via the most natural means, even at considerable cost.

Preliminary analysis of his problems and time scales suggests that a corporation president would be interested in a symbiotic association with a computer only as an avocation. Business situations usually move slowly enough that there is time for briefings and conferences. It seems reasonable, therefore, for computer specialists to be the ones who interact directly with computers in business offices.

The military commander, on the other hand, faces a greater probability of having to make critical decisions in short intervals of time. It is easy to over-dramatize the notion of the ten-minute war, but it would be dangerous to count on having more than ten minutes in which to make a critical decision.

As military system ground environments and control centers grow in capability and complexity, therefore, a real requirement for automatic speech production and recognition in computers seems likely to develop. Certainly, if the equipment were already developed, reliable, and available, it would be used.

In so far as feasibility is concerned, speech production poses less severe problems of a technical nature than does automatic recognition of speech sounds. A commercial electronic digital voltmeter now reads aloud its indications, digit by digit. For eight or ten years, at the Bell Telephone Laboratories, the Royal Institute of Technology (Stockholm), the Signals Research and Development Establishment (Christchurch), the Haskins Laboratory, and the Massachusetts Institute of Technology, Dunn,[9] Fant,[10] Lawrence,[11] Cooper,[12] Stevens,[13] and their co-workers, have demonstrated successive generations of intelligible automatic talkers. Recent work at the Haskins Laboratory has led to the development of a digital code, suitable for use by computing machines, that makes an automatic voice utter intelligible connected discourse.[14]

The feasibility of automatic speech recognition depends heavily upon the size of the vocabulary of words to be recognized and upon the diversity of talkers and accents with which it must work. Ninety-eight per cent correct recognition of naturally spoken decimal digits was demonstrated several years ago at the Bell Telephone Laboratories and at the Lincoln Laboratory.[15] To go a step up the scale of vocabulary size, we may say that an automatic recognizer of clearly spoken alpha-numerical characters can almost surely be developed now on the basis of existing knowledge. Since untrained operators can read at least as rapidly as trained ones can type, such a device would be a convenient tool in almost any computer installation.

For real-time interaction on a truly symbiotic level, however, a vocabulary of about 2000 words, e.g., 1000 words of something like basic English and 1000 technical terms, would probably be required. That constitutes a challenging problem. In the consensus of acousticians and linguists, construction of a recognizer of 2000 words cannot be accomplished now. However, there are several organizations that would happily undertake to develop an automatic recognizer for such a vocabulary on a five-year basis. They would stipulate that the speech be clear speech, dictation style, without unusual accent.

9 H. K. Dunn, 'The calculation of vowel resonances, and an electrical vocal tract,' *J. Acoust. Soc. Amer.*, vol. 22, pp. 740–753; November, 1950.

10 G. Fant, 'On the Acoustics of Speech,' paper presented at the Third Internatl. Congress on Acoustics, Stuttgart, Ger.; September, 1959.

11 W. Lawrence, *et al.*, 'Methods and Purposes of Speech Synthesis,' Signals Res. and Dev. Estab., Ministry of Supply, Christchurch, Hants, England, Rept. 56/1457; March, 1956.

12 F. S. Cooper, *et al.*, 'Some experiments on the perception of synthetic speech sounds,' *J. Acoust. Soc. Amer.*, vol. 24, pp. 597–606; November, 1952.

13 K. N. Stevens, S. Kasowski, and C. G. Fant, 'Electric analog of the vocal tract,' *J. Acoust. Soc. Amer.*, vol. 25, pp. 734–742; July, 1953.

14 A. M. Liberman, F. Ingemann, L. Lisker, P. Delattre, and F. S. Cooper, 'Minimal rules for synthesizing speech,' *J. Acoust. Soc. Amer.*, vol. 31, pp. 1490–1499; November, 1959.

15 K. H. Davis, R. Biddulph, and S. Balashek, 'Automatic recognition of spoken digits,' in W. Jackson, 'Communication Theory,' Butterworths Scientific Publications, London, Eng., pp. 433–441; 1953. J. W. Forgie and C. D. Forgie, 'Results obtained from a vowel recognition computer program,' *J. Acoust. Soc. Amer.*, vol. 31, pp. 1480–1489; November, 1959.

Although detailed discussion of techniques of automatic speech recognition is beyond the present scope, it is fitting to note that computing machines are playing a dominant role in the development of automatic speech recognizers. They have contributed the impetus that accounts for the present optimism, or rather for the optimism presently found in some quarters. Two or three years ago, it appeared that automatic recognition of sizeable vocabularies would not be achieved for ten or fifteen years; that it would have to await much further, gradual accumulation of knowledge of acoustic, phonetic, linguistic, and psychological processes in speech communication. Now, however, many see a prospect of accelerating the acquisition of that knowledge with the aid of computer processing of speech signals, and not a few workers have the feeling that sophisticated computer programs will be able to perform well as speech-pattern recognizers even without the aid of much substantive knowledge of speech signals and processes. Putting those two considerations together brings the estimate of the time required to achieve practically significant speech recognition down to perhaps five years, the five years just mentioned.

4

A Conceptual Framework for the Augmentation of Man's Intellect

Douglas C. Engelbart

In this shortened version of his original funding proposal from 1962 Douglas Engelbart provides an overview of the conceptual framework for his programme for the augmentation of human intellect. Here he elaborates upon the thought behind his Augmentation Research Center, which developed the mouse, among other interfaces, and created some of the first multi-user computer applications.

Introduction

B Y 'AUGMENTING MAN'S INTELLECT' we mean increasing the capability of a man to approach a complex problem situation, gain comprehension to suit his particular needs, and to derive solutions to problems. Increased capability in this respect is taken to mean a mixture of the following: that comprehension can be gained more quickly; that better comprehension can be gained; that a useful degree of comprehension can be gained where previously the situation was too complex; that solutions can be produced more quickly; that better solutions can be produced; that solutions can be found where previously the human could find none. And by 'complex situations' we include the professional problems of diplomats, executives, social scientists, life scientists, physical scientists, attorneys, designers— whether the problem situation exists for twenty minutes or twenty years. We do not speak of isolated clever tricks that help in particular situations. We refer to a way of life in an integrated domain where hunches, cut-and-try, intangibles, and the human 'feel for a situation' usefully coexist with powerful concepts, streamlined terminology and notation, sophisticated methods, and high-powered electronic aids.

This paper covers the first phase of a program aimed at developing means to augment the human intellect. These methods or devices can include many things, all of which appear to be but extensions of those developed and used in the past to help man apply his native sensory, mental, and motor capabilities. We consider the total system of a human plus his augmentation devices and techniques as a proper field of search for practical possibilities. This field constitutes a very important system in our society; like most systems its

From Howerton and Weeks (eds.), *The Augmentation of Man's Intellect by Machine*, Vistas in Information Handling, vol. 1 (Washington DC: Spartan Books, 1963).

performance can best be improved by considering the whole as a set of interacting elements rather than a number of isolated components.

This kind of system approach to human intellectual effectiveness does not find a ready-made conceptual framework such as exists for established disciplines. Before a research program can pursue such an approach intelligently, so as to derive practical benefits within a reasonable time in addition to results of long-range significance, a conceptual framework must be searched out—a framework that provides orientation as to the important factors of the system, the relationships among these factors, the types of change among the system factors that offer likely improvements in performance, and the kind of research goals and methodology that seem promising.

Man's population and gross product are increasing at a considerable rate, but the *complexity* of his problems grows even faster. And the *urgency* with which solutions must be found becomes steadily greater in response to the increased rate of activity and the increasingly global nature of that activity. Augmenting man's intellect, in the sense defined above, would warrant the full-time efforts of an enlightened society if its leaders could be shown a reasonable approach and some plausible benefits.

Objective of the Study

The objective of this study is to develop a conceptual framework for a coordinated research and development program whose goals would be the following: (1) to find the factors that limit the effectiveness of the individual's basic information-handling capabilities in meeting the various needs of society for problem solving in its most general sense; and (2) to develop new techniques, procedures, and systems that will better adapt these basic capabilities to the needs, problems, and progress of society. We have established the following specifications for this framework:

1. It must provide perspective for both long-range basic research and research that will yield immediate practical results.

2. It must indicate what this augmentation will actually involve in the way of changes in working environment, thinking, skills, and methods of work.

3. It must be a basis for evaluating and assimilating the possibly relevant work and knowledge of existing fields.

4. It must reveal areas where research is possible and indicate ways to assess the research; must be a basis for choosing starting points and developing appropriate methodologies for the needed research.

Two points need emphasis here. First, although a conceptual framework has been constructed, it is still rudimentary. Further search and actual research are needed for the evolution of the framework. Second, even with a basic framework, an apparently small modification can significantly alter the results of the framework. The framework must therefore be viewed as tentative, and not considered as a detailed prediction or a collection of factual statements.

Conceptual Framework

A. General

The conceptual framework we seek must orient us toward the real possibilities and problems associated with using modern technology to give direct aid to an individual in comprehending complex situations, isolating the significant factors, and solving problems. To gain this orientation, we examine how individuals achieve their present level of effectiveness, and expect that this examination will reveal possibilities for improvement.

The entire effect of an individual on the world stems essentially from what he can communicate to the world through his limited motor channels. This communication, in turn, is based on information received from the outside world through his limited sensory channels; on information, drives, and needs generated within him; and on his processing of that information. His processing is of two kinds: that which he is generally conscious of (recognizing patterns, remembering, visualizing, abstracting, deducing, inducing, etc.), and that involving self-generated information, unconscious processing and mediating of received information, and mediating of conscious processing itself.

The individual does not use this information or processing to grapple directly with the sort of complex situation in which we seek to give him help. He uses his innate capabilities in a rather indirect fashion, since the situation is generally too complex to yield directly to his motor actions, and always too complex to yield comprehensions and solutions from direct sensory inspection and use of basic cognitive capabilities. For instance, an aborigine who possesses all of our *basic* sensory-mental-motor capabilities but does not possess our background of indirect knowledge and procedure cannot organize the proper direct actions necessary to drive a car through traffic, request a book from the library, call a committee meeting to discuss a tentative plan, call someone on the telephone, or compose a letter on the typewriter.

Our culture has evolved means for us to organize and utilize our basic capabilities so that we can comprehend truly complex situations and accomplish the processes of devising and implementing problem solutions. The ways in which human capabilities are thus extended are here called *augmentation means*, and we define four basic classes of them:

1. *Artifacts*—physical objects designed to provide for human comfort, the manipulation of things or materials, and the manipulation of symbols.

2. *Language*—the way in which the individual classifies the picture of his world into the concepts that his mind uses to model that world, and the symbols that he attaches to those concepts and uses in consciously manipulating the concepts ('thinking').

3. *Methodology*—the methods, procedures, and strategies with which an individual organizes his *goal-centered* (problem-solving) activity.

4. *Training*—the conditioning needed by the individual to bring his skills in using augmentation means 1, 2, and 3 to the point where they are operationally effective.

The system we wish to improve can thus be visualized as comprising a trained human being together with his artifacts, language, and methodology.

The explicit new system we contemplate will involve as artifacts computers and computer-controlled information-storage, information-handling, and information-display devices. The aspects of the conceptual framework that are discussed here are primarily those relating to the individual's ability to make significant use of such equipment in an integrated system.

Pervading all of the augmentation means is a particular structure or organization. While an untrained aborigine cannot drive a car through traffic because he cannot leap the gap between his cultural background and the kind of world that contains cars and traffic, it is possible for him to move step by step through an organized training program that will enable him to drive effectively and safely. In other words, the human mind neither learns nor acts by large leaps, but by a series of small steps so organized or structured that each one depends upon previous steps.

Although the size of the step a human being can take in comprehension, innovation, or execution is small in comparison to the over-all size of the step needed to solve a complex problem, human beings nevertheless do solve complex problems. It is the augmentation means that serve to subdivide a large problem in such a way that the human being can walk through it in little steps. The structure or organization of these little steps or actions we designate as *process hierarchies.*

Every thought process or action is composed of subprocesses. Such subprocesses include making a pencil stroke, writing a memo, or devising a plan. An appreciable number of discrete muscle movements must be coordinated to make a pencil stroke. Similarly, making particular pencil strokes and composing a memo are complex processes in themselves which are subprocesses to the over-all writing of the memo.

Although every subprocess is a process in its own right in that it consists of further subprocesses, there is no advantage here in isolating the ultimate 'bottom' of the process-hierarchical structure. There may be no way of determining whether the apparent 'bottom' (processes that cannot be further subdivided) exist in the physical world or in the limitations of human understanding. In any case, it is not necessary to begin from the 'bottom' in discussing particular process hierarchies. No person uses a completely unique process every time he performs a new task. Instead, he begins from a group of basic, sensory-mental-motor process capabilities, and adds to these certain of the process capabilities of his artifacts. There are only a finite number of such basic human and artifact capabilities from which to draw. Moreover, even quite different higher-order processes may have in common relatively high-order subprocesses.

When a person writes a memo (a reasonably high-order process), he makes use of many processes as subprocesses that are common to other high-order processes. For example, he makes use of planning, composing, dictating. The process of writing a memo is utilized as a subprocess within many different processes of a still higher order, such as organizing a committee, changing a policy, and so on.

It is likely that each individual develops a certain repertory of process capabilities from which he selects and adapts those that will compose the processes that he executes. This repertory is like a tool kit. Just as the mechanic must know what his tools can do and how to use them, so the intellectual worker must know the capabilities of his tools and have suitable methods, strategies, and rules of thumb for making use of them. All of the process capabilities in the individual's repertory rest ultimately on basic capabilities within him or his artifacts, and the entire repertory represents an integrated, hierarchical structure (which we often call the *repertory hierarchy*).

We find three general categories of process capabilities within a typical individual's repertory: (1) those executed completely within the human integument, which we call *explicit-human* process capabilities; (2) those possessed by artifacts for executing processes without human intervention, which we call *explicit-artifact* process capabilities; and (3) those we call the *composite* process capabilities, which are derived from hierarchies containing both of the other kinds.

We assume that it is our H-LAM/T system (Human using Language, Artifacts, and Methodology, in which he is Trained) that performs a process in any instance of use of this repertory. Let us consider the process of issuing a memorandum. There is a particular concept associated with this process—that of putting information into a formal package and distributing it to a set of people for a certain kind of consideration. That the type of information package associated with this concept has been given the special name of *memorandum* shows the denominating effect of this process on the system language.

The memo-writing process may be executed by using a set of process capabilities (intermixed or repetitive form) such as planning, developing subject matter, composing text, producing hard copy, and distributing. There is a definite way in which these subprocesses are organized that represents part of the system methodology. Each of these subprocesses represents a functional concept that must be a part of the system language if it is to be organized effectively into the human's way of doing things, and the symbolic portrayal of each concept must be such that the human can work with it and remember it.

If the memo is short and simple, the first three processes may be of the explicit-human type (i.e., the memo may be planned, developed and composed within the mind), and the last two of the composite type. If it is complex, involving a good deal of careful planning and development, then all of the subprocesses may be of the composite type (at least including the use of pencil and paper artifacts), and there may be many different applications of some of the process capabilities within the total process (successive drafts, revised plans).

Executing the above-listed set of subprocesses in proper sequence represents an execution of the memo-writing process. However, the very process of organizing and supervising the utilization of these subprocess capabilities is itself a most important subprocess of the memo-writing process. Hence the subprocess capabilities as listed would not be complete without the addition of a seventh, which we call the *executive* capability. This is the capability stemming from habit, strategy, rules of thumb, prejudice, learned method, intuition, unconscious dictates, or combinations thereof, to utilize the appropriate subprocess capabilities in a particular sequence and timing. An executive process (i.e., the exercise of an executive capability) involves such subprocesses as planning, selecting, and supervising; it is within the executive processes that the methodology in the H-LAM/T system is embodied.

To illustrate the capability-hierarchy features of our conceptual framework, let the reader consider an artifact innovation appearing directly within the relatively low-order capability for composing and modifying written text, and see how this can affect his hierarchy of capabilities. Suppose you had a new writing machine—a high-speed electric typewriter with some very special features. You can operate its keyboard to cause it to write text much as with a conventional typewriter. But the printing mechanism is more complicated; besides printing a visible character at every stroke, it adds special encoding features by means of invisible selective components in the ink and special shaping of the character.

As an auxiliary device, there is a gadget that is held like a pencil and, instead of a point, has a special sensing mechanism which can be moved along a line of the special printing from your writing machine (or one like it). The signals which this reading stylus sends through the flexible connecting wire to the writing machine are used to determine which characters are being sensed, thus causing the automatic typing of a duplicate string of characters. An information-storage mechanism in the writing machine permits you to sweep the reading stylus over the characters much faster than the writer can type; the writer will catch up with you when you stop to think about what word or string of words should be duplicated next, or while you reposition the straightedge guide along which you run the stylus.

This hypothetical writing machine thus permits you to use a new process of composing text. For instance, trial drafts can rapidly be composed from rearranged excerpts of old drafts, together with new words or passages which you insert by hand typing. Your first draft may represent a free outpouring of thoughts in any order, with the inspection of foregoing thoughts continuously stimulating new considerations and ideas to be entered. If the tangle of thoughts represented by the draft becomes too complex, you can compile a reordered draft quickly. It would be practical for you to accommodate more complexity in the trails of thought you might build in search of the path that suits your needs.

You can integrate your new ideas more easily, and thus harness your creativity more continuously, if you can quickly and flexibly change your working record. If it is easier to update any part of your working record to accommodate new developments in thought or circumstance, you will find it easier to incorporate more complex procedures in your way of doing things. This will probably allow you, for example, to accommodate the extra burden associated with keeping and using special files whose contents are both contributed to and utilized by any current work in a flexible manner— which in turn enables you to devise and use even more complex procedures to better harness your talents in your particular working situation.

The important thing to appreciate here is that a direct new innovation in one particular capability can have far-reaching effects throughout the rest of your capability hierarchy. A change can propagate *up* through the capability hierarchy, higher-order capabilities that can utilize the initially changed capability can now reorganize to take special advantage of this change and of the intermediate higher-capability changes. A change can propagate *down* through the hierarchy as a result of new capabilities at the high level and modification possibilities latent in lower levels. These latent capabilities may have been previously unusable in the hierarchy and become usable because of the new capability at the higher level.

The writing machine and its flexible copying capability would occupy you for a long time if you tried to exhaust the reverberating chain of associated possibilities for making useful innovations within your capability hierarchy. This one innovation could trigger a rather extensive redesign of this hierarchy; your method of accomplishing many of your tasks would change considerably. Indeed, this process characterizes the sort of evolution that our intellect-augmentation means have been undergoing since the first human brain appeared.

For our objective of deriving orientation about possibilities for actively pursuing an increase in human intellectual effectiveness, it is important to realize that we must be prepared to pursue such new-possibility chains throughout the *entire* capability hierarchy (calling for a 'system' approach). It is also important to realize that we must be oriented to the *synthesis* of new capabilities from reorganization of other capabilities, both old and new, that exist throughout the hierarchy (a 'system-engineering' approach).

B. The Basic Perspective

Individuals who operate effectively in our culture have already been considerably 'augmented.' Basic human capabilities for sensing stimuli, performing numerous mental operations, and communicating with the outside world are put to work in our society within a system—an H-LAM/T system—the individual augmented by the language, artifacts, and methodology in which he is trained. Furthermore, we suspect that improving the effectiveness of the individual as he operates in our society should be approached as a system-engineering problem—that is, the H-LAM/T system should be studied as an interacting whole from a synthesis-oriented approach.

This view of the system as an interacting whole is strongly bolstered by considering the repertory hierarchy of process capabilities that is structured from the basic ingredients within the H-LAM/T system. The realization that any potential change in language, artifact, or methodology has importance only relative to its use within a process, and that a new process capability appearing anywhere within that hierarchy can make practical a new consideration of latent change possibilities in many other parts of the hierarchy—possibilities in either language, artifacts, or methodology— brings out the strong interrelationship of these three augmentation means.

Increasing the effectiveness of the individual's use of his basic capabilities is a problem in redesigning the changeable parts of a system. The system is actively engaged in the continuous processes (among others) of developing comprehension within the individual and of solving problems; both processes are subject to human motivation, purpose, and will. Redesigning the system's capability for performing these processes means redesigning all or part of the repertory hierarchy. To redesign a structure we must learn as much as we can about the basic materials and components as they are utilized within the structure; beyond that, we must learn how to view, measure, analyze, and evaluate in terms of the functional whole and its purpose. In this particular case, no existing analytic theory is by itself adequate for the purpose of analyzing and evaluating over-all system performance; pursuit of an improved system thus demands the use of *experimental* methods.

It need not be solely the sophisticated or formal process capabilities that are added or modified in the redesign. Even so apparently minor an advance as artifacts for rapid mechanical duplication and rearrangement of text during the course of creative thought process could yield changes in an individual's repertory hierarchy that would represent a great increase in over-all effectiveness. Normally we might expect such equipment to appear slowly on the market; changes from old procedures would be small, and only gradually would the accumulated changes create markets for more radical versions of the equipment. Such an evolutionary process has been typical of the way our repertory hierarchies have formed and grown.

But an active research effort, aimed at exploring and evaluating possible integrated changes throughout the repertory hierarchy, could greatly accelerate this evolutionary process. The research effort could guide the product development of new artifacts toward taking long-range meaningful steps; simultaneously, competitively minded individuals who would respond to demonstrated methods for achieving greater personal effectiveness would create a market for the more radical equipment innovations. The guided evolutionary process could be expected to be considerably more rapid than the traditional one.

The category of 'more radical innovations' includes the digital computer as a tool for the personal use of an individual. Here there is not only promise of great flexibility in the composing and rearranging of text and diagrams before the individual's eyes, but also promise of many other process capabilities that can be integrated into the H-LAM/T system's repertoire hierarchy.

C. Details of the H-LAM/T System

1. Synergism[1] as the Source of Intelligence

If we ask ourselves where human intelligence is embodied, our present state of knowledge forces us to concede that it appears to be elusively distributed throughout a hierarchy of functional processes—a hierarchy whose foundation extends into natural processes beyond the level of present definition. Intelligence, however, seems primarily to be associated with *organization*. All of the social, biological, and physical phenomena we observe about us seem to derive from a supporting hierarchy of organized functions (or processes), in which the principle of synergism applies to give increased phenomenological sophistication to each succeedingly higher level of organization. In particular, the intelligence of a human being, which appears to be derived ultimately from the signal-response characteristics of individual nerve cells, is a synergistic phenomenon.

2. Intelligence Amplification

During the course of this study, we had originally rejected the term *intelligence amplification*, (initially used by W. Ross Ashby 1956; 1960) to

---

1 *Synergism* is a term used by biologists and physiologists to designate (from *Webster's New International Dictionary*, 2nd edn.) the '. . . cooperative action of discrete agencies such that the total effect is greater than the sum of the two effects taken independently . . .'

characterize our objectives. Instead, we characterized them as the attempt to make a better match between existing human intelligence and problems to be solved. But we have come to accept the foregoing term in a special sense that does not imply any attempt to increase native human intelligence. *Intelligence amplification* seems applicable to our goal (of augmenting the human intellect) in that the entity to be produced will exhibit more of what can be called intelligence than an unaided human could demonstrate. That which possesses the amplified intelligence is the resulting H-LAM/T system, in which the LAM/T augmentation means represent the amplifier of the individual's intelligence.

In amplifying human intelligence we are applying the principle of synergistic structuring that pertains in the natural evolution of basic human capabilities. What our culture has done in the development of our means of augmentation is to construct a superstructure that is a synthetic extension of the biologically derived sensory-mental-motor structure on which it is built. In a very real sense, the development of 'artificial intelligence' has been going on for centuries.

3. Two-Domain System

The human together with his artifacts comprise the only physical components in the H-LAM/T system. It is upon their combined capabilities that the ultimate capability of the system will depend. This conclusion was implied in the earlier statement that every composite process of the system decomposes ultimately into explicit-human and explicit-artifact processes. There are thus two separate domains of activity within the H-LAM/T system: that represented by the human, in which all explicit-human processes occur, and that represented by the artifacts, in which all explicit-artifact processes occur. In any composite process there is cooperative interaction between the two domains, requiring interchange of energy (much of it for information exchange purposes only). Figure 1 depicts this two-domain concept and embodies other concepts discussed below.

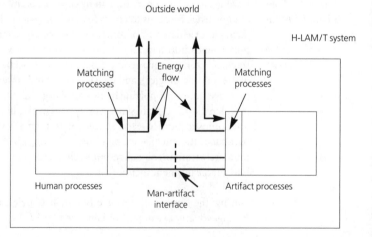

Outside world

H-LAM/T system

Matching processes

Energy flow

Matching processes

Human processes

Man-artifact interface

Artifact processes

Fig. 1.
Representation of the two active domains within the H-LAM/T system.

Where a complex machine represents the principal artifact with which a human being cooperates, the term *man-machine interface* has been used for some years to represent the boundary across which energy is exchanged between the two domains. However, the *man-artifact interface* has existed for centuries, ever since humans began using artifacts and executing composite processes.

Exchange across this 'interface' occurs when an explicit-human process is coupled to an explicit-artifact process. Quite often these coupled processes are designed for just this exchange purpose, to provide a functional match between other explicit-human and explicit-artifact processes buried within their respective domains that do the more significant things. For instance, the finger and hand motions (explicit-human processes) activate key-linkage motions in the typewriter (coupled to explicit-artifact processes). But these are only part of the matching processes between the deeper human processes that direct a given word to be typed and the more involved artifact processes that actually imprint the ink marks on the paper.

The outside world interacts with our H-LAM/T system by the exchange of energy with either the individual or his artifact. Again, special processes are often designed to accommodate this exchange. However, the direct concern of our present study lies within the system, with the internal processes that are and can be significantly involved in the effectiveness of the *system* in developing the human's comprehension and pursuing the human's goals.

4. Concepts, Symbols, and a Hypothesis

Before we pursue further direct discussion of the H-LAM/T system, let us examine some background material. There is a certain progression in the development of our intellectual capabilities—not necessarily historical—that can shed light on the human part of the system:

4.1. Concept Manipulation. Humans have the biological capability for developing abstractions and concepts. They can mentally manipulate these concepts to a certain extent, and 'think' about situations in the abstract. Their mental capabilities allow them to develop general concepts from specific instances, predict specific instances from general concepts, associate concepts, remember them, etc. We speak here of concepts in their raw, unverbalized form. For example, a person letting a door swing shut behind him suddenly visualizes a person behind him carrying a cup of hot coffee and some sticky pastries. Of all the aspects of the impending event, the spilling of the coffee and the squashing of the pastry somehow are abstracted immediately and associated with a concept of personal responsibility combined with a fear of the consequences. But a solution comes to mind immediately as an image of a quick stop and an arm extended back toward the door, with motion and timing that could prevent the collision, and the solution is accepted and enacted. With only nonverbal concept manipulation, we could probably build primitive shelter, evolve strategies of war, hunt, play games, and make practical jokes. But further powers of intellectual effectiveness are implicit in this stage of biological evolution (the same stage we are in today).

4.2. Symbol Manipulation. Humans made another great step forward when they learned to represent particular concepts in their minds with specific symbols. Here we temporarily disregard communicative speech and writing and consider only the direct value to the *individual* of being able to do his heavy thinking by mentally manipulating *symbols* instead of the more unwieldy concepts which they represent. Consider, for instance, the mental difficulty involved in herding twenty-seven sheep if, instead of remembering one cardinal number and occasionally counting, we had to remember what each sheep looked like, so that if the flock seemed too small we could visualize each one and check whether or not it was there.

4.3. Manual, External, Symbol Manipulation. Another significant step toward harnessing the biologically evolved mental capabilities in pursuit of comprehension and problem solutions came with the development of the means for externalizing some of the symbol-manipulation activity—particularly in graphic representation, which supplements the individual's memory and ability to visualize. (We are not concerned here with the value derived from human cooperation made possible by speech and writing, both forms of external symbol manipulation, but with the manual means of making graphic representations of symbols—a stick and sand, pencil and paper and eraser, straightedge or compass, and so on.) It is principally this kind of means for external symbol manipulation that has been associated with the evolution of the individual's present way of manipulating his concepts (thinking).

It is undoubtedly true that concepts which people found useful became incorporated as symbols in their language. However, Korzybski (1933) and Whorf (1956) (among others) have argued that the language we use affects our thinking to a considerable extent. They say that a lack of words for some types of concepts makes it difficult to express those concepts, and thus decreases the likelihood that we will learn much about them. If this is so, once a language has begun to grow and be used it would seem reasonable to suspect that the language also affects the evolution of the new concepts to be expressed in that language.

Apparently there are counter-arguments to this; e.g., if a concept needs to be used often but its expression is difficult, then the language will evolve to ease the situation. However, the studies of the past decade into what are called *self-organizing systems* seem to reveal that subtle relationships among interacting elements can significantly influence the course of evolution of such a system. If this is true, and if language is (as it seems to be) a part of a self-organizing system, then it appears probable that the state of a language at a given time strongly affects its own evolution to a succeeding state.

For our conceptual framework, we tend to favor the view that a language does exert a force in its own evolution. We observe that the shift over the last few centuries in matters that are of daily concern to the individual has necessarily been forced into the framework of the language existing at the time, with alterations generally limited to new uses for old words, or to the coining of new words. The English language since Shakespeare has undergone no alteration comparable to the alteration in the cultural environment; if it had, Shakespeare would no longer be accessible to us. Under such evolutionary conditions, it would seem *unlikely* that the language we now use provides the best possible service to our minds in pursuing comprehension and solving problems. It seems very likely that a more useful language form can be devised.

The Whorfian hypothesis states that 'the world view of a culture is limited by the structure of the language which the culture uses.' But there seems to be another factor to consider in the evolution of language and human reasoning ability. We offer the following hypothesis, which is related to the Whorfian hypothesis: Both the language used by a culture, and the capability for effective intellectual activity, are directly affected during their evolution by the means by which individuals control the external manipulation of symbols. (For identification, we will refer to this later on as the Neo-Whorfian hypothesis.)

If the Neo-Whorfian hypothesis could be proved readily, and if we could see how our means of externally manipulating symbols influence both our language and our way of thinking, then we would have a valuable instrument for studying human-augmentation possibilities. For the sake of discussion, let us assume the Neo-Whorfian hypothesis to be true, and see what relevant deductions can be made.

If the means evolved for an individual's external manipulation of his thinking-aid symbols indeed directly affect the way in which he thinks, then the original Whorfian hypothesis would offer an added effect. The direct effect of the external-symbol-manipulation means on language would produce an indirect effect on the way of thinking via the Whorfian-hypothesis linkage. There would then be two ways for our external symbol manipulation to affect our thinking.

One way of viewing the H-LAM/T system changes that we contemplate—specifically, integrating the capabilities of a digital computer into the intellectual activity of humans—is that we are introducing new and extremely advanced means for externally manipulating symbols. We then want to determine the useful modifications in the language and in the way of thinking that could result. This suggests a fourth stage to the evolution of our human intellectual capability.

4.4. Automated External Symbol Manipulation. In this stage, the symbols with which the human represents the concepts he is manipulating can be arranged before his eyes, moved, stored, recalled, operated upon according to extremely complex rules—all in very rapid response to a minimum amount of information supplied by the human, by means of special cooperative technological devices. In the limit of what we might now imagine, this could be a computer, with which individuals could communicate rapidly and easily, coupled to a three-dimensional color display within which *extremely sophisticated images* could be constructed, the computer being able to execute a wide variety of processes on parts or all of these images in automatic response to human direction. The displays and processes could provide helpful services and could involve concepts not hitherto imagined (e.g., the pregraphic thinker would have been unable to predict the bar graph, the process of long division, or card file system).

In searching for some simple ways to determine what the Neo-Whorfian hypothesis might imply, we might imagine some relatively straight-forward means of increasing our external symbol-manipulation capability and try to picture the consequent changes that could evolve in our language and methods of thinking. For instance, imagine that our budding technology of a few generations ago had developed an artifact that was essentially a high-speed, semiautomatic table-lookup device, cheap enough for almost everyone to afford and small and light enough to be carried on the person. Assume that individual cartridges sold by manufacturers (publishers) contained the lookup information, that one cartridge could hold the equivalent of an unabridged dictionary, and that a one-paragraph definition could always be located and displayed on the face of the device by the average practiced individual in less than three seconds. What changes in language and methodology might not result? If it were so easy to look things up, how would our vocabulary develop, how would our habits of exploring the intellectual domains of others shift, how might the sophistication of practical organization mature (if each person could so quickly and easily look up applicable rules), how would our education system change to take advantage of this new external symbol-manipulation capability of students and teachers and administrators?

The significance to our study of this discussion lies in the perspective it gives to the ways in which human intellectual effectiveness can be altered by the particular device used by individuals for their external symbol manipulation. These hypotheses imply great richness in the new evolutionary spaces opened by progressing from Stage 3 to Stage 4. We would like to study the hypotheses further, examining their possible manifestations in our experience, ways of demonstrating their validity, and possible deductions relative to going to Stage 4.

5. Capability Repertory Hierarchy

The concept of our H-LAM/T system possessing a repertory of capabilities that is structured in the form of a hierarchy is most useful in our study. We shall use it below to tie together a number of considerations and concepts.

There are two points of focus in considering the design of new repertory hierarchies: the materials with which we have to work, and the principles by which new capability is constructed from these basic materials.

5.1. Basic Capabilities. *Materials* in this context are those capabilities in the human and artifact domains from which all other capabilities in the repertory hierarchy must be constructed. Each such basic capability represents a type of functional component with which the system can be built. Thorough redesigning of the system requires making an inventory of the basic capabilities available. Because we are exploring for perspective, and are not yet recommending research activities, we are free to discuss and define in more detail what we mean by 'basic capability' without regard to the amount of research involved in making an actual inventory.

The two domains, human and artifact, can be explored separately for their basic capabilities. In each we can isolate two classes of basic capability— those classes distinguished according to whether or not the capability has been put to use within our augmentation means. The first class (those in use) can be found in a methodical manner by analyzing present capability hierarchies. For example, select a given capability at any level in the hierarchy and determine whether it can be usefully changed by any means that can be given consideration in the augmentation research contemplated. If it can, then it is not basic but can be decomposed into an eventual set of basic capabilities. Proceed through the hierarchy; capabilities encountered which cannot be usefully changed compose the basic capability inventory. Ultimately, for every such recursive decomposition of a given capability in the hierarchy, every one of the branching paths will terminate in basic capabilities. Many of the branching paths in the decomposition of a given higher-order capability will terminate in the same basic capability, since a given basic capability will often be used within many different higher-order capabilities.

Determining the class of basic capabilities not already utilized within existing augmentation systems requires a different exploration method. Examples of this method occur in technological research, where analytically oriented researchers search for new understandings of phenomena that can add to the research engineer's list of things to be used in the synthesis of better artifacts.

Before this inventorying task can be pursued in any specific instance, some criteria must be established as to what possible changes within the H-LAM/T system can be given serious consideration. For instance, some research situations might have to disallow changes which require extensive retraining, or which require undignified behavior by the human. Other situations might admit changes requiring years of special training, very expensive equipment, or the use of special drugs.

The capability for performing a certain finger action, for example, may not be basic in our sense of the word. Being able to extend the finger a certain distance would be basic, but the strength and speed of a particular finger motion and its coordination with higher actions generally are usefully changeable and therefore do not represent basic capabilities. What would be basic in this case would perhaps be the processes whereby strength could be increased and coordinated movement patterns learned, as well as the basic movement range established by the mechanical-limit loci of the muscle-tendon-bone system. Similar capability breakdowns will occur for sensory and cognitive capabilities.

5.2. Structure Types. The fundamental principle used in building sophisticated capabilities from basic capabilities is structuring—the special type of structuring (which we have termed synergistic) in which the organization of a group of elements produces an effect greater than the mere addition of their individual effects. Perhaps *purposeful* structuring (or organization) would best express the need, but how the structuring concept must mature is uncertain. We are developing growing awareness of the significant and pervasive nature of structuring within every physical and conceptual element we inspect, where the hierarchical form seems almost universally present as stemming from successive levels of organization.

The fundamental entity which is being structured in each and every case seems to be what we could call a process, where the most basic of physical processes (involving fields, charges, and moments associated with the dynamics of fundamental particles) appear in every case as the hierarchical base. Dynamic electro-optical-mechanical processes associated with the function of our artifacts, and metabolic, sensory, motor, and cognitive processes of the human, which we view as relatively fundamental components within the structure of our H-LAM/T system, each seems to be ultimately based (to our degree of understanding) on the above-mentioned basic physical processes. The elements that are organized to give fixed structural form to our physical objects (e.g., the 'element' of tensile strength of a material) are also derived from what we could call synergistic structuring of the most basic physical processes.

At the level of the capability hierarchy where we wish to work, it seems useful to distinguish several different types of structuring, even though each type is fundamentally a structuring of the basic physical processes. Tentatively we have isolated five such types, although we are not sure how many we shall ultimately want to use in considering the problem of augmenting the human intellect, nor how we might divide and subdivide these different manifestations of physical-process structuring. We use the terms *mental structuring, concept structuring, symbol structuring, process structuring,* and *physical structuring.*

5.2.1. MENTAL STRUCTURING. *Mental structuring* we apply to the internal organization of conscious and unconscious mental images, associations, or concepts which somehow manage to provide the human with understanding and the basis for judgment, intuition, inference, and meaningful action with respect to his environment. (The psychologist's 'cognitive structure' may be very near to what we need in our concept of mental structure).

We do not now try to specify the fundamental mental 'things' being structured, nor the mechanisms that accomplish the structuring or the use of that which has been structured. We feel reasonably safe in assuming that learning involves some kind of meaningful organization within the brain, and that whatever is so organized or structured represents the operating model of the individual's universe to the mental mechanisms that derive his behavior. Further, our assumption is that when the human in our H-LAM/T system makes the key decision or action that leads to the solution of a complex problem, this action will stem from the state of his mental structure at that time; the basic purpose of most of the system's activity on that problem up to that point was in developing his mental structure to permit the mental mechanisms to derive a solution from it.

We don't know whether a structure is developed in a manner analogous to (*a*) the development of a garden, where one provides a good environment, plants the seeds, keeps competing weeds and injurious pests out, but otherwise lets natural processes take their course, or (*b*) the development of a basketball team, where much exercise of skills, patterns, and strategies must be provided so that natural processes can slowly knit together an integration, or (*c*) the development of a machine, where carefully formed elements are assembled in a precise, planned manner so that natural phenomena can immediately yield planned function. We do not know the processes, but we can develop and have developed empirical relationships between the experiences given a human and the associated manifestations of developing comprehension and capability; we see the near-future course of the research toward augmenting the human intellect as depending entirely on empirical findings (past and future) for the development of better means to serve the development and use of mental structuring in the human.

We do not mean to imply by this that we renounce theories of mental processes. What we mean to emphasize is that the pursuit of our objective does not have to wait on understanding the mental processes that accomplish what we call mental structuring and that derive behavior therefrom. Not to make the fullest use of any theory that provided a working explanation for a group of empirical data would be to ignore the emphases of our own conceptual framework.

5.2.2. CONCEPT STRUCTURING. Within our framework we have developed the working assumption that the manner in which formal experiences favor the development of mental structures is based largely on *concepts* as 'media of exchange.' We view a concept to be a tool that can be grasped and used by the mental mechanisms, that can be composed, interpreted, and used by natural mental substances and processes. The grasping and processing done by these mechanisms can often be accomplished more easily if the concept is explicitly represented by a symbol. Somehow the mental mechanisms can learn to manipulate images (or something) of symbols in a meaningful way and remain calmly confident that the associated concepts are within call.

Concepts seem to be structurable in that a new concept can be composed of an organization of established concepts. For present purposes we can view a concept structure as something which we might try to develop on paper for ourselves or work with by conscious thought processes, or as something which we try to communicate to one another in serious discussion. We assume that for a given unit of comprehension to be imparted there is a concept structure (which can be consciously developed and displayed) that can be presented to an individual in such a way that it is mapped into a corresponding mental structure which provides the basis for that individual's 'comprehending' behavior. Our working assumption also considers that some concept structures would be better for this purpose than others, in that they would be more easily mapped by the individual into workable mental structures, or in that the resulting mental structures enable a higher degree of comprehension and better solutions to problems, or both.

A concept structure often grows as part of a cultural evolution—either on a large scale within a large segment of society, or on a small scale within the activity domain of an individual. But it is also something that can be directly designed or modified, and a basic hypothesis of our study is that better concept structures can be developed—structures that when mapped into a human's mental structure will significantly improve his capability to comprehend and to find solutions within his complex-problem situations. A natural language provides its user with a readymade structure of concepts that establishes a basic mental structure, and that allows relatively flexible, general-purpose concept structuring. Our concept of 'language' as one of the basic means for augmenting the human intellect embraces all of the concept structuring which the human may make use of.

5.2.3. SYMBOL STRUCTURING. The other important part of our 'language' concerns the way in which concepts are represented—the symbols and symbol structures: by means of which words as structured into phrases, sentences, paragraphs, monographs, or charts, lists, diagrams, and tables. A given structure of concepts can be represented by any one of an infinite number of different symbol structures, some of which would be much better than others for enabling the human perceptual and cognitive apparatus to search out and comprehend the conceptual matter of significance and/or interest. A concept structure involving many numerical data, for example, would generally be better represented with Arabic than Roman numerals; quite likely, a graphic structure would be better than a tabular structure.

In our special framework, it is worth noting that a given concept structure can be represented with a symbol structure that is completely compatible with the way a computer handles symbols. Such structuring has immensely greater potential for accurately mapping a complex concept structure than does the structure which an individual might practically construct and use on paper. A computer can transform back and forth between some limited view of the total structure as represented by a two-dimensional portrayal on a screen, and an aspect of the n-dimensional internal image that represents this 'view'. If the human adds to or modifies such a 'view,' the computer integrates the change into the internal-image symbol structure (in terms of the computer's favored symbols and structuring), and thereby can automatically detect a certain proportion of his possible conceptual inconsistencies. The human need no longer work on rigid and limited symbol structures, where much of the conceptual content can only be implicitly designated in an indirect and distributed fashion.

Many radical new ways of matching the dynamics of our symbol structuring to those of our concept structuring are basically available with today's technology. Their exploration would be most stimulating, and potentially very rewarding.

5.2.4. PROCESS STRUCTURING. Essentially everything that goes on within the H-LAM/T system (in relation to our direct interest here) involves the manipulation of concept and symbol structures in service to the human's mental structure. Therefore the processes within the H-LAM/T system that we are most interested in developing are those that provide for the manipulation of all three types of structure. This brings us to the fourth category of structuring, namely *process structuring*.

As we currently use it, the term process structuring includes the organization, study, modification, and execution of processes and process structures. Whereas concept structuring and symbol structuring together represent the language component of our augmentation means, process structuring represents primarily the methodology component.

Many of the process structures are applied to the task of organizing, executing, supervising, and evaluating other process structures. Others are applied to the formation and manipulation of symbol structures (the purpose of which will often be to support the conceptual labor involved in process structuring).

5.2.5. PHYSICAL STRUCTURING. Physical structuring, the last of the five types which we currently use in our conceptual framework, is nearly self-explanatory. It represents the artifact component of our augmentation means, insofar as the actual manifestation and organization of the physical devices are concerned.

5.2.6. INTERDEPENDENCE AND REGENERATION. An important feature to be noted from the foregoing discussion is the interdependence among the various types of structuring which are involved in the H-LAM/T system, where the capability for doing each type of structuring is dependent upon the capability of achieving one or more of the other types of structuring. (Assuming that the physical structuring of the system remains basically unchanged during the system's operation, we exclude its dependence on other factors in this discussion.) This interdependence has a cyclic, regenerative nature which is very significant. A good portion of the capability for mental structuring is finally dependent on the process structuring (human, artifact, composite) that enables symbol-structure manipulation. But it also is evident that this process structuring is dependent not only on basic human and artifact process capabilities but also on the ability of the human to learn how to execute processes and—no less important—on the ability of the human to select, organize, and modify processes from his repertory to structure a higher-order process that he can execute. Thus capability for structuring and executing processes is partially dependent on the human's mental structuring, which, in turn, is partially dependent on his process structuring (through concept and symbol structuring), which is partially dependent on his mental structuring, etc.

This means that a significant improvement in symbol-structure manipulation through better process structuring (initially perhaps through much better artifacts) should enable us to develop improvements in concept and mental-structure manipulations that can in turn enable us to organize and execute symbol-manipulation processes of increased power.

When considering the possibilities of computerlike devices for augmenting human capabilities, often only the one-pass improvement is visualized. This presents a relatively barren picture in comparison with that which emerges on consideration of regenerative interaction.

5.3. Roles and Levels. In the repertory hierarchy of capabilities possessed by the H-LAM/T system, the human contributes many types of capability that represent a wide variety of roles. At one time or another he will be the policy maker, the goal setter, the performance supervisor, the work scheduler, the professional specialist, the clerk, the janitor, the entrepreneur and the proprietor (or at least a major stock-holder) of the system. In the midst of some complex process, in fact, he may well be in several roles concurrently—or at least have the responsibility of the roles. For example, usually he must be aware of his progress toward a goal (supervisor), he must be alert to the possibilities for changing the goal (policy maker, planner), and he must keep records for these and other roles (clerk).

A given capability at some level in the repertory hierarchy seems to include standard grouping of lower-order capabilities which can be viewed as existing in two classes—an *executive* class and a *direct-contributive* class. In the executive class are capabilities for comprehending, planning, and executing the process. In the direct-contributive class are the capabilities organized by the executive class toward the direct realization of the higher-order capability. For example, when the telephone rings, direct-contributive processes are picking up the receiver and saying 'hello.' The executive processes comprehended the situation, directed a lower-order executive-process that the receiver be picked up and, when the receiver was in place (first process accomplished), directed the next process—the saying of 'hello.' This represents the composition of the capability for answering the telephone.

At a little higher level of capability, more of the conscious conceptual and executive capabilities become involved. To telephone someone, there must be conscious comprehension of the need for this process and how it can be executed.

At a still higher level of capability, the executive capabilities must have a degree of power that cannot be provided by unaided mental capabilities. In such a case, a sequence of steps might be drafted and checked off as each is executed. For an even more complex process, comprehending the situation in which the process is to be executed—before even beginning to plan the execution—may take months of labor and a very complex organization of the system's capabilities.

At any particular moment the H-LAM/T system is usually in the middle of executing a great number of processes. For example, the human in the process of making a telephone call may be in the middle of the process of calling a committee meeting which could be a sub-process of the process of estimating manpower needs, and so on.

Not only does the human need to play various roles (sometimes concurrently) in the execution of any given process, but he is playing these roles for the many concurrent processes that are being executed at different levels. This situation is typical for individuals engaged in reasonably demanding types of professional pursuits, and yet they have never received explicit training in optimum ways of performing any but a very few of the roles at a very few of the levels. A well-designed H-LAM/T system would provide explicit and effective concepts, terms, equipment, and methods for all these roles, and for their dynamic coordination.

5.4. Model of Executive Superstructure. It is the repertory hierarchy of process capabilities upon which the ultimate capability of the H-LAM/T system rests. This repertory hierarchy is rather like a mountain of white-collar talent that sits atop and controls the talents of the 'workers.' We can illustrate executive superstructure by considering it as though it were a network of contractors and subcontractors in which each capability in the repertory hierarchy is represented by an independent contractor whose mode of operation is to do the planning, make up specifications, subcontract the actual work, and supervise the performance of his subcontractors. This means that each subcontractor does the same thing in his turn. At the bottom of this heirarchy are those independent contractors who do actual 'production work.'

If by some magical process the production workers could still know just what to do and when to do it even though the superstructure of contractors was removed from above them, no one would know the difference. The executive superstructure is there because humans do not operate by magic, but even a necessary superstructure is a burden. We can readily recognize that there are many ways to organize and manage such a superstructure, resulting in vastly different degrees of efficiency in the application of the workers' talents.

Suppose that the applicable talent available to the total system is limited. The problem is one of distributing that talent between superstructure and workers for maximum total production and efficiency. This situation has close parallel to the H-LAM/T system in its pursuit of comprehension and problem solutions. Closer parallel exists by postulating for the contractor model that the thinking, planning, supervising, record keeping, etc., for each contractor is done by a single individual who time-shares his attention and talents over the various tasks of the entire superstructure.

Today's individual does not have special training for many of the roles he plays, and he is likely to learn them by cut-and-try and indirect imitation processes. The H-LAM/T system also often executes a complex process in multipass fashion (i.e., cut-and-try). This approach permits freedom of action which is important to the effectiveness of the system with respect to the outside world. We could expect significant gains from automating the H-LAM/T system if a computer did no more than increase the effectiveness of the executive processes. More human time, energy, and productive thought could be allocated to direct-contributive processes, which could be coordinated in a more sophisticated, flexible and efficient manner. But there is every reason to believe that the possibilities for much-improved process structuring that would stem from this automation could in turn provide significant improvements in both the executive and direct-contributive processes in the system.

5.5. Symbol Structures. The executive superstructure is a necessary component in the H-LAM/T system, and there is finite human capability which must be divided between executive and direct-contributive activities. An important aspect of the multirole activity of the human in the system is the development and manipulation of the symbol structures associated with *both* his direct-contributive roles and his executive roles.

When the system encounters a complex situation in which comprehension and problem solutions are being pursued, the direct-contributive roles require the development of symbol structures that portray the concepts involved within the situation. But executive roles in a complex problem situation also require conceptual activity—e.g., comprehension, selection, supervision—that can benefit from well-designed symbol structures and fast, flexible means for manipulating and displaying them. For complex processes, the executive problem posed to the human (of gaining the necessary comprehension and making a good plan) may be more difficult intellectually than the problem faced in the role of direct-contributive worker. If the flexibility desired for the process hierarchies (to make room for human cut-and-try methods) is not to be degraded or abandoned, the executive activity will have to be provided with fast and flexible symbol structuring techniques.

The means available to humans today for developing and manipulating symbol structures are both laborious and inflexible. To develop an initial structure of diagrams and text is difficult, but because the cost of frequent changes is often prohibitive, one settles for inflexibility. Also, the flexibility that would be truly helpful requires added symbol structuring just to keep track of the trials, branches, and reasoning thereto that are involved in the development of the subject structure. Present symbol-manipulation means would soon bog down completely among the complexities that are involved in being more than just a little bit flexible.

In H-LAM/T systems, individuals work essentially continuously within a symbol structure of some sort, shifting their attention from one structure to another as they guide and execute the processes that ultimately provide them with the comprehension and the problem solutions they seek. This view emphasizes the essential importance of the basic capability of composing and modifying efficient symbol structures. Such a capability depends heavily on the particular concepts isolated and manipulated as entities, on the symbology used to represent them, on the artifacts that help to manipulate and display the symbols, and on the methodology for developing and using symbol structures. In other words, this capability depends heavily on proper language, artifacts, and methodology, our basic augmentation means.

The course of action which must respond to new comprehension, new insights, and new intuitive flashes of possible explanations or solutions is not an orderly process. Existing means of composing and working with symbol structures penalize disorderly processes heavily. It is part of the real promise of the automated H-LAM/T systems of tomorrow that the human can have the freedom and power of disorderly processes.

5.6. Compound Effects. Since processes in many levels of the hierarchy are involved in the execution of a single higher-level process of the system, any factor that influences process execution in general will have a highly compounded total effect on the system's performance. There are several such factors that merit special attention.

Basic human cognitive powers, such as memory, intelligence, or pattern perception can have such a compounded effect. The augmentation means employed today have generally evolved among large statistical populations, and no attempt has been made to fit them to individual needs and abilities. Each individual tends to evolve his own variations, but there is not enough mutation and selection activity, nor enough selection feedback, to permit very significant changes. A good, automated H-LAM/T system should provide the opportunity for a significant adaptation of the augmentation means to individual characteristics. The compounding effect of fundamental human cognitive powers suggests further that systems designed for maximum effectiveness would require that these powers be developed as fully as possible—by training, special mental tricks, improved language, new methodology.

In the automated system contemplated here, the human should be able to draw on the explicit-artifact process capability at many levels in the repertory hierarchy. Today, artifacts are involved explicitly in only the lower-order capabilities. In future systems it should be possible for computer processes to provide direct manipulative service in the executive symbol structures at all the higher levels, which promises a compounding of the effect a computer may have.

Another factor capable of exerting a compound effect on over-all system performance is the human's unconscious processes. Clinical psychology seems to provide clear evidence that a large proportion of a human's everyday activity is significantly mediated or basically prompted by unconscious mental processes that, although 'natural' in a functional sense, are not rational. Observable mechanisms of these processes (observable by a trained person) include an individual's masking of the irrationality of his actions, and the construction of self-satisfying rationales for any action that could be challenged. Anything that might have so general an effect on our mental actions as implied here is a candidate for ultimate consideration in the continuing development of our intellectual effectiveness. It may be that the first stages of research on augmenting the human intellect will have to proceed without coping with this problem except to accommodate to it as well as possible. This may be one of the significant problems whose solution awaits our development of increased intellectual effectiveness.

Other Related Thought and Work

When we began our search, we found much literature of general significance to our objective—frankly, one is tempted to say too much. Without a conceptual framework we could not efficiently filter out the significant kernels of fact and concept from the huge mass which we initially collected as a 'natural first step' in our search. We feel rather unscholarly not to have buttressed our conceptual framework with plentiful reference to supporting work, but in truth it was too difficult to do. Developing the conceptual structure represented a sweeping synthesis job full of personal constructs from smatterings picked up in many places. Under these conditions, giving reference to a backup source would usually entail qualifying footnotes reflecting an unusual interpretation or exonerating the cited author from the implications we derived from his work. We look forward to a stronger, more comprehensive, and more scholarly presentation evolving out of future work.

However, we do want to acknowledge thoughts and work we have come across that bear most directly upon the possibilities of using a computer in real-time working association with a human to improve his working effectiveness. These findings fall into two categories. The first, which would include the present report, offers speculations and possibilities but does not include reporting of significant experimental results. Of these, Bush (1945) is the earliest and one of the most directly stimulating. Licklider (1960), who provides the most general clear case for the modern computer, coined the expression *man-computer symbiosis* to refer to the close interaction relationship between the man and computer in mutually beneficial cooperation. Ulam (1960) has specifically recommended close man-computer interaction in a chapter entitled 'Synergesis,' where he points out in considerable detail the types of mathematical work which could be aided. Good (1958) includes some conjecture about the possibilities of intellectual aid to the human by close cooperation with a computer in a rather general way, and also presents a few interesting thoughts about a network model for structuring the conceptual kernels of information to facilitate a sort of self-organizing retrieval system. Ramo has given a number of talks dealing with the future possibilities of computers for 'extending man's intellect,' and wrote several articles (1958; 1961). His projections seem slanted more toward larger bodies of humans interacting with computers, in less of an intimate personal sense than the above papers or than our initial goal. Fein, (1960), in making a comprehensive projection of the growth and dynamic interrelatedness of 'computer-related sciences,' includes specific mention of the enhancement of human intellect by cooperative activity of men, mechanisms, and automata. Fein coined the term *synnoetics* as applicable generally to the cooperative interaction of people, mechanisms, plant or animal organisms, and automata into a system whose mental power is greater than that of its components; he presents a good picture of the integrated way in which many currently separate disciplines should be developed and taught in the future to do justice to their mutual roles in the important discipline defined as 'synnoetics.'

In the second category, there have been a few papers published recently describing actual work that bears directly upon our topic. Licklider and Clark (1962), and Culler and Huff (1962), at the 1962 Spring Joint Computer Conference, gave what are essentially progress reports of work going on now in exactly this sort of thing—a human with a computer-backed display getting minute-by-minute help in solving problems. Teager (1961a; b) reports on the plans and current development of a large time-sharing system at MIT, which is planned to provide direct computer access for a number of outlying stations located in scientists' offices, giving each of these users a chance for real-time utilization of the computer.

There are several efforts we have heard about but for which there are either no publications or for which none have been discovered by us. Just before the deadline date, we have received two publications from the MIT Electronic Systems Laboratory; an Interim Engineering Report (of work done over two years ago), 'Investigations In Computer-Aided Design,' appears to contain much detailed analysis of applied work in close man-computer cooperation. A Technical Memorandum, 'Method for Computer Visualization,' by A. F. Smith, apparently elaborates on Chapter VII of the Interim Report. These documents seem extremely relevant. Mr. Douglas Ross, of the MIT Electronic Systems Laboratory has, we have recently learned, been thinking and working on real-time man-machine interaction problems for some years. In addition, an MIT graduate student, Glenn Randa (1962), developed the design of a remote display console under Ross for his graduate thesis project. We understand that another MIT graduate student, Ivan Sutherland, is currently using the display-computer facility on the TX-2 computer at Lincoln Laboratory to develop cooperative techniques for engineering design problems. At the RAND Corporation, Cliff Shaw, Tom Ellis, and Keith Uncapher have been involved in implementing a multistation time-sharing system built around their JOHNNIAC computer. Termed the JOHNNIAC Open-Shop System (JOSS for short), it apparently is near completion, and will use remote typewriter stations.

Undoubtedly there are other efforts falling into either or both categories that have been overlooked. Such oversight has not been intentional, and it is hoped that these researchers will make their pertinent work known to the present writer.

Summary and Recommendations   This paper states the hypothesis that the intellectual effectiveness of an individual is dependent on factors which are subject to direct redesign in pursuit of an increase in that effectiveness. A conceptual framework is offered to help in giving consideration to this hypothesis. The framework in part derives from recognition that human intellect is already 'augmented,' and incorporates the following attributes:

1. As principal elements, the language, artifacts, and methodology which man has learned to use.
2. Dynamic interdependence of the elements within an operating system.
3. A hierarchical system structure, best considered a hierarchy of process capabilities whose primitive components are the basic human capabilities and the functional capabilities of the artifacts, organized into increasingly sophisticated capabilities.
4. As capabilities of primary interest, those associated with manipulating symbols and concepts in support of organizing and executing processes from which are ultimately derived human comprehension and problem solutions.

The framework also pictures the development of automated symbol manipulation to accommodate minute-by-minute mental processes as a significant means of increasing intellectual capability. This can be a logical next step in the cultural evolution of the means by which humans can match their mental capabilities against their problems. This approach pertains to any problem area in which the human does his thinking with concepts that he can express in words, charts, or any other explicit symbol forms.

If the hypothesis and extrapolations discussed here and elsewhere (AFOSR 3223) are substantiated in future developments, the consequences will be exciting and assumedly beneficial to a problem-laden world. What is needed now is a test of this hypothesis and a calibration on the gains, if any, that might be realized by giving total-system design attention to human intellectual effectiveness. If the test and calibration prove favorable, then better and better augmentation systems could be developed for our problem solvers.

In this light, a research program is recommended aimed at (*a*) testing the hypothesis, (*b*) developing the tools and techniques for designing better augmentation systems, and (*c*) providing real-world augmentation systems. These goals are idealized, but results in these directions are nonetheless valuable. The approach should be on an empirical, total-system basis, i.e., coordinated study and innovation among all the factors admitted to the problem in conjunction with experiments that provide realistic action and interplay among the variables. The recommended environment for this approach is a laboratory with a computer-backed display and communication system. The experimental work of deriving, testing, and integrating innovations into a growing system of augmentation means is helped by having a specific type of human task on which to operate. From a long-range research-program point of view, characteristics of the task of computer programming make it particularly attractive as the initial such specific task.

In our view, we do *not* have to suspend such research until we learn how human mental processes work. We do *not* have to wait until we learn how to make computers more 'intelligent.' We *can* begin developing powerful and economically feasible augmentation systems on the basis of what we now know and have. We will want to integrate further basic knowledge and improved machines into existing augmentation systems. However, getting started now will provide not only orientation and stimulation for these pursuits, but also better problem-solving effectiveness with which to carry out such pursuits.

References

ASHBY, W. ROSS, *Design for a Brain*, 2nd edn., John Wiley & Sons, Inc., New York, 1960.

—— *Design for an Intelligence Amplified*, Automatic Studies, C. E. Shannon and J. McCarthy, Princeton Univ. Press, Princeton, NJ, 1956, pp. 215–234.

BUSH, VANNEVAR, 'As We May Think,' *The Atlantic Monthly,* July 1945.

CULLER, G. J., and R. W. HUFF, 'Solution of Non-Linear Integral Equations Using On-Line Computer Control,' paper for presentation at SJCC, San Francisco, Ramo-Wooldridge, Canoga Park, Calif., May 1962.

FEIN, LOUIS, 'The Computer-Related Science (Synnoetics) at a University in the year 1975,' unpublished paper, December 1960.

GOOD, I. J., 'How Much Science Can You Have at Your Fingertips?' *IBM Journal of Research and Development*, October 1958.

KORZYBSKI, A., *Science and Sanity*, International Non-Aristotelian Library Publishing Company, Lancaster, Pa., 1933.

LICKLIDER, J. C. R., 'Man-Computer Symbiosis,' *IRE Transactions on Human Factors in Electronics*, March 1960.

—— and W. E. CLARK, 'On-Line Man-Computer Communication,' *Proceedings Spring Joint Computer Conference*, National Press, Palo Alto, Calif., May 1962.

RAMO, SIMON, 'A New Technique of Education,' *IRE Transactions on Education*, June 1958.

—— 'The Scientific Extension of the Human Intellect,' *Computers and Automation*, February 1961.

RANDA, GLENN C., 'Design of a Remote Display Console,' Report ESL-R-132, MIT Cambridge, Mass., February 1962, available through ASTIA.

TEAGER, H. M., 'Real-Time, Time-Shared Computer Project,' report, M.I.T Contract Nonr-1841(69) DSR 8644, 1 July 1961(*a*).

——'Systems Considerations in Real-Time Computer Usage,' paper presented at ONR Symposium on Automated Teaching, Oct. 12, 1961(*b*).

ULAM, S. M., *A Collection of Mathematical Problems*, Interscience Publishers, Inc., New York, 1960, p. 135.

WHORF, B. L., *Language, Thought, and Reality*, MIT and John Wiley & Sons, Inc., New York, 1956.

5

The Computer as a Communication Device

J. C. R. Licklider and Robert W. Taylor

In this article from 1968 Licklider and Taylor describe the use of computers as devices for communication. In their discussion they elaborate upon early conceptions of computer supported co-operative work for face-to-face contexts as well as computer mediated communication via networked computers. Of particular interest are their descriptions of on-line interactive communities, the social benefits of these new communication possibilities, and automatic forms of communication based on an 'on-line interactive vicarious expediter and responder'.

IN A FEW YEARS, men will be able to communicate more effectively through a machine than face to face.

That is a rather startling thing to say, but it is our conclusion. As if in con-firmation of it, we participated a few weeks ago in a technical meeting held through a computer. In two days, the group accomplished with the aid of a computer what normally might have taken a week.

We shall talk more about the mechanics of the meeting later; it is sufficient to note here that we were all in the same room. But for all the communicat-ing we did directly across that room, we could have been thousands of miles apart and communicated just as effectively as people over the distance.

Our emphasis on people is deliberate. A communications engineer thinks of communicating as transferring information from one point to another in codes and signals.

But to communicate is more than to send and to receive. Do two tape recorders communicate when they play to each other and record from each other? Not really—not in our sense. We believe that communicators have to do something nontrivial with the information they send and receive. And we believe that we are entering a technological age in which we will be able to interact with the richness of living information—not merely in the passive way that we have become accustomed to using books and libraries, but as active participants in an ongoing process, bringing something to it through our interaction with it, and not simply receiving something from it by our connection to it.

From *International Science and Technology* (April 1968). Evan Herbert edited the article and acted as intermediary during its writing between Licklider in Boston and Taylor in Washington.

To the people who telephone an airline flight operations information service, the tape recorder that answers seems more than a passive depository. It is an often-updated model of a changing situation—a synthesis of information collected, analyzed, evaluated, and assembled to represent a situation or process in an organized way.

Still there is not much direct interaction with the airline information service; the tape recording is not changed by the customer's call. We want to emphasize something beyond its one-way transfer: the increasing significance of the jointly constructive, the mutually reinforcing aspect of communication—the part that transcends 'now we both know a fact that only one of us knew before.' When minds interact, new ideas emerge. We want to talk about the creative aspect of communication.

Creative, interactive communication requires a plastic or moldable medium that can be modeled, a dynamic medium in which premises will flow into consequences, and above all a common medium that can be contributed to and experimented with by all.

Such a medium is at hand—the programmed digital computer. Its presence can change the nature and value of communication even more profoundly than did the printing press and the picture tube, for, as we shall show, a well-programmed computer can provide direct access both to informational resources and to the *processes* for making use of the resources.

Communication: A Comparison of Models

To understand how and why the computer can have such an effect on communication, we must examine the idea of modeling—in a computer and with the aid of a computer. For modeling, we believe, is basic and central to communication. Any communication between people about the same thing is a common revelatory experience about informational models of that thing. Each model is a conceptual structure of abstractions formulated initially in the mind of one of the persons who would communicate, and if the concepts in the mind of one would-be communicator are very different from those in the mind of another, there is no common model and no communication.

By far the most numerous, most sophisticated, and most important models are those that reside in men's minds. In richness, plasticity, facility, and economy, the mental model has no peer, but, in other respects, it has shortcomings. It will not stand still for careful study. It cannot be made to repeat a run. No one knows just how it works. It serves its owner's hopes more faithfully than it serves reason. It has access only to the information stored in one man's head. It can be observed and manipulated only by one person.

Society rightly distrusts the modeling done by a single mind. Society demands consensus, agreement, at least majority. Fundamentally, this amounts to the requirement that individual models be compared and brought into some degree of accord. The requirement is for communication, which we now define concisely as 'cooperative modeling'—cooperation in the construction, maintenance, and use of a model.

How can we be sure that we are modeling cooperatively, that we are communicating, unless we can compare models?

When people communicate face to face, they externalize their models so they can be sure they are talking about the same thing. Even such a simple externalized model as a flow diagram or an outline—because it can be seen by all the communicators—serves as a focus for discussion. It changes the nature of communication: When communicators have no such common framework, they merely make speeches *at* each other; but when they have a manipulable model before them, they utter a few words, point, sketch, nod, or object.

The dynamics of such communication are so model-centered as to suggest an important conclusion: Perhaps the reason present-day two-way telecommunication falls so far short of face-to-face communication is simply that it fails to provide facilities for externalizing models. Is it really seeing the expression in the other's eye that makes the face-to-face conference so much more productive than the telephone conference call, or is it being able to create and modify external models?

The Project Meeting as a Model

In a technical project meeting, one can see going on, in fairly clear relief, the modeling process that we contend constitutes communication. Nearly every reader can recall a meeting held during the formulative phase of a project. Each member of the project brings to such a meeting a somewhat different mental model of the common undertaking—its purposes, its goals, its plans, its progress, and its status. Each of these models interrelates the past, present, and future states of affairs of (1) himself; (2) the group he represents; (3) his boss; (4) the project.

Many of the primary data the participants bring to the meeting are in undigested and uncorrelated form. To each participant, his own collections of data are interesting and important in and of themselves. And they are more than files of facts and recurring reports. They are strongly influenced by insight, subjective feelings, and educated guesses. Thus, each individual's data are reflected in his mental model. Getting his colleagues to incorporate his data into their models is the essence of the communications task.

Suppose you could see the models in the minds of two would-be communicators at this meeting. You could tell, by observing their models, whether or not communication was taking place. If, at the outset, their two models were similar in structure but different simply in the values of certain parameters, then communication would cause convergence toward a common pattern. That is the easiest and most frequent kind of communication.

If the two mental models were structurally dissimilar, then the achievement of communication would be signaled by structural changes in one of the models or in both of them. We might conclude that one of the communicating parties was having insights or trying out new hypotheses in order to begin to understand the other—or that both were restructuring their mental models to achieve commonality.

The meeting of many interacting minds is a more complicated process. Suggestions and recommendations may be elicited from all sides. The interplay may produce, not just a solution to a problem, but a new set of rules for solving problems. That, of course, is the essence of creative interaction. The process of maintaining a current model has within it a set of changing or changeable rules for the processing and disposition of information.

The project meeting we have just described is representative of a broad class of human endeavor which may be described as creative informational activity. Let us differentiate this from another class which we will call informational housekeeping. The latter is what computers today are used for in the main; they process payroll checks, keep track of bank balances, calculate orbits of space vehicles, control repetitive machine processes, and maintain varieties of debit and credit lists. Mostly they have *not* been used to make coherent pictures of not well understood situations.

We referred earlier to a meeting in which the participants interacted with each other through a computer. That meeting was organized by Doug Engelbart of Stanford Research Institute and was actually a progress-review conference for a specific project. The subject under discussion was rich in detail and broad enough in scope that no one of the attendees, not even the host, could know all the information pertaining to this particular project.

Face to Face Through a Computer

Tables were arranged to form a square work area with five on a side. The center of the area contained six television monitors which displayed the alphanumeric output of a computer located elsewhere in the building but remotely controlled from a keyboard and a set of electronic pointer controllers called 'mice.' Any participant in the meeting could move a near-by mouse, and thus control the movements of a tracking pointer on the TV screen for all other participants to see.

Each person working on the project had prepared a topical outline of his particular presentation for the meeting, and his outline appeared on the screens as he talked—providing a broad view of his own model. Many of the outline statements contained the names of particular reference files which the speaker could recall from the computer to appear in detail on the screens, for, from the beginning of the project, its participants had put their work into the computer system's files.

So the meeting began much like any other meeting in the sense that there was an overall list of agenda and that each speaker had brought with him (figuratively in his briefcase but really within the computer) the material he would be talking about.

The computer system was a significant aid in exploring the depth and breadth of the material. More detailed information could be displayed when facts had to be pinpointed; more global information could be displayed to answer questions of relevance and interrelationship. A future version of this system will make it possible for each participant, on his own TV screen, to thumb through the speaker's files as the speaker talks—and thus check out incidental questions without interrupting the presentation for substantiation.

Obviously, collections of primary data can get too large to digest. There comes a time when the complexity of a communications process exceeds the available resources and the capability to cope with it; and at that point one has to simplify and draw conclusions.

It is frightening to realize how early and drastically one does simplify, how prematurely one does conclude, even when the stakes are high and when the transmission facilities and information resources are extraordinary. Deep modeling to communicate—to understand—requires a huge investment. Perhaps even governments cannot afford it yet.

But someday governments may not be able *not* to afford it. For, while we have been talking about the communication process as a cooperative modeling effort in a mutual environment, there is also an aspect of communication with or about an uncooperative opponent. As nearly as we can judge from reports of recent international crises, out of the hundreds of alternatives that confronted the decision makers at each decision point or ply in the 'game,' on the average only a few, and never more than a few dozen could be considered, and only a few branches of the game could be explored deeper than two or three such plies before action had to be taken. Each side was busy trying to model what the other side might be up to—but modeling takes time, and the pressure of events forces simplification even when it is dangerous.

Whether we attempt to communicate across a division of interests, or whether we engage in a cooperative effort, it is clear that we need to be able to model faster and to greater depth. The importance of improving decision-making processes—not only in government, but throughout business and the professions—is so great as to warrant every effort.

The Computer— Switch or Interactor?

As we see it, group decision-making is simply the active, executive, effect-producing aspect of the kind of communication we are discussing. We have commented that one must oversimplify. We have tried to say why one must oversimplify. But we should not oversimplify the main point of this article. We can say with genuine and strong conviction that a particular form of digital computer organization, with its programs and its data, constitutes the dynamic, moldable medium that can revolutionize the art of modeling and that in so doing can improve the effectiveness of communication among people so much as perhaps to revolutionize that also.

But we must associate with that statement at once the qualification that the computer alone can make no contribution that will help us, and that the computer with the programs and the data that it has today can do little more than suggest a direction and provide a few germinal examples. Emphatically we do *not* say: 'Buy a computer and your communication problems will be solved.'

What we do say is that we, together with many colleagues who have had the experience of working on-line and interactively with computers, have already sensed more responsiveness and facilitation and 'power' than we had hoped for, considering the inappropriateness of present machines and the primitiveness of their software. Many of us are therefore confident (some of us to the point of religious zeal) that truly significant achievements, which will markedly improve our effectiveness in communication, now are on the horizon.

Many communications engineers, too, are presently excited about the application of digital computers to communication. However, the function they want computers to implement is the switching function. Computers will either switch the communication lines, connecting them together in required configurations, or switch (the technical term is 'store and forward') messages.

The switching function is important but it is not the one we have in mind when we say that the computer can revolutionize communication. We are stressing the modeling function, not the switching function. Until now, the communications engineer has not felt it within his province to facilitate the modeling function, to make an interactive, cooperative modeling facility. Information transmission and information processing have always been carried out separately and have become separately institutionalized. There are strong intellectual and social benefits to be realized by the melding of these two technologies. There are also, however, powerful legal and administrative obstacles in the way of any such melding.

Distributed Intellectual Resources

We have seen the beginnings of communication through a computer— communication among people at consoles located in the same room or on the same university campus or even at distantly separated laboratories of the same research and development organization. This kind of communication—through a single multiaccess computer with the aid of telephone lines—is beginning to foster cooperation and promote coherence more effectively than do present arrangements for sharing computer programs by exchanging magnetic tapes by messenger or mail. Computer programs are very important because they transcend mere 'data'—they include procedures and processes for structuring and manipulating data. These are the main resources we can now concentrate and share with the aid of the tools and techniques of computers and communication, but they are only a part of the whole that we can learn to concentrate and share. The whole includes raw data, digested data, data about the location of data—and documents—and most especially models.

To appreciate the importance the new computer-aided communication can have, one must consider the dynamics of 'critical mass,' as it applies to cooperation in creative endeavor. Take any problem worthy of the name, and you find only a few people who can contribute effectively to its solution. Those people must be brought into close intellectual partnership so that their ideas can come into contact with one another. But bring these people together physically in one place to form a team, and you have trouble, for the most creative people are often not the best team players, and there are not enough top positions in a single organization to keep them all happy. Let them go their separate ways, and each creates his own empire, large or small, and devotes more time to the role of emperor than to the role of problem solver. The principals still get together at meetings. They still visit one another. But the time scale of their communication stretches out, and the correlations among mental models degenerate between meetings so that it may take a year to do a week's communicating. There has to be some way of facilitating communication among people without bringing them together in one place.

A single multiaccess computer would fill the bill if expense were no object, but there is no way, with a single computer and individual communication lines to several geographically separated consoles, to avoid paying an unwarrantedly large bill for transmission. Part of the economic difficulty lies in our present communications system. When a computer is used interactively from a typewriter console, the signals transmitted between the console and the computer are intermittent and not very frequent. They do not require continuous access to a telephone channel; a good part of the time they do not even require the full information rate of such a channel. The difficulty is that the common carriers do not provide the kind of service one would like to have—a service that would let one have ad lib access to a channel for short intervals and not be charged when one is not using the channel.

It seems likely that a store-and-forward (i.e. store-for-just-a-moment-and-forward-right-away) message service would be best for this purpose, whereas the common carriers offer, instead, service that sets up a channel for one's individual use for a period not shorter than one minute.

The problem is further complicated because interaction with a computer via a fast and flexible graphic display, which is for most purposes far superior to interaction through a slow-printing typewriter, requires markedly higher information rates. Not necessarily more information, but the same amount in faster bursts—more difficult to handle efficiently with the conventional common-carrier facilities.

It is perhaps not surprising that there are incompatibilities between the requirements of computer systems and the services supplied by the common carriers, for most of the common-carrier services were developed in support of voice rather than digital communication. Nevertheless, the incompatibilities are frustrating. It appears that the best and quickest way to overcome them—and to move forward the development of interactive *communities* of geographically separated people—is to set up an experimental network of multiaccess computers. Computers would concentrate and interleave the concurrent, intermittent messages of many users and their programs so as to utilize wide-band transmission channels continuously and efficiently, with marked reduction in overall cost.

Computer and Information Networks

The concept of computers connected to computers is not new. Computer manufacturers have successfully installed and maintained interconnected computers for some years now. But the computers in most instances are from families of machines compatible in both software and hardware, and they are in the same location. More important, the interconnected computers are not interactive, general-purpose, multiaccess machines of the type described by David[1] and Licklider.[2] Although more interactive multiaccess computer systems are being delivered now, and although more groups plan to be using these systems within the next year, there are at present perhaps only as few as half a dozen interactive multiaccess computer *communities.*

These communities are socio-technical pioneers, in several ways out

1 Edward E. David, Jr., 'Sharing a Computer,' *International Science and Technology*, June 1966.

2 J. C. R. Licklider, 'Man–Computer Partnership,' *International Science and Technology*, May 1965.

ahead of the rest of the computer world: What makes them so? First, some of their members are computer scientists and engineers who understand the concept of man-computer interaction and the technology of interactive multiaccess systems. Second, others of their members are creative people in other fields and disciplines who recognize the usefulness and who sense the impact of interactive multiaccess computing upon their work. Third, the communities have large multiaccess computers and have learned to use them. And, fourth, their efforts are regenerative.

In the half-dozen communities, the computer systems research and development and the development of substantive applications mutually support each other. They are producing large and growing resources of programs, data, and know-how. But we have seen only the beginning. There is much more programming and data collection—and much more learning how to cooperate—to be done before the full potential of the concept can be realized.

Obviously, multiaccess systems must be developed interactively. The systems being built must remain flexible and open-ended throughout the process of development, which is evolutionary.

Such systems cannot be developed in small ways on small machines. They require large, multiaccess computers, which are necessarilycomplex. Indeed, the sonic barrier in the development of such systems is complexity.

These new computer systems we are describing differ from other computer systems advertised with the same labels: interactive, time-sharing, multiaccess. They differ by having a greater degree of open-endedness, by rendering more services, and above all by providing facilities that foster a working sense of community among their users. The commercially available time-sharing services do not yet offer the power and flexibility of software resources—the 'general purposeness'—of the interactive multiaccess systems of the System Development Corporation in Santa Monica, the University of California at Berkeley, Massachusetts Institute of Technology in Cambridge and Lexington, Mass.—which have been collectively serving about a thousand people for several years.

The thousand people include many of the leaders of the ongoing revolution in the computer world. For over a year they have been preparing for the transition to a radically new organization of hardware and software, designed to support many more simultaneous users than the current systems, and to offer them—through new languages, new file-handling systems, and new graphic displays—the fast, smooth interaction required for truly effective man-computer partnership.

Experience has shown the importance of making the response time short and the conversation free and easy. We think those attributes will be almost as important for a network of computers as for a single computer.

Today the on-line communities are separated from one another functionally as well as geographically. Each member can look only to the processing, storage and software capability of the facility upon which his community is centered. But now the move is on to interconnect the separate communities and thereby transform them into, let us call it, a supercommunity. The hope is that interconnection will make available to all the members of all the communities the programs and data resources of the entire supercommunity.

First, let us indicate how these communities can be interconnected; then we shall describe one hypothetical person's interaction with this network, of interconnected computers.

Message processing

The hardware of a multiaccess computer system includes one or more central processors, several kinds of memory—core, disks, drums, and tapes—and many consoles for the simultaneous on-line users. Different users can work simultaneously on diverse tasks. The software of such a system includes supervisory programs (which control the whole operation), system programs for interpretation of the user's commands, the handling of his files, and graphical or alphanumeric display of information to him (which permit people not skilled in the machine's language to use the system effectively), and programs and data created by the users themselves. The collection of people, hardware, and software—the multiaccess computer together with its local community of users—will become a node in a geographically distributed computer network. Let us assume for a moment that such a network has been formed.

For each node there is a small, general-purpose computer which we shall call a 'message processor.' The message processors of all the nodes are interconnected to form a fast store-and-forward network. The large multiaccess computer at each node is connected directly to the message processor there. Through the network of message processors, therefore, all the large computers can communicate with one another. And through them, all the members of the supercommunity can communicate—with other people, with programs, with data, or with selected combinations of those resources. The message processors, being all alike, introduce an element of uniformity into an otherwise grossly nonuniform situation, for they facilitate both hardware and software compatibility among diverse and poorly compatible computers. The links among the message processors are transmission and high-speed *digital* switching facilities provided by common carrier. This allows the linking of the message processors to be reconfigured in response to demand.

A message can be thought of as a short sequence of 'bits' flowing through the network from one multiaccess computer to another. It consists of two types of information: control and data. Control information guides the transmission of data from source to destination. In present transmission systems, errors are too frequent for many computer applications. However, through the use of error detection and correction or retransmission procedures in the message processors, messages can be delivered to their destinations intact even though many of their 'bits' were mutilated at one point or another along the way. In short, the message processors function in the system as traffic directors, controllers, and correctors.

Today, programs created at one installation on a given manufacturer's computer are generally not of much value to users of a different manufacturer's computer at another installation. After learning (with difficulty) of a distant program's existence, one has to get it, understand it, and recode it for his own computer. The cost is comparable to the cost of preparing a new program from scratch, which is, in fact, what most programmers usually do. On a national scale, the annual cost is enormous. Within a network of inter-active, multiaccess computer systems, on the other hand, a person at one node will have access to programs running at other nodes, even though those programs were written in different languages for different computers.

The feasibility of using programs at remote locations has been shown by the successful linking of the AN/FSQ-32 computer at Systems Development Corporation in Santa Monica, Calif., with the TX-2 computer across the continent at the Lincoln Laboratory in Lexington, Mass. A person at a TX-2 graphic console can make use of a unique list-processing program at SDC, which would be prohibitively expensive to translate for use on the TX-2. A network of 14 such diverse computers, all of which will be capable of sharing one another's resources, is now being planned by the Defense Department's Advanced Research Projects Agency, and its contractors.

The system's way of managing data is crucial to the user who works in interaction with many other people. It should put generally useful data, if not subject to control of access, into public files. Each user, however, should have complete control over his personal files. He should define and distribute the 'keys' to each such file, exercising his option to exclude all others from any kind of access to it; or to permit anyone to 'read' but not modify or execute it; or to permit selected individuals or groups to execute but not read it; and so on—with as much detailed specification or as much aggregation as he likes. The system should provide for group and organizational files within its over-all information base.

At least one of the new multiaccess systems will exhibit such features. In several of the research centers we have mentioned, security and privacy of information are subjects of active concern; they are beginning to get the attention they deserve.

In a multiaccess system, the number of consoles permitted to use the com-puter simultaneously depends upon the load placed on the computer by the users' jobs, and may be varied automatically as the load changes. Large gen-eral-purpose multiaccess systems operating today can typically support 20 to 30 simultaneous users. Some of these users may work with low-level 'assem-bly' languages while others use higher-level 'compiler' or 'interpreter' lan-guages. Concurrently, others may use data management and graphical systems. And so on.

But back to our hypothetical user. He seats himself at his console, which may be a terminal keyboard plus a relatively slow printer, a sophisticated graphical console, or any one of several intermediate devices. He dials his local computer and 'logs in' by presenting his name, problem number, and password to the monitor program. He calls for either a public program, one of his own programs, or a colleague's program that he has permission to use. The monitor links him to it, and he then communicates with that program.

When the user (or the program) needs service from a program at another node in the network, he (or it) requests the service by specifying the location of the appropriate computer and the identity of the program required. If necessary, he uses computerized directories to determine those data. The request is translated by one or more of the message processors into the pre-cise language required by the remote computer's monitor. Now the user (or his local program) and the remote program can interchange information.

When the information transfer is complete, the user (or his local program) dismisses the remote computer, again with the aid of the message processors. In a commercial system, the remote processor would at this point record cost information for use in billing.

Who Can Afford It?

The mention of billing brings up an important matter. Computers and long-distance calls have 'expensive' images. One of the standard reactions to the idea of 'on-line communities' is: 'It sounds great, but who can afford it?'

In considering that question, let us do a little arithmetic. The main elements of the cost of computer-facilitated communication, over and above the salaries of the communicators, are the cost of the consoles, processing, storage, transmission, and supporting software. In each category, there is a wide range of possible costs, depending in part upon the sophistication of the equipment, programs, or services employed and in part upon whether they are custom-made or mass-produced.

Making rough estimates of the hourly component costs per user, we arrived at the following: $1 for a console, $5 for one man's share of the services of a processor, 70 cents for storage, $3 for transmission via line leased from a common carrier, and $1 for software support—a total cost of just less than $11 per communicator hour.

The only obviously untenable assumption underlying that result, we believe, is the assumption that one's console and the personal files would be used 160 hours per month. All the other items are assumed to be shared with others, and experience indicates that time-sharing leads on the average to somewhat greater utilization than the 160 hours per month that we assumed, Note, however, that the console and the personal files are items used also in individual problem solving and decision making. Surely those activities, taken together with communication, would occupy at least 25% of the working hours of the on-line executive, scientist or engineer. If we cut the duty factor of the console and files to one quarter of 160 hours per month, the estimated total cost comes to $16 per hour.

Let us assume that our $16/hr interactive computer link is set up between Boston, Mass., and Washington, D.C. Is $16/hr affordable? Compare it first with the cost of ordinary telephone communication: Even if you take advantage of the lower charge per minute for long calls, it is less than the daytime direct-dial station-to-station toll. Compare it with the cost of travel: If one flies from Boston to Washington in the morning and back in the evening, he can have eight working hours in the capital city in return for about $64 in air and taxi fares plus the spending of four of his early morning and evening hours en route. If those four hours are worth $16 each, then the bill for the eight hours in Washington is $128—again $16 per hour. Or look at it still another way: If computer-aided communication doubled the effectiveness of a man paid $16 per hour then, according to our estimate, it would be worth what it cost if it could be bought right now. Thus we have some basis for arguing that computer-aided communication is economically feasible. But we must admit that the figure of $16 per hour sounds high, and we do not want to let our discussion depend upon it.

Fortunately, we do not have to, for the system we envision cannot be bought at this moment. The time scale provides a basis for genuine optimism about the cost picture. It will take two years, at least, to bring the first interactive computer networks up to a significant level of experimental activity. Operational systems might reach critical size in as little as six years if everyone got onto the bandwagon, but there is little point in making cost estimates for a nearer date. So let us take six years as the target.

In the computer field, the cost of a unit of processing and the cost of a unit of storage have been dropping for two decades at the rate of 50% or more every two years. In six years, there is time for at least three such drops, which cut a dollar down to 12½ cents. Three halvings would take the cost of processing, now $5 per hour on our assumptions, down to less than 65 cents per hour.

Such advances in capability, accompanied by reduction in cost, lead us to expect that computer facilitation will be affordable before many people are ready to take advantage of it. The only areas that cause us concern are consoles and transmission.

In the console field, there is plenty of competition; many firms have entered the console sweepstakes, and more are entering every month. Lack of competition is not the problem. The problem is the problem of the chicken and the egg—in the factory and in the market. If a few companies would take the plunge into mass manufacture, then the cost of a satisfactory console would drop enough to open up a mass market. If large on-line communities were already in being, their mass market would attract mass manufacture. But at present there is neither mass manufacture nor a mass market, and consequently there is no low-cost console suitable for interactive on-line communication.

In the field of transmission, the difficulty may be lack of competition. At any rate, the cost of transmission is not falling nearly as fast as the cost of processing and storage. Nor is it falling nearly as fast as we think it should fall. Even the advent of satellites has affected the cost picture by less than a factor of two. That fact does not cause immediate distress because (unless the distance is very great) transmission cost is not now the dominant cost. But, at the rate things are going, in six years it will be the dominant cost. That prospect concerns us greatly and is the strongest damper to our hopes for near-term realization of operationally significant interactive networks and significant on-line communities.

On-line Interactive Communities

But let us be optimistic. What will on-line interactive communities be like? In most fields they will consist of geographically separated members, sometimes grouped in small clusters and sometimes working individually. They will be communities not of common location, but of *common interest*. In each field, the overall community of interest will be large enough to support a comprehensive system of field-oriented programs and data.

In each geographical sector, the total number of users—summed over all the fields of interest—will be large enough to support extensive general-purpose information processing and storage facilities. All of these will be interconnected by telecommunications channels. The whole will constitute a labile network of networks—ever-changing in both content and configuration.

What will go on inside? Eventually, every informational transaction of sufficient consequence to warrant the cost. Each secretary's typewriter, each data-gathering instrument, conceivably each dictation microphone, will feed into the network.

You will not send a letter or a telegram; you will simply identify the people whose files should be linked to yours and the parts to which they should be linked—and perhaps specify a coefficient of urgency. You will seldom make a telephone call; you will ask the network to link your consoles together.

You will seldom make a purely business trip, because linking consoles will be so much more efficient. When you do visit another person with the object of intellectual communication, you and he will sit at a two-place console and interact as much through it as face to face. If our extrapolation from Doug Engelbart's meeting proves correct, you will spend much more time in computer-facilitated teleconferences and much less en route to meetings.

A very important part of each man's interaction with his on-line community will be mediated by his OLIVER. The acronym OLIVER honors Oliver Selfridge, originator of the concept. An OLIVER is, or will be when there is one, an 'on-line interactive vicarious expediter and responder,' a complex of computer programs and data that resides within the network and acts on behalf of its principal, taking care of many minor matters that do not require his personal attention and buffering him from the demanding world. 'You are describing a secretary,' you will say. But no! Secretaries will have OLIVERS.

At your command, your OLIVER will take notes (or refrain from taking notes) on what you do, what you read, what you buy and where you buy it. It will know who your friends are, your mere acquaintances. It will know your value structure, who is prestigious in your eyes, for whom you will do what with what priority, and who can have access to which of your personal files. It will know your organization's rules pertaining to proprietary information and the government's rules relating to security classification.

Some parts of your OLIVER program will be common with parts of other people's OLIVERS; other parts will be custom-made for you, or by you, or will have developed idiosyncrasies through 'learning' based on its experience in your service.

Available within the network will be functions and services to which you subscribe on a regular basis and others that you call for when you need them. In the former group will be investment guidance, tax counseling, selective dissemination of information in your field of specialization, announcement of cultural, sport, and entertainment events that fit your interests, etc. In the latter group will be dictionaries, encyclopedias, indexes, catalogues, editing programs, teaching programs, testing programs, programming systems, data bases, and—most important—communication, display, and modeling programs.

All these will be—at some late date in the history of networking—systematized and coherent; you will be able to get along in one basic language up to the point at which you choose a specialized language for its power or terseness.

When people do their informational work 'at the console' and 'through the network,' telecommunication will be as natural an extension of individual work as face-to-face communication is now. The impact of that fact, and of the marked facilitation of the communicative process, will be very great—both on the individual and on society.

First, life will be happier for the on-line individual because the people with whom one interacts most strongly will be selected more by commonality of interests and goals than by accidents of proximity. Second, communication will be more effective and productive, and therefore more enjoyable. Third, much communication and interaction will be with programs and programmed models, which will be (a) highly responsive, (b) supplementary to one's own capabilities, rather than competitive, and (c) capable of representing progressively more complex ideas without necessarily displaying all the levels of their structure at the same time—and which will therefore be both challenging and rewarding. And, fourth, there will be plenty of opportunity for everyone (who can afford a console) to find his calling, for the whole world of information, with all its fields and disciplines, will be open to him—with programs ready to guide him or to help him explore.

For the society, the impact will be good or bad, depending mainly on the question: Will 'to be on line' be a privilege or a right? If only a favored segment of the population gets a chance to enjoy the advantage of 'intelligence amplification,' the network may exaggerate the discontinuity in the spectrum of intellectual opportunity.

On the other hand, if the network idea should prove to do for education what a few have envisioned in hope, if not in concrete detailed plan, and if all minds should prove to be responsive, surely the boon to humankind would be beyond measure.

Unemployment would disappear from the face of the earth forever, for consider the magnitude of the task of adapting the network's software to all the new generations of computer, coming closer and closer upon the heels of their predecessors until the entire population of the world is caught up in an infinite crescendo of on-line interactive debugging.

6

Personal Dynamic Media

Alan Kay and Adele Goldberg

In this article from 1977 Kay and Goldberg describe their vision for personal computing as represented by the epochal Dynabook. In their discussion they elaborate upon the significance of this device as a reactive, flexible, personal medium for everyday use.

Introduction

THE LEARNING RESEARCH GROUP at Xerox Palo Alto Research Center is concerned with all aspects of the communication and manipulation of knowledge. We design, build, and use dynamic media which can be used by human beings of all ages. Several years ago, we crystallized our dreams into a design idea for a personal dynamic medium the size of a notebook (the *Dynabook*) which could be owned by everyone and could have the power to handle virtually all of its owner's information-related needs. Towards this goal we have designed and built a communications system: the SmallTalk language, implemented on small computers we refer to as 'interim Dynabooks.' We are exploring the use of this system as a programming and problem solving tool; as an interactive memory for the storage and manipulation of data; as a text editor; and as a medium for expression through drawing, painting, animating pictures, and composing and generating music.

We offer this paper as a perspective on our goals and activities during the past years. In it, we explain the Dynabook idea, and describe a variety of systems we have already written in the SmallTalk language in order to give broad images of the kinds of information-related tools that might represent the kernel of a personal computing medium.

Background

Humans and Media

'Devices' which variously store, retrieve, or manipulate information in the form of messages embedded in a medium have been in existence for thousands of years. People use them to communicate ideas and feelings both to others and back to themselves. Although thinking goes on in one's head, external media serve to materialize thoughts and, through feedback, to augment the actual paths the thinking follows. Methods discovered in one medium provide metaphors which contribute new ways to think about notions in other media.

From *Computer* (March 1977): 10; 31–41 (and amended by Adele Goldberg, April 1988, to compensate for missing pictures). © 1977 IEEE. Reprinted with permission. (The illustrations from the 1988 reprint are not included; small changes to text have been made accordingly.)

For most of recorded history, the interactions of humans with their media have been primarily nonconversational and passive in the sense that marks on paper, paint on walls, even 'motion' pictures and television, do not change in response to the viewer's wishes. A mathematical formulation—which may symbolize the essence of an entire universe—once put down on paper, remains static and requires the reader to expand its possibilities.

Every message is, in one sense or another, a *simulation* of some idea. It may be representational or abstract. The essence of a medium is very much dependent on the way messages are embedded, changed, and viewed. Although digital computers were originally designed to do arithmetic computation, the ability to simulate the details of any descriptive model means that the computer, viewed as a medium itself, can be *all other media* if the embedding and viewing methods are sufficiently well provided. Moreover, this new 'metamedium' is *active*—it can respond to queries and experiments—so that the messages may involve the learner in a two-way conversation. This property has never been available before except through the medium of an individual teacher. We think the implications are vast and compelling.

A Dynamic Medium for Creative Thought: The Dynabook

Imagine having your own self-contained knowledge manipulator in a portable package the size and shape of an ordinary notebook. Suppose it had enough power to outrace your senses of sight and hearing, enough capacity to store for later retrieval thousands of page-equivalents of reference materials, poems, letters, recipes, records, drawings, animations, musical scores, waveforms, dynamic simulations, and anything else you would like to remember and change.

We envision a device as small and portable as possible which could both take in and give out information in quantities approaching that of human sensory systems. Visual output should be, at the least, of higher quality than what can be obtained from newsprint. Audio output should adhere to similar high-fidelity standards.

There should be no discernible pause between cause and effect. One of the metaphors we used when designing such a system was that of a musical instrument, such as a flute, which is owned by its user and responds instantly and consistently to its owner's wishes. Imagine the absurdity of a one-second delay between blowing a note and hearing it!

These 'civilized' desires for flexibility, resolution, and response lead to the conclusion that a user of a dynamic personal medium needs several hundred times as much power as the average adult now typically enjoys from time-shared computing. This means that we should either build a new resource several hundred times the capacity of current machines and share it (very difficult and expensive), or we should investigate the possibility of giving each person his own powerful machine. We chose the second approach.

Design Background

The first attempt at designing this metamedium (the FLEX machine: Kay 1969) occurred in 1967–69. Much of the hardware and software was successful from the standpoint of computer science state-of-the-art research, but lacked sufficient expressive power to be useful to an ordinary user. At that time we became interested in focusing on children as our 'user community.' We were greatly encouraged by the Bolt Beranek and Newman/MIT Logo work that uses a robot turtle that draws on paper, a CRT version of the turtle, and a single music generator to get kids to program.

Considering children as the users radiates a compelling excitement when viewed from a number of different perspectives. First, the children really can write programs that do serious things. Their programs use symbols to stand for objects, contain loops and recursions, require a fair amount of visualization of alternative strategies before a tactic is chosen, and involve interactive discovery and removal of 'bugs' in their ideas.

Second, the kids love it! The interactive nature of the dialogue, the fact that *they* are in control, the feeling that they are doing *real* things rather than playing with toys or working out 'assigned' problems, the pictorial and auditory nature of their results, all contribute to a tremendous sense of accomplishment to their existence. Their attention spans are measured in hours rather than minutes.

Another interesting nugget was that children really needed as much or more computing power than adults were willing to settle for when using a timesharing system. The best that timesharing has to offer is slow control of crude wire-frame green-tinted graphics and square-wave musical tones. The kids, on the other hand, are used to finger-paints, water colors, color television, real musical instruments, and records. If the 'medium is the message,' then the message of low-bandwidth timesharing is 'blah.'

An Interim Dynabook

We have designed an interim version of the Dynabook on which several interesting systems have been written in a new medium for communication, the SmallTalk programming language (Goldberg and Kay 1976). We have explored the usefulness of the systems with more than 200 users, most notably setting up a learning resource center in a local junior high school.

The interim Dynabook is a completely selfcontained system. To the user, it appears as a small box in which a disk memory can be inserted; each disk contains about 1500 page-equivalents of manipulable storage. The box is connected to a very crisp high-resolution black and white CRT or a lower-resolution high-quality color display. Other input devices include a typewriter keyboard, a 'chord' keyboard, a pointing device called a 'mouse' which inputs position as it is moved about on the table, and a variety of organ-like keyboards for playing music. New input devices such as these may be easily attached, usually without building a hardware interface for them. Visual output is through the display, auditory output is obtained from a built-in digital-to-analog converter connected to a standard hi-fi amplifier and speakers.

We will attempt to show some of the kinds of things that can be done with a Dynabook; a number of systems developed by various users will be briefly illustrated. All photographs of computer output in this paper are taken from the display screen of the interim system.

Remembering, The Dynabook can be used as an interactive memory or file cabinet. The
Seeing, and owner's context can be entered through a keyboard and active editor,
Hearing retained and modified indefinitely, and displayed on demand in a font of
publishing quality.

Drawing and painting can also be done using a pointing device and an
iconic editor which allows easy modification of pictures. A picture is thus a
manipulable object and can be animated dynamically by the Dynabook's
owner.

A book can be read through the Dynabook. It need not be treated as a
simulated paper book since this is a new medium with new properties. A dynamic search may be made for a particular context. The non-sequential nature of the file medium and the use of dynamic manipulation allows a story
to have many accessible points of view; Durrell's *Alexandria Quartet*, for instance, could be one book in which the reader may pursue many paths
through the narrative.

Different Fonts One of the goals of the Dynabook's design is *not* to be *worse* than paper in any
for Different important way. Computer displays of the past have been superior in matters
Effects of dynamic writing and erasure, but have failed in contrast, resolution, or
ease of viewing. There is more to the problem than just the display of text in
a high-quality font. Different fonts create different moods and cast an aura
that influences the subjective style of both writing and reading. The
Dynabook is supplied with a number of fonts which are contained on the file
storage.

The Dynabook as a personal medium is flexible to the point of allowing an
owner to choose his own ways to view information. Any character font can
be described as a matrix of black and white dots. The owner can draw in a
character font of his own choosing. He can then immediately view font
changes within the context of text displayed in a window. With the Dynabook's fine grain of display, the rough edges disappear at normal viewing distance to produce high-quality characters. [. . .]

Editing Every description or object in the Dynabook can be displayed and edited.
Text, both sequential and structured, can easily be manipulated by combining pointing and a simple 'menu' for commands, thus allowing deletion,
transposition, and structuring. Multiple windows allow a document (composed of text, pictures, musical notation) to be created and viewed simultaneously at several levels of refinement. Editing operations on other viewable
objects (such as pictures and fonts) are handled in analogous ways.

Filing The multiple-window display capability of SmallTalk has inspired the
notion of a dynamic *document*. A document is a collection of objects that
have a sensory display and have something to do with each other; it is a way
to store and retrieve related information. Each subpart of the document, or
frame, has its own editor which is automatically invoked when pointed at by
the 'mouse.' These frames may be related sequentially, as with ordinary
paper usage, or *inverted* with respect to properties, as in cross-indexed file

systems. *Sets* which can automatically map their contents to secondary storage with the ability to form unions, negations, and intersections are part of this system, as is a 'modeless' text editor with automatic right justification.

The current version of the system is able to automatically cross-file several thousand multifield records (with formats chosen by the user), which include ordinary textual documents indexed by content, the SmallTalk system, personal files, diagrams, and so on.

Drawing/
Painting

The many small dots required to display high-quality characters (about 500,000 for an 8-½"×11" sized display) also allow sketching-quality drawing, 'halftone painting,' and animation. The subjective effect of gray scale is caused by the eye fusing an area containing a mixture of small black and white dots. [...]

Curves are drawn by a *pen* on the display screen. (Straight lines are curves with zero curvature.) In the Dynabook, *pens* are members of a class that can selectively draw with black or white (or colored) ink and change the thickness of the trace. Each *pen* lives in its own *window*, careful not to traverse its window boundaries but to adjust as its window changes size and position. [...]

Animation and
Music

Animation, music, and programming can be thought of as different *sensory views* of dynamic processes. The structural similarities among them are apparent in SmallTalk, which provides a common framework for expressing those ideas.

All of the systems are equally controllable by hand or by program. Thus, drawing and painting can be done using a pointing device or in conjunction with programs which draw curves, fill in areas with tone, show perspectives of three-dimensional models, and so on. Any graphic expression can be animated, either by reflecting a simulation or by example (giving an 'animator' program a sample trace or a route to follow).

Music is controlled in a completely analogous manner. The Dynabook can act as a 'super synthesizer' getting direction either from a keyboard or from a 'score.' The keystrokes can be captured, edited, and played back. Timbres, the 'fonts' of musical expression, contain the quality and mood which different instruments bring to an orchestration. They may be captured, edited, and used dynamically.

Simulation

In a very real sense, simulation is the central notion of the Dynabook. Each of the previous examples has shown a simulation of visual or auditory media. Here are a number of examples of interesting simulations done by a variety of users.

An Animation
System Programmed
by Animators

Several professional animators wanted to be able to draw and paint pictures which could then be animated in real time by simply showing the system roughly what was wanted. Desired changes would be made by iconically editing the animation sequences.

Much of the design of SHAZAM, their animation tool, is an automation of the media with which animators are familiar: *movies* consisting of sequences of *frames* which are a composition of transparent *cels* containing foreground and background drawings. Besides retaining these basic concepts of conventional animation, SHAZAM incorporates some creative supplementary capabilities.

Animators know that the main action of animation is due not to an individual frame, but to the change from one frame to the next. It is therefore much easier to plan an animation if it can be seen moving as it is being created. SHAZAM allows any cel of any frame in an animation to be edited while the animation is in progress. A library of already-created cels is maintained. The animation can be single-stepped; individual cels can be repositioned, reframed, and redrawn; new frames can be inserted; and a frame sequence can be created at any time by attaching the cel to the pointing device, then *showing* the system what kind of movement is desired. The cels can be stacked for background parallax; *holes* and *windows* are made with *transparent* paint. Animation objects can be painted by programs as well as by hand. The control of the animation can also be easily done from a SmallTalk simulation. For example, an animation of objects bouncing in a room is most easily accomplished by a few lines of SmallTalk that express the class of bouncing objects in physical terms.

A Drawing and Painting System Programmed by a Child

One young girl, who had never programmed before, decided that a pointing device *ought* to let her draw on the screen. She then built a sketching tool without ever seeing ours. She constantly embellished it with new features including a menu for brushes selected by pointing. She later wrote a program for building tangram designs.

This girl has taught her own SmallTalk class; her students were seventh-graders from her junior high school. One of them designed an even more elaborate system in which pictures are constructed out of geometric shapes created by pointing to a menu of commands for creating regular polygons. The polygons can then be relocated, scaled, and copied; their color and line width can change.

A Hospital Simulation Programmed by a Decision-Theorist

The simulation represents a hospital in which every *department* has resources which are used by *patients* for some *duration of time*. Each patient has a *schedule* of departments to visit; if there are no resources available (doctors, beds), the patient must *wait* in line for service. The SmallTalk description of this situation involves the class of *patients* and the class of *departments*. The generalization to any hospital configuration with any number of patients is part of the simulation. The particular example captured in the pictures shows patients lining up for service in *emergency*. It indicates that there is insufficient staff available in that important area.

An Audio Animation System Programmed by Musicians

Animation can be considered to be the coordinated parallel control through time of images conceived by an animator. Likewise, a system for representing and controlling musical images can be imagined which has very strong analogies to the visual world. Music is the design and control of images (pitch and duration changes) which can be *painted* different *colors* (timbre choices); it has synchronization and coordination, and a very close relationship between audio and spatial visualization.

The SmallTalk model created by several musicians, called TWANG, has the notion of a *chorus* which contains the main control directions for an overall piece. A chorus is a kind of *rug* with a warp of parallel sequences of 'pitch, duration, and articulation' commands, and a woof of synchronizations and global directives. The control and the *player* are separate: in SHAZAM, a given movie sequence can animate many drawings; in TWANG, a given chorus can tell many different kinds of instrumentalists what should be played. These *voices* can be synthetic timbres or timbres captured from real instruments. Musical effects such as vibrato, portamento, and diminuation are also available.

A chorus can be *drawn* using the pointing device, or it can be *captured* by playing it on a keyboard. It can be played back in real time and dynamically edited in a manner very similar to the animation system.

We use two methods for real-time production of high-quality timbres; both allow arbitrary transients and many independent parallel voices, and are completely produced by programs. One of these allows independent dynamic control of the spectrum, the frequency, the amplitude, and the particular collection of partials which will be heard.

For children, this facility has a number of benefits: the strong similarities between the audio and visual worlds are emphasized because a single vernacular *which actually works* in both worlds is used for description; and second, the arts and skills of composing can be learned at the same time since tunes may be drawn in by hand and played by the system. A line of music may be copied, stretched, and shifted in time and pitch; individual notes may be edited. Imitative counterpoint is thus easily created by the fledgling composer.

A Musical Score Capture System Programmed by a Musician

OPUS is a musical score capture system that produces a display of a conventional musical score from data obtained by playing a musical keyboard. OPUS is designed to allow incremental input of an arbitrarily complicated score (full orchestra with chorus, for example), editing pages of the score, and hard copy of the final result with separate parts for individual instruments.

Conclusion

What would happen in a world in which everyone had a Dynabook? If such a machine were designed in a way that *any* owner could mold and channel its power to his own needs, then a new kind of medium would have been created: a metamedium, whose content would be a wide range of already-existing and not-yet-invented media.

An architect might wish to simulate three-dimensional space in order to peruse and edit his current designs, which could be conveniently stored and cross-referenced.

A doctor could have on file all of his patients, his business records, a drug reaction system, and so on, all of which could travel with him wherever he went.

A composer could hear his composition while it was in progress, particularly if it were more complex than he was able to play. He could also bypass the incredibly tedious chore of redoing the score and producing the parts by hand.

Learning to play music could be aided by being able to capture and hear one's own attempts and compare them against expert renditions. The ability to express music in visual terms which could be filed and played means that the acts of composition and self-evaluation could be learned without having to wait for technical skill in playing.

Home records, accounts, budgets, recipes, reminders, and so forth, could be easily captured and manipulated.

Those in business could have an active briefcase which travelled with them, containing a working simulation of their company, the last several weeks of correspondence in a structured cross-indexed form—a way to instantly calculate profiles for their futures and help make decisions.

For educators, the Dynabook could be a new world limited only by their imagination and ingenuity. They could use it to show complex historical inter-relationships in ways not possible with static linear books. Mathematics could become a living language in which children could cause exciting things to happen. Laboratory experiments and simulations too expensive or difficult to prepare could easily be demonstrated. The production of stylish prose and poetry could be greatly aided by being able to easily edit and file one's own compositions.

These are just a few ways in which we envision using a Dynabook. But if the projected audience is to be 'everyone,' is it possible to make the Dynabook generally useful, or will it collapse under the weight of trying to be too many different tools for too many people? The total range of possible users is so great that any attempt to specifically anticipate their needs in the design of the Dynabook would end in a disastrous feature-laden hodgepodge which would not be really suitable for anyone.

Some mass items, such as cars and television sets, attempt to anticipate and provide for a variety of applications in a fairly inflexible way; those who wish to do something different will have to put in considerable effort. Other items, such as paper and clay, offer many dimensions of possibility and high resolution; these can be used in an unanticipated way by many, though *tools* need to be made or obtained to stir some of the medium's possibilities while constraining others.

We would like the Dynabook to have the flexibility and generality of this second kind of item, combined with tools which have the power of the first kind. Thus a great deal of effort has been put into providing both endless possibilities and easy tool-making through the SmallTalk programming language.

Our design strategy, then, divides the problem. The burden of system design and specification is transferred to the user. This approach will only work if we do a very careful and comprehensive job of providing a general medium of communication which will allow ordinary users to casually and easily describe their desires for a specific tool. We must also provide enough already-written general tools so that a user need not start from scratch for most things she or he may wish to do.

We have stated several specific goals. In summary, they are:

- to provide coherent, powerful examples of the use of the Dynabook in and across subject areas;
- to study how the Dynabook can be used to help expand a person's visual and auditory skills;
- to provide exceptional freedom of access so kids can spend a lot of time probing for details, searching for a personal key to understanding processes they use daily; and
- to study the unanticipated use of the Dynabook and SmallTalk by children in all age groups.

References

BAEKER, RONALD, 'A Conversational Extensible System for the Animation of Shaded Images,' *Proc. ACM SIGGRAPH Symposium*, Philadelphia, Pennsylvania, June 1976.

GOLDBERG, ADELE and ALAN KAY (eds.), *SmallTalk-72 Instruction Manual*, Xerox Palo Alto Research Center, Technical Report No. SSL 76–6, March 1976.

GOLDEEN, MARIAN, 'Learning About SmallTalk', *Creative Computing*, September–October 1975.

KAY, ALAN, 'The Reactive Engine', doctoral dissertation, University of Utah, September 1969.

Learning Research Group, 'Personal Dynamic Media', Xerox Palo Alto Research Center, Technical Report No. SSL 76–1, March 1976.

SAUNDERS, S., 'Improved FM Audio Synthesis Methods for Realtime Digital Music Generation,' *Proc. ACM Computer Science Conference*, Washington, DC, February 1975.

SMITH, DAVID C., 'PYGMALION: A Creative Programming Environment', Doctoral dissertation, Stanford University Computer Science Department, June 1975.

SNOOK, TOD, 'Three-dimensional Geometric Modelling', Masters thesis, University of California, Berkeley, September 1976.

7

A New Home for the Mind

Ted Nelson

In this article from 1982 Ted Nelson elaborates upon his ideas for a computer-based publishing system which incorporates automatic version control and linked, nonsequential text, or 'hypertext'. Building upon this, Nelson describes the components of his system for managing royalties and copyright in a 'whole new pluralistic publishing form'. In concluding his discussion, he offers a vision of the social benefits of implementing these concepts.

S IMPLICITY ALMOST NEVER happens by itself; it must be designed. There are many computer programs for dealing with complexity. Unfortunately, as a rule, they generate more complexity. Many systems that start out simply, like order processing or invoicing, are appallingly complex in their full-blown computer regalia. As a result, many computer people see their jobs as the management and perpetuation of this complexity.

An alternative to this care and feeding of ever more complex systems based on simplistic frameworks is to seek a framework that holds and deals with ideas and their relationships in their natural form and structure, in their full and exact intricacy. To face squarely and early the natural implications of a process brings simplicity in the long run.

A situation where this choice can be made is upon us now with the arrival of cheap word processing systems. These machines help create, manipulate and store people's ideas in the form of written documents. Many of these documents relate to each other, quoting in part or whole, referencing through footnotes and bibliographies, or merely sharing similar ideas. It is often necessary to store many copies of one document to assure safety from accidental deletions, provide a means for backtracking through successive states of the document and for repeated use by other documents.

The safety of documents should be taken care of automatically; that it is still a problem shows the low state of the art. Backtracking is an important consideration. Although we do not need to go back through previous material often, we should be able to do it right when we do. Here is what doing it right entails:

Suppose we create an automatic storage system that takes care of backtracking automatically. As a user makes changes, they go directly into the storage system, filed chronologically. The user may then refer not merely to

From *Datamation* (March 1982).

the present version of a document, but may go back in time to any previous version. He must also be able to follow a specific section of a document back through time, studying its previous states. We need not go into technical details here, but it is obvious that such a system departs from conventional block storage. It would store material in fragments under control of a master directory which indexes by time and other factors.

This same scheme can be expanded to handle alternative versions, more than one arrangement of the same materials, a facility that writers and programmers could certainly use. Alternative versions are important in many boiler plate applications, such as law and public relations writing, where the same materials are churned out repeatedly in different arrangements and variations. A master indexing scheme could greatly reduce storage requirements in these applications, and make the relations among documents much clearer.

Of course, a facility that holds many versions of the same material and allows historical backtracking is not terribly useful unless it can help intercompare different versions in detail, unless it can show you, word for word, what parts of two versions are the same.

Lawyers could use this facility to compare wordings. Congressmen could compare different draft versions of legislative bills. Authors could see what has happened to specific passages in their writings between drafts. Biologists and anatomists could compare corresponding parts of animals using a graphical database of physiology that shows evolving structure.

By creating such a capable storage system, we have greatly simplified the life of the text user. The nuisance of backup, and the spurious nonsense-task of finding names for backup files, is eliminated. More importantly, we have unified all versions (previous and alternative) in a single structure for ready reference. The user could scroll through any two versions to see corresponding parts, and much more.

Adding A Link Facility

So far we imagine a new reading-and-writing box that behaves pretty much like a high-power word processor. Let us add one more facility, links.

To begin with, let us think of a link as simply an opportunity to jump away from some point in the text. A conventional footnote is a good example. An asterisk, say, signals that 'there's something to jump to from here.' If you point at it with your light-pen (or mouse or whatever), bingo!—you're now at the footnote, or whatever else the author took you to. If you don't like it there, hit a return button and you're back to where the asterisk appeared. No harm has been done.

This simple facility—call it the jump-link capability—leads immediately to all sorts of new text forms: for scholarship, for teaching, for fiction, for poetry.

Marginal notes, like those scribbled in books, are another simple and important type of link. (Where the 'margins' of the computer screen are—that is, how to show them—is a matter particular to your own screen setup.)

The link facility gives us much more than the attachment of mere odds and ends. It permits fully nonsequential writing. Writings have been sequential because pages have been sequential. What is the alternative? Why, *hypertext*—nonsequential writing.

Many, perhaps most, writers have been frustrated by the problem of choosing a sequence for the ideas they are presenting. Any sequence is generally arbitrary, and what is right for one reader may be wrong for another. Indeed, many writers have experimented with nonsequential forms—one of my favorites is Nabokov's *Pale Fire*—and I think such forms have proved gratifying. They are not necessarily easy to work with, however. That is because existing mechanisms push us toward sequency. Even the best of commercial word processors.

I have so far presented several new capabilities that I think are important: alternative versions and historical backtrack, both with sameness display, and links.

These work together; they have to. The links allow the creation of nonsequential writings and jump-structured graphics of many kinds. But if you are going to have links you really need historical backtrack and alternative versions. Why? Because if you make some links on Monday and go on making changes, perhaps on Wednesday you'd like to follow those links into an updated version. They'd better still be attached to the right parts, even though the parts may have moved. And the sameness display allows the complex linked alternatives to be studied and intercompared in depth.

Let us call this Stage One: a system of computer storage that holds small pieces of a document, not big blocks, and instantly assembles them into any part of whichever version you ask for. That allows you to create links of any kind you want between any things you want, and shows you which parts are the same between related versions. Let us call such a storage system a hyperfile.

Electronic publishing is coming; this much we all agree on. Just what it will be is not so clear. For some five hundred years the public has been reading from books and magazines of paper. Now all that may change.

As computer crt screens become more and more available, there is less and less reason for printing on paper. The costs of wood pulp and gasoline, the long lead times of editorship and production, the increasing divergence of specialized interests, and the lowering cost of computers with screens, of disk storage, and digital communications, all suggest this.

Beginning thinkers in this area often suppose that what will be offered to the screen reader will be merely individual stored documents, available online quickly, but based somehow on conventional documents nestling in conventional sequential computer files. My view is quite different.

Consider the hyperfile we just finished expounding. Why can't we extend it into a full publishing system? Once the package allows linkage and backtracking, why not extend it? Why not allow anyone to create links between documents, allowing jumps straight from one to another? If documents can be reached and used on-line by anyone, all we need additionally is the ability to create links among them—to make our own bookmarks and marginal notes, to quote from them by direct excision. And why not, indeed, allow users to assemble collections of documents into larger ones?

Royalties will have to be paid, of course. Since there is no controlling what happens at the user end, this royalty should be automatically recorded and largely based on *transmission time*. An hour, five minutes, or one second of a thing, each contribute proportionally to the copyright holder's account. I will bypass the question of whether different rates of royalty should be allowed.

Original Document Remains

The logic of such compound documents is simple and derives from the concept of document ownership. Every document has an owner. The integrity of this document is maintained; no one may change it but the owner.

Someone else, however, may create a document which quotes it or revises it; this document, too, retains its integrity. That means you can indefinitely create new documents from old ones, making whatever changes seem appropriate. Originals remain unchanged.

What's more, since the copyright holder gets an automatic royalty, anything may be quoted without permission. That is, publishing through such a net requires implicit permission for your work to be quoted ad lib. You publish something, anyone can use it, you always get a royalty automatically. Fair. Especially if the reader can always say, 'Show me what this was originally.'

But this means a whole new pluralistic publishing form. If anything which is already published can be included in anything newly published, any new viewpoint can be fairly presented. For example, my great-grandfather, Edmund Gale Jewett, believed that one word in *Hamlet* was incorrect. It should have been 'siege,' not 'sea of troubles,' in the well-known soliloquy, he thought.

Very well. If *Hamlet* is on the system, then E. G. Jewett could publish his own *Hamlet* very easily: a quote-link to the whole original, except for 'sea,' which is changed to 'siege.'

Now, the obvious rules of the road should be as follows:

1. Shakespeare's *Hamlet* is of course unchanged and available instantly.

2. Jewett's modified version of *Hamlet*, composed almost entirely of the original, is also available instantly. Jewett may give it any title he wants.

3. Shakespeare—or presumably some Needy Author's Fund—gets the royalties for the portion of Shakespeare's *Hamlet* summoned by readers.

4. When people read Jewett's *Hamlet*, the author's fund still gets the royalty on Shakespeare's behalf almost all the time. But Jewett gets a minute proportion of the royalty for the change he has made, whenever a reader encounters that part.

5. Anyone reading Jewett's version can say, 'Show me the original of this next to it,' or just, 'Take me to the original.'

6. Anyone reading Shakespeare's *Hamlet* can say: 'What documents have links to this?' or 'Are there any alternative versions?' and get a list that includes Jewett's version.

Note also the modest cost to Jewett should he 'publish' his text: the storage cost for a few hundred bytes to hold ID, pointers, and changes. Also, note that this arrangement is fair, orderly, and simple. These seem to me very important features.

The overarching vision I propose, then, we might call a 'hyperworld'—a vast new realm of published text and graphics, all available instantly; a grand library that anybody can store anything in—and get a royalty for—with links, alternate versions, and backtrack available as options to anyone who wishes to publish them. It is a world:

- whose documents window and link freely to one another,
- where every quotation may be traced instantly, and seen in its original context;
- where minority interpretations and commentary may be found everywhere;
- where any point of view disagreed with may at once be restated 'in the margin,' with only minor changes, by any commentator; thus good explanations of everything soon become available;
- where a collage of parts can be assembled by anyone into a new unifying vision, but the doubtful reader may wander off into a constituent part and not return;
- where an article published on Wednesday is festooned with disagreements by Friday, widely windowed the following week, forgotten the next year, rediscovered in a decade.

Scholarship becomes piled high with popularizations. Good quotations, good diagrams, propagate through this electronic literature like wildfire, as everybody uses them.

The tangle of links will grow. Professional indexers will create directories of what they think we'll want to see, and collect a whiff of royalty every time you veer through their directory. (The system must not have an official directory; that implies an official set of categories—a bias best left to users.)

Is this chaos? Not at all. Because at any one time you are within one specific document, the work of a specific author. If this work is windowing to other documents, nevertheless you are still not 'in' the others, but viewing them through the present author's textual filter.

Think of the present document as a sheet of glass. It may have writing painted on it by the present author; it may have windows to something else, but these windows may have, as it were, colored cellophane or opaquing on them. It is only when you step through the window—which you may do at any time—that you reach the original. But stepping through the window means turning one glass page and going on to the next. Now you are in another work.

Simple and Orderly

Now reconsider what we said before about simplicity. Simplicity must be designed, but it should reflect the true inner structure of something. Many approaches to electronic publishing are very complicated. But that can't work on a broad scale: the word publishing itself suggests use by the public.

Meaning simplicity. For thousands of years we have had a tradition we call literature. Its inner structure has been that of documents, each with an owner/creator, which quote and refer to one another in an ever-growing snowball. All I am proposing here is to electronify and hasten access to this very traditional structure—but with suitable enhancements arising from available software techniques.

The result is a seemingly anarchic pool of documents, true, but that's what literature has been anyhow. Yet I see this new world as orderly in two ways. Its orderliness is not, as some would suppose, imposed by the computer or its administrators, but by something which arose long ago in the natural structure of literature, and which we are merely retaining.

One kind of order, order on the small scale, is simply the distinction between documents and the enforcement of ownership. You know who created whatever you're looking at; despite the staggering pluralism, each thing is kept separate and intact because only its author, or publisher, controls it. No one can ever be misquoted except by making a copy, rather than a quotation-link, and that can be easily recognized as suspicious.

The other form of order is the long-term orderliness of ideas, which is ever created and re-created by commentators, paraphrasers, anthologizers.

I see a world where people are brought together by the computer, rather than driven apart by television. The computer screen is really a very social instrument. Not many people have noticed that the crt is an ideal two-person device. Sure, much of the time there's only one person at it, but often there are two. And when there are two people, the situation is socially interesting: they are usually in a colleague relationship. Two people sit, chat, exchange ideas as they browse, decide together what to do next. Bossy authority does not fit well when two people are looking at a tube and chatting. 'Suppose we try this,' one will say, or, 'Let's do that.' One may be officially the other's boss or teacher, but the relationship is softened, made more sensible and open to ideas from both. One moral is that every computer screen should have a jump seat. As crt furniture and mountings are better designed, the computer and screen will no longer be a stack of boxes to be placed on a wooden desk, but an integrated piece of furniture with suspended tube, coordinated work surfaces, and bucket seats. Or rather a pilot's bucket seat and a colleague's less comfortable pullout seat. Kibitzers will have to stand.

As explorable graphics and simulations are added to our hyperworld, the computer screen will be more and more a new kind of shared social environment. I see little kids at play in spaceships and far galaxies, but with characters on the screen that they've borrowed from here and there. Barbie, the Wizard of Oz, Captain Midnight, and Shaft can be toys in Eriador or the palace of Ming the Merciless, because graphical pieces may be drawn from everywhere. The kids build worlds and castles in two-dimensional collages, which can always be there when they come back, unlike wooden blocks that clutter the living room. Later, as 3D imaging systems like CHARGE become available, the hyperworld can include three-dimensional dataspaces.

I see adults who were 'afraid of science' learning physics at the wheel of a video game, combining one author's graphics with another's simulations and still another's sound synthesis; where dings and roars and acceleration make the ideas come alive.

I see families together again, actively sharing. Imagine a kid and her father browsing through an illustrated hypertext:

'Gee, daddy, a brontosaurus! Let's animate him!'

'Like this?' The father finds several animations that have been published for this brontosaurus. Choosing one, he makes the brontosaurus walk and eat.

'I wonder what the bones of the dinosaur look like while he's walking,' ruminates the child.

Father links to bones while maintaining the animation. Now the skeleton walks inside its outline, still munching from trees.

'Oh, save that, daddy!'

Daddy hits a button and a private link is created to the original dinosaur picture, the animation frame, and the skeleton—all of which may be brought together again, with time and date, when the child wants to see her 'dinosaur picture.'

Hey, here we are in *Snow White and the Seven Dwarfs.* A Disney vision. Shall we jump sideways on links to older illustrations? Yikes, the 19th century engravings are too sinister. Let's see if this passage has a corresponding part in the Donald Barthelme version.

Once we can have full and independent linking and windowing, scholarship changes dramatically. A commentator or critic can underline precisely what he is referring to at any time, and gather together whatever pieces support his thesis. Intercomparison and exegesis become easier to do and easier to follow. Detailed annotations to existing writings may easily be published, anthologies of related materials can easily be put together.

Perhaps most important, this richness and completeness becomes available to students who before have had to deal with simplified, bowdlerized, and gutless materials.

Consider schools. From the one-room schoolhouse, a cooperative endeavor fostering individual goals and abilities in a sharing atmosphere, we went to a batch-processing system with inane fixed curricula, arbitrary and meaningless standards of success and failure (what in hell does a 'B' in geometry *mean*?), and teaching as a platoon-control process. Human mentality, even for the 'well educated,' has been kept by the educational system and popular outlook far below the levels we can, and ought to, attain.

Why is it that schools are by their nature boring and oppressive, yet museums, which may cover the same subjects, are liberating and exciting to kids? The answers are fairly simple: one is dull, the other is vivid; one is confining, the other is free.

Now there ought to be a way—there's going to be a way—to combine the freedom of a museum with a reasonable criterial system for monitoring achievement.

Aside from the merest basics, it is not important *what* you learn, it is important *that* you learn, and if there are a lot of choices then you are going to choose for yourself and succeed for yourself; thus you feel gratified from the learning process and competent to continue it, and those are two outcomes the schools have studiously avoided.

How to bring out the excitement, controversy, drama, of all the world's subjects, put this in a voluntaristic and uncontrolled framework, and keep it orderly? By creating, I think, a whole new hyperworld where we fly our crts through text and graphics of every kind, and a social world built around it—where ideas become important.

There are several key problem areas.

1. *Curriculum.* It is unfathomable to me, when so little education is cumulative, and when adults say over and over that they don't remember what they 'learned' in school, why curriculum is assumed to be of any importance, thought to be anything other than a pointless and painful charade. Nobody learns it anyway; it's simply an administrative runaround. ('Curriculum' originally meant 'racetrack.')

2. *'Subjects.'* There are no 'subjects.' Everything is deeply intertwingled. Supposed subjects are arbitrary divisions in the infinite tapestry of human ideas and concerns. The true interconnectedness of knowledge, as well as the sweeping disagreements that make scholarship interesting, should be available to students at all levels.

3. *Personal conflicts.* The problems between teacher and student of personality, authority, and outlook often swamp whatever else is supposed to be going on. There has got to be a way around this.

4. *Cognitive style.* Different people learn best in different ways, and anything could be taught in any style—but much energy is wasted on promoting cognitive style as well.

There is a crucial distinction between hypertext and computer assisted instruction. It is simply one of freedom. In computer assisted instruction, the author can lock you into a specific situation and there you are—constrained to do the task that has been set for you, however long it takes, however oppressive and stupid it may be. And there is typically no way to register a disagreement.

In compound hypertext, however, we retain one of the great traditions of Western literature: freedom to turn the page or close the book. You are free to write marginalia of disagreement anywhere—which everyone else is in turn free to ignore. I believe that the rigidity and narrow-mindedness of today's computer assisted instruction will open out into the freedom of hyperworld exploration.

And the two-seat hypertext screen may just restore the convivial qualities of bygone education and of personal tutoring, as the teacher drops into the jump seat at the student's computer and makes suggestions rather than gives orders.

If there is a published, widely pluralistic tapestry of writings on all topics, then each reader, old or young, can find the style that best suits him or her for pursuing a specific topic.

One of the dullest subjects I took in school was 'history.' It was a tiresome enumeration of names, wars and dates with no particular meaning. But I loved historical movies; they had heroes with a purpose. Now in fact historical scholars are often vitally concerned with heroes and their purposes. How do the schools manage to make these things dull?

Why shouldn't the students have access to material that makes the motivating controversies, the heroes and high spots of history come alive—and then link sideways between documents to the more factual material? By what paths did the tribes reach Europe? (What universal rules of tribalism are there, if any?) Was the legend of Valhalla really inspired by the Roman colosseum? What really happened before the Thera/Atlantis explosion? What did the Tower of Babel look like?

An Ever-Widening Tree

We can't know, but we can conjecture; there is an ever-widening tree of possibilities. I want to explore it, and I'm sure other kids would love it too.

Imagine: Hyper-poetry—collages of pieces of text that cleverly intertwine, or even rhyme.

Hyper-valentines—send a loved one a picture with little doors that open into all kinds of wonderful places in the hyperworld.

Minority voices—every viewpoint should be easily heard. Of course, this does not mean people will listen. But the problem of 'media coverage,' a chafing-point for minorities who feel that their views cannot be heard, is in a sense solved.

High ideals—what passes for high ideals often isn't worth a gumball. The drabness of most computer ideals is a downer, like being sprayed with wet concrete: 'New tools for management,' 'Better through-put,' 'Instant file cards for libraries.' This is worth spending your life on? With word processing and shoot-'em-up arcade games, interactive computing and graphics have at last reached The People, and indeed threaten to transform society. But is this the kind of transformation we ought to be thinking about?

Those of us who grew up believing passionately in ideals that made our country great, such as liberty and pluralism and the accessibility of ideas, can hardly ignore the hope of such an opening-out. Libertarian ideals of accessibility and excitement might unseat the video narcosis that now sits on our land like a fog. I want to see the writings of Herodotus, Nostradamus, and Matthew Brann as accessible as those of Rod McKuen, along with the art of the Renaissance and movies of tomorrow—an all-encompassing picture-book encyclopedia tumult graffiti-land, the Whole Works.

If this all seems like a wild idea, that means you understand it. These are times wild with possibility. In an age of pocket calculators, the Pill, hydrogen bombs by rocket, and soap opera by satellite, we can try to create whatever wildness we want in our society.

And when the kids start being born up in the space colonies—do we want them to lose touch? Paper's too heavy to send up, but hypertext might be about right.

I say these worlds are possible soon. We need them, and they will make lots of money. The software is on the way. But what is really lacking are the visionary artists, writers, publishers, and investors who can see the possibilities and help carry such ideas into reality.

8

Computer Software

Alan Kay

In this article, Alan Kay expands upon the idea of the computer as a medium. Via an analogy to the shaping of clay, Kay discusses the nature of computer software and the significance of user interface design while arguing for a comprehensive vision of computer literacy for understanding computer media. Discussing spreadsheet software as well as software agents, Kay illustrates the protean nature of the computer and its unique capacities for representation and simulation.

COMPUTERS ARE TO computing as instruments are to music. Software is the score, whose interpretation amplifies our reach and lifts our spirit. Leonardo da Vinci called music 'the shaping of the invisible,' and his phrase is even more apt as a description of software. As in the case of music, the invisibility of software is no more mysterious than where your lap goes when you stand up '[. . .]'

The materials of computing are the tersest of markings, stored by the billions in computer hardware. In a musical score the tune is represented in the hardware of paper and ink; in biology the message transmitted from generation to generation by DNA is held in the arrangement of the chemical groups called nucleotides. Just as there have been many materials (from clay to papyrus to vellum to paper and ink) for storing the marks of writing, so computer hardware has relied on various physical systems for storing its marks: rotating shafts, holes in cards, magnetic flux, vacuum tubes, transistors and integrated circuits inscribed on silicon chips. Marks on clay or paper, in DNA and in computer memories are equally powerful in their ability to represent, but the only intrinsic meaning of a mark is that it is there. 'Information,' Gregory Bateson noted, 'is any difference that makes a difference.' The first difference is the mark; the second one alludes to the need for interpretation.

The same notation that specifies elevator music specifies the organ fugues of Bach. In a computer the same notation can specify actuarial tables or bring a new world to life. The fact that the notation for graffiti and for sonnets can be the same is not new. That this holds also for computers removes much of the new technology's mystery and puts thinking about it on firmer ground.

As with most media from which things are built, whether the thing is a cathedral, a bacterium, a sonnet, a fugue or a word processor, architecture dominates material. To understand clay is not to understand the pot. What a pot is all about can be appreciated better by understanding the creators and

From *Scientific American*, vol. 251, no. 3 (1984), pp. 41–7. The text of the original article has been amended for publication in this volume.

users of the pot and their need both to inform the material with meaning and to extract meaning from the form.

There is a qualitative difference between the computer as a medium of expression and clay or paper. Like the genetic apparatus of a living cell, the computer can read, write and follow its own markings to levels of self-interpretation whose intellectual limits are still not understood. Hence the task for someone who wants to understand software is not simply to see the pot instead of the clay. It is to see in pots thrown by beginners (for all are beginners in the fledgling profession of computer science) the possibility of the Chinese porcelain and Limoges to come.

Here I need spend no more time on computing's methods for storing and reading marks than molecular biology does on the general properties of atoms. A large enough storage capacity for marks and the simplest set of instructions are enough to build any further representational mechanisms that are needed, including even the simulation of an entire new computer. Augusta Ada, Countess of Lovelace, the first computer-software genius, who programmed the analytical engine that Charles Babbage had designed, understood well the powers of simulation of the general-purpose machine. In the 1930's Alan M. Turing stated the case more crisply by showing how a remarkably simple mechanism can simulate all mechanisms.

The idea that any computer can simulate any existing or future computer is important philosophically, but it is not the answer to all computational problems. Too often a simple computer pretending to be a fancy one gets stuck in the 'Turing tar pit' and is of no use if results are needed in less than a million years. In other words, quantitative improvements may also be helpful. An increase in speed may even represent a qualitative improvement. Consider how speeding up a film from two frames per second to 20 (a mere order of magnitude) makes a remarkable difference; it leads to the subjective perception of continuous movement. Much of the 'life' of visual and auditory interaction depends on its pace.

As children we discovered that clay can be shaped into any form simply by shoving both hands into the stuff. Most of us have learned no such thing about the computer. Its material seems as detached from human experience as a radioactive ingot being manipulated remotely with buttons, tongs and a television monitor. What kind of emotional contact can one make with this new stuff if the physical access seems so remote?

One feels the clay of computing through the 'user interface': the software that mediates between a person and the programs shaping the computer into a tool for a specific goal, whether the goal is designing a bridge or writing an article. The user interface was once the last part of a system to be designed. Now it is the first. It is recognized as being primary because, to novices and professionals alike, what is presented to one's senses is one's computer. The 'user illusion,' as my colleagues and I called it at the Xerox Palo Alto Research Center, is the simplified myth everyone builds to explain (and make guesses about) the system's actions and what should be done next.

Many of the principles and devices developed to enhance the illusion have now become commonplace in software design. Perhaps the most important principle is WYSIWYG ('What you see is what you get'): the image on the screen is always a faithful representation of the user's illusion. Manipulating the image in a certain way immediately does something predictable to the state of the machine (as the user imagines that state). One illusion now in vogue has 'windows,' 'menus,' 'icons' and a pointing device. The display frames called windows make it possible to present a number of activities on the screen at one time. Menus of possible next steps are displayed; icons represent objects as concrete images. A pointing device (sometimes called a mouse) is pushed about to move a pointer on the screen and thereby select particular windows, menu items or icons.

All of this has given rise to a new generation of interactive software that capitalizes on the user illusion. The objective is to amplify the user's ability to simulate. A person exerts the greatest leverage when his illusion can be manipulated without appeal to abstract intermediaries such as the hidden programs needed to put into action even a simple word processor. What I call direct leverage is provided when the illusion acts as a 'kit,' or tool, with which to solve a problem. Indirect leverage will be attained when the illusion acts as an 'agent': an active extension of one's purpose and goals. In both cases the software designer's control of what is essentially a theatrical context is the key to creating an illusion and enhancing its perceived 'friendliness'.

The earliest computer programs were designed by mathematicians and scientists who thought the task should be straightforward and logical. Software turned out to be harder to shape than they had supposed. Computers were stubborn. They insisted on doing what was said rather than what the programmer meant. As a result a new class of artisans took over the task. These test pilots of the binary biplane were often neither mathematical nor even very scientific, but they were deeply engaged in a romance with the material—a romance that is often the precursor of new arts and sciences alike. Natural scientists are given a universe and seek to discover its laws. Computer scientists make laws in the form of programs and the computer brings a new universe to life.

Some programmers breathed too deeply of the heady atmosphere of creating a private universe. They became what the eminent designer Robert S. Barton called 'the high priests of a low cult.' Most discovered, however, that it is one thing to be the god of a universe and another to be able to control it, and they looked outside their field for design ideas and inspiration.

A powerful genre can serve as wings or chains. The most treacherous metaphors are the ones that seem to work for a time, because they can keep more powerful insights from bubbling up. As a result progress is slow—but there is progress. A new genre is established. A few years later a significant improvement is made. After a few more years the improvement is perceived as being not just a 'better old thing' but an 'almost new thing' that leads directly to the next stable genre. Interestingly, the old things and their improvements do not disappear. Strong representatives from each past era thrive today, such as programming in the 30-year-old language known as FORTRAN and even in the ancient script known as direct machine code. Some people might look on such relics as living fossils; others would point out that even a very old species might still be filling a particular ecological niche.

The computer field has not yet had its Galileo or Newton, Bach or Beethoven, Shakespeare or Molière. What it needs first is a William of

Occam, who said 'Entities should not be multiplied unnecessarily.' The idea that it is worthwhile to put considerable effort into eliminating complexity and establishing the simple had a lot to do with the rise of modern science and mathematics, particularly from the standpoint of creating new aesthetics, a vital ingredient of any growing field. It is an aesthetic along the lines of Occam's razor that is needed both to judge current computer software and to inspire future designs. Just how many concepts are there really? And how can metaphor, the magical process of finding similarity and even identity in diverse structures, be put to work to reduce complexity?

The French mathematician Jacques S. Hadamard found, in a study of 100 leading mathematicians, that the majority of them claimed to make no use of symbols in their thinking but were instead primarily visual in their approach. Some, including Einstein, reached further back into their childhood to depend on 'sensations of a kinesthetic or muscular type.' The older parts of the brain know what to say; the newer parts know how to say it. The world of the symbolic can be dealt with effectively only when the repetitive aggregation of concrete instances becomes boring enough to motivate exchanging them for a single abstract insight.

In algebra the concept of the variable, which allows an infinity of instances to be represented and dealt with as one idea, was a staggering advance. Metaphor in language usually accentuates the similarities of quite different things as though they were alike. It was a triumph of mathematical thinking to realize that various kinds of self-comparison could be even more powerful. The differential calculus of Newton and Leibniz represents complex ideas by finding ways to say 'This part of the idea is like that part, except for . . . .' The designers of computing systems have learned to do the same thing with differential models, for example with programming methods that have the property called inheritance. In recent years models based on the idea of recursion have been formulated in which some of the parts actually are the whole: a description of the entire model is needed to generate the representation of a part. An example is the fractal geometry of Benoit B. Mandelbrot, where each subpart of a structure is similar to every other part. Chaos is captured in law.

Designing the parts to have the same power as the whole is a fundamental technique in contemporary software. One of the most effective applications of the technique is object-oriented design. The computer is divided (conceptually, by capitalizing on its powers of simulation) into a number of smaller computers, or objects, each of which can be given a role like that of an actor in a play. The move to object-oriented design represents a real change in point of view—a change of paradigm—that brings with it an enormous increase in expressive power. There was a similar change when molecular chains floating randomly in a prebiological ocean had their efficiency, robustness and energetic possibilities boosted a billionfold when they were first enclosed within a cell membrane.

The early applications of software objects were attempted in the context of the old metaphor of sequential programming languages, and the objects functioned like colonies of cooperating unicellular organisms. If cells are a good idea, however, they really start to make things happen when the cooperation is close enough for the cells to aggregate into supercells: tissues and organs. Can the endlessly malleable fabric of computer stuff be designed to form a 'superobject'?

The dynamic spreadsheet is a good example of such a tissuelike superobject. It is a simulation kit, and it provides a remarkable degree of direct leverage. Spreadsheets at their best combine the genres established in the 1970's (objects, windows, what-you-see-is-what-you-get editing and goal-seeking retrieval) into a 'better old thing' that is likely to be one of the 'almost new things' for the mainstream designs of the next few years.

A spreadsheet is an aggregate of concurrently active objects, usually organized into a rectangular array of cells similar to the paper spreadsheet used by an accountant. Each cell has a 'value rule' specifying how its value is to be determined. Every time a value is changed anywhere in the spreadsheet, all values dependent on it are recomputed instantly and the new values are displayed. A spreadsheet is a simulated pocket universe that continuously maintains its fabric; it is a kit for a surprising range of applications. Here the user illusion is simple, direct and powerful. There are few mystifying surprises because the only way a cell can get a value is by having the cell's own value rule put it there.

Dynamic spreadsheets were invented by Daniel Bricklin and Robert Frankston as a reaction to the frustration Bricklin felt when he had to work with the old ruled-paper versions in business school. They were surprised by the success of the idea and by the fact that most people who bought the first spreadsheet program (VisiCalc) exploited it to forecast the future rather than to account for the past. Seeking to develop a 'smart editor,' they had created a simulation tool.

Getting a spreadsheet to do one's bidding is simplicity itself. The visual metaphor amplifies one's recognition of situations and strategies. The easy transition from the visual metaphor to the symbolic value rule brings the full power of abstract models to bear almost without notice. One powerful property is the ability to make a solution generic by 'painting' a rule in many dozens of cells at once without requiring users to generalize from their original concrete level of thinking.

The simplest kind of value rule makes a cell a static object such as a number or a piece of text. A more complex rule might be an arithmetic combination of other cells' values, derived from their relative or absolute positions or (much better) from names assigned to them. A value rule can test a condition and set its own value according to the result. Advanced versions allow a cell's value to be retrieved by heuristic goal seeking, so that problems for which there is no straightforward method of solution can still be solved by a search process.

The strongest test of any system is not how well its features conform to anticipated needs but how well it performs when one wants to do something the designer did not foresee. It is a question less of possibility than of perspicuity: Can the user see what is to be done and simply go do it?

Suppose one wants to display data as a set of vertical bars whose height is normalized to that of the largest value, and suppose such a bar-chart feature was not programmed into the system. It calls for a messy program even in a high-level programming language; in a spreadsheet it is easy. Cells serve as the 'pixels' (picture elements) of the display; a stack of cells constitutes a bar.

In a bar displaying one-third of the maximum value, cells in the lowest third of the stack are black and cells in the upper two-thirds are white. Each cell has to decide whether it should be black or white according to its position in the bar: 'I'll show black if where I am in the bar is less than the data I am trying to display; otherwise I'll show white'.

Another spreadsheet example is a sophisticated interactive 'browser,' a system originally designed by Lawrence G. Tesler, then at the Xerox Palo Alto Research Center. Browsing is a pleasant way to access a hierarchically organized data base by pointing to successive lists. The name of the data base is typed into the first pane of the display, causing the subject areas constituting its immediate branches to be retrieved and displayed in the cells below the name. One of the subject areas can be chosen by pointing to it with a mouse; the chosen area is thereby entered at the head of the next column, causing its branches in turn to be retrieved. So it goes until the desired information is reached. Remarkably, the entire browser can be programmed in the spreadsheet with just three rules.

The intent of these examples is not to get everyone to drop all programming in favour of spreadsheets. Current spreadsheets are not up to it; nor, perhaps, is the spreadsheet metaphor itself. If programming means writing step-by-step recipes as has been done for the past 40 years, however, then for most people it never was relevant and is surely obsolete. Spreadsheets, and particularly extensions to them of the kind I have suggested, give strong hints that much more powerful styles are in the offing for novices and experts alike. Does this mean that what might be called a driver-education approach to computer literacy is all most people will ever need—that one need only learn how to 'drive' applications programs and need never learn to program? Certainly not. Users must be able to tailor a system to their wants. Anything less would be as absurd as requiring essays to be formed out of paragraphs that have already been written.

In discussing this most protean of media I have tried to show how effectively design confers leverage, particularly when the medium is to be shaped as a tool for direct leverage. It is clear that in shaping software kits the limitations on design are those of the creator and the user, not those of the medium. The question of software's limitations is brought front and center, however, by my contention that in the future a stronger kind of indirect leverage will be provided by personal agents: extensions of the user's will and purposes, shaped from and embedded in the stuff of the computer. Can material give rise to mentality? Certainly there seems to be nothing mindlike in a mark. How can any combination of marks, even dynamic and reflexive marks, possibly show any properties of mentality?

Atoms also seem quite innocent. Yet biology demonstrates that simple materials can be formed into exceedingly complex organizations that can interpret themselves and change themselves dynamically. Some of them even appear to think! It is therefore hard to deny certain mental possibilities to computer material, since software's strong suit is similarly the kinetic structuring of simple components. Computers 'can only do what they are programmed to do,' but the same is true of a fertilized egg trying to become a baby. Still, the difficulty of discovering an architecture that generates mentality cannot be overstated. The study of biology had been under way some hundreds of years before the properties of DNA and the mechanisms of its expression were elucidated, revealing the living cell to be an architecture in process. Moreover, molecular biology has the advantage of studying a system already put together and working; for the composer of software the computer is like a bottle of atoms waiting to be shaped by an architecture he must invent and then impress from the outside.

To pursue the biological analogy, evolution can tell the genes very little about the world and the genes can tell the developing brain still less. All levels of mental competence are found in the more than one and a half million surviving species. The range is from behavior so totally hard-wired that learning is neither needed nor possible, to templates that are elaborated by experience, to a spectrum of capabilities so fluid that they require a stable social organization—a culture—if full adult potential is to be realized. (In other words, the gene's way to get a cat to catch mice is to program the cat to play—and let the mice teach the rest.) Workers in artificial intelligence have generally contented themselves with attempting to mimic only the first, hard-wired kind of behavior. The results are often called expert systems, but in a sense they are the designer jeans of computer science. It is not that their inventors are being dishonest; few of them claim for a system more than it can do. Yet the label 'expert' calls up a vision that leads to disillusionment when it turns out the systems miss much of what expert (or even competent) behavior is and how it gets that way.

Three developments have very low probabilities for the near future. The first is that a human adult mentality can be constructed. The second is that the mentality of a human infant can be constructed and then 'brought up' in an environment capable of turning it into an adult mentality. The third is that current artificial-intelligence techniques contain the seeds of an architecture from which one might construct some kind of mentality that is genuinely able to learn competence. The fact that the probabilities are low emphatically does not mean the task is impossible. The third development is likely to be achieved first. Even before it is there will be systems that look and act somewhat intelligent, and some of them will actually be useful.

What will agents be like in the next few years? The idea of an agent originated with John McCarthy in the mid-1950's, and the term was coined by Oliver G. Selfridge a few years later, when they were both at the Massachusetts Institute of Technology. They had in view a system that, when given a goal, could carry out the details of the appropriate computer operations and could ask for and receive advice, offered in human terms, when it was stuck. An agent would be a 'soft robot' living and doing its business within the computer's world.

What might such an agent do? Hundreds of data-retrieval systems are now made available through computer networks. Knowing every system's arcane access procedures is almost impossible. Once access has been gained, browsing can handle no more than perhaps 5,000 entries. An agent acting as a librarian is needed to deal with the sheer magnitude of choices. It might serve as a kind of pilot, threading its way from data base to data base. Even better would be an agent that could present all systems to the user as a single large system, but that is a remarkably hard problem. A persistent 'go-fer' that for

24 hours a day looks for things it knows a user is interested in and presents them as a personal magazine would be most welcome.

Agents are almost inescapably anthropomorphic, but they will not be human, nor will they be very competent for some time. They violate many of the principles defining a good user interface, most notably the idea of maintaining the user illusion. Surely users will be disappointed if the projected illusion is that of intelligence but the reality falls far short. This is the main reason for the failure so far of dialogues conducted in ordinary English, except when the context of the dialogue is severely constrained to lessen the possibility of ambiguity.

Context is the key, of course. The user illusion is theater, the ultimate mirror. It is the audience (the user) that is intelligent and can be directed into a particular context. Giving the audience the appropriate cues is the essence of user-interface design. Windows, menus, spreadsheets and so on provide a context that allows the user's intelligence to keep choosing the appropriate next step. An agent-based system will have to do the same thing, but the creation of an interface with some semblance of human mentality will call for a considerably subtler approach.

Any medium powerful enough to extend man's reach is powerful enough to topple his world. To get the medium's magic to work for one's aims rather than against them is to attain literacy. At its simplest, literacy means fluency. Familiarity (knowing the 'grammar') is not enough. People who can recognize a book and its words, a typewriter and its keyboard or a computer and its input-output devices are not literate unless they can spend most of their time dealing with content rather than with the mechanics of form.

Is the computer a car to be driven or an essay to be written? Most of the confusion comes from trying to resolve the question at this level. The protean nature of the computer is such that it can act like a machine or like a language to be shaped and exploited. It is a medium that can dynamically simulate the details of any other medium, including media that cannot exist physically. It is not a tool, although it can act like many tools. It is the first metamedium, and as such it has degrees of freedom for representation and expression never before encountered and as yet barely investigated. Even more important, it is fun, and therefore intrinsically worth doing.

If computers can be cars, then certainly computer literacy at the level of driver-education courses is desirable. Indeed, the attempt is now being made to design user interfaces giving access to the computer's power by way of interactions even easier to learn than driving a car. Integrated programs for word processing, graphics, simulation, information retrieval and person-to-person communication will be the paper and pencil of the near future. The driver-education level of paper-and-pencil literacy is taught, however, in kindergarten and first grade, implying that what can be called mark-making literacy in computers should be attained as early as possible; children should not be made to wait until they can get in a half year of it just before they graduate from high school, as recent reports by educational commissions suggest. Children need informational shoes, bicycles, cars and airplanes from the moment they start to explore the universe of knowledge.

Paper-and-pencil literacy does not stop, moreover, when children know how to manipulate a pencil to make certain kinds of marks on paper. One reason to teach reading and writing is certainly that people need these skills to get through daily life in the 20th century, but there are grander and more critical goals. By reading we hope not only to absorb the facts of our civilization and of those before us but also to encounter the very structure and style of thought and imagination. Writing gets us out of the bleachers and onto the playing field; old and new knowledge becomes truly ours as we shape it directly.

In short, we act as though learning to read and write will help people to think better and differently. We assume that starting with centuries' worth of other people's knowledge is more efficient than starting from scratch and will provide a launch pad for new ideas. We assume that expressing and shaping ideas through metaphor and other forms of rhetoric makes the ideas more fully our own and amplifies our ability to learn from others in turn. (Oliver Wendell Holmes said, 'The mind, once expanded to the dimensions of larger ideas, never returns to its original size.') We hold all of this to be important even though reading and writing seem to be quite hard and take years to master. Our society declares that this kind of literacy is not a privilege but a right, not an option but a duty.

What then is computer literacy? It is not learning to manipulate a word processor, a spreadsheet or a modern user interface; those are paper-and-pencil skills. Computer literacy is not even learning to program. That can always be learned, in ways no more uplifting than learning grammar instead of writing.

Computer literacy is a contact with the activity of computing deep enough to make the computational equivalent of reading and writing fluent and enjoyable. As in all the arts, a romance with the material must be well under way. If we value the lifelong learning of arts and letters as a springboard for personal and societal growth, should any less effort be spent to make computing a part of our lives?

PART TWO

Systematic Studies

9

Modernity Modernised— The Cultural Impact of Computerisation

Niels Ole Finnemann

In this article Niels Ole Finnemann describes the computer as a symbol processing machine and discusses its consequences for modernity. Finnemann offers a far-reaching analysis of the significance of computerization for modern culture. In so doing, he provides an ontological description of the specific nature of the computer as a multi-semantic machine. By focusing on the semiotic nature of the computer, and the implications of this for the variety of forms of representation that the computer can accommodate, Finnemann's analysis helps not only to better understand the nature of the computer, but also exactly how the computer as a medium has effected a revolution in the technology of knowledge representation. Finnemann's analysis provides a fundamental framework in which to understand better the nature of computers as media as well as their cultural impact.

I T IS NOT A matter of discussion whether the computer is part of the social and cultural transformations we are witnessing today, both in the modern or western societies and in any other society in the world. Although there are many different interpretations of these transformations, one can hardly find any which does not ascribe an important role to the computer—whether as a main cause or as an important means of contemporary cultural changes.

If nothing else unites these various theories, they are uniform in their reference to the significance of the computer. This being so, one might expect it to be easy to find a basic and commonly acknowledged description of the properties of the computer on which such predictions concerning the cultural effects were founded. Despite the plenitude of descriptions to be found, I have not succeeded in finding one able to meet the demand, on the one hand, of being valid for any possible use of computers and, on the other, of taking into account the fact that the computer is a mechanical machine, a medium, and is based on a specific set of principles for the representation of symbolic content.

Finnemann, Niels Ole (1997), 'Modernity Modernised—The Cultural Impact of Computerisation', Aarhus, Denmark: Center for Cultural Research—University of Aarhus.

Consequently, I had to make such a description, and since it deviates from previous descriptions I shall start with a short summary of my answer to the question, what is a computer?

It might be helpful to point out a few of the previously given answers, as for instance:

- the computer is a computer (i.e. it is a calculating machine);
- the computer is a machine by which data are processed by means of a programme;
- the computer is only an artefact comparable to any other kind of artefact.

I shall not give a detailed account of the various mistakes inherited in these answers, but only say the following:

1. Strictly speaking a computer is not a computer, since it does not operate as other known calculating devices. It actually does not calculate at all. The computer is not a calculating machine but a machine in which we can simulate calculating machines as well as many other kinds of devices and processes in a mechanical way.

2. The computer is not a machine in which data are processed with the help of a programme. Of course we do use programmes. But we should always keep in mind that the programmes themselves need to be represented and processed in exactly the same way as any other kind of data. That is: as sequences/strings of bits, each one processed and editable. In the machine there is no difference between data and programme.

3. The computer is not an artefact on a par with other artefacts, since it can only function as an artefact—i.e. simulate artefacts—with the help of symbolic representations.

I shall return to the central points in these statements very soon, but first I will give a general definition of the computer and use it to explain why the question of having a definition does matter.

As mentioned above, if we want to discuss the cultural impact of the computer, we need a concept of the computer that is valid for any possible kind of use. We cannot take any specific and current use as the point of departure. The reason for this is very simple. If we don't use a definition which is valid for any possible use, we have no way to determine what the cultural impact will be, since this may depend on and vary with not yet known ways to use the machine which may evolve in the years to come. What we need is a description that is valid not just for all currently existing kinds of use but also for any kind of possible use; that is: we need to describe the invariant properties of the computer, or in other words the constraints manifested regardless of the purpose for which the machine is used.

There are three such constraints inherent in all kinds of use:

1. Any process which is to be performed in a computer needs to be represented and processed by means of a mechanically effective notation system—or what I will describe as a specific and new type of alphabet.

2. Any process performed needs to be governed by means of some algorithmic syntax.

3. Finally, any process performed is performed by means of an interface determining the semantic content of the algorithmic (or syntactical) processes.

I will now describe some of the implications. First, it is worth emphasizing that these three conditions need to be met in any kind of use. There will always be a notational representation, an algorithmic syntax, and an interface defining the semantic content of the syntax. But there is also an important difference between the first condition and the other two conditions. While all processes performed in the computer need to be performed in the very same alphabet—there is only one alphabet available in the machine—there are no definable limits either for the variation of algorithms used to govern the process or for the definition of the semantical content of the syntactical processes. The need for a syntax and a semantics will always exist, but both syntax and semantics are open for free variation according to our own choices and ideas.

We can specify the basic principles for the possible syntactical variation in four aspects:

1. We are free to use any of all the existing algorithms or to create new algorithms under the sole condition that it can be processed through a finite set of steps (as described by Alan Turing in his definition of a finite, mechanical procedure).
   No single formal procedure exists which is necessarily a part of any computer process.

2. We are free to use a given algorithmic procedure for different purposes—i.e. giving the same formal procedure new semantic content. The very same algorithm can be used for various purposes by redefining the semantic content (and it can be done on the level of the interface).

3. The same purposes might be achieved by using various/different algorithms.

4. It is always possible to modify any syntactical structure as well as its function and semantic content, implying that no non-optional, syntactical determination exists by which previous steps determine following steps.

For the semantic level we can specify the freedom of choice in two aspects:

1. First we can chose between a range of various formal interpretations, (some of which can be used to calculate or to perform logical operations) and a range of informal semantical regimes—as we do when we use the computer as a typewriter or to represent pictures.

2. Second, we are free to use a combination of more than one semantic regime simultaneously, as we do when using the computer to simulate a typewriter, in that we control the process both by an iconographic semantics and by the semantics of ordinary language.

Since we are not able to predict or point out specific limitations for the future development either of new algorithms or of possible semantics, it follows that predictions of the cultural impact cannot be predictions concerning the semantic content of the effects of computerisation. (Just as knowledge of the medium of the book does not allow us to say anything about the content of the next book to be written.) What we are able to predict, however, is that any present as well as any future use will be constrained by the demand that the content represented has to be manifested in the above-mentioned alphabet.

One may wonder why the binary notation is denoted as an alphabet, a point I shall now explain. One should first of all be aware that the binary notation system used in the computer is not defined according to the principles for the use of notations in formal symbol systems. In formal symbol systems each notational unit needs to be defined as representing a semantic value either as data value or as a rule, while the binary—or informational notation—units used in the computer are defined independently of any semantic content. Since they are in themselves always semantically empty units, they can never have any semantic value of their own. Semantic content in the computer is always related to a sequence of units, never to a single unit, as is always the case in formal notation systems.

The reason for this can be found in the principles of the universal computing machine. As it was principally shown by the English mathematician Alan Turing in 1936, such a machine had to function independently of any specific formal rule or programme (any specific semantic content), since it should be able to perform any rule or programme. (If the machine was determined by some specific formal rule, it would be deprived of its universality.)

We can illustrate the basic difference between the principles of formal and informational notation by comparing the use of binary notation as a formal notation system (the binary number system) and the use of the very same two units in the computer. Used in a formal system, the two units are always defined by their data value according to their position in the expression. They can never represent a rule for addition or subtraction (for this purpose other notation units are necessary), while in the computer they shall both represent data (numbers) and various rules, such as the rules of addition for instance—and they shall not only represent the rule, they are also used to carry out the process of addition in a mechanical way. While a formal notation unit is defined as a physical representation of a semantic value, informational units are defined as physical forms which are legitimate units but without any semantic value of their own. On the other hand, they need to be defined as mechanical operative units in the physical machine.

Consequently, there is also another important difference. While we are always free to introduce new units in formal systems—by defining the semantic content of the unit—we are never able to introduce new units in the informational notation system. The number of units needs to be finite (actually we use two, but this is arbitrary, although practical; theoretically we could use 17, for instance) since it shall be defined at the time the machine is built—as part of the hardware. The number of notation units cannot be modified since it cannot be a part of the editable software.

Hence, informational notation systems can be defined as notation systems consisting of a finite number of members each of which is defined by a unambiguous physical form and a lack of any semantic content of its own. On the other hand, this is exactly why the very same notation system can be used to represent formal expressions, whether data or rules, the alphabet of ordinary language, pictorial and musical expressions, as well as a huge amount of non-symbolic phenomena and processes—due only to our own choices.

Since the units are the physical operative units—performing the process as a step by step process in the machine, we are always able to manipulate computer processes on the level of the individual units, that is: on a level lower than that of the semantic content and lower than the formal level, rules and hence independently of the semantic content and the syntactical rules. This is why we can say that the previous processes or programme never predetermine the later process in a nonoptional way.

Of course, most of us would never use the machine if we were to use it on the level of binary notation. It is not very convenient and we do use programmes to determine many processes. But we do it for our own convenience. Programmes are not a constraint determining what can be done. Accordingly, we can state that the notation system (and the presence of a computer) represents the only invariant constraints for any computer process. If something can be represented in this system it can be processed in a computer, and thus we can say that the computer is basically defined by a new kind of alphabet. Some of the characteristics of this alphabet are similar to the characteristics of the alphabet of written language, others are not.[1]

For our purposes, the most important difference, however, is that the linguistic alphabet can only be used as an alphabet of linguistic representations, while the informational alphabet can be used to represent a multitude of semantic regimes. For example: linguistic regimes, whether phonetically or alphabetically represented, formal regimes, pictorial and musical regimes, and these can even be represented simultaneously.

For this reason the computer can be defined as a multisemantic machine. Its multisemantic properties can be specified in the three following points:

- It is possible to use this machine to *handle* symbolic expressions which belong to different semantic regimes (linguistic, formal— including mechanical, mathematical and logical—as well as pictorial and auditive regimes, and so on) with the sole restriction that the expression which is handled can be represented in a notation system comprising a finite number of expression units.

- It is also possible to *control* the machine (or the computational process) with different semantic regimes with the same restriction, as this control, however, can only be performed mechanically for a

---

1 Both similarities and differences are described at length in my book, *Thought, Sign and Machine*, and here I shall mention only that both notation systems are 'subsemantic' (based on double articulation, i.e. letters beneath the level of the smallest semantic unit) and both consist of a limited set of units. But while the units in the linguistic alphabet do have certain qualities—as they are either vocals or consonants and as they in some cases do have semantic content of their own (e.g. in the grammatical endings and in the words 'a' and 'I')—this is never the case in the informational system. The letters in this alphabet are completely empty of any specifying qualities. We could say that the new alphabet is totally clean and in this respect the perfect alphabet, also allowing us to represent any other known alphabet in it.

limited class of procedures, while for others it requires the semantic regime to be exercised through continuous human intervention.

- Any process executed in the machine runs as a relationship between *at least two semantic regimes*, namely one laid down in the system and one contained in the use. The two regimes may coincide, as can happen when a programmer is editing a programme, or when a closed semantic procedure is executed, such as in the form of the automatic execution of a mathematical proof. Usually, however, this is more a question of a plurality of semantic regimes, but always at least two.

With this description it now becomes possible to add yet another criterion both to the distinction between the computer and other machines and to the distinction between the computer and other symbolic means of expression. While other machines can be described as mono-semantic machines in which a given, invariant rule set is physically implemented and defines the functional architecture as an invariant architecture, the computer is a multi-semantic machine based on informational architecture which is established by the materials the machine processes. While other symbolic expression systems can be described as mono-semantic regimes in which the semantic regime is closely connected to a given notation and syntax, the computer is a multisemantic symbolic medium in which it is possible to simulate both formal and informal symbolic languages as well as non-symbolic processes, just as this simulation can be carried out through formal and informal semantic regimes.

Together, these two delimitations contain a third, important criterion for the definition of the computer, in that the computer, contrary to other machines and media, can be defined as a medium in which there are no invariant thresholds between:

- the machine and the material processed by the machine. If there is no software there is only a heating device.
- the programme and the data, since any programme or structure of rules is to be represented and executed in the binary notation system in exactly the same way and form as any other data.
- the information which is implemented in the functional architecture of the machine and the information processed by that architecture.

On the basis of this description of the properties of the computer it is possible to conclude that the computer is a medium for the representation of knowledge in general, whether formally coded or not, and that it not only has the same general properties as written language, but also properties providing a new historical yardstick both for the concept of a mechanical machine and for the concept of the representation of knowledge and any other kind of symbolic content.

We can use this description to delineate a whole range of 'first-time-in-history' features according to the functions we can perform with computers as well as to the symbolic formats we can represent. Concerning functional innovations, at least three main points can be indicated, as the computer performs the following operations.

- First, it is a medium for *producing, editing, processing, storing, copying, distributing and retrieving* knowledge, thereby integrating for instance the production of knowledge, the production and selling of books, and the library into a single system.

- Second, it is a medium for presenting *linguistically (spoken and written), formally, pictorially and auditorily* expressed knowledge, thereby integrating all stable forms of knowledge in modern society into the same medium and in the same symbolic system of representation.

- Third, it is a medium for communication, thereby integrating the most important previous means of communication, such as mail, telegraph, radio, telephone, television, etc., whether one-to-one, one-to-many, many-to-many, and both close to real-time interactive communication and rapid communication independent of the presence of the receiver.

In itself, the integration of all these functions, which were formerly distributed between *different* media and functions, is epoch-making, but in addition to this comes the fact that the properties of the computer also change the conditions and possibilities in each of these individual areas. Although these cannot be described under the same heading, they have, however, a common background in the general properties of the machine. There is one important aspect which will be of significance in all areas: a great number of the restrictions which were formerly connected with the physically bound architecture of the symbolic media are here transformed into facultative symbolic restrictions which are implemented in a physically variable (energy-based) and serialized textual form. Symbolic representation is thus available in a permanently editable form.

I shall concentrate on three of these unprecedented features:

- First, we have a new alphabet in which we are able to represent knowledge represented in any of the formats used in the prior history of modern societies.

- Second, we now have a means of textualised—serial—representation of pictures.

- Third, we are on the way to having one globally distributed, electronically integrated archive of knowledge.

For this reason we can conclude that the multisemantic machine represents a revolution in the technology of knowledge representation, a revolution based on a new alphabet, a new format for written, textualised—sequentially manifested and processed—representation. Since the computer provides new ways to produce, represent and organize knowledge in general as well as new ways of communication, it also provides a change in the societal infrastructure, in so far as society is defined by the methods of knowledge representation and communication.

Basic Constraints of the New Medium—Seriality and Machinery

Although the symbolic properties of the computer go far beyond the capacities of any previously known means of representation, there are two basic limitations. First, as previously mentioned, any representation in computers is conditioned by a series of sequentially processed notational units.

No matter the specific function and semantic format used, and no matter the specific purpose, any use of computers is conditioned by a representation in a new type of alphabet, implying that the content is manifested in an invisible, textual form, which can be edited at the level of this alphabet. Second, the global scope is conditioned and limited by the actual presence of and access to the machinery.

Taken together, these limits delineate a system for the representation of knowledge which is most properly conceived of as a new electronically integrated, globally distributed archive of knowledge, in which anything represented is manifested and processed sequentially as a permanently editable text. Hence, the computer is basically a technology for textual representation, but as such it changes the structures and principles of textual representation as known from written and printed texts, whether they belong to common or formal languages. The character of this structural change, however, goes far beyond the internal structure of textual representations, because—due to the integration of both linguistic, formal, visual and auditive formats of knowledge—it widens the range and logic of textual representation and—due to the integration of globally distributed archives in one system—widens the social and cultural scope of any kind of textual representation.

Therefore, we can say that as an agent of change the computer provides a new textual infrastructure for the social organization of knowledge. The basic principle in this change is inherent in the structural relation between the hidden text and its visible representation. While the informational notation shares linear sequencing with other kinds of textual representation, it is always randomly accessible. The whole 'text' is synchronically manifested in the storage from which a plenitude of 'hypertexts' can be selected independently of previous sequential constraints. What is at stake here, however, is not—as often supposed—a change from seriality to non-seriality, but a change in which any sequential constraint can be overcome with the help of other sequences, since anything represented in the computer is represented in a serially processed substructure.

One of the significant implications is that sequences defined by a sender can be separated—and rearranged and reinterpreted—with sequences defined by any receiver—while the position of the receiver in the same act is changed to the more active role of 'writer', 'co-writer', or simply of user. Interactivity thus becomes a property inherent in the serial substructure and available as an optional choice for the user, limited only by his or her skills and intentions.

Seriality persists, even in the case of non-serial expressions such as photographs and paintings, since non-serial representation is only the result of an iteration of a selected set of serially processed sequences. The same is true for the representation of any stable expression, whether of a certain state or of a dynamically processed repetitive structure and even in those cases where some binary sequence is made perceptible for editing as a first order representation. Thus, since an interplay between the textual substructure and any superstructure (whether textual or not) is indispensable in any computer process, this interaction is the core of the structural change in the principles of textual representation.

The Textualisation of Visual Representations

A Triumph For the Culture of the Text

The inclusion of pictorial representation seems to be one of the most significant indicators of the new range and logic of textual representation, as now, for the first time in history, we have an alphabet in which any picture can be represented as a sequential text.

Textual representation is a feature common to all computer-based pictures, and defines their specificity compared to other pictures. Since any picture in a computer has to be processed in the very same—binary—alphabet, it follows that any picture can be edited at this level, implying that any computer-based picture can be transformed into any other picture in this alphabet.

In many cases, morphing may perhaps be only a curiosity, but the basic principle that any computerized picture is always the result of an editable textualised process performed in time is far from a curiosity, since it changes the very notion of a picture as a synchronously and not serially manifested whole.

Seriality and time are not only introduced into the notion of pictures as an invisible background condition, they are also introduced at the semantic and perceptible levels, since the textualised basis allows the representation of—editable—time to be introduced at both these levels.

The pictures on the screen are always played in time—even if there is no change in the picture.

While the synchronously manifested whole is an axiomatic property of a painting or a photograph—even though they are produced and perceived serially in time—the same property in the computer has to be specified and declared as a variable at the same level as any other feature, whether it belongs to the motive, to the compositional structure, or to the relation between foreground and background. Variability and invariance become free and equal options on the same scale, applicable to any pictorial element, which implies that there is no element of the picture whatsoever which is not optionally defined and permanently editable.

There is of course a price to be paid for this new triumph of modern typographic and textual culture, as the textual representation presupposes a coding of the picture into an alphabet. The basic principle in this coding is the substitution of physically defined notational units for physical substance, implying a definition of a fixed set of legitimate physical differences (i.e. differences in colours) which are allowed to be taken into account. Since we cannot go back to the original if we only have a digitized version, the coding is irreversible and the possible secondary codings and transformations will therefore always be constrained by the primary coding which always defines a specific borderline between informational and noisy aspects of the original.

Various Aspects of these Constraints

The relevance and weight of this constraint is itself a variable which has to be taken into account in the use of computer-based representations, but in general there are two main aspects. First, some of the substance qualities of the original will always be missing since there is a change of expression substance. There will therefore always be some doubt about the validity of the reference to the original. This is obviously a serious constraint on the scholarly study of art represented in computers. Second, the definition of a fixed set of legitimate physical differences at the time of the original coding may later prove to be misleading, in that physical differences which are not taken into account may be of significance. Since the digitized picture is conditioned by the definition of a—later invariant—distinction between differences which are regarded as either noise or information in the substance, there may be cases—in medical diagnostics, for instance—in which a reinterpretation of this distinction is needed but not possible.

The constraint here is directly related to the logical interrelation between noise and information, which implies that information can only be defined by treating potential information as noise, since information is always manifested in some kind of substance. While missing information concerning some qualities of substance cannot be completely avoided, at the same time computerization allows a broad repertoire of possible enrichments concerning global accessibility, as well as analytical and interpretational procedures. Since the constraints on informational representation are basically those of notation and processing time, it is not possible to define any other invariant semantic or syntactic limitations for the digitized representation of pictures.

The significance of the textualization of the picture can be seen by comparing previously known pictorial representations for which some kind of textual representation exists, such as those described in Euclidean geometry for instance, in the analytical geometry of Descartes, or in the various other forms of syntactically defined pictures, whether based on a well-defined perspective (like linear perspective) or a well-defined iconic or diagrammatic system.

The basic and general change in representational form towards any of these representations can be described as a transition from representation at a syntactic level to representation at the level of letters (those of the new alphabet). The textual representation of geometrical figures defines a naked syntactic structure, whether two-dimensional or three-dimensional, without regard to substance qualities such as colours and so forth, while any syntactic structure in a computer-based representation of a picture can be dissolved into a series of notation units, including the representation of some kind of substance.

Although this is a change from a higher to a lower level of stable organization, for this very reason it is a change from a more restricted set to a more elaborate set of variation potentialities in which the higher level structures become accessible to manipulation at the lower level. In the first case the picture is defined by a stable syntactic structure—to which can be added certain rules for variation; while in the latter, (the digitized version) stability is defined solely at the level of notational representation—to which it is possible to ascribe a plenitude of—editable—syntactic and compositional structures as well as to integrate representations (only partially, however) of substance qualities such as colours and backgrounds at the same textual level. Form, structure and rule become editable on the same scale as substance. The representation of substance is necessary, but need not, however, be a simulation of the substance of the original. The representation of an arbitrarily defined and itself editable background on the screen will do the job.

Moreover, informational notation is a common denominator in which some substance qualities, the syntax as well as the motive, are manifested on a par with each other. As any sequence representing one or another element of a picture can be selected and related to other sequences in various ways and possibly ascribed various functions as well (i.e. add a referential function, which is itself editable, to other sequences), it follows that any fragment of a picture or a picture as a whole can be integrated into a continuously increasing—or decreasing—syntactic and semantic hierarchy completely independently of the original form and source. The insecurity in the referential relation to the original is thus complementary to the enrichment of possible hierarchies and frames of reference.

Perspective becomes optional and variable and so do other kinds of representational structures such as representation based on the size and positioning of motifs and the choice of colours in accordance with semantic importance, as was often the case during the Middle Ages. The resurrection of—or return to—the Middle Ages, however, is not on the agenda of computerization, since no single, non-optional hierarchy of values can be established.

Considered from a cognitive point of view, this is a radical extension of the ways in which cognitive content can be manifested in pictorial representations, whether in iconic, diagrammatic or geometrical form. Considered from a pictorial point of view, it is a radical extension of the ways in which the representation of both physical objects and pictures can be made subject to cognitive treatment.

Much of this is a result of the fact that the computer-based representation of stable structures has to be 'played' in time, but since time has already been represented in film and on the television screen, the proposition must be qualified accordingly. In the case of film making the basic difference is that the definition or selection of perspective is constrained by the optical artefacts used—the lenses of the camera, while the definition of perspective in the computer has to be defined as—a still editable—part of the same text as the motif, which implies that the very division between the optical constraints and motif becomes editable. So with regard to freedom of choice the computerized picture more closely resembles the animated cartoon than the film.

In the case of television the difference is primarily the result of the notational definition of the signals, as the stable picture on the TV screen is only the—perceptible—result of serial processes. As will be familiar, a basic constraint on real time digital television is the enormous amount of binary letters needed to represent what was formerly an analogue signal.

This is a constraint, however, which at the same time transgresses a series of other constraints characterizing the old-fashioned television of the twentieth century. The most far-reaching of these is probably the possible breakdown of one-way transmission and communication. Since a receiving computer can also be a sender, the receiver can also become the editor of the editors, able to decide what and when he will receive from whom. And since the computer is not only a medium for communication but also for storing in a completely editable form, the new medium transgresses the documentation monopoly of senders too.

Summary

If, as it has often been argued in media studies, other modern electronic media contribute to a revitalization of visual and oral culture—although in a mediated secondary form, as claimed by Walter J. Ong—at the expense of the hegemonic regime of 'typographic culture', as it was claimed by Marshall McLuhan, the computer can more properly be understood as a medium by which the scope of modern discursive culture is extended to embrace vision and pictorial expressions by the textualisation of electronics, which at the same time allows the representation of other media, but now as optional genres within this medium.

Not only the picture or any other visual object can now be embraced by a text. As the author of a discursive text is able to represent himself in the text, so the observer or spectator is now able to represent himself as an interacting part of any picture—given the appropriate paraphernalia of 'virtual reality', in both cases, however, only as a fragmentary representation. Under any circumstances, computerization implies that some physical and organizational constraints and invariants (whether substantial, structural or conventional) are converted to text and hence become optional variables.

On the Global Archive: One World, One Archive

The fact that the computer—due to the properties described—has the potential to become a new general and globally distributed network medium for the representation of knowledge does not necessarily imply that it will actually become such a medium.

There are, however, strong indications that it will.

First of all, it seems beyond reasonable doubt that the use of computers will spread almost everywhere—whether this is rational or not—due to a widespread, powerful human fascination. The spread of computers into an ever-increasing number of fields—throughout the world—indicates that a profound change in the basic infrastructural level of all societies has already begun.

Although we are not able to predict what will happen in the future, there are very few reasons to believe that this process can be stopped and the only argument which should not be marginalized seems to be the risk of a breakdown due to inadequate supplies of electricity. Computerization in general need not be argued for, and arguments given in the past have often turned out to be wrong or have had no particular impact. If we are only able to guess at what may happen anyway, we might ask why we should bother about this matter at all. In this connection I should therefore like to mention two arguments possibly able to indicate a high degree of social and cultural relevance which might give the grounds for the process of computerization.

The first argument is closely related to changes in the global scope of modernity. While the global perspective—inherent both in the claim of universality for human rights and western rationality in general, as well as in the process of colonization—is as old as modernity itself, most decisions in modern societies have until recently depended mainly on knowledge based on a more limited—locally restricted—scale. Today, however, a rapidly increasing number of local decisions on local issues depend on knowledge based on global considerations. This is true for economical, political, military and especially ecological information and, in consequence, there is also a need for a global scale for cultural issues. While some might argue that it would be better to attempt to re-establish a local economy and local political and military government, there no longer appears to be any room left for the idea of a locally restricted ecology.

Given that an increasing number of local decisions concerning ecological issues need to be based on a corpus of knowledge of global dimensions, there is no real alternative to the computer. While this is an argument based on the natural conditions for cultural survival, the second argument comes from within culture and is a consequence of the exponential growth in the production of knowledge (anticipated by the English scientist J. D. Bernal in the 1930s and the US scientist Vannevar Bush in the 1940s, and later described in the steadily growing number of books, papers and articles which have appeared since the pioneering work of Derek de Solla Price, among others,[2] in the early 1960s).

Whether measured as the number of universities, academic journals, published articles, the number of scientists and scholars in the world, or the number of reports prepared for politicians for making decisions, etc., the overall tendency is the same. Limits to the growth of paper-based knowledge production are in sight—whether seen from an economical or organizational point of view, or in a general perspective: as a chaotic system in which nobody can keep abreast of what is known even within his or her own specialized field.

Basic structural changes are inevitable, be they in the form of a cultural collapse or a cultural reorganization. The computer is obviously not the only solution to the handling and reorganization of this exponential growth, but is an inevitable part of any viable solution, since any cultural reorganization must include a repertoire of remedies for storing, editing, compressing, searching, retrieving, communication and so forth, which can only be provided by computers. The computer may widen some cultural gaps, but if it were not used there might not be any cultural gaps to bridge, since there might not be any culture.

**Modernity
Modernised**

I shall now address my last and perhaps rather more intriguing question concerning the general cultural impact of computerization, and I will do so by placing the computer in the history of media in modern societies.

The basic idea is that we are able to delineate three main epochs in the history of the media, and that we can relate these epochs of the media to a set of more general concepts which forms a history of modern thinking as well. The concepts chosen will be: the notion of the self and the relation between the observer and the observed. The notion of perspective and the notion of laws and rules.

In the following the model of this history is presented along with a few words to lend it some plausibility.

---

2 J. D. Bernal, 1939. Vannevar Bush (1945), 1989. Derek de Solla Price (1961), 1975.

Three Epochs of the Media History of Modernity

1. The Epoch of the Printed Text—(Orality + Script + Print)

Dominant from the Renaissance to the Enlightenment (1500–1800)

Main ideas: the world (nature) is seen as a reversible mechanical machine (static) consisting of passive particles—'atomic' and 'indivisible' entities held together by immaterial forces.

The human observer is seen as an ideal observer able to conceive the world as if positioned outside the world (in a divine perspective). The main argument for this being so was the idea that God has written not one but two books. The Holy Bible and the book of nature, which can be read because God has 'written' nature according to a set of eternal natural laws which we can recognize by our human reason. Since nature is a readable book, man can look into it and detect and describe the laws of nature. We can discover divine will directly by studying nature and describing what we see, without asking the priests or the pope.

Although there was no denial of God, there is a secularization of the relation to physical nature—made possible by God himself, so to speak—as he created this nature according to a set of rational natural laws. Consequently, the idea of truth is directly identified with the notion of eternal and universally given laws. Truth is defined as knowledge of the rules governing the system and these rules are established as given prior to and from outside the system they govern. As a consequence of this axiom, the laws are not accessible for human intervention. Since the laws are universal and eternal they are also detectable from any place and at any time. They are independent of human subjectivity. Truth is objective knowledge and objective knowledge is knowledge of universal laws manifested in nature and described in the printed texts of the philosophers and scientists.

Thus the printed text became the new medium of truth by which the secularization of the relation to physical nature took place. There was, however also a dichotomy established between the observer as observer of the natural laws and the human self as a free and reasoning individual, leading to the dichotomy between the idea of a deterministic nature and the free will of man.

Among the ideas related to this general frame we also find the idea of linear perspective (representing a model for the formalized repeatable and mechanical production of pictorial representations), the idea of the author as the independent creator writing on his own authority, and the idea of the sovereignty of human reason—which during history leads to the development of public discourse, enlightenment and democracy—and the fragmentation of reason in descriptive (scientific) reason, normative (ethical) reason and evaluative (aesthetic) reason (concerning nature, society and culture/art/taste respectively).

This is of course a very broad overview in which many different positions are reduced to a common and maybe somewhat reductive denominator. But it seems to me that it actually depicts some very important notions, since they are all changed and reinterpreted during the 19th century, which we can see as a transformed and second edition of modernity.

2. The Epoch of Analog Electronic Media: From 1843 until the Late Twentieth Century (Speech + Script + Print + Analog Electric Media)

Considered in the perspective of media history, the nineteenth century is characterized by the emergence of analog, electronic media, starting with the electrical telegraph in 1843 and continuing ever since, including devices such as the telephone, the camera, the radio, the tape recorder, the television, the video, and a huge amount of other media and measuring instruments all based on the use of energy and especially electricity for symbolic purposes.

Compared to the static, printed text the new media are all dynamic, they are a means of communication more than of storing knowledge and not least because of that: the printed text maintains its sacred position as the basic means of representing true knowledge in modern society. However, the new media contributes to a far-reaching development of the whole social media matrix and we need to take all the media present—and their interrelations—into consideration if we want to study the function of any single medium, since new media also contribute to changing the function of older media.

So a new media matrix is formed around both the old and new media including speech + script + print + telegraph/radio/movie and later television and video, etc. The new energy-based media adds dynamic properties and they imply a revolution in pictorial representation (photo, movie, television) and in the means of global communication, as simultaneous communication now exists on a global scale.

Basic concepts in science, philosophy and culture are changed as well. This is not caused by the new media—but probably the new ideas co-evolved in a kind of interdependency. New paradigms are emerging in physics, biology, psychology, sociology and the humanities. In spite of many differences they are all concerned with the interpretation of dynamic processes, development, evolution, change (and in some cases even irreversibility), and they see the world not as the traditional Newtonian—and reversible—machine but as a dynamic and all embracing, integrated energy system, in which the observer is also included in one form or another. For example, as in the Hegelian idea of history as the unfolding of the universal *weltgeist*, in the pantheistic ideas of Romanticism, or in the historical materialism of Marx, and most remarkably in the various new physical theories developed around the study of energy in general and—at the end of the century—resulting in the paradigms of thermodynamics, soon after the turn of the century followed by the theories of relativity and quantum physics.

In spite of the differences and contradictions between these new physical theories they all take the relation between the observer and the observed into account, as they include and localise the observer in the same universe as the observed—in one way or another. Still, many of the previous axioms are maintained during the nineteenth century, as for instance the idea that the truth about nature and society can be found in a set of universal laws or rules, which can assure that we still have access to universal knowledge—a divine perspective.

Although the notion of a rational and rule-based universe is maintained, the status of the rules themselves are often reinterpreted, as according for instance to Kant they should rather be regarded as a set of logical or rational principles for the functioning of human reason rather than as natural laws as such. In both cases the rules are still given as the axiomatic and invariant basis for human cognition, and they are inaccessible to human intervention, but in the latter case they are now given within the universe as rules for mental processes. The notion of truth is still identified with the notion of universal laws, but the observer and the human self are brought on the bench as dynamic figures in the very same dynamic world they inhabit, as is the notion of laws.

Accordingly, new concepts of visual representation emerge too, as for instance manifested in the attempts to describe how the human sense apparatus influences our sensations, in the development of new kinds of visual representations such as the panorama, the panoptikon and other similar attempts to create what we could call an all-encompassing system perspective, either included in one mechanism or in the combination of many mechanisms which should be added together to visualize the totality. The world is seen as one integrated dynamic system or as a set of many different dynamic systems—but they are all seen as rule-based. However, the interrelations between various systems remain a basically unsolved mystery.

Again, much could be added to this picture, but it still includes some of the important notions, which again are changed and reinterpreted during the twentieth century, in which we see a transition into a third epoch of modern thinking.

3. The Epoch of Digital Electronic Media From 1936 (Speech + Script + Print + Analog Electric Media + Digital Media)

From the notions of the world as a mechanical and reservible machine and as an all-embracing dynamic energy system (leading to pragmatic functionalism) we are now on the way to regarding the world as an ecological information system—a system in which it seems that we need to reinterpret the notion of the self, the observer, the idea of universal knowledge, the notion that rules and laws as being given outside and independently of the systems they regulate, as well as basic ideas on visual representation and perspective. These are of course vast questions which deserve many years of analysis and discussion, so now I will only give a rough sketch of a few aspects implied in contemporary conceptual changes.

Concerning the notion of laws and rule-based systems it seems that we need to acknowledge the existence of systems in which the rules are processed in time and space as part of and on a par with the ruled system, implying that there are systems in which the rules can be changed, modified, suspended or ascribed new functions during the process, influenced by any component part of the system or according to new inputs whether intended or not. In such systems the rules are not able to provide the stability, and thus we need to explain how stability can exist in such systems.

I see basically three arguments in favour of the need for a concept for this kind of system:

- First, the idea of rule-based systems does not allow or explain the existence of individual cases, or such cases are treated as irrelevant noise.

- Second, the idea of rule-based systems does not allow or explain the existence of deviations from and modifications of the rules if the deviations cannot be traced back to some other rules.

- Third, rule-based systems only allow the formation of new rules as the result of previously existing rules.

Not only does the computer not fit the notion of rule-based systems, as is the case for many—if not most—human and cultural phenomena, like for instance ordinary language and even biological phenomena. As a consequence of these arguments, it seems reasonable—or even inevitable—to introduce a concept for what one could label rule-generating systems, as distinct from rule-based systems.

Rule-based systems can be defined as systems in which the processes are governed by a set of previously given rules outside the system (and inaccessible from within the ruled system). The rules govern the system and guarantee its stability. Contrary to this, rule-generating systems can be defined as systems in which the rules are the result of processes within the system and hence open for influence from other processes in the same systems as well as from higher or lower levels and the surroundings. Such systems are to some extent, but not completely, governed by the rules, as these are themselves open for modification, change and suspension. Since they are not completely governed by the rules, the stability needs to be provided in other ways, and this is obtained by using redundancy functions in some way, as is the case in ordinary language, computers, and many other areas of culture.

A main point here is that objective knowledge need not be universal knowledge. Individual phenomena, the existence of singularities and so-called exceptions are as real as the existence of universals. Truth should not to be identified with universally valid laws. Another important aspect concerning the notion of knowledge and truth follows from the fact that we are always and only concerned with fragmentary representations selected among a number of possibilities. Any phenomenon in the world may have more than one representation. The implication is that we cannot stick to the notion of complete representation as was done in the former stages of modern thinking.

Parallel to this we are also able to recognize new ideas concerning visual representation and the notion of perspective. While both linear perspective and the various system perspectives in previous epochs were seen as models for universal representation, we are now heading towards a new concept of fragmented perspective, which could be labelled a scanning perspective, since scanning processes do not give the complete representation but a picture of some selected indicators.

An interesting point is that more or less parallel conceptual changes to those mentioned here can be found in many other contemporary sources. (recursive systems, Luhmann, autopoeisis, Giddens, temporal logic). It seems that they all come as a logical consequence of previous modern thinking, as a further elaboration of modern thinking, and—in my view the most important—as a transgression of the basic axioms of the previous epoch, in that the axioms are moved from the field of axioms to the field of analysis, moved from the area of invariance to the area of variability—as a broadening of the potential of modern thinking.

This applies to the notion of rules, which were first moved into the system, then regarded as processes in the system and later as the resultant effects of various other processes, bringing us from the notion of homogenous rule-based systems to the notion of heterogenous and reciprocally interfering systems—and as I would suggest to the notion of rule-generating systems. It also applies to the notion of the observer, who was originally conceived of as positioned outside the system, then brought into the system, and later regarded as an interactive component.

Since these evolving concepts can be seen as consequence of attempts to give an answer to unsolved questions in previous modern thinking, we may assume that we are still in the modern tradition. So we are in many other respects, but we are so in a manner which might be called a process of modernizing modernity, that is, a process in which former axioms are placed on the agenda and made into objects for analysis and description. This is actually the way the process of secularisation has always worked. We are only taking a small new step in continuation of this process.

If, as I assume, the previous axioms, which are now placed on the agenda, are the axioms concerning the concepts of the human mind, human reason, knowledge, symbolic representation, language, and the text as the medium of truth, we can state that the secularisation of the relation to nature has now come to include and embrace the very means of the same process. A secularisation in the relation to the (symbolic) means by which the previous secularisation towards other parts of nature was carried out. If so, we may say that we are facing a secularising process of a second order.

References

BOLTER, DAVID (1984) *Turing's Man. Western Culture in the Computer Age.* Chapel Hill: University of North Carolina Press.

BOLTZ, NORBERT (1993) *Am Ende der Gutenberg, Galaxis: die neuen Kommunikations verhältnisse.*

BUSH, VANNEVAR (1945) 'As We May Think'. Munich: Fink Verlag. (= Ch. 1 above.)

CROWLEY, D. J. and DAVID MITCHELL, eds. (1994) *Communication Theory Today.* Stanford, Calif.: Stanford University Press.

DERRIDA, JACQUES (1967) 1979 *De la grammotologie.* Paris: Éditions de Minuit.

EISENSTEIN, ELISABETH (1979) *The Printing Press as an Agent of Change: Communications and Cultural Transformations in Early Modern Europe.* New York: Cambridge University Press.

FINNEMANN, N. O. (1996) *Modernitet og Medier*, Inst. for Informations—og Medievidenskab, Århus.

—— (1997) *Kommunikative Rum*, Work Paper Series, no. 43, Center for Cultural Research, Aarhus Universitet, Århus.

—— (1994) *Tanke, Sprog og Maskine.* Akademisk Forlag, København. Engl. translation by Gary Pickering 'Thought, Sign and Machine, The Computer Reconsidered' manuscript available by request to finnemann @ cfk.hum.aau.dk.

INNIS, HAROLD and MARY INNIS (1949) *Empire and Communications.* Toronto: University of Toronto Press.

INNIS, HAROLD (1950) *The Bias of Communication.* Toronto: University of Toronto Press.

LATOUR, BRUNO (1991, 1993) *We Have Never Been Modern.* London: Harvester Wheatsheaf.

LYOTARD, FRANÇOIS (1979) *La Condition Postmoderne: rapport sur le savoir.* Paris: Éditions de Minuit.

McLUHAN, MARSHALL (1962) *The Gutenberg Galaxy. The Making of Typographic Man.* Toronto: University of Toronto Press.

—— (1964) 1994 *Understanding Media—The Extensions of Man.* Cambridge, Mass.: MIT.

MEYROWITZ, JOSHUA (1985) *No Sense of Place: The Impact of Electronic Media on Social Behavior.* New York: Oxford University Press.

—— (1993) 'Images of Media'. *Journal of Communication* 43: 3, pp. 55–66.

—— (1994) 'Medium Theory', in Crowley and Mitchell (eds.), *Communication Theory Today.*

ONG, WALTER J. (1982) *Orality and Literacy—The Technologizing of the Word*. London: Routledge.

TURING, ALAN, M. (1936) 1965 'On Computable Numbers—With an Application to the Entscheidungsproblem', *Proceedings of the London Mathematical Society*, ser. 2 vol. 42. 1936–7: 230–65 with corrections in vol. 43, 1937: 544–6. Davis (ed.), 1965: 115–54.

ZUBOFF, SHOSHANA (1989) *In the Age of the Smart Machine: The Future of Work and Power*. New York: Basic Books.

10

'Interactivity'—Tracking a New Concept in Media and Communication Studies

Jens F. Jensen

In this essay, Jens F. Jensen provides an important survey of theories about the concept of interactivity and elaborates a new typological description of forms of interactivity, which focuses on patterns of information flow. In his review and categorization of a broad spectrum of computer media forms, Jensen offers a framework for identifying classes of applications and forms of information flow as well as means for describing the forms of interaction they may engender.

> *... interactivity is quintessentially a communication concept...*
> *its time has come for communication research. Interactivity is a*
> *special intellectual niche reserved for communication scholars.*
> *(Sheizaf Rafaeli, 1988)*

'in´ter.ac´tive
1. new technology that will change the way you **shop, play** and **learn**
2. a zillion-dollar **industry** (maybe)'

The above quote is a quick, dictionary-like keyword definition of the concept 'interactive' as it appeared on the cover of *Newsweek* on May 31, 1993. Inside the magazine, under the title 'An interactive Life. It will put the world at your fingertips . . .', readers were told that the ultimate promise of 'interactivity' was:

a huge amount of information available to anyone at the touch of a button, everything from airline schedules to esoteric scientific journals to video versions of off-off-off Broadway. Watching a movie won't be a passive experience. At various points, you'll click on alternative story lines and create your individualized version of "Terminator XII." Consumers will send as well as receive all kinds of data . . . Video-camera

This is a newly revised version of an article originally published in Danish: Jensen, Jens F., ' "Interactivitet"—på sporet af et nyt begreb i medie- og kommunikationsvidenskaberne'. *MedieKultur*, 26 (April 1997), 40–55.

owners could record news they see and put it on the universal network
... Viewers could select whatever they wanted just by pushing a button
... Instead of playing rented tapes on their VCRs ... [the customers] may
be able to call up a movie from a library of thousands through a menu
displayed on the TV. Game fanatics may be able to do the same from
another electronic library filled with realistic video versions of arcade
shoot-'em-ups ... (1993: 38).

The cover and quote are in many ways characteristic.[1] In recent years, expectations of 'interactivity' and new 'interactive media' have been pushed to the breaking point in terms of what will become technologically possible, in terms of services that will be offered, in terms of economic gain, etc. Along with terms like 'multimedia', 'hypermedia', 'media convergence', 'digitization' and 'information superhighway', 'interactivity' is presumably among the words currently surrounded by the greatest amount of *hype*. The concept seems loaded with positive connotations along the lines of high tech, technological advancement, hypermodernity and futurism, along the lines of individual freedom of choice, personal development, self determination—and even along the lines of folksy popularization, grassroots democracy, and political independence.

At the same time, it seems relatively unclear just what 'interactivity' and 'interactive media' mean. The positiveness surrounding the concepts and the frequency of their use seem, in a way, to be reversely proportional to their precision and actual content of meaning. Americans often use the expression *buzzwords* to refer to words which, within a certain topic, appear to refer to something very important and which—for a given time—are heard constantly, but are often difficult to understand since in reality nobody seems to know what they mean. 'Interactivity' is currently one of the media community's most used *buzzwords*. In that sense, it's easy to agree with Sheizaf Rafaeli who starts his article on 'interactivity' by maintaining that, 'Interactivity is a widely used term with an intuitive appeal, but it is an underdefined concept. As a way of thinking about communication, it has high face validity, but only narrowly based explication, little consensus on meaning, and only recently emerging empirical verification of actual role' (1988: 110).

Maybe this isn't so surprising after all. The meaning of professional terms—including scientific and academic terms—is often watered down once they win popular acceptance in daily usage. And with the explosive growth and decided success of interactive technologies and the interactive approach in recent years in the form of video recorders, videotext, telephone-based voice response systems, ATM cards, automatic tellers, on-line services, information kiosks, 'intelligent' household appliances and most importantly, computers and multimedia, Internet, intranets, WWW, networked computers—where it can be said that culture has lived out what we might call 'the interactive turn'—'interactivity' has naturally entered common usage. And this watering down of the concept has not become less significant after the worlds of advertising and entertainment have annexed the term as a common, value added word in the effort to sell new products and services.

1 Although in this case there is also a certain ironic distance.

This kind of confusion of concepts is, however, inappropriate in an academic situation where it is necessary to know relatively precisely what terms refer to and which differences they make. At the same time, the concept of 'interactivity' (as will be shown) has a longer and more complicated tradition behind it than first meets the eye. There are, therefore, many good reasons to leave the *hype* and *buzz* behind and take a closer look instead at the background and construction of the concept of 'interactivity'.

The following is an attempt to track the concept of 'interactivity'.[2] First the concept's current placement in the fields of media and communication will be discussed, and its background in other traditions will be touched on. This will be followed by various representative attempts at definitions from academic studies and finally, based on this presentation, a new definition of 'interactivity' will be suggested.

'Interactivity'— media studies' blind spot?

... scholars are going to have to shift toward models that accommodate the interactivity of most of the new communication technologies. New paradigms are needed, based on new intellectual terminology.

(*Rogers & Chaffee, 1983*)

While *Newsweek*, as previously cited, dared to publish a cover with a refreshing keyword definition, more serious definitions are harder to find in common reference works and handbooks from the fields of media and communication. Here the term 'interactivity' is most notable for its absence. The *Dictionary of Mass Media & Communication* doesn't list it. *A Dictionary of Communication and Media Studies* doesn't list it, nor does the *Handbook of Communication*. Even relatively new and updated handbooks like *Key Concepts in Communication and Cultural Studies* (O'Sullivan *et al.*, 1994) are silent when it comes to 'interactivity'. It certainly looks as though the authors of the handbooks completely disagree with this article's introductory quote, which cites Rafaeli's opinion that 'interactivity' should be of central and essential concern to students of communication.

Naturally, this blind spot, when it comes to the concept of 'interactivity' and 'interactive media', has an explanation. One way to clarify what may be blocking the view—and at the same time establish a framework for understanding the various concepts of interactivity currently in circulation—is to use the media typology developed by Bordewijk and Kaam.[3] Their typology is based on two central aspects of all information traffic: the question of who owns and provides the information, and who controls its distribution in terms of timing and subject matter.

By cross-tabulating these two aspects in relation to whether they are controlled by either a centralized information provider or a decentralized

---

2 There are several general articles which each deal with the concept of interactivity in different ways, e.g. Heeter (1989), Goertz (1995), Jäkel (1995), and Toscan (1995). Articles which I have borrowed from for this paper, in varying degrees.

3 The media typology can only be suggested here. See Jensen (1996e, 1997b, 1998c) for a more in-depth presentation.

information consumer, a matrix appears with four principally different communication patterns, as illustrated in Figure 1.

	Information produced by a central provider	Information produced by the consumer
Distribution controlled by a central provider	1) TRANSMISSION*	4) REGISTRATION
Distribution controlled by the consumer	3) CONSULTATION	2) CONVERSATION

1) If information is produced and owned by a central information provider and this center also controls the distribution of information, we have a communication pattern of the *transmission* type. This is a case of one way communication, where the significant consumer activity is pure reception. Examples would be classical broadcast media such as radio and TV but also, for example, listservs, or live broadcasts of conferences, real time radio, TV, multimedia etc. via the MBone.

2) If the exact opposite occurs and information is produced and owned by the information consumers who also control distribution, we have a *conversation* pattern of communication. This is a case of traditional two way communication, where the significant consumer activity is the production of messages and delivery of input in a dialog structure. Typical examples would be the telephone but also e-mail, mailing lists, newsgroups, IRC, etc.

3) If information is produced and owned by an information provider, but the consumer retains control over what information is distributed and when, it is a *consultation* communication pattern. In this case, the consumer makes a request to the information providing center for specific information to be delivered. Here the characteristic consumer activity is one of active selection from available possibilities. Typical examples would be various *on-demand* services or on-line information resources such as FTP, Gopher, WWW etc.

4) Finally if information is produced by the information consumer, but processed and controlled by the information providing center, we have a *registration* communication pattern. In this communication pattern the center collects information from or about the user. In this case, the characteristic aspect is the media system's storage, processing, and use of the data or knowledge from or about the user. Typical examples would be various types of central surveillance, registration systems, logging of computer systems, etc.

Among these four information patterns, *transmission* is the only one that is characterized by one-way communication from the information-providing center to the consumer. In other words, there is no return or back-channel that makes an information flow possible *from* the information consumer to the media system. Until now, communication and media studies has primarily based its models and insights on the transmission pattern because of the dominant role played by mass communication research. This model has also followed certain preconceptions and basic concepts such as: sender, receiver, intention, effect, channel, media, etc. Communication patterns of the conversational type have naturally been studied within the field of interpersonal communication, but actually the work has been based on models from the transmission pattern. The two last communication patterns (consultation and registration) have been left practically unexplored by media researchers.

Current media developments including the arrival of 'new media' (such as the Internet, intranets, networked multimedia, WWW, Gopher, etc.) have been more or less singularly characterized by a movement away from the transmission pattern toward the other three media patterns. These new media, which open up the possibility for various forms of input and information flow from information consumers to the system, can hardly be described using traditional one way models and terminology. Seen from this perspective, it might well be claimed that as developments proceed, existing media theory is increasingly less able to explain current media phenomena. Or it could be said that the new media represent a growing challenge to traditional media and communication research that necessitates a thorough rethinking of all central models and concepts.

There are already many who have pointed out this situation. Aside from Rogers & Chaffee, whose quote leads this section, Carrie Heeter's article, with the telling title: 'Implications of New Interactive Technologies for Conceptualizing Communication' speaks out for 'a need to reconceptualize communication, in part because of changes brought about by new telecommunication technologies' (1989: 217). Rice & Williams point out that 'new media may, in fact, necessitate a considerable reassessment of communication research. Intellectual changes must occur to match the growing changes in communication behavior' (1984: 80). And Everett M. Rogers maintains that 'The Communication Revolution now underway in Information Societies is also a revolution in communication science, involving both models and methods' (1986: 213), and that 'Driving the epistemological revolution in communication science is the interactivity of the new communication technologies' (194).

Another, related problem that stems from historical, institutional politics rather than logical reasoning or scholarship has led mass media and interpersonal communication to split into two separate research institutions and scholarly traditions. In many ways, the new media provide mediation between, or a combination of, mass media and interpersonal media—a kind of 'interpersonal mass media'—which falls outside of (or into the no-man's land between) the two traditional areas of research interest.

Perhaps for these reasons, among others, the established media and communication research community has developed blind spots in relation to new interactive media. This general problem can only be mentioned briefly here,[4] as we proceed to follow another, more specific trail . . .

---

4 See Jensen (forthcoming) for more in-depth treatment.

'Interactivity'— The Background Behind the Concept

As Michael Jäckel (1995), among others, has pointed out, the concept 'interactivity' extends—perhaps not surprisingly—from the concept of 'interaction'. A concept which generally means: 'exchange', 'interplay', 'mutual influence'.

However, if we focus on individual fields of scholarship, the concept takes on many, very different meanings. In medical science, 'interaction' describes the interplay between two medications given at the same time. In engineering, 'interaction' refers to the relationship between, and actions of, two different materials under stress. In statistics, 'interaction' represents the common effect of several variables on an independent variable. In linguistics, it refers to the influence on language bahavior of bi-lingual children (Jäckel 1995). In other words, the meaning of the concept 'interaction' depends on the context in which it is used. Concepts are called *multi-discursive* 'when they can be found with significantly different meanings or connotations according to their use within different discourses' and thus 'depend to a very large extent on their context for their meaning to be clear' (O'Sullivan 1994: 190). 'Interaction' can certainly be said to be a multi-discursive concept.[5]

However, none of the above definitions are particularly relevant in this context. Of primary importance in establishing the concept of 'interactivity' in this case, is how the term is understood in three other academic fields (cf. Goertz 1995; and Jäckel 1995): (1) The interaction concept of sociology; (2) the interaction concept(s) of communication studies; and finally (3) the interaction concept of informatics.

(1) What does sociology's concept of 'interaction' look like? The *Wörterbuch der Soziologie* writes: 'Interaction is the most elemental unit of social events, where people adapt their behavior to each other, whether or not they follow mutual expectations or reject them. As coordinated action is not preprogrammed, a minimum of common meaning and linguistic understanding is necessary' (Krappmann, 1989: 310, emphasis deleted). Similarly, the *International Encyclopedia of Communications* writes: 'interaction occurs as soon as the actions of two or more individuals are observed to be mutually interdependent', i.e. 'interaction may be said to come into being when each of at least two participants is aware of the presence of the other, and each has reason to believe the other is similarly aware', in this way establishing a 'state of reciprocal awareness' (Duncan, 1989: 325). Understood in this way, according to sociology, interaction makes up 'a basic constituent of society' (326).

The basic model that the sociological interaction concept stems from is thus the relationship between two or more people who, in a given situation, mutually adapt their behavior and actions to each other. The important aspects here are that clear-cut social systems and specific situations are involved, where the partners in the interaction are in close physical proximity, and 'symbolic interaction' is also involved. In other words, a mutual exchange and negotiation regarding meaning takes place between partners

---

5 There is an added finesse in the concept 'multi-discursive' here, since 'the words used in other discourses will continue to resound, so to speak, in each case' (190).

who find themselves in the same social context. A situation which communication and media studies would call communication. Within sociology then, it is possible to have communication without interaction (e.g. listening to the radio and/or watching TV) but not interaction without communication.

(2) As regards the concept of 'interaction' in communication and media studies, there is no such clear-cut answer since there appears to be several different concepts of 'interaction' involved.

If we look at the dominant trend within current communication and media studies, what might generally be called the 'cultural studies' tradition, one recurring trait is that the term 'interaction' is used as a broad concept that covers processes that take place between receivers on the one hand and a media message on the other. For the sake of simplicity, attention will be drawn to an example, more as a source of inspiration to than as a central representative of the 'cultural studies' tradition:

Wolfgang Iser wrote an essay in 1980 actually entitled 'Interaction Between the Text and the Reader'. He starts by claiming that 'Central to the reading of every . . . work is the interaction between its structure and its recipient' (160). In brief, his approach is that the work can neither be reduced to the author's text nor the reader's subjectivity, but must be found somewhere between these two poles. And if 'the virtual position of the work is between the text and the reader, its actualization is clearly the result of an interaction between the two'. It seems fairly obvious[6] that this is not 'interaction' in the sociological sense. What's missing is genuine reciprocity and an exchange between the two elements involved in that the text naturally can neither adapt nor react to the reader's actions or interpretations. The concept of 'interaction', as it is used here, seems to be a synonym for more noncommittal terms such as 'relation', 'relationship', 'interpretation' or 'reading', etc.

The question immediately becomes whether it is relevant to use the concept of 'interaction', with its strongly sociological connotations, in connection with these phenomena which are actually certain types of active reception. O'Sullivan *et al.* point out a related problem in this conceptual watering-down process when in *Key Concepts in Communication and Cultural Studies*, under the reference 'interaction/social interaction', they warn: 'The phrase "social interaction" has perhaps been used too frequently within communication studies—to the point of obscuring any one agreed interpretation. It would be inappropriate, for example, to describe an audience as "socially interacting" when reading a book, or witnessing the death of Hamlet within a hushed and darkened theatre . . . because of the lack of observable reciprocation from others the social criteria are not satisfied' (1994: 155).

There are, however, also traditions within media and communication studies where use of the concept of 'interaction' comes closer to the sociological meaning. One example might be research in interpersonal communication, where the object of study by definition lies within a sociological framework of understanding (see e.g. Corner & Hawthorn, 1993). Another

6 Which Iser also draws attention to—in an otherwise rather inconsistent argument—both by pointing out differences, and similarities between social interaction and reading and thereby between the general (here, psychoanalytical) concept of interaction and the special text–reader relationship.

example might be traditional media sociology which often takes over the sociological interaction concept and uses it in a sense that shows solidarity with the sociological, primarily in relation to communication within groups of (media) audiences (e.g. McQuail 1987: 228 ff.).

A third example might come from sociologically oriented media effect research which arose in connection with the so-called 'two-step flow' model (Lazarsfeld). It starts with a critical look at the more simple and mechanistic one way models of the transfer of messages to an audience and instead shows that media messages are transmitted and processed during several steps. At first, the information is transmitted to relatively well informed individuals (*opinion leaders*); and in the next phase the information is brought to a broader, less well-informed public via interpersonal communication. This model combines a mass communication model with a model for interpersonal communication within a mass media audience where the latter represents 'interaction' in a traditional sociological sense. Related understandings of interaction in connection with media can be observed in 'uses and gratification' studies, symbolic interactionism, etc.

And a fourth example is Horton and Wohl's concept of 'para-social interaction'. Horton and Wohl's (1956) central insight is that the new mass media—particularly TV—has an especially characteristic ability to create an illusion of apparently intimate face-to-face communication between a presenter and an individual viewer. This illusion is created by close-ups of the presenter's face and gestures, simulated direct eye contact, the use of a direct address, personal *small talk*, a private conversational style, etc. To a certain degree, the technique makes the members of the audience react—and participate—as though they were in a face-to-face interaction in a primary group. Together these conditions create what Horton and Wohl call '[the] simulacrum of conversational give and take' (215) or 'intimacy at a distance'. It is this relationship between the TV presenter and the viewer which they call 'para-social interaction'. Horton and Wohl are fully convinced that this new form of (media) interaction is different from traditional social interaction and that the significant difference is precisely that media interaction is necessarily 'one-sided, nondialectical, controlled by the performer, and not susceptible of mutual development' and can be characterized by the lack of effective reciprocity (215). Even so, their main point is that the relationship between TV performers and viewers is in principle experienced and treated in the same way as daily communication and interaction. In other words, para-social interaction 'is analogous to and in many ways resembles social interaction in ordinary primary groups' (228), which is also why it can (and should) advantageously be studied as interaction in the sociological sense.

To review, then, it can be noted that the concept of interaction in media and communication studies is often used to refer to the actions of an audience or recipients in relation to media content. This may be the case *even though* no new media technology is being used which would open up the possibility for user input and two-way communication, but on the contrary, to refer to traditional one-way media. These references may also occur *even though* they (often) don't refer to social situations where an interactive partner is physically present and *even though* the social situations are (often) not characterized by reciprocity and the exchange or negotiation of a common understanding. This is why we cannot speak of interaction in the strictly sociological sense.

In terms of media technologies which actually open up for input from the user, media researchers have not used the concept 'interaction' for quite a while. Instead, they have used concepts which more technically refer to this possibility, for example: two-way communication or 'return channel' systems. It was with the use of the interaction concept in informatics that this first began to change, which brings us to the third and final tradition mentioned previously.

(3) How is the informatic concept of 'interaction' constructed? The basic model which this concept uses as its starting point is, contrary to the sociological tradition (even though the concept has been partially taken from there) the relationship between people and machines which in this tradition is often called human-computer interaction (HCI) or man-machine interaction. Historically, this terminology originated from batch processing, where a large amount of data or programs were collected before being processed by a computer. Using a so-called 'dialogue' function, it was possible for the user to observe partial results, menu choices and dialog boxes and thereby continually influence the performance of the program via new input to 'dialogue traffic' or in what came to be called an 'interactive mode' (cf. Goertz 1995). 'Interaction' in the informatic sense refers, in other words, to the process that takes place when a human user operates a machine. However, it doesn't cover communication between two people, mediated by a machine, a process often referred to as *computer mediated communication* (CMC). Within informatics, then, (in contrast to sociology) it is possible to have (human-machine) interaction without having communication, but not (computer mediated) communication without also having (human-computer) interaction.

A central characteristic of the informatic concept of 'interaction' is that the process between the human and the machine is, to a large degree, seen as *analogous* with communication between people. Another important trait is the central placement of the concept of 'control'. For example, in 1979 when a number of the leading researchers in the field gathered in Seillac, France, for a workshop with the title 'The Methodology of Interaction', it turned out that there was considerable disagreement about the definition of the 'interaction' concept. After lengthy debate, they arrived at this consensus definition: 'Interaction is a style of control' (1979: 69). This is another instance where the informatic concept of interaction has a complicated double relationship to that from sociology. As far as an understanding of human-machine interaction as being *analogous with* communication between people, it can be said to have a certain—if metaphoric—affinity with the sociological concept. On the other hand, the 'control' aspect clashes with it since control can be seen as the opposite of mutuality, reciprocity, and negotiation.

The informatic concept of interaction is, as suggested, the most recent arrival of the three. Even so, as a field of research it (HCI) is perhaps the most well-defined and well established, with its own conferences, journals, and paradigms, and it has also had a major influence on the media concept of 'interaction'.[7]

---

7 As seen in the above discussion of the 'multi-discursive' concept in note 5.

In summary, it can be said that while 'interaction' in the sociological sense refers to a *reciprocal* relationship between two or more people, and in the informatic sense refers to the relationship *between people and machines* (but not communication between people mediated by machines), in communication studies it refers, among other things, to the relationship between the text and the reader, but also to reciprocal human actions and communication associated with the use of media as well as (para-social) interaction via a medium. Obviously, as far as the concept of interaction is concerned, there is already considerable confusion.

But now let's start to track the concept of 'interactivity'. While sociology doesn't usually use the derivative 'interactivity', the concepts of 'interaction' and 'interactivity' in informatic and media studies appear to be synonymous. At the Seillac workshop mentioned above, the two concepts were connected by the consensus definition: 'Interaction is a style of control and interactive systems exhibit that style' (1980: 69). Synonymous usage that, in connection with the arrival of 'new media', has also become widespread in the field of media studies. In this sense, the concept 'interactivity' or the combination 'interactive media' is most often used to characterize a certain trait of new media which differs from traditional media. The question is, which trait is it?

'Interactivity': Prototype, Criteria, or Continuum?

INTERACTIVE. *Media as a computer smorgasbord—and you get to vary the recipes. Customers control what they see and can talk back to their machines.*

(*Newsweek, 1993*)

Taking a look at the collection of existing definitions of 'interactivity' spread throughout media studies and computer science, it seems that there are three principle ways of defining the concept: (1), as prototypic examples; (2) as criteria, i.e. as a given feature or characteristic that must be fulfilled; or (3) as a continuum, i.e. as a quality which can be present to a greater or lesser degree.

1. Interactivity as Prototype

A representative of the first type—definition by prototypic example—can be found in Jerome T. Durlak's 'A Typology for Interactive Media', where among the introduction's qualifying definitions it says: 'Interactive media systems include the telephone; "two-way television"; audio conferencing systems; computers used for communication; electronic mail; videotext; and a variety of technologies that are used to exchange information in the form of still images, line drawings, and data' (1987: 743).[8] This type of definition is, by it's very nature, never very informative, partly because it doesn't point out which traits qualify a given media as interactive or which aspects connect them, etc. Aside from that, the definition raises another principle question.

8 See also Rafaeli (1988: 110 f.)

Among the examples of 'interactive media' listed above are also media which are used for interpersonal communication, in other words, media using the conversation pattern, such as the telephone, e-mail, etc. In certain academic traditions (and possibly national languages) it isn't readily apparent that this type of interpersonal media should be considered 'interactive'. However, it isn't uncommon in large parts of the English/American academic literature.[9] Durlak and many others claim that interpersonal communication and especially face-to-face communication is the ideal type of interactive communication: 'Face-to-face communication is held up as the model because the sender and receiver use all their senses, the reply is immediate, the communication is generally closed circuit, and the content is primarily informal or "ad lib"' (1987: 744). According to this way of thinking, media whose communication form comes closest to face-to-face communication are therefore also the most 'interactive', whereby conversational media, such as video conferencing, are considered more interactive than consultative media such as, say, computer-based online services.

As seen here, and in upcoming examples, the concept of 'interactivity' refers both to media patterns of the consultative and the conversational type. It also becomes clear that the concept of interactivity, understood in this way (in the form of the conversation communication pattern), is related to the sociological concept of 'interaction', understood as 'actions of two or more individuals observed to be mutually interdependent' and (in the form of the consultation communication pattern) borrows from the informatic concept of interaction, understood as 'actions between a human user and a machine' (cf. Goertz 1995).

2. Interactivity as Criteria

Examples of the second type of definition—interactivity defined as criteria, that is, as a certain trait or feature that must be fulfilled—can be found, e.g., in Rockley Miller's writing. He offers definitions of the terms 'interactivity', 'interactive', and 'interactive media'. 'Interactivity' is defined as 'A reciprocal dialog between the user and the system', where both sociology's (mutual dialog) and informatic's (user and system) conceptual constructions appear once again; the adjective 'interactive' is understood as: 'Involving the active participation of the user in directing the flow of the computer or video program; a system which exchanges information with the viewer, processing the viewer's input in order to generate the appropriate response within the context of the program...'; and the compound term 'interactive media' is said to mean: 'Media which involves the viewer as a source of input to determine the content and duration of a message, which permits individualized program material' (1987).[10]

The strength of this set of definitions is that it is relatively exact. Its weakness is that it is narrowly tied to specific technologies (computer and video); that it primarily looks at interactivity from within the consultation communication pattern; and that even within the consultation pattern it excludes a number of services which are commonly considered interactive—services in

---

9 Aside from Durlak (1987) see also Steuer (1995), Scharpe (1995), and Rafaeli (1988: 110).

10 For examples of other criteria-based definitions, see Feldman (1991: 8).

which choices can only be made from continual transmissions (primarily TV services such as *near-video-on-demand, be-your-own-editor, teletext*, etc.) but where there is no actual processing of the user's input. On a more general level, there are problems with defining 'interactivity' as criteria, or a given feature, as this example certainly should have demonstrated. Such definitions have a tendency to include and exclude very differing types of media which today are commonly thought of as interactive, in a relatively casual way. And, by extension, they have a tendency toward obsolescence and being quickly outdated by technological developments. Finally, based on criteria definitions, it is impossible to differentiate between different forms or levels of interactivity.

Another, perhaps more useful, criteria definition, can be found in the *International Encyclopedia of Communications*, where John Carey suggests the following provisions for the keyword 'interactive media': 'Technologies that provide person-to-person communications mediated by a telecommunications channel (e.g., a telephone call) and person-to-machine interactions that simulate an interpersonal exchange (e.g., an electronic banking transaction)' (1989: 328). The last example is explained in more depth a little further on: 'most of the content is created by a centralized production group or organization', and 'individual users interact with content created by an organization' (328). This conceptual construction points more or less directly toward the conversational media type and the consultative media type respectively (and as a result, at the sociological and informatic concepts of interaction) which collectively make up 'interactive media'.

Once again there is a certain vagueness to the definition of the concept. For example, when Carey exemplifies 'person-to-machine interaction', and the user as 'interacting with content' he writes, 'For example, in some interactive cable television systems, viewers can respond to questions posed in programming. Typically their response is limited to pressing one of a few alternative buttons on their cable converter box, thereby indicating agreement with one of the opinion statements set out by the program producers' (328). This example doesn't seem to point to the selection of pre-produced content and thereby at a consultation pattern, but rather shows the possibility of creating input which the media system processes and is able to use. In other words, a registration pattern—a (pattern) example, which the general definition seems to ignore.

More problematic perhaps, is the fact that the definition also excludes services based on the transmission pattern, such as teletext, *near-video-on-demand, be-your-own-editor*, datacasting, which make up the bulk of some TV systems so-called 'interactive services'. Carey himself seems aware of the problem and asks the question whether or not it is possible to draw such narrow boundaries. He writes, 'Most scholars would not classify as interactive media those technologies that permit only the selection of content such as a broadcast teletext service with one hundred frames of information, each of which can be selected on demand by a viewer. However, the boundary between selection of content and simulation of an interpersonal communication exchange is not always definable in a specific application or service' (328). This definition of the concept has some of the same weaknesses as its predecessor: the tendency to exclude various media which are generally considered interactive and an inability to use the definition to differentiate between various forms and levels of interactivity, etc.

3. Interactivity as Continuum

The third possibility, which solves some of these problems (but at the same time may creates others) is to define interactivity not as criteria, but rather as a continuum, where interactivity can be present in varying degrees. One possible way to structure this type of definition is to base it on the number of dimensions it includes, so that we could speak of 1-dimensional, 2-dimensional, 3-dimensional ... and n-dimensional interactivity concepts. This will be explained in more depth in the following section.

Interactivity's Continuum and Dimensions

... interactivity as it relates to communication technologies is a multidimensional concept.

(*Carrie Heeter, 1989*)

1. 1-Dimensional Concepts of Interactivity

One relatively simple model of interactivity as a continuum, which operates from only one dimension, can be found in the writing of Everett M. Rogers (1986). Rogers defines 'interactivity' as 'the capability of new communication systems (usually containing a computer as one component) to "talk back" to the user, almost like an individual participating in a conversation' (1986: 34). And—a bit farther down—'interactivity is a variable; some communication technologies are relatively low in their degree of interactivity (for example, network television), while others (such as computer bulletin boards) are more highly interactive' (211). Based on this definition, Rogers has created a scale, reprinted in Fig. 2, in which he lists 'degrees of interactivity' for a number of selected communication technologies on a continuum from 'low' to 'high'.

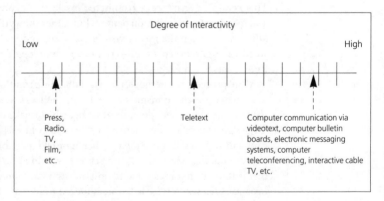

Degree of Interactivity

Low   High

Press,   Teletext   Computer communication via
Radio,   videotext, computer bulletin
TV,   boards, electronic messaging
Film,   systems, computer
etc.   teleconferencing, interactive cable
                                     TV, etc.

Fig. 2.
E. M. Rogers'
1-dimensional scale of
'selected communication
technologies on an
interactivity continuum'
(1987: 34)

As can be seen in Fig. 2, Rogers primarily refers to the concept of 'interactivity' within the consultation pattern. The basic model is clearly 'human-machine interaction', understood in the context of interpersonal communication ('talking back'). It is also because of this consultative aspect (selection available between channels and programs) that classical transmission mass media such as TV and radio can be considered 'interactive'—although to a lesser degree. As is presumably also apparent, this attempt to sort and define is relatively rough and lacking in information—a trait that is intensified by Rogers failure to deliver explicit criteria for the placement of each media.

But there are several other—and perhaps more influential—unidimensional concepts of interactivity. As early as 1979, in connection with the development of videodisc technology, the Nebraska Videodisc Design/Production Group had already established a definition of various levels of interactivity. A classification, which was later accepted as an international ad hoc standard. The levels are as follows:

Level 0: Linear playback only.

Level 1: Linear playback plus search and automatic stops.

Level 2: Videodiscs controlled by a computer program placed either directly on the videodisc or manually *loaded*. . . . They include all of the level 1 capabilities plus program *looping*, branching and faster access time.

Level 3: Videodiscs controlled by an external computer . . . More than one videodisc can be controlled by the same computer. Computer-generated text and graphics can be superimposed over videodisc images . . . A variety of user input devices can be employed and user input can be registered and documented. (Lambert 1987: p. xi.)

In this case, the definition and division of levels of interactivity are closely related to specific videodisc technology and, perhaps therefore, the concept of interactivity is primarily related to the consultation pattern of communication (although level 3 hints at the registration pattern).

Similar, but technologically more up-to-date, scales have since been defined by Klaus Schrape (1995), among others, who operates with 5 levels of interactivity:

Level 0: Turn on/turn off and change channel (zapping).

Level 1: A supply consists of more transmitted channels mutually displaced in time (parallel transmitted TV, multi-channel TV, multi-perspective TV), between which the viewer is able to choose.

Level 2: Transmission of optional relevant supplementary information to the TV-signal, with or without relation to the program (e.g. videotext).

Level 3: Any form of stored content by individual request (passive user orientation).

Level 4: Communicative interaction, active user orientation (direct return channel), two way communication: e.g. videophone, interactive services etc.[11]

This division of levels and definitions also reveals close association with the technology of its time—now interactive and digital TV. However, it includes several types of information patterns, where the transition from level 0 to

---

[11] For similar scales see also Next Century Media's 7-level scale (Hackenberg, 1995).

level 1 marks the transition from transmission to consultation media and the transition from level 3 to level 4 marks the transition from consultation media to conversation media, referred to here as passive and active user orientation or stored content versus communicative interaction. An obvious criticism of this model is that it places different types of interactivity, which don't appear to be similar, within the same dimension and on the same scale. It isn't readily apparent why a telephone conversation should be more interactive than searching an information database, since they involve very different types of communication traffic (conversation versus consultation) with very different user goals and functions. If, e.g., the purpose is to find exact, verifiable information, it obviously makes different qualitative and not just quantitative demands on the 'interactivity' than if the purpose is to negotiate a mutual agreement with a partner.

Sheizaf Rafaeli (1988) has also constructed a concept of interactivity based on one continual dimension, but with quite a different accent. Rafaeli's definition centers on the concept 'responsiveness', as a measure of a media's ability to be receptive and react in response to a given user, or more precisely, a measure of how much one message in an exchange is based on previous messages. This model uses three progressive levels in its continuum: (1) Two-way communication takes place when messages are delivered both ways. (2) Reactive communication also requires that a later message reacts to a previous message. (3) Finally, full interactivity requires that a later message responds to a sequence of previous messages.[12] In this conceptual construction recursiveness plays a central role. A graphic illustration is shown in Figure 3.

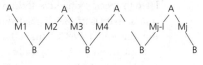

Two-way communication

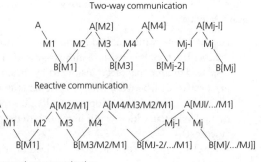

Reactive communication

Interactive communication

Fig. 3.
S. Rafaeli's
1-dimensional concept of
interactivity defined as
'responsiveness' or
'recursiveness' and
elaborated in three
progressive levels on the
continuum: Two way
communication, reactive
communication and
interactive
communication.

'Responsiveness' obviously requires that the media registers and stores information about a given user's input and actions and can then adjust to the user's wishes and distinctive characteristics. This concept of interactivity

---

12 Rafaeli's own more formal definition sounds like this: '*interactivity* is an expression of the extent that in a given series of communication exchanges, any third (or later) transmission (or message) is related to the degree to which previous exchanges referred to even earlier transmissions' (1988: 111).

refers therefore (contrary to e.g. Rogers's) primarily to the registration communication pattern. This aspect can be stated such that a media—in one sense or another—'understands' the user, and in this way approaches themes related to 'smart technologies', 'artificial intelligence', etc. Once again, interpersonal communication functions as an ideal to be measured up to with characteristics similar to the sociological concept of interaction, and its requirement of reciprocity.

Finally, Jonathan Steuer (1995) represents the transition from 1-dimensional to 2-dimensional concepts of interactivity in that he has developed a 2-dimensional matrix based on a parameter of 'vividness' which refers to 'the ability of a technology to produce a sensorially rich mediated environment' (41) and 'interactivity', which refers to 'the degree to which users of a medium can influence the form or content of the mediated environment' (41). This definition focuses on the user's ability to input information (primarily the conversation pattern) which, among other things, means that the telephone and video games are considered much more interactive than *home-shopping* and *pay-per-view*. The reason that this 2-dimensional model has been placed as a subsection of the 1-dimensional concept of interaction is obviously that 'vividness' is not an aspect of interactivity but an independent dimension. Figure 4 shows Steuer's classification of a wide range of media technologies on the basis of the two dimensions. This chart also illustrates the classification's relatively noncommittal relationship to the

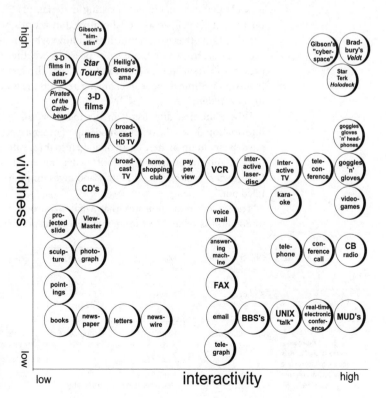

Fig. 4.
J. Steuer's (1995: 52) classification of various media technologies using the dimensions 'vividness' and 'interactivity'.

empirical, since purely fictional media such as the 'Holodeck' from the science fiction movie *Star Trek* and 'cyberspace' from William Gibson's *Neuromancer* have been included on an equal basis with actual media (cf. Goertz 1995). Like many of the other attempts at systemization, Steuer's fails to deliver explicit criteria for placement on the continuum, but seems to follow more or less subjective—possibly arbitrary—criteria (51 f.).

2.
2-Dimensional
Concepts of
Interactivity

Bohdan O. Szuprowicz, among others, has presented a 2-dimensional concept of interactivity in *Multimedia Networking* (1995). Szuprowicz maintains that if you are to understand all the questions and problems in connection with what he calls 'interactive multimedia networking and communications', it's necessary 'to define and classify the various levels and categories of interactivity that come into play' (14). For Szuprowicz, 'interactivity' is 'best defined by the type of multimedia information flows' (14), and he divides these information flows into three main categories: (1) 'User-to-documents' interactivity is defined as 'traditional transactions between a user and specific documents' and characterized by being quite restricted since it limits itself to the user's choice of information and selection of the time of access to the information. There is little or no possibility of manipulating or changing existing content. (2) 'User-to-computer' interactivity is defined as 'more exploratory interactions between a user and various delivery platforms' characterized by more advanced forms of interactivity which give the user a broader range of active choices, including access to tools that can manipulate existing material. (3) Finally, 'User-to-user' interactivity is defined as 'collaborative transactions between two or more users' (14) in other words, information flows which make direct communication between two or more users possible, whether it is point-to-point, person-to-person, multipoint, multiuser, etc. This last form, contrary to the first two mentioned above, is characterized, among other things, by operating in *real time*.

Where the first dimension in the matrix is made up of these various information flows, the other is made up of other aspects, which these flows are dependent upon, here again divided into three categories: 'access, distribution, and manipulation of multimedia content' (15). Figure 5 unfolds Szuprowicz' 2-dimensional matrix and gives examples of how it might be filled out.

The description indicates that what Szuprowicz calls, 'user-to-user' interaction is related to the sociological concept of interaction, 'user-to-

Object-oriented manipulation	Mail	Database	Groupware
Broadcast	Newsletter	Information kiosk	Presentation
Interactive access	Hypermedia	Graphical user interface	Conferencing, training
	User-to-documents	User-to-computer	User-to-user

Fig. 5.
B. O. Szuprowizs'
2-dimensional matrix
showing 'interactive
multimedia information
flows' (1995: 15).

computer'-interaction is related to the informatic concept of interaction, while 'user-to-documents' interaction has an affinity to the interaction concept used by communication studies, as it is drawn up in Iser's text-reader model. Along the same lines, the 'user-to-user' information flow is similar to what has been called the conversation communication pattern. The 'user-to-documents' information flow parallels the consultation communication pattern, while the 'user-to-computer' information flow can be said to be a particularly elaborate version of the consultation communication pattern (or alternatively, to combine several communication patterns). From this perspective, it also becomes clear that Szuprowicz's differentiation between 'user-to-documents' and 'user-to-computer' is relatively unclear. In most specific cases, it would be difficult to determine whether the 'interactivity' is directed toward a document or toward a platform. The very formulation of the difference appears to refer mostly to the 'degree of manipulability' rather than an actual qualitative difference. This is why the difference is difficult to handle in practice—and to maintain in theory. Instead, this seems to be various forms of the consultation information pattern.

3.
3-Dimensional
Concepts of
Interactivity

Continuing along the trail to the 3-dimensional concepts of 'interactivity', Brenda Laurel's writing gives us a privileged example. In several contexts (1986 and 1990), Laurel has argued that 'interactivity exists on a continuum that could be characterized by three variables', specifically: (1) 'frequency', in other words, 'how often you could interact'; (2) 'range', or 'how many choices were available'; and (3) 'significance', or 'how much the choices really affected matters' (1991: 20). Judged by these criteria, a low degree of interactivity can be characterized by the fact that the user seldom can or must act, has only a few choices available, and choices that make only slight difference in the overall outcome of things. On the other hand, a high degree of interactivity is characterized by the user having the frequent ability to act, having many choices to choose from, choices that significantly influence the overall outcome—'just like in real life', she adds (20).[13] Laurel doesn't provide a graphic illustration of the 3-dimensional continuum, but it might be

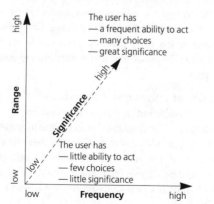

Fig. 6.
An illustration of
Brenda Laurel's
3-dimensional continuum,
consisting of: 'frequency',
'range' and 'significance'

13 In *Computers as Theatre*, 'Interactivity and Human Action', Laurel modifies this model in favor of a more intuitively based definition, as well as pointing out other dimensions of meaning (1991: 20 f.).

illustrated by Figure 6. As the description of variables indicates, this concept of interactivity moves mostly within the framework of the consultation communication pattern since 'choice' is the recurring term. Understood in this way, the concept can be said to point out three aspects of 'interactivity' within the consultation communication pattern.

4.
4-Dimensional
Concepts of
Interactivity

An example of a 4-dimensional concept of interactivity, in other words, where four dimensions of meaning constitute interactivity, can be found in the writing of Lutz Goertz, who simultaneously presents a considerably more elaborate attempt at a definition.[14] After a thorough discussion of various other attempts at definitions, Goertz isolates four dimensions, which are said to be meaningful for 'interactivity': (1) 'the degree of choices available'; (2) 'the degree of modifiability'; (3) 'the quantitative number of the selections and modifications available'; and (4) 'the degree of linearity or non-linearity'. Each of these four dimensions also makes up its own continuum which Goertz places on a scale. The higher the scale value, the greater the interactivity.

(1) The 'degree of choice available' concerns the choices offered by the media being used. There is considerable difference between, say, TV media where the receiver only chooses between various programs and perhaps the quality (sound level, brightness, etc.) of the program being received, and, on the other hand, a video game such as a flight simulator, where the user can select his position and speed in virtual space, various degrees of difficulty, opponents, points of view, perspective, etc. Goertz proposes the following scale for the continuum of choice:

0 No choice available except a decision about when reception starts and ends ...
1 Only basic changes available in the quality of the channel (such as: light/dark, high/low or fast/slow),
2 As in 1, plus the ability to choose between selections in one choice dimension; choices occur simultaneously (such as television or radio programs) ...
3 As in 2, but the selections available within the choice dimension are not time dependent (such as newspapers or video-on-demand),
4 As in 3, but there are two or more choice dimensions for a user to choose from (e.g. video games with various levels of play, forms of presentation, forms of action and story lines to choose from). (Goertz 1995: 486)

This dimension of interactivity falls within what has previously been described as the consultation communication pattern.

(2) The 'degree of modifiability' refers to the user's own ability to modify existing messages or add new content where these modifications and additions, it should be noted, are saved and stored for other users. In this dimension, there would be a great difference between TV media on the one hand, which doesn't offer any possibility of user input, and Internet news groups,

14 Another 4-dimensional concept of interactivity can be found in Dunn 1984, who operates with 350 possible combinations.

on the other hand, which open up the possibility of letting the user type and send any kind of written message which can then be read by all participants. Goertz draws up the following scale:

0   No modification possible with the exception of storing or erasing messages,
1   Manipulation or 'verfremdung' of messages is possible (e.g. through the choice of sound or color),
2   Modification to some degree of random additions, changes, or erasure of content is possible,
3   Modification possible through random additions to, changes in, or erasure of any type of content (e.g. computer word processors or graphics software, and in most media as a means of communication. (Goertz 1995: 486–7)

As the users possibility of input, the modifiability dimensions falls within what has previously been described as the conversation communication pattern.

(3) Besides the selection and modifiability dimensions the 'quantitative size of the available selections and modifications' refers to the quantitative number of selections possible within each of the available dimensions. In this dimension, for example, there will be a significant difference between the choices available by terrestrially distributed television and the many choices and modifications possible in a word processing program. Goertz's scale is as follows:

0   No choice possible,
1   Some choice available (between 2 and 10 choices) within at least one selection or modification dimension (e.g. television reception via terrestrial frequencies),
2   As in 1, plus more than 10 choices within one selection or modification dimension (a reader can choose from several hundred newspaper articles and reviews, teletext offers more than 100 pages though no other choices are available),
3   More than 10 choices available in *more than two* selection and/or modification dimensions (limited selection available as e.g. in branched choices . . .
     or: an infinite or seamless selection available from *one* selection or modification dimension respectively (e.g. video games which allow the user to write in a random name at the beginning),
4   An infinite or seamless selection available from all selection and/or modification possibilities (applies to media uses which allow participants random messages, e.g. word processing programs, but first actually for all media which function as a means of communication). (Goertz 1995: 487)

(4) Finally, the 'degree of linearity/non-linearity' functions as a measure of the user's influence on the time, tempo and progression of the reception or communication. This dimension is to capture the difference between, e.g., on the one hand a movie, where the moviegoer doesn't have any influence on when the movie starts, where, or in which order the scenes are shown; and on

the other hand a hypertext where the reader is free to determine what, when and in which order something will be read:

0   The time and order of the material is completely controlled by the information producer or the sender (e.g. television, radio, film),

1   The order of the material is determined by the information producer or sender, the user initiates the communication process and can stop or re-start it (video, records, other sound media),

2   As in 1, but the user determines the tempo of the reception (e.g. books),

3   As in 2, the user can select single elements of information which have little or no connection to each other (e.g. newspapers),

4   As in 3, the user can now retrieve elements of information which are highly connected (e.g. references in an encyclopedia or via hypertext functions on a World Wide Web site). (Goertz 1995: 487)

Both the 3rd and the 4th dimensions refer primarily to the possibility of choice and thus fall into the consultation communication pattern.

According to Goertz, the actual (interactive) media landscape could be depicted in highly differentiated ways by using these four dimensions. As a simple multiplication also demonstrates, this 4-dimensional concept of interactivity results in no fewer than 500 different combination possibilities. Obviously, such a large number of possible combinations is impossible to deal with in actual practice. A system with more categories than actual media to put in those categories (where the map is bigger than the country to be mapped) is obviously not suitable. The purpose of constructing typologies or systems is to reduce the complexity, not to increase it. Aside from that, Goertz fails to observe one of his own premises. One of the fundamental preconditions specified is that the various interactive dimensions must be selective but must not contradict themselves. As the above shows, the definition and scale for the 3rd dimension the 'quantitative number of selections and modifications available' can't help but conflict with the two first dimensions which also apply to 'selection' and 'modification' possibilities, just as the 4th dimension the 'degree of linearity/non-linearity' also expresses a certain aspect of the 'selection' dimension. This redundancy appears to be symptomatic when Goertz graphically illustrates the dimensions by means of 21 specific contemporary uses of media. In practice, only the first two dimensions, represented as 'selection' and 'modification' respectively are used. The resulting 2-dimensional matrix is shown in Figure 7.[15]

Among many other things, this chart can be used to show that there are media which give the user a high degree of modifiability but a low degree of choice (such as e-mail) and, on the contrary, there are other media which give the user a low degree of modifiability but a very high degree of choice (such as multi-channel TV, pay-per-view, Gopher, World Wide Web). In

---

15 It should be noted that in another effort Goertz does establish an index or measurement of interactivity based on all four dimensions. This is a so-called 'sum-index' which results from scale values for each of the four dimensions simply being added together.

Selection possibilities/ modification possibilities	0	1	2	3	4
0	Cinema Book: novel		Television, terrestrial TV cable TV radio pay-per-view	Newspapers videotext Book: non-fiction	Information via online-service VR-walk-through, e.g. virtual museum
1					
2				Home-banking	Video game
3		E-mail		Mailbox	VR-walk through, e.g. office arrangements CONVERSATION Electronic word-processing TELEPHONE VIDEO-CONFERENCE

Fig. 7. L. Goertz's placement of 21 specific media uses based on the dimensions 'degree of selections available' and 'degree of modifiability' (1995: 489).

this case as well, classical broadcast media such as radio and television are judged to have a certain—relatively low—measure of interactivity. And once again, media which use interpersonal communication (in other words, conversational media) are considered to have the highest degree of interactivity.

5. N-Dimensional Concepts of Interactivity

Finally, there are concepts of interactivity which operate with more than four dimensions, only one of which will be dealt with here. In an article from 1989, 'Implications of New Interactive Technologies for Conceptualizing Communication', Carrie Heeter starts by acknowledging the changes in new media technologies. Changes which according to the author necessitate a fundamental reconceptualization of the traditional communication models and understanding used in communication research. The author especially points at 'increased interactivity' as 'a primary distinction of new technologies', and proposes to understand interactivity in relation to communication technologies as 'a multidimensional concept', where six such 'dimensions of interactivity' (211) are defined.

The 1st dimension, also called 'selectivity', concerns, '*the extent to which users are provided with a choice of available information*' (222);

The 2nd dimension concerns '*the amount of effort users must exert to access information*' (223);

The 3rd dimension concerns '*the degree to which a medium can react responsively to a user*' (223);

The 4th dimension concerns '*the potential to monitor system use*' (224), understood as a form of feedback that automatically and continuously registers all user behavior while on the media system;

The 5th dimension concerns '*the degree to which users can add*

information to the system that a mass, undifferentiated audience can access
(224) ('many-to-many' communication).

And the 6th dimension concerns '*the degree to which a media system
facilitates interpersonal communication between specific users*' (225)
('person-to-person' communication).

An interactivity concept of this type will naturally also allow a much finer division of interactive media, but once again the many dimensions and the
high degree of complexity make it very difficult to deal with the concept on a
practical basis. (Just illustrating a 6-dimensional graph leads to considerable
difficulties.) It also becomes apparent that a number of the dimensions
listed—as with Goertz—are not exclusive, but have a tendency to overlap
each other. For example, there will be a fluid boundary between a user's ability to add information to the system (5th dimension) and several users ability to communicate with each other (6th dimension). The system's ability to
monitor users (4th dimension) will be connected with its ability to respond
sensitively (3rd dimension). The number of choices available (1st dimension) will unavoidably influence efforts to access the system (2nd dimension). This also implies that while the 5th dimension ('ease of adding
information') and the 6th dimension ('facilitation of interpersonal communication') largely cover what has been called the conversation communication pattern, the 3rd dimension ('responsiveness') and 4th dimension
('monitoring of information use') are related to what has been called the registration communication pattern; and the 1st dimension ('choice available')
and 2nd dimension ('effort users must exert') fall into the consultation communication pattern.

At the End of the Trail?

One possible and reasonably risk-free conclusion from this long tracking effort, might well be that the concept of interactivity (as well as the concept of
interaction) is outrageously complex and has a long list of very different, specific variations. But it would be unsatisfactory to stop this tracking session
with such a disappointing conclusion. In order to arrive at a more satisfactory narrative closure of our quest, a final attempt will therefore be made to
suggest a more suitable concept of interactivity, based on the preceding presentations and discussions of the concept. Due to a lack of space, however, it
will only be a brief suggestion.[16]

As indicated above there are good reasons to (re)establish a conceptual
distinction between the concept of interaction and the concept of interactivity. Without being able to go into a detailed argumentation in this
context, it would be expedient to retain the concept of 'interaction' in its
original, strong sociological sense to refer to 'actions of two or more
individuals observed to be mutually interdependent' (but not mediated
communication), and to use the concept of 'interactivity' to refer to media
use and mediated communication. Here derived concepts such as 'para-
social interaction'—or perhaps even better 'social para-interaction'—may

[16] For a more detailed presentation, see Jensen (forthcoming).

cover communication in media which in some way simulates interpersonal interaction.

The above review of the various concepts of interactivity has pointed out, among other things, the inappropriateness of definitions which are based too rigidly on specific historic technologies. It has also pointed out the inappropriateness of defining interactivity via a prototype or as criteria. A definition as a continuum appears to be more appropriate, and at least more flexible, in relation to the many varied levels of interactivity, the many differing technologies and rapid technological developments. It has also become clear that there are different forms of interactivity, which cannot readily be compared or covered by the same formula. There appears to be a particular difference in interactivity which consists of a choice from a selection of available information content; interactivity which consists of producing information via input to a system, and interactivity which consists of the system's ability to adapt and respond to a user. It might, therefore, be appropriate to operate with different—mutually independent—dimensions of the concept of interactivity. As it may have been apparent from the beginning, or has at least continually been made apparent by this review, the various important aspects of the concept of interactivity can to a great extent be reduced to four dimensions which can be understood using the communication patterns: transmission, consultation, conversation and registration.

Based on this understanding interactivity may be defined as: *a measure of a media's potential ability to let the user exert an influence on the content and/or form of the mediated communication.* This concept of interactivity can be divided up into four sub-concepts or dimensions which could be called:

1. *Transmissional interactivity*—a measure of a media's potential ability to let the user choose from a continuous stream of information in a one way media system without a return channel and therefore without a possibility for making requests (e.g. teletext, near-video-on-demand, be-your-own-editor, multi-channel systems, datacasting, multicasting).

2. *Consultational interactivity*—a measure of a media's potential ability to let the user choose, by request, from an existing selection of pre-produced information in a two-way media system with a return channel (video-on-demand, on-line information services, CD-ROM encyclopedias, FTP, WWW, Gopher, etc.)

3. *Conversational interactivity*—a measure of a media's potential ability to let the user produce and input his/her own information in a two-way media system, be it stored or in real time (video conferencing systems, news groups, e-mail, mailing lists, etc.).

4. *Registrational interactivity*—a measure of a media's potential ability to register information from and thereby also adapt and/or respond to a given user's needs and actions, whether they be the user's explicit choice of communication method or the system's built-in ability to automatically 'sense' and adapt (surveillance systems, intelligent agents, intelligent guides or intelligent interfaces, etc.).

The difference between consultational and registrational interactivity is thus the difference between the user's choice of information content and the media system's choice of, or adaptation to, a method of communication, in other words, the *way* in which the communication system functions.

Since transmissional and consultational interactivity both concern the availability of choice—respectively with and without a request—it is possible

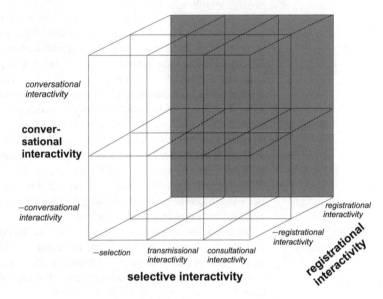

Fig. 8.
The 'cube of interactivity':
a 3-dimensional represen-
tation of the dimensions of
interactivity

to represent them within the same (selection) dimension. The four types of interactivity can then be presented in a 3-dimensional graphic model—an 'interactivity cube'—as attempted in Figures 8 and 9, which in this form results in 12 different types of interactive media.

So this is where the trail ends, for the moment. Not a dead end, but not the complete resolution of our quest either, in the sense of finding the ultimate definition for 'interactivity'. Instead, this is a temporary and contemporary attempt at synthesizing a conceptual construction. Perhaps, more importantly, this is a contribution toward a hopefully greater understanding of the meaning of the concept of 'interactivity' in media and communication studies, and the importance of media and communication studies to the meaning of the concept of 'interactivity'.

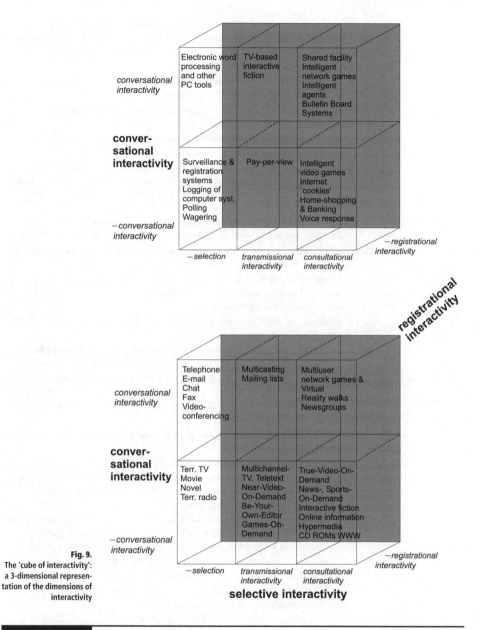

Fig. 9.
The 'cube of interactivity':
a 3-dimensional represen-
tation of the dimensions of
interactivity

References BORDEWIJK, JAN L. and BEN VAN KAAM, 1986: 'Towards a new classification of
TeleInformation Services', in *Inter Media*, vol. 14, nr. 1.

CAREY, JOHN, 1989: 'Interactive media', in *International Encyclopedia of
Communications*, New York: Oxford University Press.

CORNER, JOHN and JEREMY HAWTHORN (eds.): *Communication Studies. An
Introductory Reader*, London: Edward Arnold.

DUNCAN, STARKEY, Jr., 1989: 'Interaction, Face-to-Face', in *International Encyclopedia
of Communications*, New York: Oxford University Press.

DUNN, ROBERT M., 1984: 'The Importance of Interaction', in *Computer Graphics World*, June.

DURLAK, JEROME T., 1987: 'A Typology for Interactive Media', in Margaret L. McLaughlin (ed.): *Communication Yearbook* 10, Newbury Park: Sage publications.

FELDMAN, T., 1991: *Multimedia in the 90s*, British National Bibliography Research Fund Report 54, London 1991.

GOERTZ, LUTZ, 1995: 'Wie interaktiv sind Medien? Auf dem Weg zu einer Definition von Interaktivität', in *Rundfunk und Fernsehen*, 4/1995.

GUEDJ, R. A. *et al.* (eds.) 1980: *Methodology of Interaction*, North-Holland Publishing Company.

HAYKIN, RANDY (ed.), 1994: *Multimedia Demystified. A Guide to the World of Multimedia from Apple Computer*, Inc., New York: Random House.

HEETER, CARRIE, 1989: 'Implications of New Interactive Technologies for Conceptualizing Communication', in Jerry L. Salvaggio and Jennings Bryant (eds.): *Media Use in the Information Age: Emerging Patterns of Adoption and Consumer Use*, Hillsdale, New Jersey.

HORTON, DONALD, and R. RICHARD WOHL, 1956: 'Mass Communication and Para-social Interaction. Observations on Intimacy at a Distance', in: *Psychiatry* 19.

—— 1997: 'Massekommunikation og parasocialt interaktion: Et indlæg om intimitet på afstand', in *MedieKultur*, nr. 26.

ISER, WOLFGANG, 1989 (org. 1980): 'Interaction between text and reader', in John Corner and Jeremy Hawthorn (eds.): *Communication Studies. An Introductory Reader*, London: Edward Arnold.

JÄCKEL, MICHAEL, 1995: 'Interaktion, Soziologische Anmerkungen zu einem Begriff', in *Rundfunk und Fernsehen*, 4/1995.

JENSEN, JENS F., 1995: *Multimedier og teknologiudvikling*. Rapport udarbejdet for Statsministeriets Medieudvalg, Statsministeriet/Medieudvalget, København.

—— 1996a: 'Interaktivt TV.—"Coming soon at a screen near you" ', in *Fjernsyn i forvandling, K&K*, nr. 80, Medusa.

—— 1996b: *Interaktivt TV*, Arbejdspapir fra forskningsprojektet TV's æstetik, nr. 12, Aarhus.

—— 1996c: *Mapping Interactive Television*, Arbejdspapir fra forskningsprojektet TV's æstetik, nr. 15, Aarhus.

—— 1996d: *Mapping Interactive Television. A New Media Typology for Information Traffic Patterns on the Superhighway to the Home*, paper to' 'Interactive Television 1996', The Superhighway through the Home? A World Conference Dedicated to Interactive Television', University of Edinburgh, Scotland.

—— 1996e: *Mapping the Web. A Media Typology for Information Traffic Patterns on the Internet Highway*, in Herman Mauer (ed.): *Proceedings of WebNet 96. World Conference of the Web Society*, San Francisco (Proceedings, CD-ROM, WWW).

—— 1997a: 'Interaktivitet—på sporet af et nyt begreb i medie- og kommunikationsforskningen', in *MedieKultur*, nr. 26.

—— 1997b: 'Vejkort til Informationsmotorvejen. En medietypologi for informationstrafikmønstre på Internet', in *MedieKultur*, nr. 27.

—— 1997c: ' "Interactivity"—Tracking a New Concept', in Suave Lobodzinski and Ivan Tomek (eds.) *Proceedings of WebNet 97—World Conference of the WWW, Internet & Intranet*, Toronto: Canada (proceedings, CD-ROM, WWW).

—— (red.), 1998a (forthcoming): *Multimedier, Hypermedier, Interaktive Medier*, (FISK-serien 3), Aalborg: Aalborg Universitetsforlag.

—— 1998b (forthcoming): 'Interaktion & Interaktivitet', in Jens F. Jensen (ed.): *Multimedier, Hypermedier, Interaktive medier* (FISK-serien 3), Aalborg: Aalborg Universitetsforlag.

—— 1998c: 'Roadmap of the Information Highway', Working Paper from the project 'The Aesthetics of Television', Aarhus, Denmark: University of Aarhus, Department of Information and Media Studies.

KANTROWITZ, BARBARA et al., 1993: 'An Interactive Life', in Newsweek, d. 31. May.

KRAPPMANN, LOTHAR, 1989: 'Interaktion', in Günter Endruweit & Gisela Trommsdorff (eds.): Wörterbuch der Soziologie, band 2, Stuttgart.

LAMBERT, STEVE, and JANE SALLIS (eds.), 1987: CD-I and Interactive Videodisc Technology, Howard W. Sams and Co.

LAUREL, BRENDA, 1986: 'Interface as Mimesis', in D. A. Norman and S. Draper (eds.): User Centered System Design: New Perspectives on Human-Computer Interaction, Hillsdale: Lawrence Erlbaum.

—— 1990: 'Interface Agents: Metaphors with Character', in Brenda Laurel (ed.): The Art of Human-Computer Interface Design, Reading, Mass.: Addison-Wesley.

—— 1991: Computers as Theatre, Reading, Mass.: Addison-Wesley.

McQUAIL, DENIS, 1987: Mass Communication Theory. An Introduction, London: Sage Publications.

—— 1986: 'Is Media Theory Adequate to the Challenge of New Communications Technologies?', in Marjorie Ferguson (ed.): New Communication Technologies and the Public Interest. Comparative Perspectives on Policy and Research, London.

MILLER, ROCKEY (ed.), 1988: Videodisc and Related Technologies: A Glossary of Terms, The Videodisc Monitor.

Newsweek, d. 31. May, 1993.

O'SULLIVAN et al. (1994): Key Concepts in Communication and Cultural Studies, London: Routledge.

PAVLIK, JOHN V. (1996): New Media and the Information Superhighway, Boston: Allyn and Bacon.

POWELL, BILL et al., 1993: 'Eyes on the Future', in: Newsweek, d. 31. May.

QUARTERMAN, JOHN S., 1996: User Growth of the Internet and of the Matrix, http://www.mids.org/mn/605/usergrow.html (også publiceret i Matrix News 6 (5), May 1996)

—— 1997: 1997 Users and Hosts of the Internet and the Matrix, http://www.mids.org

—— and SMOOTH CARL-MITCHELL, 1994: What is the Internet, Anyway?, http://www.mids.org/what.html (også publiceret i Matrix News, 4 (8), August 1994).

RAFAELI, SHEIZAF, 1988: 'Interactivity. From New Media to Communication', in Robert P. Hawkins, John M. Wiemann, and Suzanne Pingree (eds.): Advancing Communication Science: Merging Mass and Interpersonal Processes, Newsbury Park.

REARDON, KATHLEEN K. and ROGERS M. EVERETT, 1988: 'Interpersonal versus Mass Media Communication. A False Dichotomy', in Human Communication Research 15.

RICE, RONALD E. (ed.), 1984: The New Media. Communication, Research and Technology, Beverly Hills: Sage Publications.

ROGERS, EVERETT M., 1986: Communication Technology. The New Media in Society, New York.

ROGERS, E. and S. CHAFFEE, 1983: 'Communication as an Academic Discipline: A Dialog', in Journal of Communication, 33.

SCHRAPE, KLAUS, 1995: Digitales Fernsehen. Marktchancen und ordnungspolitischer Regelungsdedarf, Munich.

STEUER, JONATHAN, 1992: 'Defining Virtual Reality: Dimensions Determining Telepresence', in Journal of Communication.

—— 1995: 'Defining Virtual Reality: Dimensions Determining Telepresence', in Frank Biocca and Mark R. Levy (eds.): Communication in the Age of Virtual Reality, Hillsdale, NJ: Lawrence Erlbaum Associates.

SZUPROWICZ, BOHDAN O., 1995: Multimedia Networking, New York: McGraw-Hill.

TOSCAN, CATHY, 1993: 'A Basic Survey of Interactivity in Multimedia', paper, Aalborg Universitet, upubliceret.

—— 1995: 'Networked Multimedia. An Evolution in Communication?', Thesis, Aalborg Universitet, upubliceret.

11

One Person, One Computer: The Social Construction of the Personal Computer

Klaus Bruhn Jensen

In this article Klaus Bruhn Jensen offers a framework for examining the cultural construction of communication technologies via an analysis of the personal computer in advertising. Focusing on the social contexts of media, Jensen employs the concept of a media environment to help illuminate relations between media forms and their content, particularly in relationship to the introduction of new forms like the personal computer. Jensen's discourse-analytical methodology provides an example of communications research designed to address the meanings of technology. Furthermore, Jensen's review and use of concepts from communication research, like intertextuality and symbolic diffusion, helps clarify relationships between media forms as aspects of the so-called information society.

To understand the dominating role played by technics in modern civilization, one must explore in detail the preliminary period of ideological and social preparation. Not merely must one explain the existence of the new mechanical instruments: one must explain the culture that was ready to use them and profit by them so extensively. For note this: mechanization and regimentation are not new phenomena in history: what is new is the fact that these functions have been projected and embodied in organized forms which dominate every aspect of our existence. Other civilizations reached a high degree of technical proficiency without, apparently, being profoundly influenced by the methods and aims of technics. All the critical instruments of modern technology—the clock, the printing press, the water-mill, the magnetic

From Peter Bøgh Andersen, Berit Holmqvist, and Jens F. Jensen (eds.), *The Computer as Medium* (Cambridge University Press, 1993). Research for this chapter was conducted, in part, during 1988–89, when the author was a Fellow of the American Council of Learned Societies at the Annenberg School of Communications, University of Southern California, USA. He wishes to acknowledge the assistance of the ACLS and of Bill Dutton and Everett Rogers at Annenberg. Special thanks are due to the staff of the Documentation Center at the United States Embassy, Copenhagen, Denmark.

compass, the loom, the lathe, gunpowder, paper, to say nothing of mathematics and chemistry and mechanics—existed in other cultures. The Chinese, the Arabs, the Greeks, long before the Northern European, had taken most of the first steps toward the machine. And although the great engineering works of the Cretans, the Egyptians, and the Romans were carried out mainly on an empirical basis, these peoples plainly had an abundance of technical skill at their command. They had machines; but they did not develop 'the machine.'(Mumford, 1934: 4)

In his classic study of the mechanization of modern societies, *Technics and Civilization* (1934), Lewis Mumford raised issues that remain relevant for, but largely unaddressed by communication research. One fundamental issue is how new technologies are assimilated to specific political, economic, and cultural practices in a particular historical context, thus developing into resources with a characteristic social form. In the area of information and communication technology, the process of assimilation has gone further than in most other areas of social life. It is evident that two generations after Mumford's study, the mass media have become integrated into everyday life to the extent of being in some respects constitutive of social reality. Increasingly, the audience-public can be said to live *inside* 'the machine' of mass media, in a qualitatively new form of media environment.

The social implications of this development have, to a degree, been examined from the perspective of media institutions and other infrastructures, frequently with the assumption that an information society is emerging (Nora and Minc, 1980; Porat, 1977; Toffler, 1980). However, the perspective of the audience-public on the many issues relating to that political and cultural change has been given less attention. This chapter outlines a framework for examining the social construction of communication technologies, and presents findings from a study of the introduction and reception of the personal computer in the United States.

Drawing on historical research about the rise of literacy and the development of new genres of communication, I suggest a definition of the social contexts of media use as *media environments*. The contexts of media use set the historical conditions for cultural practices in a way that is broadly analogous to the limiting function of the natural environment for economic enterprise. The introduction of new media as social resources entails a reconstruction of the total media environment, as a new division of labor among the media is negotiated. Simultaneously, 'new' media rely on 'old' media to present, position, and legitimate an unfamiliar technology to the public acting as consumers and citizens. The empirical findings from a study of computer advertisements in American general-interest magazines over a ten-year period suggest the importance of the symbolic representation of this new medium during the process of its diffusion. Of particular salience in this process has been the intertextuality of the contemporary media environment—the references in one medium to another medium, genre, or discourse. For communication theory, the findings thus highlight the need to develop a perspective on mass communication that is both historical and discursive, social and semiotic. A medium is frequently the message of another medium.

Media In and On History

Early film audiences reportedly were frightened by the representation of a train approaching on the screen. Today, audiences are said to zip, zap, and graze the television medium, seeking ever greater stimulation and fascination. It is plausible that media recipients, while drawing on decoding skills developed for older media, are continually socialized to the tasks of new media environments (Jensen, in press).

Previous studies on the development of literacy have concluded that a system of writing generally constitutes a cultural resource with important social consequences (Goody, 1987; Goody and Watt, 1963; Innis, 1972; Havelock, 1963; Lowe, 1982; Scribner and Cole, 1981; Thomas, 1989). In the sciences, alphabetic writing, in contrast to oral forms of intercourse, may ensure a systematic and cumulative form of analysis. In politics, literacy makes possible a complex governmental system by providing a resource for organization and communication across time and space. In contrast to the technological schematism of McLuhan (1962; 1964), later work has noted how the modes of communication are shaped not just by the media, but as importantly by their social and contextual uses (see also Ong, 1982). As shown by Eisenstein (1979), it was the scribal culture of the medieval monasteries, as related by Umberto Eco in *The Name of the Rose* (1981), rather than an oral culture, which was transformed by the printing press from the mid-fifteenth century. By putting an end to the monopoly of the Church on the dissemination and legitimation of knowledge, print technology became instrumental in the cultural revolutions summed up as Renaissance and Reformation.

Current developments, perhaps equally fundamental, may entail a reconstruction of the contexts of media reception. It is not only the *private* domain that has become a new form of media environment as television has brought social issues and the 'backstage' behavior (Meyrowitz, 1985) of other people into the home in a seemingly unmediated way. Also in *public* life, the total availability of mass communication particularly in urban areas has resulted in a saturation of much of social time and space with cultural products— from billboard advertising and print media read in transit, to television and recorded music in the shopping center and the workplace. If, traditionally, cultural activities have served as a time-out from everyday life, the merging of mass communication with the everyday may be producing a next-to-constant time-in—a specifically modern set of media environments.

Intertextuality

One key feature of contemporary media environments is intertextuality, defined as the structured interrelations between otherwise distinct texts, genres, and media. Originating in Julia Kristeva's structuralist theory of texts, intertextuality may be understood as 'a use of language that calls up a vast reserve of echoes from similar texts, similar phrasings, remarks, situations, characters' (Coward and Ellis, 1977: 51). The intertextual aspect of discourse appears especially prominent in mass communication, because the mass media in various ways feed on each other's content. Accordingly, whatever 'effect' one medium or discourse may produce is in principle reinforced by intertextuality.

Two main forms of intertextuality can be distinguished. *Thematic* intertextuality refers to narrative elements that are reiterated in other texts. A characteristic example would be recurring literary figures, such as the theme of Oedipus or the legend of Faust in Western arts. More important in this context is *structural* intertextuality, which refers to the configuration of texts in relation to each other as part of a particular mode or purpose of communication. A familiar example is the sequential structure of television programming, comprising also commercials and pre-announcements. Another variety of structural intertextuality is advertising and criticism about new cinema releases in print media and broadcasting. Such recycling of cultural symbols through the media carries major implications for the history and social impact of mass communication, which are only beginning to be examined by research (Bennett and Woollacott, 1987; Pearson and Uricchio, 1991).

An overlooked form of intertextuality is the portrayal of one medium in other media. In particular, mass media serve as vehicles for introducing new communication technologies for general consumption. If consumers are to spend a significant amount of money on a new medium, they must perceive it as relevant or meaningful to their specific social context. Without meaning, no effects. Without symbols, no diffusion.

Symbolic Diffusion   The terminology of symbolic diffusion is employed here to specify what is traditionally referred to as the social construction of reality (Berger and Luckmann, 1966). Within the general process of everyday interaction that serves to construct a shared, intersubjective reality and to posit its agents as social subjects, symbolic diffusion refers the specific process by which new cultural resources are disseminated and appropriated. At issue, then, is not merely the marketing question of who acquires what device, from which manufacturer, resulting in what degree of satisfaction, but the cultural question of how the technology is represented to users and non-users alike.

Earlier research has examined the diffusion of various technological innovations and, to some degree, their social consequences. While Rogers (1983) offers a general framework of such inquiry, analyses of the spread of the personal computer (Dutton, Rogers, and Jun, 1987) and earlier studies of the telephone (Pool, 1977) have offered necessary baseline information on the spread of these technologies to different user groups. The development of videotex and its apparent failure as a general service democratizing information, has been examined in several studies (see, for example, Branscomb, 1988; Charon, 1988; Noll, 1985). And computer games, being one of the most widely used genres of computer communication, have been described both in a historical perspective (Haddon, 1988) and as a discursive form similar to earlier forms of story-telling (Skirrow, 1986). Still, little attention has been given to the further significance of these and other communication technologies in the perspective of social or cultural history (but see Rogers and Larsen, 1984; also Schudson, 1991).

Recently, a number of studies have begun to examine the implications of the personal computer for the general audience-public, with Turkle (1984) representing an early and methodologically innovative approach to the cultural significance of the computer as perceived by different user groups.

Within a different, philosophical approach to computing, Heim (1987) has analyzed the possible impact of word processing on people's sense of language—the Word—as a means of expression, communication, and ultimately communion. The development of hypertext systems as a phase in the history of literacy has been examined by Bolter (1991). Furthermore, Roszak (1986) has offered a critical assessment of the promises to the public that are implied by the notion of an information society, as symbolized by the personal computer. Finally, a few studies have documented the values and meanings that have been associated with the personal computer during the course of its introduction (Pfaffenberger, 1988) and more generally the visual representation of new communication technologies in media discourses (Kaplan, 1990). So far, however, little research has examined the representation of the personal computer in other mass media and hence its symbolic diffusion.

The symbolic diffusion of the personal computer is of special interest for a critical evaluation of the current state of the information society. The promise that technologies such as the personal computer can help to democratize politics and culture, may lead the audience-public to accept the substantial, direct and indirect costs of introducing a new technological infrastructure in society. In this scenario, the personal computer represents a point of access to the greatly enhanced networks of knowledge and communication at the local, national, as well as international levels. Advertising for computers during the 1980s did indeed rely, in part, on a theme of democracy through technology. An illustrative example is found in advertisements from the Apple company that refer to the twin principles of one person, one vote, and 'one person, one computer' (*Newsweek*, Special Election Issue, November/December 1984). The personal computer, then, offers both a symbol and a touchstone of the information society.

Methodology   The empirical study examined a sample of computer advertisements from *Time* and *Newsweek* covering the period 1977–88. These general-interest news magazines were selected for analysis because, in the United States, they are perhaps the closest approximation to a national press (Gans, 1979: xi). In addition to choosing media that reach a wide segment of the American public, one aim of the analysis was to explore the discursive forms employed by an 'old' print medium to represent a 'new' electronic and increasingly visual medium to prospective users. Print media remain an important, but somewhat overlooked constituent of contemporary media environments.

All issues of *Newsweek* and *Time* from the years 1977, 1981, 1984, and 1988 were included in the analysis. These years may be taken as strategic junctures in the life of the personal computer. Taking the introduction of the Apple II in 1977 as the point of departure, the analysis centers on the period starting four years later in 1981 (the year of the introduction of the IBM PC) and ending in 1984 (the introduction of the Macintosh), while adding another year sample taken four years later in 1988. The main advantage of the sample is that it facilitates a characterization of the long waves of symbolic diffusion, which might be lost in other forms of sampling—for example, a selection of magazines from a few weeks in each consecutive year of the entire period. The present sample, further, makes possible a discourse analysis of each advertisement with reference to its context of other media discourses, including various thematic advertising campaigns during a particular period.

The criteria for selecting the advertisements served to identify any advertising for computer products or services as well as commercial messages on behalf of computer companies, such as corporate or image advertising. The purpose of this rather wide-ranging sample was to make possible a comparative analysis of the representation of, for example, the home user versus the business user and of the personal computer versus other types of computing. This called for inclusion of advertising for computer games as well as for whole computer systems aimed at business. The criteria called for exclusion, on the other hand, of computer products or services that were advertised as one element of a company's line of products within one advertisement. Among other things, this would exclude communication systems that comprise elements of computing, such as telephony. These aspects of telecommunications and computing, while relevant for a comprehensive analysis of the symbolic diffusion of informatics and telematics, fell outside the scope of this study. Moreover, advertisements placed by non-computer companies, even when referring to computers as an element of their service to customers, were excluded. Finally, printers referred to as 'typewriters' rather than 'word processors' or similar items interfacing with a 'computer' were excluded from the sample.

The intersubjectivity of the selections made by the primary researcher according to these criteria was verified by another analyst with reference to one whole issue of either *Newsweek* or *Time* from each of the four years (two issues of each magazine). Only one case in which an advertisement had been excluded by the primary researcher was disputed, while none of the ads included was questioned by the secondary analyst.

This procedure, of course, is standard in social-scientific communication research, and it offers a valuable check at the level of selecting particular types of media content. However, when it comes to describing and interpreting the discursive forms through which symbolic diffusion is accomplished, a similar procedure of coding the advertisements by a pre-defined set of categories is insufficient. For the purpose of studying how cultural and political significance is ascribed to technology, one must analyze media contents as discourses.

Discourses of   Recent communication studies have developed discourse analysis as a sys-
Advertising   tematic tool for qualitative research on the content and reception of mass communication (for surveys, see Jensen, 1987; Van Dijk, 1991). Unlike formal content analysis, which employs independent coders and decontextualized categories of analysis as part of a quantitative design, discourse analysis serves to establish the meaning of linguistic and visual elements in their discursive context. Hence, measures of contextual meaning are given priority over measures of recurrence. Counts of particular discursive structures are seldom meaningful since the explanatory value of the analytical categories appears only from specimen analyses.

The approach entails a detailed procedure of verbal and visual analysis, which may combine qualitative and quantitative modes of inquiry. First, the discourse analysis of magazine advertising is taken as the basis for assigning advertisements to a further set of categories of theoretical interpretation. These categories serve to produce a quantitative characterization of the sample of advertisements as a whole. Second, the discourse analysis is qualitative or exploratory, in the sense that it makes possible a further interpretation of key themes in the advertising discourses concerning the social uses of the personal computer. The empirical study thus also reflects on methodological issues of how qualitative and quantitative modes of inquiry may complement each other within a theoretical framework of symbolic diffusion (see also Jensen and Jankowski, 1991).

Concretely, the verbal and visual analysis of advertisements focused on three discursive categories: *actors* (the participants in events represented in advertising); *coherence* (the structure of the advertising discourse, including the functional relations between linguistic statements and images); and *implications* (assumptions serving as implicit premises of an argument or narrative). Most details of the discourse analysis cannot be reported within the scope of this chapter. The section on findings presents, first, the aggregated categorization of computer advertisements that resulted from the discourse analysis, and, second, a more detailed examination of the advertising discourses with respect to their implications concerning the social uses of the personal computer. To illustrate the nature of the discourse approach, a brief exemplary analysis will now be given of the well-known television commercial introducing the Macintosh during the Super Bowl of 1984 (see also Berger, 1989).

The commercial introduces several sets of *actors* who are in conflict, and who are contrasted with each other through their visual representation as well as their actions. Seated in a murky hall before a giant television screen showing some form of Big Brother, a congregation of skinhead zombies dressed in grey are the audience of a propagandistic political speech. Intercut with this scene, the viewer sees a young female athlete, dressed in bright colors and carrying a large hammer, who is apparently approaching the hall while being pursued by helmeted, faceless police. An important narrative device in the overall structure of the commercial is its *coherence*, particularly as established through the intercutting of scenes. This aspect of coherence serves to emphasise the several dichotomies that are acted out in the commercial as the confrontation reaches its climax. Arriving at the hall, the athlete hurls the hammer at the screen, which explodes. Among the *implications* that may thus be activated in the audience are various intertextual structures, aesthetic forms, and myths. Most obviously, an intertextual relation is established to George Orwell's *1984*, which is made explicit in the final text informing viewers that, because Apple is introducing the Macintosh, 1984 will not be like *1984*. Furthermore, the visual and narrative universe of the commercial may recall for viewers *Blade Runner* and other films by Ridley Scott, who also directed the commercial, suggesting the kind of future that the Macintosh can help them to avoid. Finally, the promise may be that, unlike the Big Brother and Goliath of computers (IBM), David (Apple) will empower the individual in the information society of 1984 and beyond, through a truly personal computer.

Findings The discourse analysis of the sample of computer advertisements from *Time* and *Newsweek* provided the foundation for a categorization of the advertising discourses with reference to a traditional model of communication. Both in the social sciences and the humanities, questions about the communication process—who / says what / to whom / in which context / through which channel and code / with what effect—tend to structure the process of inquiry. While Lasswell (1948) asks about effects in a concrete, material or *social* sense, Jakobson (1960) and other humanistic studies pose their questions with regard to *discursive* impact, meaning, or implications. The discursive mode of inquiry, then, focuses on the actual discourse of communication, examining its structure and the conditions of understanding, while reserving judgement about its further impact on individuals or cultures.

Adopting a discursive approach to computer advertising, the study framed one set of questions to the data in terms of the basic communication model: Who proffers what to whom, in which context, through which channel and code, and with what implications? Special attention is given to the questions of what types of computer products are proffered to which user groups and, above all, with what implications regarding the social uses of the personal computer. These questions are especially important for understanding the process of symbolic diffusion and social construction of new technologies. Several of the other questions call for further historical and discursive analysis, and fall outside the scope of the present study. 'In Which Context' addresses the place of the personal computer in social and cultural history, and awaits further work in media history. 'Through Which Channel' suggests the need for further work on differences between media as they serve to construct technologies socially as consumer products, while 'Through Which Code' points to a great many unresolved issues of communication theory, particularly the specificity of visual and verbal signs and their configuration in advertising and other genres of mass communication.

Who Although the senders or addressers of communication are defined, in part, by the criteria for selecting the advertisements, there are several noteworthy aspects of the computer companies that are the implied senders of the advertising discourses. First of all, while the advertising is mainly that of individual companies, some advertisements are also designed to build the legitimacy of the computer sector as a whole. This appears to be the case especially with advertising from IBM, even if some other companies refer to the services of the computer to mankind or society in general. An example of such image advertising is a recurring item from IBM showing a line-up of suspects including a computer, asserting that 'The computer didn't do it' (*Newsweek* (N), October 12, 1981; *Time* (T), September 21, 1981). The further argument is that even though computers can be misused, they cannot 'commit crimes.' Presumably, action with social consequences is the prerogative, not of anonymous technologies, but of human individuals.

Moreover, some advertisements refer to the singularity of a company and its approach to business, rather than its products and services. From 1977 onward, advertising from Wang argues that this company is 'hungrier than IBM' (T, 2/28/77). Similar references to a general competitive spirit abound in the sample. Another example is a reference to three businessmen who made their (computer) company the greatest (business) success in history (T, 3/12/84; 3/26/84). Survival and success in market terms may thus serve as an indicator of quality also in terms of the technology or service offered.

Finally, some advertisements associate a sense of community with computer companies. In some cases, the vocabulary suggests that just as the company is responsive to customer needs ('We listen'), its computers are 'compatible' with users and speak their 'language.' In other cases, advertisements appeal to the concept of family as experienced both in the workplace and the home. Computers may furnish a means of contact to various 'families,' and they may defend the larger family of the nation from external threats, notably Japan. Computers, like other communication technologies, may represent avenues to community.

What   The findings concerning the particular aspects of computing that were advertised during the four years of the study, are summarized in Tables 1a and 1b. For ease of reference, the tables also list the total number of advertisements for each year in each magazine.

The most noticeable development is the overall growth in the volume of computer advertisements in the first part of the period, followed by an equally marked decline between 1984 and 1988. This trend applies to both *Time* and *Newsweek.* However, the yearly number of items in *Time* is about twice the number in *Newsweek.* This may be explained by differences in the educational, occupational, and income characteristics of readers, which suggest that readers of *Time* are more likely to be in a position to decide to purchase a computer either for a business or for home use (Gans, 1979: 222). In addition, *Time* may be perceived as catering more to the business market, partly because of its relatively more conservative editorial line.

More interestingly, the figures suggest a process of symbolic diffusion gaining momentum from the late 1970s, climaxing in the early to mid-1980s, and subsiding in the late 1980s. This is consistent with the development of the industry reaching a climax and crisis around 1984, with the Apple company as a case in point (Sculley, 1987: chs. 8–9).

TABLE 1A. *Newsweek:* The What of Computer Advertising

	1977	1981	1984	1988
No. of items	11	48	155	70
Hardware	—	—	15	16
Software	—	—	27	—
No distinction	11	48	113	54
(Hereof word processing)	4	12	—	11

TABLE 1B. *Time:* The What of Computer Advertising

	1977	1981	1984	1988
No. of items	33	92	245	130
Hardware	—	1	27	19
Software	—	1	65	34
No distinction	33	90	153	77
(Hereof word processing)	6	27	—	9

The distinction between hardware and software appears to have been established in advertising discourse between 1981 and 1984, even if the majority of the advertisements from 1984 still do not refer exclusively to one or the other. This may be interpreted as a sign that by the mid-1980s the audience-public could be considered familiar with the basic elements of computer technology. This interpretation is supported by the fact that, despite the overall decline in advertising volume from 1984 to 1988, in *Time* the proportion of advertising making the distinction between hardware and software, relative to advertisements without this distinction, was higher in 1988 than 1984, thus suggesting a continued trend toward differentiation. The picture is complicated, however, by the total absence of software advertisements in *Newsweek* during 1988, which calls for further research.

Perhaps the most interesting suggestion of the two tables arises from the figures concerning word processing. The analysis noted whenever reference was made to the designated use of computers for word processing. The findings for both 1977 and 1981 show references to word processing in both magazines without a distinction being made between hardware and software. By 1984, as total volume increases and the hardware-software distinction appears, the references to word processing disappear from both magazines. In 1988, the references have re-appeared despite the decrease in volume. This implies that around the top of the curve of its introduction, the personal computer was constructed in advertising discourse as a 'general machine' with various social uses, including but not restricted to word processing. By contrast, 1988 may have witnessed an attempt by companies to reclaim part of their market after the concept of the general machine apparently had failed.

To Whom   A number of related conclusions are suggested by the representation of computer users in the advertisements. These findings are summarized in Tables 2a and 2b, again listing the volume of advertising.

It should be noted that the term *public* refers to the general public as affected by computers and addressed by advertising as citizens. In discourse terms, the public is addressed grammatically as an Afficative element, being affected by computers. The term *home* refers to the private user, who is potentially an Agentive using the computer for various purposes in the home context, but also as part of other social and cultural activities. *Youth* includes children and teenagers.

The first conclusion with respect to user groups is that while the number of advertisements addressed respectively to business and private users rises and falls in accordance with the general curve of symbolic diffusion already noted, the most noteworthy figure documents the growth of advertising in both magazines which is addressed to *any* prospective computer customer, irrespective of context and uses, between 1981 and 1984. This is consistent with the conclusion that the personal computer was constructed socially as a 'general machine' that could be assimilated to different uses in different sectors. The development of a home market, while significant, may have been less important, also in social and cultural terms, than the development of a market across user groups and sectors of application.

Second, of the advertisements directed specifically at the home market, a significant portion makes reference to children and youth. An important argument for introducing the personal computer into the home, as discussed further later on, has been that these groups need a computer to get ahead, or stay ahead, in the educational system and later in the job market. So-called computer literacy arguably will become a pre-condition for successful participation in many areas of social life in the information society.

TABLE 2A. *Newsweek:* Computer Advertising To Whom

	1977	1981	1984	1988
No. of items	11	48	155	70
Business	5	31	60	20
(Hereof small)	—	11	1	3
Public	6	5	2	6
Home	—	12	27	8
(Hereof youth)	—	7	19	2
No distinction	—	—	66	36

TABLE 2B. *Time:* Computer Advertising To Whom

	1977	1981	1984	1988
No. of items	33	92	245	130
Business	22	71	11	58
(Hereof small)	10	22	5	14
Public	11	7	6	7
Home	—	14	26	16
(Hereof youth)	—	3	20	12
No distinction	—	—	102	49

Third, a relatively large portion of the advertising addressed to companies makes reference to small business. Even though it was to be expected that small businesses will need small computers, the many references particularly in *Time* suggest that, in order to market small computers at all, advertising is relying on a familiar theme of a general American business ideology—namely, that small is where a business starts, not where it ends. A personal computer may become a resource for building and expanding one's own business.

Fourth and finally, the number of image advertisements directed at the general public remains at the same low level throughout the period. As is the case also with the other figures in the tables, there are no major differences between *Time* and *Newsweek* in this respect. The occasional example of such advertisements may serve to bolster the image of the computer and the companies in the eyes of the audience-public. However, the low figure also suggests that if, indeed, advertising has a general impact on the public's perception of and action vis-à-vis computers, this impact must be traced, above all, to the discourses of actual sales advertising. The entire sample of advertisements carries a variety of implications, finally, regarding the social uses of the personal computer.

With What Implications The presence of particular implications in the sample during each of the four years of the study is noted and discussed here. Rather than counting the *recurrence* of implications during each year, the discourse analysis served to identify the *occurrence* of social, political, and cultural implications at different times. The methodological assumption underlying this approach was that it is the presence or absence of implications in a specific context that may suggest the rise and fall of themes in the process of symbolic diffusion. Hence, whereas the preceding sections on 'What' and 'To Whom' have presented quantitative measures based on the discourse analysis, this section examines and interprets the qualitative categories of the discourse analysis only. (Again, differences between *Time* and *Newsweek* are negligible, and will not be commented on.)

1977 Two sets of implications can be singled out during the first year of the study. In advertisements addressed to the general *public*, computers are presented as a new technology serving the public interest. Computers can help companies and organizations to give consumers better service and to make production more efficient. More generally, information, as administered through computers, is seen as a resource enabling mankind to manage material resources better as world population continues to increase. The common theme, which becomes explicit in some advertisements, is that of 'the information age.' It is summarized in an advertisement from IBM, featuring various examples of how this company is 'helping put information to work for people' (T, 11/21/77).

The second set of implications is found in advertising addressed to *business*. Not surprisingly, computers are presented as a means to business success: 'In other words, results' (T, 4/18/77). More specifically, the means is presented as individual solutions and state of the art equipment. By contrast, low cost is referred to infrequently, and is not a prominent sales argument or theme.

The advertisements further reflect an awareness that computers must somehow be compatible with people and their work routines. This implication is developed as a key theme in advertising to all user groups during later years, but is found during 1977 in a preliminary form addressed to business. The theme of user friendliness is commonly found in references to companies and machines mastering more than one 'language,' such as a representative of one computer company speaking both English and 'medical' (T, 5/2/77). But, also for the operator of the machine, compatibility is key: 'Alice your bookkeeper,' on being introduced to a new computer system, initially thinks that her bosses have 'flipped out,' but she quickly learns how accessible that particular system is and becomes 'Alice your computer operator' (T, 11/21/77). At the same time, questions of job satisfaction are seen from the perspective of (male) management, as suggested by references to 'your' people.

1981   An important implication in the first advertisements directed at the *home* market is that computers are now accessible for everybody. The Atari company, for example, advertises 'computers for people' and proposes to 'bring the computer age home.' Furthermore, a distinction is introduced between games and other uses of the personal computer, implying that different social uses of the computer may be more or less worthy and legitimate. Thus, the producer of one video game emphasizes that it offers not only 'the excitement of a game,' but also 'the mind of a computer' (T, 11/2/81). More generally, the range of possible uses of a computer by ordinary people is emphasised, most clearly perhaps in advertising for the IBM PC that refers to both work, learning, and pleasure. In addition to programming and word processing, the personal computer is presented as a resource for planning your budget, keeping an eye on your calories, and tapping into data banks. The assumption that personal computers have become a staple of the home and family life, is summed up in a headline from IBM: 'Dad, can I use the IBM computer tonight?' (N, 11/23/81). However, during 1981 the personal computer was not yet constructed as an indispensable resource for the education of youth, even if learning was presented as one application.

The implications in advertising addressed to the general *public* remain relatively unaffected as the role of computing in other sectors grows. Computers help people and make for efficient production—for example, by saving energy. The computer's helping function is given a new dimension in an IBM advertisement reporting that some computers now have a general 'Help' button explaining the system to users (T, 10/5/81). Another development in computer advertising overall is the increasing use, compared to 1977, of slogans about the social consequences of computers. Digital: 'We change the way the world thinks.' Wang: 'Making the world more productive.' Such advertising discourse is addressed, in part, to the public as citizens, and it may contribute to the agenda for public debate about computers and hence to symbolic diffusion.

As for *business* users, the implications are in keeping with those noted for 1977. Computer companies offer state of the art service and equipment that is accessible in the user's own 'language.' There are some additional indications that because computers are now used in a variety of job functions, flexibility increasingly must be presented as a quality of the systems advertised. As mentioned in the section 'To Whom,' the spread of computers to small businesses is also a prominent theme. Moreover, with reference to intensifying competition, some advertisements during 1981 emphasise that computers are a necessary instrument in order to remain on top of things and accordingly make the right decisions. One advertisement even makes the argument that a particular computer 'works for less than the minimum wage' (T, 8/17/81). The right computer can help you avoid 'your business running you,' and in the process it may give a sense of 'freedom' (T, 6/22/81). A sense of intensified competition may also have made itself felt in the computer business, since several companies refer both to the complexity of making a decision to buy a computer system and to the need to explore the uniqueness of *their* system. Under the heading of 'How do you explain something that's never existed before?,' one advertisement suggests that it may be as difficult to explain this particular office system as it was for a cave man to explain the concept of the wheel to his fellow cave men (T, 6/8/81).

1984   At the height of the symbolic diffusion of the personal computer, 1984 was the first year when some advertising in the sample was directed to *all users*, carrying implications about its general nature. One common implication is that in the future, everybody will use personal computers; the question is which type. The Apple company made this point in its campaign for the Macintosh, arguing that this machine is for 'the rest of us' who cannot or do not want to use more complicated personal computers. And, in addition to the qualities of accessibility and flexibility noted earlier, new possibilities arguably are offered to new users by portable computers and more sophisticated software.

Two aspects of the social uses of the personal computer stand out in advertising from 1984. First, the computer is associated with success in a society that is constantly under transformation. One computer is offered to 'Today's Upward Mobile Society' (T, 1/2/84). The underlying assumption is made explicit in one advertisement for diskettes: 'Somebody has to be better than everybody else' (T, 8/13/84).

The other major implication has to do, not with success within current society, but with a possible transformation of society. One product is presented as 'The most dangerous computer in the world,' possibly leading to 'a social revolution,' because it decentralizes authority and empowers individuals to transcend time and space. This vision of a different future is associated in the text with Thomas Jefferson (T, 7/2/84). A similar, more elaborate concept of (more) democracy through technology was developed by the Apple company in their Macintosh campaign during the presidential election in late 1984: 'One person, one vote. One person, one computer' (N, November/December 84).

Other uses of the personal computer as part of a social change and emancipation arise from new types of software that 'multiply thought' (T, 7/16/84), the production of an underground newsletter (T, 12/10/84), and the application of the personal computer as a means of communication with the entire world. The 'Era 2' communications software is depicted as a means of plugging a keyboard directly into the Earth (T, 3/12/84). In this scenario, the Orwell of *1984* is proven wrong (T, 1/2/84), and the right computer system will give us 'the future without the shock' (T, 4/9/84). How that scenario relates to the other set of implications concerning personal success, is elaborated next.

The implications associated with the *home* user are similar in most respects to those noted for 1981. The personal computer has a variety of uses for the whole family, and as such it is a way for the family, in the terminology of IBM's Chaplin campaign, to plug into 'modern times.' (Interestingly, another company appropriates the Chaplin figure and suggests that IBM 'could make a tramp out of anyone' (T, 5/7/84).) Whereas adults can now take work home, the home use of the personal computer is depicted primarily as the road to educational success for the children, including preparation for college. This theme is articulated in a variety of ways throughout the sample for 1984, so that a personal computer is constructed as a necessary resource in any form of education, also with reference to equal opportunities for ethnic minorities (T, 10/1/84). The Apple company, for example, suggests that because ordinary children are kept away from computers at school by 'bully nerds,' every child needs an 'Apple' after school (T, 9/17/84).

The advertising addressed to the general *public* again refers to the computer working in the public interest, for example, by processing medical information and by bringing computing power inexpensively to the children who need it most. And readers are reminded that since it is in everybody's interest to keep information secure, 'there are rules for driving a computer, too' (T, 2/6/84). The public interest, incidentally, is defined as the American interest when a computer chip is said to be a way of meeting Japan's challenge.

Finally, also for *business* users, the implications remain largely unchanged. If computer systems are up-to-date and flexible, they will enable all levels of a business, large or small, to work together toward success. Furthermore, an employee is said to be able to 'save' his/her boss by suggesting the right software (T, 9/24/84). Pricing remains a minor consideration, even though a few companies introduce low prices as a sales argument. Humor is used, in part, to poke fun at decision-makers who still cannot make up their mind to buy a computer (now, of course, the solution to their worries is here, T, 6/4/84). And a database program is advertised as exactly what 'a big-time executive' like Santa Claus needs to keep an eye on everybody world-wide (N, 4/30/84).

1988   It is significant that the theme of social revolution has disappeared from the advertising discourses by 1988, while the theme of success remains a major implication of advertisements addressed to *all users.* Success is measured in terms of achievement, power, and survival, as suggested by the text of two advertisements: The company behind a flexible system argues that 'survival belongs not merely to the fittest, but to those who remain fittest, longest' (N, 10/17/88). And, the producer of a portable computer states that 'you can never be too powerful or too thin' (N, 5/16/88). The disappearance of the theme of social revolution will be interpreted and discussed in the conclusion.

Furthermore, some advertising now takes an aggressive approach to marketing by implying that anybody who does not (own and) use a computer is unreasonably backward. One advertisement, showing a very old typewriter, asks in the headline, 'Just how simple do word processors have to get before you begin using one?' (N, 2/29/88). Using a computer may have become a prerequisite for being a part of the good society of the information society.

A few specific social uses of computing first appear in the 1988 sample. The personal computer is associated with the work routines of the yuppie, who may use it to transcend time and space: One product is meant 'for people whose minds are at work even when their bodies aren't' (T, 7/25/88). And another computer terminal is presented as the monitor on which the (presumably male) reader will meet women when applying to a computerized dating service in AD. 2025 (N, 11/14/88). Moreover, the increasing use of the personal computer for graphic and other visual representation has become a major sales argument. Graphics may help users, for example, to do away with dull presentations. One advertisement even exclaims, with a touch of irony, but nevertheless stressing the visual potential of the personal computer: 'Move over, Michelangelo' (T, 4/11/88).

In advertising addressed to the *home* market, educational uses of the personal computer continue to be a major implication. A simple 'pre-computer' is advertised as a way to 'turn on a mind' (N, 11/7/88). However, the intensive campaign of 1984, suggesting that a computer is a necessary condition of education at any level, had subsided by 1988. Instead, it may have been assumed that the theme of computing as an educational resource had already been established, at least among important segments of the likely market for personal computers. Given this assumption, advertising could focus on additional reasons for acquiring a computer, such as its simplicity ('it works on common sense' (N, 5/23/88)), and its rapidly decreasing price. Several companies including IBM now refer to low prices as the main sales argument in some advertisements.

In image advertising to the general *public*, computers are said to produce benefits for society and profits for companies, especially as accessible and applicable systems become more widespread. Throughout the period studied, then, the advertising discourses make no distinction between the public interest and the interests of American business. Apple, for example, asserts that other companies have begun to copy their general concept of joining 'human nature and common sense' and that 'American business is reaping the benefits' (T, 11/14/88). Computer simulation can also help society avoid 'white elephants' (T, 3/21/88). In the area of news and information, similarly, the computer is seen to be serving the public interest: Under the heading of 'Once again the world is flat,' *Time* runs a campaign offering an educational version of the magazine on diskette. In the very general terms of another campaign, a company is said to 'bring us all together,' in one case with reference to black and white groups in the context of the NAACP (National Association for the Advancement of Colored People) (T, 10/31/88). Yet, this notion of cooperation is never linked to specific political ends and means, such as computing as a means of social revolution.

In *business* sector advertising, finally, the flexibility of the personal computer and its contribution to efficient production remain key themes. There are many references to the compatibility of different items, both hardware and software, within a total system of administration and communication. This is the innovative means to a familiar end: success and growth. One advertisement suggests that even if individual enterprise is necessary to start a business, expansion requires the right technology: 'Your brains built the business. Ours can expand it' (T, 4/4/88). A key requirement toward this end is control, especially because of the complexity of contemporary business organisations. One company reassures the business reader that with its computer in hand, 'being out of town no longer means being out of control' (N, 4/18/88). Interestingly, the issue of control applies across several different levels of social organization, from the level of one company to an entire industry and ultimately the nation in a world context. Control and leadership at one level may help to ensure leadership one level up. One advertisement suggests that the technology of that particular company has made an important contribution to 'the world-wide competitiveness of American manufacturing,' which is only natural, because 'we're both leaders' (T, 5/16/88). What is good for computer companies, may be good for America.

Conclusion

In summary, the discourse analysis and the categorization of magazine advertising support the conclusion that the personal computer was constructed socially as a 'general machine' with diverse social uses for many different user groups within the prospect of an emerging information society. The process of diffusion reached a climax and crisis around 1984. It is significant that, increasingly, the same sales advertising was addressed to all user groups and, further, that the image of companies also was built primarily through sales advertising.

The implications or themes that were identified in the discourse analysis, initially refer to the computer both as an increasingly accessible service for the general public, sometimes with explicit reference to the notion of the information society, and as a source of business profits. The public interest is presented as equal to the interests of business in general and American business in particular. In the course of the period examined, the information society becomes an implicit premise of the advertisements, which instead begin to detail the specific uses of the personal computer by individuals, especially its status as an indispensable resource for education and information, as opposed to games and other entertainment genres.

One of the most interesting implications is posed by the rise and fall of the theme of social revolution. Whereas the themes of individual success and social revolution appeared side by side during 1984, only the more conventional theme in the context of American culture—namely individual success—was found during 1988. This may be interpreted to mean that during a phase of introduction, new communication technologies come to represent a social imagination that normally remains unarticulated in media discourses. Symbolic diffusion, accordingly, can be seen as a process of projecting social utopias that may resonate with the audience-public onto new technologies. These utopias may be the positive counterpart of the dystopias envisioned by the moral panics to which new media traditionally also give rise. When the first phase of introduction is over, or when the promise of utopia is seen not to materialize in social practice or in the experience of the audience-public, advertising and similar discourses may re-emphasise more conventional, consensual themes, depending of course on other developments in the given social and historical context. Nevertheless, such utopias remain a source of appeal and fascination that may be tapped during later phases of diffusion. Even though almost a decade has passed since *Time* chose, not a Person of the Year, but the computer as the Machine of the Year (T, 1/3/83), the question of whether the computer may become a general machine for everybody to use, still produces magazine cover stories (*Business Week*, September 10, 1990).

This chapter has presented a study of the social construction of the personal computer in advertising discourses. The empirical findings have substantiated the importance of studying also the symbolic or semiotic aspects of the diffusion of new communication technologies. The methodological approach, furthermore, has pointed to the specific relevance of discourse analysis as a means of integrating qualitative and quantitative modes of inquiry regarding media. In particular, more research on the personal computer as a medium is called for from the perspective of discourse analysis and semiotics (see also Andersen, 1990). Finally, the theoretical framework, focusing on media environments that are characterized by intertextuality, has suggested the need to examine the interaction and the division of labor between media in a specific historical and cultural context. Since one important site of the interaction between media is the audience, further empirical research on media environments should include not just media discourses, but also the reception and social uses of new media. The symbolic diffusion of new media ultimately is enacted by the audience-public in everyday contexts of communication and social action.

References

ANDERSEN, P. BØGH. (1990). *A Theory of Computer Semiotics.* Cambridge: Cambridge University Press.

BENNETT, T. and WOOLLACOTT, J. (1987). *Bond and Beyond,* London: Methuen.

BERGER, A. (1989). 1984—The Commercial. In *Political Culture and Public Opinion* (pp. 175–86), ed. A. Berger. New Brunswick, NJ: Transaction Publishers.

—— and LUCKMANN, T. (1966). *The Social Construction of Reality.* London: Allen Lane.

BOLTER, J. (1991). *Writing Space.* Hillsdale, NJ: Lawrence Erlbaum Associates.

BRANSCOMB, A. (1988). Videotext: Global Progress and Comparative Policies. *Journal of Communication, 38,* 50–59.

CHARON, J. (1988). Videotex: From Interaction to Communication. *Media, Culture & Society, 9,* 301–32.

COWARD, R. and ELLIS, J. (1977). *Language and Materialism.* London: Routledge Kegan Paul.

DUTTON, W., ROGERS, E., and JUN, S. (1987). Diffusion and Social Impacts of Personal Computers. *Communication Research, 14,* 219–50.

ECO, U. (1981). *The Name of the Rose.* London: Picador.

EISENSTEIN, E. (1979). *The Printing Press as an Agent of Change.* London: Cambridge University Press.

GANS, H. (1979). *Deciding What's News.* New York: Vintage.

GOODY, J. (1987). *The Interface Between the Written and the Oral.* Cambridge: Cambridge University Press.

GOODY, J. and WATT, I. (1963). The Consequences of Literacy. *Comparative Studies in Society and History, 5,* 304–45.

HADDON, S. (1988). Electronic and Computer Games. *Screen, 29,* 52–73.

HAVELOCK, E. (1963). *Preface to Plato.* Oxford: Blackwell.

HEIM, M. (1987). *Electric Language.* New Haven: Yale University Press.

INNIS, H. (1972). *Empire and Communications.* Toronto: University of Toronto Press.

JAKOBSON, R. (1960). Linguistics and Poetics. In *Selected Writings* (vol. 3, pp. 18–51), ed. S. Rudy. The Hague: Mouton, 1981.

JENSEN, K. B. (1987). News as Ideology: Economic Statistics and Political Ritual in Television Network News. *Journal of Communication, 37,* 8–27.

—— (in press). Print Cultures and Visual Cultures: A Critical Introduction to Research on New Media Environments. In *Approaches to Mass Communication,* ed. J. Stappers. London: Sage.

—— JANKOWSKI, N. W. eds. (1991). *A Handbook of Qualitative Methodologies for Mass Communication Research.* London: Routledge.

KAPLAN, S. (1990). Visual Metaphors in the Representation of Communication Technology. *Critical Studies in Mass Communication, 7,* 37–47.

LASSWELL, H. (1948). The Structure and Function of Communication in Society. In *Reader in Public Opinion and Communication* (pp. 178–90), eds. B. Berelson, M. Janovitz (1966), Glencoe, Ill.: The Free Press.

LOWE, D. (1982). *History of Bourgeois Perception. Chicago: University of Chicago Press.*

McLUHAN, M. (1962). *The Gutenberg Galaxy.* Toronto: University of Toronto Press.

—— (1964). *Understanding Media.* New York: McGraw-Hill.

MEYROWITZ, J. (1985). *No Sense of Place.* New York: Oxford University Press.

MUMFORD, L. (1934). *Technics and Civilization.* London: Routledge.

NOLL, A. M. (1985). Videotex: Anatomy of a Failure. *Information & Management, 9,* 99–109.

NORA, S. and MINC, A. (1980). *The Computerization of Society.* Cambridge, Mass.: MIT Press.

ONG, W. (1982). *Orality and Literacy.* London: Methuen.

PEARSON, R. and URICCHIO, W. eds. (1991). *The Many Lives of the Batman.* London: British Film Institute.

PFAFFENBERGER, B. (1988). The Social Meaning of the Personal Computer: Or, Why the Personal Computer Revolution Was No Revolution. *Anthropological Quarterly, 61,* 39–47.

POOL, I. ed. (1977). *The Social Impact of the Telephone.* Cambridge, Mass.: MIT Press.

PORAT, M. (1977). *The Information Economy: Definition and Measurement.* Washington, DC: Government Printing Office.

ROGERS, E. (1983). *Diffusion of Innovations* (3rd edn.). New York: The Free Press.

—— LARSEN, J. (1984). *Silicon Valley Fever.* New York: Basic Books.

ROSZAK, T. (1986). *The Cult of Information.* New York: Pantheon.

SCHUDSON, M. (1991). Historical Approaches to Communication Studies. In *A Handbook of Qualitative Methodologies for Mass Communication Research* (pp. 175–189), eds. K. B. Jensen and N. W. Jankowski. London: Routledge.

SCRIBNER, S. and COLE, M. (1981). *The Psychology of Literacy.* Cambridge, Mass.: Harvard University Press.

SCULLEY, J. (1987). *Odyssey: Pepsi to Apple.* Glasgow: Fontana.

SKIRROW, G. (1986). Hellivision: An Analysis of Video Games. In *High Theory/Low Culture* (pp. 115–142), ed. C. MacCabe. New York: St Martin's Press.

THOMAS, R. (1989). *Oral Tradition and Written Record in Classical Athens.* Cambridge: Cambridge University Press.

TOFFLER, A. (1980). *The Third Wave.* New York: Bantam.

TURKLE, S. (1984). *The Second Self.* New York: Simon & Schuster.

van DIJK, T. (1991). The Interdisciplinary Study of News as Discorse. In *A Handbook of Qualitative Methodologies for Mass Communication Research* (pp. 108–120), eds. K. B. Jensen and N. W. Jankowski. London: Routledge.

12

Who Will We Be in Cyberspace?

Langdon Winner

In this essay Langdon Winner focuses on relations and conditions that are shaping the form of information society. Asking 'Who will we be in cyberspace?', Winner probes selfhood and civic culture in the face of (yet another) period of significant technological and social change. Focusing on the effects of automation and information technology on society as a whole, Winner offers social criticism both of the manner in which information technology has been introduced into society and of the forms of interaction it is changing and spawning. In particular he argues that impudent marketing strategies applied during the American invention of consumerism in the early part of the twentieth century are being repeated in the present technological renovation of society, with a range of confounding consequences. In his challenge to computer professionals to 'help a democratic populace explore new identities and horizons of a good society', we are reminded of the fact that the digital future is still malleable, and still very much under development, in need of leadership committed to values that carry beyond the short-term vision of market economics.

TO THOSE WHO view America from other parts of the world, it must sometimes seem that we are a compulsively restless people, continually reinventing ourselves, renovating our ways of living at the drop of a hat. There seems to be no idea too extravagant, no project too far fetched that some sizable segment of the populace won't take up, try it out, see how it works. Birthplace of new ideas, discoveries, practices, styles, gadgets, and institutions, the United States has gained renown as a laboratory for the exploration of human identities and relationships that later spread to other parts of the globe.

The propensity to personal and social reinvention goes back to the earliest days of our national experience. In the middle eighteenth century, it seemed likely that the British monarchy and a stable monarchical way of life in the American colonies would endure forever. Rooted in notions of hierarchy, inequality, patriarchy, and highly structured relations between patrons and clients, monarchy gave people's lives meaning and coherence. But efforts to sustain this pattern sparked discontent and eventual revolt. The colonists' successful war against King George III was also a revolution in political

From *The Information Society*, 12 (1996).

culture, one that overthrew monarchy as a tightly woven fabric of human relations.

During their turn at the helm, leaders of the uprising, the founding fathers, did their best to create a new society, building political, legal, and economic institutions based on models adapted from the ancient republics. Individual liberty and consent of the governed became the guiding principles. But the political institutions of the republican system were to depend on the guidance of a small group of enlightened, virtuous men, people with great souls and abilities, an arrangement that many Americans found disagreeable. It did not take long, therefore, for the republican conception of social and political relations to itself be challenged by the proliferation of rules, roles, and relations far more democratic in character. By the early nineteenth century, Americans were again busily self-transforming, affirming that the promise of the country was for the mass of common working people to achieve material prosperity and genuine self-government (Wood, 1992).

In sum, a lifetime that stretched from 1750 to 1820 would have undergone a sequence of three radically different ways of defining what society was about, three ways of defining who a person was and where a person stood in the larger order of things. I call attention to this segment of American history to recall the fact that times of rapid transformation are not new to us. Today's zealots for the information age and cyberspace often insist that we are confronted with circumstances totally unprecedented, circumstances that require rapid transformation of society. That may be true in some respects. But it is also true that we Americans are past masters in reinventing ourselves and sometimes proceed thoughtfully to good effect.

Since the middle nineteenth century, episodes of person and social transformation have focused as much upon people's relationship to technological systems as they have to political institutions. By now it is a familiar story: To invent a new technology requires that (in some way or another) society also invents the kinds of people who will use it; older practices, relationships, and ways of defining people's identities fall by the wayside; new practices, relationships, and identities take root. From that standpoint, as technological devices and systems are being introduced, it is important that those who care about the future of society to go beyond questions about the utility of new devices and systems, beyond even questions about economic consequences. One must also ask:

1. Around these instruments, what kinds of bonds, attachments, and obligations are in the making?
2. To whom or to what are people connected or dependent upon?
3. Do ordinary people see themselves as having a crucial role in what is taking shape?
4. Do people see themselves as competent, able to make decisions?
5. Do they feel that their voices matter in making decisions that will affect family, workplace, community, nation?
6. Do they feel themselves to be fairly treated?

These are issues about conditions that sustain selfhood and civic culture, issues that should always be addressed as technological innovations emerge.

If we limit our attention to powerful technical applications, their uses and market prospects, we tend to ignore what may be the single most consequential feature of technological change, the shaping of the conditions that affect people's sense of who they are and why they live together.

In our time the most important occasion for addressing such questions is the digital transformation of an astonishingly wide range of material artifacts interwoven with social practices. In one location after another, people are saying in effect: Let us take what exists now and restructure or replace it in digital format. Let's take the bank teller, the person sitting behind the counter with little scraps of paper and an adding machine, and replace it with an ATM accessible 24 hours a day. Let's take analog recording and the vinyl LP and replace it with the compact disc in which music is encoded as a stream of digital bits. Or let's take the classroom with the teacher, blackboard, books, and verbal interchange and replace it with materials presented in computer hardware and software and call it 'interactive learning' (as if earlier classrooms lacked an interactive quality). In case after case, the move to computerize and digitize means that many preexisting cultural forms have suddenly gone liquid, losing their former shape as they are retailored for computerized expression. As new patterns solidify, both useful artifacts and the texture of human relations that surround them are often much different from what existed previously. This process amounts to a vast, ongoing experiment whose long-term ramifications no one fully comprehends.

The opportunities and challenges presented by digital liquification have generated great waves of enthusiasm. Entrepreneurs are busily at work creating new products and services. Organizational innovators are experimenting with all kinds of computer-mediated collaborative work. Artists, even ones highly skeptical of information technology's overall effects, are exhilarated by the new varieties of aesthetic expression that have become available in computing and telecommunications. It is no surprise that the widespread rapture about computing has achieved ideological expression as well. The old bromides of Alvin Toffler's simplistic wave theory of history, barely fizzing a couple of years ago, have received a new injection of seltzer in the right-wing manifesto, 'Cyberspace and the American Dream: A Magna Carta for the Knowledge Age' (Dyson *et al.*, 1994). In this and similar paeans to the digital age, there is a rekindling of the millennial expectations that often arise during times of technological and social change, accompanied by the ill-founded hopes of 'mythinformation,' for example, the expectation that the spread of information machines is somehow inherently democratic and that no one needs to lift a finger to achieve democratization and create a good society (Winner, 1986).

But along with the excitement and sense of limitless possibilities arise some serious misgivings. As the sweeping digital liquification of social practices and institutions proceeds, one sees closely associated processes of economic liquidation that erode the former livelihoods of many working class and middle class people. As jobs and activities and organizational structures undergo digital transformation, structures that were formerly funded are now defunded, liquidated as capital takes the opportunity to move elsewhere. In businesses, universities, government agencies, and other organizations, the connection between the introduction of new computing systems and widespread announcements of layoffs and downsizing seems obvious. Digital liquification has become the cultural solvent that enables financial and organization liquidation. In this process, whole vocations—secretaries, phone operators, bank tellers, postal clerks—have been eliminated or abolished or drastically reduced. During the two decades in which automation and information have entered their workplaces, the level of real wages for much of the population has declined. The erosion of income is no longer limited to blue collar and clerical workers. Recent manpower studies by the American Association of Engineering Societies show a decline in the real wages of technical professionals as well (Bell, 1995). Firms are laying off high-level, high-salaried senior managers and technical staff, hiring younger, cheaper workers right out of college. The infomated knowledge base of organizations provides a stable framework from which leaders of the firm can experiment with audacious programs in restructuring and reengineering.

Gurus on the business seminar circuit—Tom Peters, Daniel Burrus, Michael Hammar, James Champy, and the like—prefer to see these upheavals as an exhilarating challenge. Thus, Peters advises people in the throes of career change to embrace 'perpetual adolescence' because 'we all need to be in the leaping business these days' (Peters, 1994, pp. 301 and 308). Other observers describe these developments as potentially cataclysmic for much of the population, as the 'end of work' and 'end of career' present society with conditions for which it is ill prepared (Bridges, 1994; Rifkin, 1995; Glassner, 1994). Whatever one's anticipations on that score may be, it is certainly true that in our time some basic conditions of human identity and association are being powerfully redefined. Who will we become as such developments run their course? What kind of society and political order will emerge?

Rather than seek guidance on these matters from today's giddy manifestoes of cyberspace, perhaps we should consider relevant chapters in our own history, chapters in which technological transformation involved profound alterations in self and society, periods in which momentous choices about the future were up for grabs. Of particular relevance, in my view, are several recent studies by historians and social scientists that have tried to identify what is distinctive about human selfhood in what came to be called modern, industrial society. A number of scholars in widely different fields— David Hounshell (1984), Terry Smith (1993), Jeffrey Meikle (1979), David Noble (1977), Adrian Forty (1986), Ruth Schwarz Cowan (1983), Dolores Hayden (1981), Roland Marchand (1985), David Nye (1990), David Harvey (1989), and others—have looked at the first half of twentieth century America, noticing such developments as the creation of the Ford assembly line, the spread of scientific management, the development of large, long linked systems in electricity, water supply, transit, telephone, radio, and television, seeking to explain how they achieved the form they did, how they were received by the populace as a whole, how the rise of the consumer economy with its appliances and other goods came to be defined as necessary for the good life, and how associated developments in advertising, industrial design, public relations, education, and other methods fields helped shape public opinion and channel social development.

What emerges from these studies that might be useful today? What can we take from them that might help us think about contemporary developments that link computing with society's future? I briefly underscore several issues that seem especially important.

One consistent finding in histories of the modern period is that power over the most important decisions about how technologies were introduced was far from evenly distributed. Those who had the financial and technical wherewithal to create new technologies in earlier decades of our century often found it feasible and desirable to mold society to match the needs of emerging technological systems and organizational plans. Many leaders in the corporate sector regarded society as mere putty that could be shaped with minimal resistance from the populace affected.

Greatest latitude for overt social control was present in the workplaces where employees were often seen as malleable, subject to the routines and disciplines of work. This attitude was clearly displayed in the paternalism of F. W. Taylor's *Principles of Scientific Management* and the practices it advanced. 'In the past the man has been first,' Taylor explained. 'In the future the system must be first' (Taylor, 1911, p. 7). In Taylor's vision and in similar approaches to modern American management, the authority relations of modern industry were perfectly clear. When a worker accepted employment at a particular firm, the worker was required to follow an intricate schedule specifying what to do and how to do it. The employer named the job, specified its content, and determined the extent to which the work required any knowledge or competence. Thus, as the workplaces of industrial society were organized, people were mobilized not only for productive tasks, but for fairly stable, predictable, reproducible identities as well. Such efforts carried a strong moral component. Cultural historians note that during the middle decades of the twentieth century, virtues appropriate to the development of machines—productive order, efficiency, control, forward-looking dynamism—became prevailing social virtues as well (Smith, 1993).

For industrial leaders like Henry Ford, Henry Luce, and Alfred Sloan, men able to achieve an overview of unfolding developments, a key realization was that continuing economic growth required the mobilization of great numbers of people not merely as producers but as consumers as well. By the 1920s it was common for corporate planners to aspire to reach deeply into people's lives, offering items and opportunities for consumption along with carefully tailored images and slogans that helped depict identities, attitudes, and lifestyles that could guide people's inclinations in home life and leisure. Industrial design, advertising, and corporate-sponsored journalism and public education combined with industrial planning to promote a series of strongly endorsed social role identities that were depicted in photos, newspaper and magazine articles, and school text books (Marchand, 1985). In Michael Schudson's apt summary, 'Where buying replaced making, then looking replaced doing as a key social action, reading signs replaced following orders as a crucial modern skill' (Schudson, 1984, pp. 156–157).

In this light, historians Roland Marchand and Terry Smith note the widely displayed tableaux vivants of modern life, combinations of advertising text and photography that from the 1920s to 1950s depicted:

The executive in the office tower
The worker in the clean, well-organized factory

The housewife in her appliance filled kitchen
Children surrounded with goods for the little ones
The automobile driver speeding along a wide open highway

The purpose of these images was to project possibilities for living in modern society at a time in which many of those possibilities were still novel. Crucial to the effect of these projections was a story about the world, a story in which people's orderly role in production was to be rewarded with an equally orderly, rational, modern role in consumption. Within well-managed corporate strategies that linked the shape of consumer goods to advertising slogans, photographs, magazine stories, and other widely promulgated inducements, people were encouraged to seek meaning and fulfillment within prescribed channels. It would be absurd to suggest that these efforts succeeded in determining the content of people's lives completely. But I think it is true to say that there were deliberate and effective moves to frame and to guide how ordinary people understood life's possibilities. One has only to live for a while in societies in which these accomplishments have not taken root—for example, prosperous societies in contemporary Europe in which consumerism as a way of life does not yet dominate the ways people understand self, family, and society—to appreciate the artificiality and pungency of modern American strategies of social control.

Histories of these developments clearly suggest that the basic terms of this social contract were nonnegotiable. The ideas and plans of everyday citizens were not regarded as crucial for corporate planning. In the advertisements and tableaux vivants, the future was always depicted something whole and inevitable. People were to be propelled forward by forces larger than themselves into a world that was rational, dynamic, prosperous, and harmonious. One visited spectacles like the 1939 World's Fair in New York to be swept up in the excitement of it all. There were no pavilions to solicit the public's suggestions about emerging devices, systems, or role definitions. As millions of visitors strolled through the fair, they learned how to orient themselves to changes in living that seemed to have their own undeniable trajectory.

Presenting the future in this way served an important purpose. Those making choices about the direction of social priorities and investments—for example, Robert Moses and other organizers of the New York World's Fair—had no desire to open the planning of sociotechnical innovations to make the process more inclusive. Spreading the broad umbrella of 'progress' over the details of policy, economic and political elites were able to defuse public criticism. The well-managed social consensus that unfolding developments were basically nonnegotiable was reflected in the silence of public discourse about alternatives, for example, the almost complete absence of popular forums in print or elsewhere from the 1920s through the 1950s where the meaning of the new technologies and their consequences could be discussed, criticized, or debated.

Held out to the American populace as the ultimate promise of modern society was individual, material satisfaction. The modern world was to be a place in which personal desires would be fulfilled through the consumption of industrially produced commodities. So glorious was the expected bounty, that any request to negotiate its terms would have seemed positively impudent. Missing from the picture was any attention to collective goods and collective problems. Long-term social commitments and the social costs of 'progress' were obscured by the belief that individual fulfillment was all that mattered. Thus, buying and driving this automobile would give the driver and family members a sense of thrill and belonging. Then as now, the automobile was always shown on highways miraculously free of other vehicles, well-paved roads that seemed to extend infinitely, wherever happy drivers turned the steering wheel. As a 1930s ad for ethyl gasoline in the 1930s proclaimed: 'There's always room out front' (Marchand, 1985, p. 362).

Another key finding from social and cultural studies of modernism takes note of the design of artifacts. Those in a position to make decisions were aware that as everyday folks looked at the novelties that bombarded them, they were apt to find these transformations complex and confusing. In that light, a commonly chosen design strategy was to conceal the complexity of devices, systems, and social arrangements and to make them appear simple and manageable. Thus, for example, streamlining and other varieties of shiny metal styling were adopted to complex, technical mechanisms within soothing, attractive surfaces. As people became comfortable with these forms, the workings of the artificial world that surrounded people seemed less and less intelligible. The same is true of the texts and pictures of advertising. Extremely simple solutions—often ones involving personal uplift with the aid of consumer purchases—were proposed for complicated, real-world problems. Eventually some of those complex problems—congestion, pollution, urban and environmental decay—emerged as difficult issues, made even more vexing by the fact that they festered for decades.

As we ponder horizons of computing and society today—for example, choices in the creation and use of computer networks on a widespread scale—it seems likely that American society will reproduce some of the basic tendencies of modernism:

- Unequal power over key decisions about what is built and why.

- Concerted attempts to enframe and direct people's lives in both work and consumption.

- The presentation of the future society as something nonnegotiable.

- The stress on individual gratification rather than collective problems and responsibilities.

- Design strategies that conceal and obfuscate important realms of social complexity.

Patterns of this kind persist because the institutions of planning, finance, management, advertising, education, and design that shaped modernity earlier this century are still extremely powerful. Occasional calls for resistance and reform by labor unions, environmentalists, consumer groups, feminists, and others have, for the most part, been neutralized or absorbed. Thus, for example, the push for ecological limits is repackaged as 'Green consumerism' and demands for participation in workplace decisions rechanneled to become 'empowerment' through the ownership and use of personal computers. Possibilities for self-conscious social choice and deliberate social action are often sidetracked to become obsessions focused on the purchasing and possessing of commodities.

As strong as these basic tendencies remain, however, it is doubtful that the world taking shape within and around today's information systems will simply reproduce the terms of previous decades. In fact, many of the forms of selfhood and social organization carefully nurtured for modern society seem ill-suited for conditions that increasingly confront Americans in the workplace and elsewhere. For example, the focus of personal identity based upon holding a lasting enduring job seems destined to become a relic of the industrial past (Glassner, 1994). Within the context of the global communications, global enterprise, lean production, organizational flexibility, the idea that one might become a permanent employee of one organization or even one industry is less and less sensible. Much blue collar and clerical work is now temporary. To an increasing extent even well-educated technical professionals are required to define themselves as contractors able to move from project to project, task to task, place to place among many organizations. The assumption in computer-centered enterprises is no longer that of belonging to and being crucial to any enduring framework of social relations. To an increasing extent our organizations assume perpetual expendability. How people will respond to that, how they will recreate selfhood in an era in which everyone is expendable, could well become a far more serious issue in coming decades than even the often lamented decline of real wages.

Another crisis brewing in the information society has to do with where and how people will experience membership. For modernism the prescribed frame for social relations was that of city and suburb. People were situated geographically and expected to find meaningful relationships close to home. But today it is increasingly obvious that for sizeable, economically important segments of our society, attachment is no longer defined geographically at all. Many activities of work and leisure take place in global, electronic settings and that is how people define their attachments. Robert Reich, among others, worries that the symbolic analysts of today's global webs of enterprise are now shedding traditional loyalties to their fellow citizens, leaving the less well-to-do, the less well wired to suffer in decaying cities (Reich, 1991). Indeed, attitudes of this sort can be found in the sociopathic cyberlibertarianism of the 1990s as represented, for example, in the 'Cyberspace and the American Dream' of the Progress and Freedom Foundation (Dyson *et al.*, 1994) and in much of the hyperventilated prose of *Wired* magazine. What is affirmed in such thinking is a fierce desire for market freedom and unfettered self-expression with no expectation that inflated cyber-egos owe anything to geographically situated others. Increasingly prevalent conditions of work and communication seem to encourage the development of ways of being human that correspond to hypertextual movements on the World Wide Web. 'Don't count on me for anything; I'm out of here with the click of a mouse.' Key virtues expressed in this context no longer involve the staid pursuit of efficiency, predictability, and order favored in classic modernism. Valued now are protean flexibility, restless entrepreneurialism, and a willingness to dissolve social bonds in the pursuit of material gain. Of course, there are many social conflicts this breast-thumping individualism conceals. Many of those enthralled with globalization as the wellspring of economic vitality also bemoan 'the weakened family,' 'collapse of community,' and 'chaos of the inner cities,' failing to notice any connection. As the power of global computing expands, it seems increasingly difficult for computers at home to add 2 + 2 and get 4.

There are many, of course, who expect that desirable new forms of community will emerge, that people will use their computers and the Internet to forge new social relationships and identities, including ones that might bolster local community life. Time will tell whether those lovely hopes pan out. It's anyone's guess what sorts of personalities, styles of discourse, and social norms will ultimately flourish in these new settings. Will digital media sustain healthy attachments to persons both near and far away? Or will they foster insouciance, resentment, and mutual contempt that distance has spawned in other historical settings? If the habits of expression commonly found in mid-1990s Internet news groups are any indication, the kinds of interpersonal respect, civility, and friendship that formed the basis of traditional, geographically based communities seem ill suited to the Net. Frequently encountered on-line nowadays is a Nietzschean tyro for the twenty-first century: the irascible, self-absorbed, white male cyber-boor (Winner, 1995).

One feature of early twentieth century modernism that American society seems likely to reproduce in years to come is the habit of excluding ordinary citizens from key choices about the design and development of new technologies, including information systems. Industrial leaders still indulge the old habit of presenting as *faits accomplis* what otherwise might have been choices open for diverse public imaginings, investigations, and debates. In magazine cover stories, corporate advertising campaigns, and political speeches, announcements of the arrival of the Information Superhighway and similar metaphors are still pitched in the language of inevitability. Get ready for it folks, here it comes: the set-top box!

The Firesign Theater dramatized this predicament many years ago in a biting satire about an electronic future. In the sketch a fellow dressed like a clown gets onto a van headed to an enticing theme park. A recording intones: 'Live in the Future! It's just starting now!' The traveler looks at the other people on the bus, squeaks his squeaker and comments: 'You know, I think we're all Bozos on this bus.' Much the same could be said of those corporate and political leaders who expect to herd the populace toward the on-ramps of 'The Information Superhighway' with extravaganzas like those that promoted the unveiling of Windows 95.

These are matters in which people doing research on computing and the future could have a positive influence. If we're asking people to change their lives to adapt to the introduction of new information systems, it seems responsible to solicit very broad participation in deliberation, planning, decision making, prototyping, testing, evaluation, and the like. Some of the best models, in my view, come from the Scandinavian social democracies where a variety of social and political circumstances makes close consultation with ordinary workers and citizens a much more common practice than it is in the United States (Sandberg *et al.*, 1992). Broad participation of this kind is warranted by principles of democracy and social justice, but it also makes sense because it is likely to produce better systems, ones that have a better fit with genuine human needs. Unfortunately, models for innovation of this kind have been seldom tried in the United States, perhaps because they are too democratic for those who oversee our intensely inegalitarian 'market' system.

At the same time, it is fascinating to notice what even the modest forms of citizen response found in the tightly controlled contexts of market testing seem to reveal. Despite the enormous corporate and political push for high-definition television in the late 1980s, for example, the American public never warmed to the idea. After all, why would more lines on the screen be desirable? By the mid-1990s when the television industry discovered more lucrative uses for video bandwidth, the campaign for HDTV was discretely shelved. In a similar development, recent reports suggest that after all the hype about the version of the so-called information superhighway stressing interactive TV, companies have found that 'consumers yawned in the face of its most hotly promoted applications—movies-on-demand and interactive home shopping' (Caruso, 1993). In contrast, what people seem to be excited about—a possibility that many socially concerned computer professionals have anticipated for a long while—are networks that have open architecture, networks of many-to-many communication in which people can be more than passive consumers of information, but also producers, creative actors able to tinker with new possibilities and perhaps give them a distinctive personal stamp. Denise Caruso, business writer for the *New York Times*, reports that corporate designers, sensing the public mood, have gone back to the drawing boards, setting aside the push for set-top boxes, and are now perfecting cable modems.

While it is encouraging to see the influence of the general populace crop up in this way, its expected contributions are always muted and indirect. The attitude of many leaders in the computing and telecommunications industry still seems to be that only they know what is good for their fellow citizens and that somewhere down the line they are going to enforce corporate closure on the shape of information systems, capture those markets, and place their distinctive brand on people's lives. As Caruso observes, 'the telephone companies . . . , preparing [their own] networks and services, agree that fiber co-ax is the right design' (Caruso, 1995).

How reassuring; evidently the 'right design' is headed our way and again we have not had to lift a finger. Developments of this kind echo the first words of Jean-Jacques Rousseau's *Social Contract* written two centuries ago: 'Men are born free, but everywhere they are in chains.' An equivalent maxim today might be: 'People are not born with brass rings in their noses, but much technological development quietly supposes that they are.'

But why should we settle for effrontery so blatant? Rather than exclude the energy and ideas of the American populace, rather than try to predetermine what the horizons of computing and society will be, research and developments in computing ought to involve the public—ordinary people from all walks of life—in activities of inquiry, exploration, dialogue, and debate. Here computer professionals could, if they so chose, exercise much-needed leadership. While it is sometimes tempting to conclude that we are merely going 'where the technology is taking us,' or that social outcomes are and should be 'determined by market forces,' the fact of the matter is that deliberate choices about the relationship between people and new technology are made by someone, somehow, every day of the year. Persons whose professional work gives them insight into the choices that matter must be diligent in expressing their knowledge and judgments to a broad public. Otherwise they may find themselves employed as mere ranch hands, helping fit the citizenry with digital brass rings.

As the twentieth century draws to a close, it is evident that, for better or worse, the future of computing and the future of human relations—indeed, of human being itself—are now thoroughly intertwined. Foremost among the obligations this situation presents is the need to seek alternatives, social policies that might undo the dreary legacy of modernism: pervasive systems of one-way communication, preemption of democratic social choice corporate manipulation, and the presentation of sweeping changes in living conditions as something justified by a univocal, irresistible 'progress.' True, the habits of technological somnambulism cultivated over many decades will not be easily overcome. But as waves of overhyped innovation confront increasingly obvious signs of social disorder, opportunities for lively conversation sometimes fall into our laps. Choices about computer technology involve not only obvious questions about 'what to do,' but also less obvious ones about 'who to be.' By virtue of their vocation, computer professionals are well situated to initiate public debates on this matter, helping a democratic populace explore new identities and the horizons of a good society.

References

BELL, T. E. 1995. Surviving in the Reengineered Corporate Environment: The Freelance Engineer. *IEEE Power Eng. Rev.* May: 7–11.

BRIDGES, W. 1994. *Jobshift: How to Prosper in a Workplace Without Jobs.* New York: Addison-Wesley.

CARUSO, D. 1993. Digital Commerce: On-line Browsing Got You Down? Don't Get Mad, Get Cable. *New York Times* June 5:D3.

COWAN, R. S. 1983. *More Work for Mother: The Ironies of Household Technology From the Open Hearth to the Microwave.* New York: Basic Books.

DYSON, E., GILDER, G., KEYWORTH, G., and TOFFLER, A. 1994. Cyberspace and the American Dream: A Magna Carta for the Knowledge Age. Release 1.2. August 22. Washington, DC: Progress and Freedom Foundation.

Firesign Theatre. 1971. I Think We're All Bozos on This Bus. Columbia Records C30737.

FORTY, A. 1986. *Objects of Desire.* New York: Pantheon.

GLASSNER, B. 1994. *Career Crash: America's New Crisis and Who Survives.* New York: Simon & Schuster.

HARVEY, D. 1989. *The Condition of Postmodernity: An Enquiry into the Origins of Cultural Change.* Cambridge, Mass.: Blackwell.

HAYDEN, D. 1981. *The Grand Domestic Revolution: A History of Feminist Designs for American Homes, Neighborhoods, and Cities.* Cambridge, Mass.: MIT Press.

HOUNSHELL, D. A. 1984. *From the American System to Mass Production, 1800–1932: The Development of Manufacturing Technology in the United States.* Baltimore: Johns Hopkins University Press.

MARCHAND, R. 1985. *Advertising the American Dream: Making Way for Modernity, 1920–1940.* Berkeley: University of California Press.

MEIKLE, J. L. 1979. *Twentieth Century Limited: Industrial Design in America, 1925–1939.* Philadelphia: Temple University Press.

NOBLE, D. F. 1977. *America by Design: Science, Technology and the Rise of Corporate Capitalism.* New York: Knopf.

NYE, D. E. 1990. *Electrifying America: Social Meanings of a New Technology, 1880–1940.* Cambridge, Mass.: MIT Press.

PETERS, T. 1994. *The Pursuit of Wow!: Every Person's Guide to Topsy-Turvy Times.* New York: Vintage Books.

REICH, R. B. 1991. *The Work of Nations: Preparing Ourselves for 21st-century Capitalism.* New York: Knopf.

RIFKIN, J. 1995. *The End of Work: The Decline of the Global Labor Force and the Dawn of the Post-Market era.* New York: G. P. Putnam's Sons.

SANDBERG, A., BROMS, G., GRIP, A., SUNDSTROM, L., STEEN, J., and ULLMARK, P. 1992. *Technological Change and Co-Determination in Sweden.* Philadelphia: Temple University Press.

SCHUDSON, M. 1984. *Advertising: The Uneasy Persuasion.* New York: Basic Books.

SMITH, T. 1993. *Making the Modern: Industry Art and Design in America.* Chicago: University of Chicago Press.

TAYLOR, F. W. 1911. *The Principles of Scientific Management.* New York: Harper & Brothers.

WINNER, L. 1986. Mythinformation. In *The Whale and the Reactor.* Chicago: University of Chicago Press, pp. 98–117.

—— 1995. Privileged Communications. *Technol. Rev.* March/April, p. 70.

WOOD, G. S. 1992. *The Radicalism of the American Revolution.* New York: Knopf.

13

Understanding Community in the Information Age

Steven G. Jones

In this essay Steven G. Jones offers an informative discussion of central issues and ideas related to Computer Mediated Communication in general and on-line community in particular. Jones's discriminating treatment of the notion of on-line community relates diverse historical and contemporary perspectives while providing a broad and insightful understanding of these new on-line 'spaces'. Referring to Licklider and Taylor's text (Chapter 5 in this volume), Jones asks, 'Can CMC be understood to build communities and form a part of the conduct of public life, as many other forms of communication seem to, or does CMC problematize our very notions of community and public life?' Through his considered response to this question, Jones furthers understanding of ideas about of community, on-line identity, and the nature of virtual communities.

WHETHER BY CHOICE or accident, by design or politics (or some complex combination of each), the United States (followed closely by many other countries) is embarking on a building project the likes of which have not been seen since the Eisenhower era. Indeed, there are startling parallels between the current project, the 'information highway,' and the one spurred on by both world wars, the interstate highway system—not the least of which is the reliance on the word 'highway' and the romantic connotations of the open road (and that Vice President Al Gore, Jr.'s father was instrumental in the development of the federal highway system). Another parallel is the initially military motivation for highway building (established by Thomas Jefferson, among others) and the military origins of the most prominent information highway, the Internet, in defense department computer networks linked to university research centers.

Patton (1986), in his history of the US interstate system, says that it was

> the most expensive and elaborate public works program of all time, offer[ing] a vision of social and economic engineering. It was planned to be at once a Keynesian economic driver and a geographic equalizer, an instrument for present prosperity and the armature of a vision of the future. It was at once the last program of the New Deal and the first space program. (p. 17)

From Steven G. Jones (ed.), *CyberSociety: Computer-Mediated Communication and Community* (London: Sage, 1995). The original chapter has been amended for publication in this volume.

The information highway being vociferously championed by the Clinton administration and by Vice President Al Gore also combines ideas about the economic and social direction of the United States. It is in a sense the first program of the new New Deal and, some say, the last space program. Patton's comments about the effects that interstates have had on cities and communities bear especially close scrutiny, as they evoke images of what the information highway may as well do to social formations. Highways, Patton says,

> have had monstrous side effects. They have often rolled, like some gigantic version of the machines that build them, through cities, splitting communities off into ghettos, displacing people, and crushing the intimacies of old cities. . . .
>
> While promising to bring us closer, highways in fact cater to our sense of separateness. (p. 20)

Critical to the rhetoric surrounding the information highway is the promise of a renewed sense of community and, in many instances, new types and formations of community. Computer-mediated communication, it seems, will do by way of electronic pathways what cement roads were unable to do, namely, connect us rather than atomize us, put us at the controls of a 'vehicle' and yet not detach us from the rest of the world.

If that is to be so, it is not premature to ask questions about these new formations. What might electronic communities be like? Most forecasters, like Howard Rheingold (1993), envision them as a kind of ultimate flowering of community, a place (and there is no mistaking in these visions that it is place that is at stake) where individuals shape their own community by choosing which other communities to belong to. Thus a paradox long haunting America is solved in a particularly American way; we will be able to forge our own places from among the many that exist, not by creating new places but by simply choosing from the menu of those available. Another of the many questions we must ask about electronic communities is: What is the nature of individual members' commitments to them? In the physical world, community members must live together. When community membership is in no small way a simple matter of subscribing or unsubscribing to a bulletin board or electronic newsgroup, is the nature of interaction different simply because one may disengage with little or no consequence?

Perhaps the most important question for the [present] purpose [. . .] is: how do we study computer-mediated community? Like other social groups, these are palpable, yet evanescent to CMC users. Although we can 'freeze' electronic discourse by capturing the text and information it may contain, how do we ascertain the interpretive moment in electronic discourse, particularly as it engages both reading and writing? [A number of] authors [have] attempt[ed] to answer that question in a variety of ways. *[Many] of them are aware of and alert to the possibilities and pitfalls of embracing traditional methods of social research to study nontraditional social formations, and all cultivate what Chayko (1993) calls a 'special sensitivity' to distinctions between the virtual and the real. As she writes, that sensitivity is required for us to study the

---

* Jones refers here and below to contributors to his volume *CyberSociety*. Further instances are indicated by an asterisk.

new ways in which we 'carve out' reality by framing experience, and to the nature of such newly constituted 'realities.' It is one of the tasks of sociologists to problematize 'what is real.' Rather than assume that the real world is 'out there' to be learned about and internalized, we recognize that there is no reality apart from what social actors make of it. (p. 172)

This is particularly important ground as it relates, in Berger and Luckmann's (1967) terms, to the 'social construction of reality.' That reality is not constituted *by* the networks CMC users use; it is constituted *in* the networks. It would be far easier to understand the physical, or hardwired, connections than to understand the symbolic connections that emerge from interaction. To again borrow from Carey (1989), much of our energy has been directed toward understanding the speed and volume with which computers can be used as communication tools. Conspicuously absent is an understanding of how computers are used as tools for connection and community. Carey makes the distinction between transmission and ritual views clear: 'Communication under a transmission view is the extension of messages across geography for the purposes of control, the . . . case under a ritual view is the sacred ceremony that draws persons together in fellowship and commonality' (p.18).

The distinctions between the two views of communication Carey draws are critical to understanding the full range and scope of CMC. It would seem we now have our global village or community, not just via CMC but by way of the many media of communication ever present. Everywhere we go we can 'tap into' that community with a cellular telephone, a personal digital assistant, a modem, or a satellite dish. But connection does not inherently make for community, nor does it lead to any necessary exchanges of information, meaning, and sense making at all. Barnes and Duncan (1992) borrow from James Clifford: 'When we write we do so from a necessarily local setting' (p. 3). The primary act involved in CMC is that of writing. Like Ong's (1982) description of authorship, that act is *intensely* local, for, although we may be certain of an audience, we are unable to verify its existence just as we are unable to verify its interpretation of our writing.

That uncertainty is central to the act of writing, as Ong sees it. It may also be central to the desire for control and feedback that Beniger (1986) believes caused the 'control revolution.' Beniger's thoughts are focused on the rapid technological innovation at the end of the late nineteenth century that heralded the introduction of basic communication technologies and, he says, restored the economic and political control lost during the Industrial Revolution:

> Before this time, control of government and markets had depended on personal relationships and face-to-face interactions; now control came to be reestablished by means of bureaucratic organization, the new infrastructure of transportation and telecommunications, and system-wide communication via the new mass media. (p. 14)

The need for control is obvious when viewed as a problem of geography, at once created and solved by transportation and communication. But when viewed as outside the frame of transportation and from the perspective of ritual, the predicament is one that we continue to face: How do we attend to the social connections impinging on us, the connections we at once desire (e-mail, telephone, fax, etc.) and despise (for they take up more and more of our time and energy)? Again, control is sought after, but it is not sought for the purposes of power but for the purposes of its inverse, restraint. As Carey (1993) put it, 'Human intelligence has lodged itself, extrasomatically, in the very atmosphere that surrounds and supports us. Yet, back at home, we have a surplus of disorder and disarray' (p. 172). The very surfeit of knowledge and information leads toward chaos, and ever greater efforts are made at controlling the disorder with information-navigating devices like Hyper-Card®, Gopher, Veronica, and Mosaic.

Such disorder and the attempts to control it underscore the mythic invest-ment we have in computer technology. The chaos and confusion generated by the opening of new frontiers led us to devise means of communication and transportation as if those means were one, part and parcel of the same process. Rail and road followed river and stream, to be supplanted by tele-graph wire, telephone wire, and fiber-optic cable. (One ought to wonder what wireless communication as it develops in all its manifestations will truly bring, as the link between communication and transportation, forged by his-tory, dissolves.) Jenkins and Fuller [in the volume *CyberSociety*, writing about] new world narratives and Nintendo is precisely the analysis needed to make explicit the links between our new media and our history.

It is important, too, for us to not only understand the parallels between new world narratives and CMC narratives but to understand their differ-ences. In a modern world, there is a need for control related to structure and homogenization, to the reversal of entropy. Such reversal comes to us in the guise of connections and associations that overcome geography and physical space. Computer-mediated communication will, it is said, lead us toward a new community: global, local, and everything in between. But the presence of chaos inexorably draws us away from that ideal as the need for control be-comes greater and greater. It is most accurate to claim, as Carey (1993) does, that when it comes to proselytizing CMC, 'these are ideas that people want or need to be true merely because it would be bewildering to be without them' (p. 172).

It may as well be 'bewildering' for us to create and learn the norms of on-line worlds, for to learn them is a complex process. It may bring people together insofar as such learning is often collaborative, but it is equally as often frustrating and off-putting. Nevertheless, there is a sense that we are embarking on an adventure in creating new communities and new forms of community, and that sense is fueled by two motives: first, that we *need* new communities and, second, that we *can* create them technologically. Such motives, in turn, arise from what Soja (1989) has called 'postmodern geog-raphies.' the tensions caused by differentiation and homogenization in the (re)production of space. In the case of CMC, what allows for the reproduc-tion of space is the malleability with which identity can be created and nego-tiated [. . .]. Consequently, one must question the potential of CMC for production of social space. Could it perhaps *re*produce 'real' social relations in a 'virtual' medium?

It is more likely that social relations emerging from CMC are between the two poles of production and reproduction. Pushing too close to either pole puts at risk whatever new social construction of reality may arise. And yet any new social formations are at risk of being mythologized and incorporated into the 'rhetoric of the electrical sublime' that Carey (1989) identifies. All media, for instance, have been touted for their potential for education. Radio and television, in particular, were early on promoted as tools for education, and CMC is no different. In an article on computer technology in schools, one author wrote, 'At a time when American schools are receiving less and less money to cope with growing social upheaval, telecomputing seems to offer a glimmer of hope, enlivening both teachers and students even as it compels a striking realignment of relationships within the classroom' (Leslie, 1993, p. 90).

There is no doubt that CMC is linked inextricably to education. Even the Corporation for Public Broadcasting (CPB) now seeks

> to develop community-wide education and information services. These publicly accessible interactive services will take full advantage of widely available communications and information technologies, particularly in-expensive computers linked by telephone lines.
>
> Who will mobilize the development of high-quality, non-commercial, educational and public services that will provide all Americans with the opportunities for learning, staying healthy, and participating in cultural and civic affairs—services crucial to the well-being of society as a whole? (from 1993 solicitation guidelines)

The CPB's comments parallel those made when radio and TV were introduced (the emphasis then was on broadcasting in the public interest, convenience, and necessity). Even Jaron Lanier, a pioneering virtual reality programmer and engineer, has said, 'Television wasn't planned well enough and I think it's been a real disaster in this country' ('Virtual Reality,' 1992, p. 6). Similarly, Quarterman (1993) has said, 'Radio and television produced a different society. Computer networks will, too. Perhaps this time we can avoid a few mistakes' (p. 49). Such comments obfuscate the power behind decisions that go into planning and organizing media. Who will plan, how will we plan, and how will we account in our planning for unanticipated consequences? Media regulation in the US has hardly been the most successful enterprise. Why should we believe regulating CMC will be different?

At the heart of comments like Lanier's and Quarterman's is a pervasive sense that we can learn from the 'mistakes' we believe we've made using older media. Computer-mediated communication (and computers generally) gives us a sense that we can start over and learn from the past. Their comments point out that we have a fundamental need, or at least hope, for something better to come from future media.

But what exactly are we hoping *for*? The answer to that question is necessarily linked to questions about who we are hoping to be as a society, and that, in turn, is tied to issues of identity and discourse. Who are we when we are on-line? The question becomes even more important as new technologies are developed for creating 'agents' or 'alters' that roam the network for us when we are away from our terminals.

The possibility of new social formations is certainly alluring and is one of those ideas we seem to 'want or need to be true.' Another related idea we seem to need is, of course, the concept of virtual reality. What is most interesting, though, is that virtual reality is hardly less 'bewildering' than non-virtual reality. The systems of cultural significance and methods of social control that [a number of writers]* describe in on-line worlds in some instances parallel ones we are already accustomed to and in some instances do not. In all instances, though, they do form a new matrix of social relations. What impulses those formations are propelled by is an important matter that should not be overlooked. Cybersocieties are not organized simply for the transmission of information, nor do they 'have to do something nontrivial with the information they send and receive' (Licklider & Taylor, this vol. Chap. 5, p. 97). In fact, much of what is done with CMC is trivial. As Chesebro and Bonsall (1989) note, CMC may 'promote efficiency at the expense of social contact' (p. 221). However, it is unlikely that many in contemporary society find the values explicit in Chesebro and Bonsall's statement antagonistic. CMC brings us a form of efficient social contact.

I believe that is an important point, for it speaks to the issue of community formation in a postmodern world. CMC allows us to customize our social contacts from fragmented communities. Few have studied this phenomenon comprehensively, although a step in the right direction was taken by Linda Harasim, editor of the anthology *Global Networks*. Harasim (1993) finds that social communication is a primary component of computer-mediated communication and is well able to organize thoughts about the use of CMC around social rather than solely work functions. However, none of those contributing to the anthology she edited probe satisfactorily into the nature of CMC's social use, preferring to claim, in the final analysis, that we simply seek community by whatever means it is available.

This is probably true, particularly insofar as we seek community in other places as it dissolves in the spaces we physically inhabit. But we then must ask, as Benedikt (1991, p. 125) does, 'What is space?' Forceful arguments about the ways technology shapes social relations have been made by numerous social scientists and philosophers, including Lewis Mumford and Marshall McLuhan. But space is not social relations, and vice versa. Mumford (1934) in particular notes a shift in society's interests, away from the abstraction of time and space and toward a desire to *use* space and time. CMC gives us a tool with which to use space for communication.

CMC, of course, is not just a tool; it is at once technology, medium, and engine of social relations. It not only structures social relations, it is the space within which the relations occur and the tool that individuals use to enter that space. It is more than the context within which social relations occur (although it is that, too) for it is commented on and imaginatively constructed by symbolic processes initiated and maintained by individuals and groups. The difficulty in defining space is clear in the zeal with which many have latched onto other derivative terms. For instance, yet more evidence of the prophetic nature of rhetoric about CMC is the pervasive use of the word 'cyberspace,' coined by William Gibson, a writer of fiction, to put a finger on a space at once real in its effects and illusory in its lack of physical presence. The 'space race' of the 1950s and 1960s is indeed over. We no longer look to the stars and the thermodynamic engines that will transport us to them but to sites unknown and unseen (perhaps unseeable) and the ever smaller electronic engines that seem to effortlessly and without danger bring this space to us.

But is it even possible to pin down space to any particular definition? As Benedikt (1991) correctly observes, 'Space, for most of us, hovers between ordinary, physical existence and something other' (p. 125). Where we find it hovering is, as Soja (1989) notes, in 'socially produced space, [where] spatiality can be distinguished from the physical space of material nature and the mental space of cognition and representation, each of which is used and incorporated into the construction of spatiality but cannot be conceptualized as its equivalent' (p. 120). [...]

The importance of CMC and its attendant social structures lies not only in interpretation and narrative, acts that can fix and structure, but in the sense of mobility with which one can move (narratively and otherwise) through the social space. Mobility has two meanings in this case. First, it is clearly an ability to 'move' from place to place without having physically traveled. But, second, it is also a mobility of status, class, social role, and character. Like the boulevardiers or the denizens of Nevsky Prospect described by Berman (1982), the citizens of cyberspace (or the 'net,' as it is commonly called by its evanescent residents) 'come here to see and be seen, and to communicate their visions to one another, not for any ulterior purpose, without greed or competition, but as an end in itself' (p. 196). The difference between those on the net and those on the street is encompassed in a distinction made by Soja (1989): 'Just as space, time, and matter delineate and encompass the essential qualities of the physical world, spatiality, temporality, and social being can be seen as the abstract dimensions which together comprise all facets of human existence' (p. 25).

In cyberspace, spatiality is largely illusory (at least until Gibson's accounts of its visualization are realized), and temporality is problematized by the instantaneity of CMC and the ability to roam the net with 'agents,' software constructs that are automated representatives able to retrieve information and/or interact on the net. What is left is social being, and that too is problematic. Is the social actor in cyberspace mass-mediated, a massmediator, a public figure, or a private individual engaged in close, special interrelation? As Soja sees it in a summary of the dialectic between space and social life,

> The spatio-temporal structuring of social life defines how social action and relationship (including class relations) are materially constituted, made concrete. The constitution/ concretization process is problematic, filled with contradiction and struggle (amidst much that is recursive and routinized). Contradictions arise primarily from the duality of produced space as both outcome/embodiment/product and medium/presupposition/producer of social activity. (p. 129)

No matter how ill-defined the space of cyberspace, the space we occupy as social beings is as affected by CMC. As Gillespie and Robins (1989) note, 'New communications technologies do not just impact upon places; places and the social processes and social relationships they embody also affect how such technological systems are designed, implemented and used' (p. 7).

Soja's comments and the questions that arise from them speak to the heart of the many contradictions and problems embodied in CMC. On the one hand, it appears to foster community, or at least the sense of community, among its users. On the other hand, it embodies the impersonal communication of the computer and of the written word, the 'kind of imitation talking' Ong (1982, p. 102) aptly describes. In that fashion, CMC wears on its sleeve the most important dichotomy that Jensen (1990) identifies in her book *Redeeming Modernity*. Jensen writes that traditional life, supposedly, 'was marked by face-to-face, intimate relationships among friends, while modern life is characterized by distant, impersonal contact among strangers. Communities are defined as shared, close, and intimate, while societies are defined as separate, distanced, and anonymous' (p. 71).

Can CMC be understood to build communities and form a part of the conduct of public life, as other forms of communication seem to, or does CMC problematize our very notions of community and public life? CMC may yet be the clearest evidence of Beniger's (1987) 'pseudo-community,' part of the 'reversal of a centuries-old trend from organic community—based on interpersonal relationships—to impersonal association integrated by mass means' (p. 369). Even if it is, the most important question is: How is it that a mass medium can be so closely related to (in some cases, equated with) a community?

A danger in the current assessments of cyberspace and cyberspatial social relations is the implacability of Carey and Quirk's 'mythos of the electronic revolution' previously mentioned. For instance, Benedikt (1991) has claimed that in cyberspace, 'to which every computer is a window, seen or heard objects are neither physical nor, necessarily, representations of physical objects but are, rather, in form, character and action, made up of data, of pure information' (pp. 122–3). Now, one most imminent danger (arising in part from the commodification of information) is that information is itself understood as a physical entity. It is important to remind one's self that computer data is essentially binary information based on the manipulation of strings of ones and zeros, themselves no more 'physical' than our imagination allows them to be. In the operation of an audio compact disc player, the compact disc's bits of information are decoded by the player and converted to sound waves representative of (although nevertheless analogous to) the sound waves encoded during recording. The sound certainly retains 'high fidelity,' thanks largely to the enormous quantities of information encoded by the disc. In the operation of cyberspatial social relations, bits of information are decoded by users and converted to analogues of mediated and interpersonal social relations. The danger lies in the sense that cyberspatial social relations maintain 'high fidelity' to those analogues. First, there is no prerequisite for such a homology. Second, any presupposition of a homology also assumes and fixes the rebirth of prior social relations, engineered along with the machines that make them palpable.

The importance of the disappointment that engineered communities have brought cannot be understated. We can no more 'build' communities than we can 'make' friends or, at least, as David Harvey (1989) points out, 'the potential connection between projects to shape space and encourage spatial practices . . . and political projects . . . can be at best conserving and at worst downright reactionary in their implications' (p. 277). Harvey follows Heidegger through to his connections to fascism, a condition the nets have generally avoided, but his points, particularly as they concern political life, ought to be heeded by CMC users. Definitions of community have largely centered around the unproblematized notion of place, a 'where' that social scientists can observe, visit, stay, and go. Their observations had largely been formed by examination of events, artifacts, and social relations within distinct geographic boundaries. The manifestation of political struggle as boundaries shift, break apart, and re-form has largely been overlooked, and the perspectives [developed by a number of contemporary writers]* are a first step toward redirecting observation and interrogation.

Communities formed by CMC have been called 'virtual communities' and defined as 'incontrovertibly social spaces in which people still meet face-to-face, but under new definitions of both "meet" and "face". . . . [V]irtual communities [are] passage points for collections of common beliefs and practices that united people who were physically separated' (Stone, 1991, p. 85). In that sense, cyberspace hasn't a 'where' (although there are 'sites' or 'nodes' at which users gather). Rather, the space of cyberspace is predicated on knowledge and information, on the common beliefs and practices of a society abstracted from physical space. Part of that knowledge and information, though, lies in simply knowing how to navigate cyberspace. But the important element in cyberspatial social relations is the sharing of information. It is not sharing in the sense of the *transmission* of information that binds communities in cyberspace. It is the ritual sharing of information (Carey, 1989) that pulls it together. That sharing creates the second kind of community that Carey (1993) identifies as arising from the growth of cities during the late nineteenth and early twentieth century, the one

> formed by imaginative diaspora—cosmopolitans and the new professionals who lived in the imaginative worlds of politics, art, fashion, medicine, law and so forth. These diasporic groups were twisted and knotted into one another within urban life. They were given form by the symbolic interactions of the city and the ecology of media, who reported on and defined these groups to one another, fostered and intensified antagonisms among them, and sought forms of mutual accommodation. (p. 178)

Such a formation is reoccuring in the discourse within CMC and without it, in the conversations its participants have on-line and off, and in the media coverage of electronic communication, electronic communities, and virtual reality.

The Community Along the Highway

In *The Postmodern Condition*, geographer and theorist David Harvey (1989) refers frequently to 'time-space compression': 'processes that so revolutionize the objective qualities of space and time that we are forced to alter, sometimes in quite radical ways, how we represent the world to ourselves' (p. 240). Harvey finds such compression central to understanding the now commonplace (and perhaps dated) concepts of the world as a 'global village' or 'spaceship earth.' As part of his analysis of shifts in the history of capitalism, he identifies a change in spatial organization from feudal to Renaissance Europe. As regards the former, he writes,

> In the relatively isolated worlds . . . of European feudalism, place as-
> sumed a definite legal, political, and social meaning indicative of a rela-
> tive autonomy of social relations and of community inside roughly given
> territorial boundaries. . . . External space was weakly grasped and gener-
> ally conceptualized as a mysterious cosmology populated by some exter-
> nal authority, heavenly hosts, or more sinister figures of myth and
> imagination. (pp. 240–1)

Morris (1992) has criticized Harvey's reduction of complex problems to simple dualities. In particular, Morris writes, 'Global problems are posed with a sense of urgency verging on moral panic, but then existing practical experiments in dealing with these on a plausible scale are dismissed for the usual vices ("relativism," "defeatism"), reclassified as what they contest ("postmodernism"), or altogether ignored' (pp. 271–2). Still, at least two points that Harvey makes are important for the study of CMC and commu-nity. First, external space is in some sense no more firmly grasped today, al-though it is conceptualized in a variety of ways linked to objective representation via maps, photographs, and other visual media. Second, the relative autonomy of which Harvey speaks has given way since the Renais-sance 'to the direct influence of [the] wider world through trade, intra-territorial competition, military action, the inflow of new commodities, of bullion and the like' (Morris, 1992, p. 244). Social isolation becomes a diffi-cult proposition for any contemporary community. Computer-mediated communities are in a sense 'practical experiments' dealing with 'global prob-lems,' and Morris's critique is all the more sharp as she points out Harvey's fallacy that 'geographically "global" space requires a philosophically *tran-scendent* space of analysis' (Morris, 1992, p. 273). Which of these spaces, if any (or all), is to be addressed in studies of CMC?

It is clear that studies of community have embedded a similar fallacy. The study of community followed a course similar to that which Harvey describes and Morris critiques as it evolved from attempts to describe and 'write' communities in an isolated (almost antispatial) fashion to attempts to grapple with the complexities of overlapping and interlinked communities.

In assessing the history of community studies one finds that space was un-derstood less as socially produced and more as that which produced social re-lations. So, for instance, Stacey (1974) identified the threads running through definitions of community in the sociological study of community. These include territory, social system, and sense of belonging. The first elem-ent, territory, however, is meant as a boundary within which a community maintains the other two elements. Similarly, Bell and Newby (1974) identi-fied a variety of elements present in most definitions of community: social interaction based on geographic area, self-sufficiency, common life, con-sciousness of a kind, and possession of common ends, norms, and means. Bell and Newby also included ideas about social systems, individuality, total-ity of attitudes, and process as commonalities in approaches to community studies.

The most useful deconstruction of conceptions of community comes from Effrat (1974), who categorizes three main ones:

1. Community as solidarity institutions
2. Community as primary interaction
3. Community as institutionally distinct groups

Effrat's categories betray not only a Western sociological bias (which she admits) but a root in structured social action particularly well-defined in the Chicago school of sociology. It is an 'instrumentalist' perspective based on involvement and interaction, concepts somewhat easier to measure, at least, than community but nonetheless difficult to describe qualitatively. Such a perspective stems also from one of the earliest community studies, Warner's (1963) *Yankee City*, which Warner claimed would cross-sectionally represent American communities. The desire driving these studies is that of the social scientist who seeks to generalize from conditions of study as close to the 'laboratory' as possible.

It is difficult to import definitions that use these elements and ideas to computer-mediated communication. Of Effrat's categories, the third, community as institutionally distinct groups, makes the most sense in the context of computer use. CMC is rarely a solidarity institution in Effrat's terms; that is, it rarely functions to produce solidarity. It may be a primary interaction, in a particularly narrow sense, insofar as relationships that CMC engenders may be close ones, and the content of communication may also make computer mediation the primary source of interaction. Yet viewed that way, primary interaction is virtually a function of a community defined as an institutionally distinct group, that is, a function of belonging to some social group or category.

It is most critical to attend to Etzioni's (1991) 'I am We' paradigm:

the idea that both individual and community have a basic moral standing; neither is secondary or derivative. To stress the interlocking, mutually dependent relationship of individual and community, and to acknowledge my mentor, Martin Buber, I refer to this synthetic position . . . (the We signifies social, cultural and political, hence historical and institutional forces, which shape the collective factor—the community). (p. 137)

[A number of writers]* attend precisely to that paradigm and to the three criteria that Etzioni uses to focus community: scope, substance, and dominance (pp. 144–149). Each criterion focuses too, in its way, on the argument Calhoun (1980) makes that 'we need to develop a conceptualization of community which allows us to penetrate beneath simple categories . . . to see a variable of social relations. The relationship between community as a complex of social relationships and community as a complex of ideas and sentiments has been little explored' (p. 107). The former has been an element of CMC study from the start. Some of the earliest ideas about CMC recognize that computer-mediated community will affect our considerations of space. As Licklider and Taylor saw it in 1968,

What will on-line interactive communities be like? In most fields they will consist of geographically separated members, sometimes grouped in small clusters and sometimes working individually. They will be communities not of common location, but of *common interest*. In each geographical sector, the total number of users ... will be large enough to support extensive general-purpose information processing and storage facilities ... life will be happier for the on-line individual because the people with whom one interacts most strongly will be selected more by commonality of interests and goals than by accidents of proximity. (Licklider and Taylor, this vol. Chap. 5, pp. 108–10)

The relation between 'fields' and 'interests' is not questioned in that article, nor is the connection between 'common interest' and Calhoun's concept of 'community as a complex of ideas and sentiments' followed up, but of greater importance is the belief that 'accidents of proximity' lead one to be unhappy. Serendipity in its usual sense plays no part in either world that Licklider and Taylor (1968) describe; only a kind of will to interact among others with (undefined) 'common interests' is operational. Yet geography does play a role, for it, at the very least, serves as the site and center of the machine that they state will serve us as we escape the social constraints that location has placed on us.

Walls (1993), in a chapter on global networks, attempts to subdivide community into those that are 'relationship focused' and those that are 'task focused,' but the subdivision only provides insight into the functions of particular user groups rather than into the connections between users and hardly accounts for Calhoun's conception of community. Frederick (1993) borrows from Harasim's (1993) concept of 'networlds' and Rheingold's (1993) notion of 'virtual communities' to identify 'nonplace' communities. None of these all too brief forays into CMC and community hit the mark. What is missing is the concomitant conceptualization of space and the social, the inquiry into connections between social relations, spatial practice, values, and beliefs. The ability to create, maintain, and control space (whatever we call it—virtual, nonplace, networld) links us to notions of power and necessarily to issues of authority, dominance, submission, rebellion, and cooptation, notions that Etzioni (1991) establishes as primary criteria of community. Just because the spaces with which we are now concerned are electronic it is not the case that they are democratic, egalitarian, or accessible, and it is not the case that we can forego asking in particular about substance and dominance.

Concerns about these issues have not only been underrepresented in the study of CMC, they have also been lost in community studies. In his classic study of communities and social change in America, Bender (1978) critiques community sociology as the study of 'locality-based action' that emphasizes territory at the expense of culture:

The identification of community with locality and communal experiences with rather casual associations has quietly redefined community in a way that puts it at odds with its historical and popular meaning ... drain[ing] the concept of the very qualities that give the notion of community cultural, as opposed to merely organizational, significance. (p. 10)

For Bender, communities are defined not as places but as social networks, a definition useful for the study of community in cyberspace for two reasons.

First, it focuses on the interactions that create communities. Second, it focuses away from place. In media that shift not only the sense of space but the sense of place, decentering (although not removing) the consideration of territory is necessary to permit entry of notions of power and its analysis.

Pseudocommunity and the Decentering of Place

Several authors, most notably Beniger (1987) and Peck (1987), have written about pseudocommunity: 'the great societal transformations of the 19th century . . . a sharp drop in interpersonal control of individual behavior: from traditional communal relationships (*Gemeinschaft*) to impersonal, highly restricted association or *Gesellschaft* . . . from face-to-face to indirect or symbolic group relations' (Beniger, 1987, p. 353). Beniger borrows from Tonnies's (1967) work to bring the distinctions between Gemeinschaft and Gesellschaft into a discussion of mass-mediated discourse. For Beniger, a pseudocommunity is one in which impersonal associations constitute simulated personalized communication, what he calls 'a hybrid of interpersonal and mass communication' (p. 369). His and Peck's criticisms of pseudocommunity center on the insincerity (or inauthenticity) of communication that it represents and the goals toward which that communication may be directed. It is natural that such criticisms ought to be part of an awareness of CMC, for it is, to say the least, difficult to judge sincerity in electronic text. Rheingold (1993) asks the appropriate questions:

> Is telecommunication culture capable of becoming something more than what Scott Peck calls a 'pseudo-community,' where people lack the genuine personal commitments to one another that form the bedrock of genuine community? Or is our notion of 'genuine' changing in an age where more people every day live their lives in increasingly artificial environments? New technologies tend to change old ways of doing things. Is the human need for community going to be the next technology commodity? (pp. 60–1)

The most important of these questions is the one that asks whether or not our notions of the 'genuine' are changing. One of the measures of genuine community ought to be its relationship to action (political or otherwise). As Taylor (1992) notes in *The Ethics of Authenticity*, political powerlessness feeds alienation from community. Does participation in on-line communities increase or decrease individuals' feelings of power? Is it a technology that embodies Taylor's ethic as its users spin off identities, or is it one that technologizes and reduces that ethic by problematizing identity and, with it, authenticity? As others [. . .] have noted, perhaps it does, but it probably does not. Part of the reason for such an assessment is that it is difficult to determine just what would constitute on-line political and personal action. The connections between computer-mediated community and the social and political worlds that users are part of offline are unclear, much like the connections between advertising and consumer behavior or between television and direct effects. Moreover, it is important to not slide by questions of access to computer-mediated communities, as they are related to power. Quarterman (1993) claims that 'although power may come from the barrel of a gun, as Chairman Mao said, it is often preserved by secrecy. In networking, secrecy is not power and may not even be possible. Therefore, networking is subversive' (pp. 48–9). Yet Quarterman does not explain why secrecy may be impossible, nor does he seem sensitive to the powerful role that information and its absence may play in society. As Robert Doolittle (1972) has noted, the rhetorical and political elements that most often constitute communities include common understandings that action and effort will lead to the realization of achievements for the common good. The situation in which we find computer-mediated communities at present is that their very definition as communities is perceived as a 'good thing,' creating a solipsistic and self-fulfilling community that pays little attention to political action outside of that which secures its own maintenance. Community and power do not necessarily intersect, but such solipsism is a form of power itself, wielded by those who occupy the community. Branscomb (1993) has pointed out, 'More important than the substance of the legal rules that are likely to arise governing electronic communications is the question of what group will determine which laws or operating rules shall apply' (p. 99).

Part of what is already occurring is the creation of multitechno/cultural groups that determine operating rules for their own domain.* But what is occurring additionally as the Internet and other computer networks sprout commercial nodes is the agglomeration of capital and its concomitant pressures on groups that already have some power. The arguments those groups (and others) often marshal to persuade government, industry, and citizens that computer networks must remain 'free' are based on the very idea that it is only for lack of constraint that community could exist via CMC. However, community itself is a structuring concept—and a strong one given the almost primordial pull of symbolic force the word 'community' continues to have.

Community as Culturally Constructed Category

Creating and maintaining community has traditionally been valued as a commendable goal. Bell and Newby (1974) wrote of the theoretical inheritance brought to definitions of community that '"community" was thought to be a good thing, its passing was to be deplored, feared and regretted' (p. 21). That inheritance was left by modernism, and in some ways is part of post-modernism too, at least insofar as the tensions between modernity and post-modernism are sometimes still implicated in its theoretical discourse. The importance of that inheritance is the rhetorical use of community in social planning and the strength of persuasion the term 'community' contains. In her book, *Redeeming Modernity*, Jensen (1990), borrowing from Robert Nisbet, identifies 'the community/society dichotomy [that] references social relations,' and claims that 'what is at stake in this dichotomy, in American social thought, is the issue of connection—how we are to link up to each other in America' (p. 71). Jensen's questions about the ties that bind us ought to be asked in light of CMC. How is computer-mediated communication to link us up?

We have some answers insofar as links have already been made and others are envisioned. The scholarly literature examining computer-mediated communication has been expanding, as scholars in various fields probe and examine the nature of this form of communication. What can be learned from these forays that seek to assess not only the present state of CMC but its future?

Several threads, or categories, emerge from a close reading of the literature, predicated on the notion of CMC's effects on social relations. CMC, it is claimed, will

1. Create opportunities for education and learning
2. Create new opportunities for participatory democracy
3. Establish countercultures on an unprecedented scale
4. Ensnarl already difficult legal matters concerning privacy, copyright, and ethics
5. Restructure man/machine interaction

It is instructive and interesting to examine each claim in its own right. [. . .] Interestingly, the unifying principle among these claims is that organizational change will precipitate their occurrence. As Marvin (1988) notes in her brilliant study of the earliest electrical communication devices, *When Old Technologies Were New*, assumptions about technological change tell us what we believe the technology is supposed to do, which in turn reveals much about what we believe *we* are supposed to do. It would seem, then, that rather than reinvent or re-create social relations, or even reexamine culturally constructed definitions of community we already have, we believe we are supposed to reorganize social relations around a new technology.

The most important reorganization is the force with which the ideal of face-to-face communication is brought to the center of arguments about the structure of communication technology. Some evidence of this is found in the use of terms like 'interactivity' to describe (and promote) new technology that allows for user feedback. As Rafaeli (1988) sees it,

> Interactivity is generally assumed to be a natural attribute of face-to-face conversation, but it has been proposed to occur in mediated communication settings as well.
>
> [I]nteractivity is an expression of the extent that in a given series of communication exchanges, any third (or later) transmission (or message) is related to the degree to which previous exchanges referred to even earlier transmissions. . . . This complex and ambitious definition misrepresents the intuitive nature of interactivity. In fact, the power of the concept and its attraction are in the matter-of-factness of its nature. The common feeling is that interactivity, like news, is something you know when you see it. (pp. 110–11)

Rafaeli goes on to criticize the use of interactivity as a 'buzzword' but does not overlook a fundamental question: Why should face-to-face communication serve as an ideal? The most likely answer is that it is a form of communication that we identify and associate with community, with Gemeinschaft, and face-to-interface communication we associate with the impersonal communication that Beniger decries has led to 'pseudocommunity'.

Yet Michael Schudson (1978) has noted that

> when we criticize the reality of the mass media, we do so by opposing it to
> an ideal of conversation which we are not inclined to examine. We are
> not really interested in what face-to-face communication is like; rather,
> we have developed a notion that all communication *should* be like a
> certain model of conversation, whether that model really exists or not.
> (p. 323)

Computer-mediated communication permits us the 'feeling' that Rafaeli
emphasizes, but we are too media-savvy to be misled to believe that CMC has
achieved the face-to-face ideal. We thus totter between the belief that CMC
will, to borrow from Marshall McLuhan, 'retribalize' us by engaging us in an
ideal form of communication we have abandoned, and the belief that our
interaction will become mechanized and lack the 'richness' of face-to-face
conversation. The development of CMC fits Schudson's (1978) idea that the
face-to-face ideal is 'in part a consequence of mass media': 'First, the mass
media have contributed to making the "egalitarian" criterion of ideal communication more prominent and more possible to realize. . . . The mass
media have had a second effect in making the conversational ideal more frequently realizable' (p. 326).

Creating software (and hardware) for CMC has become a race to provide
the most 'lifelike' interaction possible, a race characterized by extreme atten-
tiveness to information richness and simulation. Each checkpoint in this race
asks whether or not we have taken a step toward realizing the 'conversational
ideal' about which Schudson writes. Yet, even in face-to-face interaction,
much of what is most valuable is the absence of information, the silence and
pauses between words and phrases. Cohen (1985) critiques the idyllic (and
often romantic) view of face-to-face interaction, too:

> The idea that, in small-scale society, people interact with each other as
> 'whole persons' is a simplification. They may well encounter each other
> more frequently, more intensively and over a wider range of activities
> than is the case in more anonymous large-scale milieux. But this is not to
> say that people's knowledge of 'the person' overrides their perception of
> the distinctive activities (or 'roles') in which the person is engaged.
> (p. 29)

Nevertheless, we are reassured by the belief that the reality our eyes perceive
in face-to-face communication is more real (or less manipulable) than other
media by which we perceive reality. That belief reasserts itself in the understanding we have that what mediated reality lacks is sufficient 'richness' to
convey nonmediated reality. Each belief fuels the bias toward filling cyberspace with information and gives rise to two distinct ideas: first, that unused
space is wasteful and, second, that more information is desirable and better.
The trend in CMC, as in other areas of computing, has been to provide
greater speed and more levels of organization to cope with that bias, and
computer-mediated communication has been viewed from the perspective
of organizational communication scholarship for quite some time. That perspective brings a bias, and I will examine it in a moment. Regarding community most directly, though, the bias most readily discernible is toward the

removal of boundaries. Yet, as Cohen (1985) notes, it is 'boundary [that] encapsulates the identity of the community' (p. 12). Face-to-face interaction does not necessarily break down boundaries, and to adopt it as an ideal will likewise not necessarily facilitate communication, community building, or understanding among people.

CMC and Organization

Although the study of organizational communication has only recently begun to intersect with community studies, particularly in the field of health communication, much of the literature examining CMC is from an organizational perspective and stems from studies of the introduction of computers in the workplace. The work of Rice (1984, 1987, 1989; Rice & Love, 1987; Rice & McDaniel, 1987) as well as that of Sproull and Kiesler (1991) is exemplary and develops ideas about the changes that electronic mail brings to organizations. The main body of their scholarship examines patterns of interaction and communication through telecommuting, teleconferencing, e-mail, and the like and asks questions about management, work, and the future of traditional organizational structures unbound from 'the conventional patterns of who talks to whom and who knows what' (Sproull & Kiesler, 1991, p. 116).

There are two key elements to this form of analysis of CMC. First, it assumes that distance and space are to be centrally overcome and controlled, not in the sense that an individual is to control them but in the sense that a technology centrally and universally used will permit 'almost unlimited access to data and to other people' (Sproull & Kiesler, 1991, p. 116). Almost in the same breath, however, Sproull & Kiesler argue for centralized oversight and control of access, claiming that

> it is up to management to make and shape connections. The organization of the future will depend significantly not just on how the technology of networking evolves but also on how managers seize the opportunity it presents for transforming the structure of work. (p. 123)

The issue, however, is less changes to 'the structure of work' and more the control of access to information and people. That access is based on two principal assumptions about the use of computers found in many analyses of CMC: Computers cut across/break down boundaries, and computers break down hierarchies. Both of these assumptions are based on the idea that modifications to present social systems and reactions to social concerns can best be achieved by using a new technology on old problems. It is not unusual to find such assumptions when any new technology is put to use, as Marvin (1988) notes. Similarly, Hiltz and Turoff (1978) note, in relation to electronic mail, that there is a tendency to view new technology as simply a more efficient method or tool for confronting or improving an existing technology or situation.

Yet [. . .] computers just as easily create boundaries and hierarchies. As Ross (1990) points out in a terrific essay, itself available on-line, there is a 'tendency to use technology to form information elites,' and evidence of such formations can be found in the romanticizing of the hacker as a countercultural hero (p. 15), in the elevation of privacy as a critical issue for computer users, and in the fervor with which PGP and other data encryption devices are being adopted.

The speed with which we may form new hierarchies and reorganize existing ones, particularly such as those on Usenet, does little to mitigate the fact that they are indeed present. They may rise and fall more quickly, but they are just as ubiquitous. Rheingold (1993) goes so far as to determine that computer-mediated communities will 'grow into much larger networks over the next twenty years' (p. 58) but does not question or examine how that growth will be accompanied by structuring and hierarchies within networks.

Indeed, it is difficult to understand just how hierarchy and community can coexist via CMC, in part because of the seemingly anarchic (or at least unstructured) nature of many computer networks. A common denominator linking hierarchy and community is identity, not only in terms of one's sense of self but also in terms of one's sense of others. CMC provides ample room for identity but not for its fixing and structuring. Ross (1990) notes that 'access to digital systems still requires only the authentication of a signature or pseudonym, not the identification of a real surveillable person, so there exists a crucial operative gap between authentication and identification' (p. 24). As some authors point out,* one can have multiple identities in cyberspace; moreover, one can shift identities rather easily, taking on characteristics of others' identities. It even is possible, as MacKinnon shows,* to functionally locate personae via CMC.

The Illusion of Community

Issues of identity ought to be front and center with those of community as CMC develops. As Cheney (1991) correctly claims, 'One's identity is somehow related to the larger social order. However [there is] disagree[ment] ... on what kind of relationship this entails' (p. 10). What is most important is that identity is related directly to the increase in size of social organizations. The necessity to 'keep track' of individuals by way of Social Security numbers and other bureaucratic devices that connect an individual to a larger entity make identification a matter of organization too, rather than a matter of self-definition. Cheney's (1991) comment that 'there has been a transformation of the term "identity" from its "sameness" meaning to its "essence" meaning' (p. 13) is significant precisely because identity as mediated in cyberspace carries no essential meanings. Alliances based on 'sameness' may form and dissolve. Yet the ideas that Cheney borrows from Burke that assist him in developing a definition of identity 'associated with the individual that must draw upon social and collective resources for its meaning' (p. 20) do not apply equally in CMC. CMC users may use similar resources to develop and structure meaning but without the effective alliances that Cheney implies are necessary.

Rheingold (1993) attempts to define how identity will be constructed via CMC:

> We reduce and encode our identities as words on a screen, decode and unpack the identities of others. The way we use these words, the stories

(true and false) we tell about ourselves (or about the identity we want
people to believe us to be) is what determines our identities in
cyberspace. The aggregation of personae, interacting with each other,
determines the nature of the collective culture. (p. 61)

One might suppose the same is true as to the aggregation of particular traits
that determine the nature of the individual. However, the symbolic processes
that Rheingold elides through use of such words as 'encode' and 'unpack'
(themselves taken from the language of computer software) are fraught with
unproblematized assumptions about the work that humans perform in
search of their own identities and those of others. Interaction ought not be
substituted for community, or, for that matter, for communication, and to
uncritically accept connections between personae, individuals, and community inadvisable.

It will be unfortunate, too, if we uncritically accept that CMC will usher in
the great new era that other media of communication have failed to bring us.
It is not, as virtual reality pioneer Jaron Lanier says, that television has failed
us because it 'wasn't planned well enough' ('Virtual Reality,' 1992, p. 6); it is
that organization and planning are not necessarily appropriate processes for
constructing or recapturing the sense of community for which we are nostalgic. Bender (1978) sharply criticizes those who seek 'to recapture community
by imputing it to large-scale organizations and to locality-based social activity regardless of the quality of human relationships that characterize these
contexts' (p. 143). Instead, Bender finds community in the midst of a transformation and asks us to heed his call that we not, by way of our nostalgia,
limit definitions of community to that which 'seventeenth-century New
Englanders knew' (p. 146), although with electronic town hall meetings and
the like we seem to be doing precisely that. One example can be found in
Rheingold's work. Although often critical in much of his writing, it is clear
from the comparisons that Rheingold (1993) makes to other forms of community that what he calls 'virtual communities' are predicated on nostalgic
(and romantic) ideals:

It's a bit like a neighbourhood pub or coffee shop. It's a little like a salon,
where I can participate in a hundred ongoing conversations with people
who don't care what I look like or sound like, but who do care how I
think and communicate. There are seminars and word fights in different
corners. (p. 66)

Virtual communities might be real communities, they might be pseudo-
communities, or they might be something entirely new in the realm of
social contracts, but I believe they are in part a response to the hunger for
community that has followed the disintegration of traditional communities around the world. (p. 62)

Of course, it is difficult to imagine what new on-line communities may be
like, and it is far easier to use our memories and myths as we construct them.
What is more important than simply understanding the construction we are
undertaking is to notice that it is peculiar and particular to the computer. Because these machines are seen as 'linking' machines (they link information,
data, communication, sound, and image through the common language of

digital encoding), to borrow from Jensen (1990), they inherently affect the ways we think of linking up to each other, and thus they fit squarely into our concerns about community. Media technologies that have largely been tied to the 'transportation' view of communication mentioned earlier were developed to overcome space and time. The computer, in particular, is an 'efficiency' machine, purporting to ever increase its speed. But unlike those technologies, the computer used for communication is a technology to be understood from the 'ritual' view of communication, for once time and space have been overcome (or at least rendered surmountable) the spur for development is connection, linkage. Once we can surmount time and space and 'be' anywhere, we must choose a 'where' at which to be, and the computer's functionality lies in its power to make us organize our desires about the spaces we visit and stay in.

The question remains, though, whether or not the communities we may form by way of CMC will, or even ought to, be part of our public culture. If so, then perhaps it would be best to not understand them as communities. As Bender (1978) writers, 'Our public lives do not provide an experience of community. The mutuality and sentiment characteristic of community cannot and need not be achieved in public. We must be careful to distinguish between these two contexts of social experience' (p. 148). The manner in which we seek to find community, empowerment, and political action all embedded in our ability to use CMC is thereby troubling. No one medium, no one technology, has been able to provide those elements in combination, and often we have been unable to find them in any media. CMC has potential for a variety of consequences, some anticipated, some not. A critical awareness of the social transformations that have occurred and continue to occur with or without technology will be our best ally as we incorporate CMC into contemporary social life.

References   BARNES, T. J., & DUNCAN, J. S. (1992). *Writing Worlds*. London: Routledge.

BELL, C., & NEWBY, H. (1974). *The Sociology of Community*. London: Frank Cass & Company, Ltd.

BENDER, T. (1978). *Community and Social Change in America*. New Brunswick, NJ: Rutgers University Press.

BENEDIKT, M. (1991). Cyberspace: Some Proposals. In M. Benedikt (ed.), *Cyberspace* (pp. 119–224). Cambridge, Mass.: MIT Press.

BENIGER, J. (1986). *The Control Revolution*. Cambridge, Mass.: Harvard University Press.

—— (1987). Personalization of Mass Media and the Growth of Pseudo-Community. *Communication Research, 14*(3), 352–71.

BERGER, P. L., & LUCKMANN, T. (1967). *The Social Construction of Reality*. New York: Anchor Books.

BERMAN, M. (1982). *All That Is Solid Melts into Air*. New York: Simon & Schuster.

BRANSCOMB, A. W. (1993). Jurisdictional Quandaries for Global Networks. In L. M. Harasim (ed.), *Global Networks* (pp. 57–80). Cambridge, Mass.: MIT Press.

CALHOUN, C. J. (1980). Community: Toward a Variable Conceptualization for Comparative Research. *Social History, 5*, 105–29.

CAREY, J. (1989). *Communication as Culture*. Boston, Mass.: Unwin-Hyman.

—— (1993). Everything that Rises must Diverge: Notes on Communications, Technology and the Symbolic Construction of the Social. In P. Gaunt (ed.), *Beyond Agendas* (pp. 171–84). Westport, Conn.: Greenwood.

CHAYKO, M. (1993). What is Real in the Age of Virtual Reality? 'Reframing' Frame Analysis for a technological World. *Symbolic Interaction, 16*(2), 171–81.

CHENEY, G. (1991). *Rhetoric in an Organizational Society: Managing Multiple Identities.* Columbia: University of South Carolina Press.

CHESEBRO, J. W., & BONSALL, D. G. (1989). *Computer-mediated Communication.* Tuscaloosa: University of Alabama Press.

COHEN, A. (1985). *The Symbolic Construction of Community.* London: Tavistock.

DOOLITTLE, R. J. (1972). Speech Communication as an Instrument in Engendering and Sustaining a Sense of Community in Urban and Poor Neighborhoods: A Study of Rhetorical Potentialities. Unpublished doctoral dissertation, Pennsylvania State University.

EFFRAT, M. P. (1974). *The Community: Approaches and Applications.* New York: Free Press.

ETZIONI, A. (1991). *The Responsive Society.* San Francisco: Jossey-Bass.

FREDERICK, H. (1993). Computer Networks and the Emergence of Global Civil Society. In L. M. Harasim (ed.), *Global Networks* (pp. 283–96). Cambridge, Mass.: MIT Press.

GILLESPIE, A., & ROBINS, K. (1989). Geographical Inequalities: The Spatial Bias of the New Communications Technologies. *Journal of Communication, 39*(3), 7–18.

HARASIM, L. M. (ed.). (1993). *Global Networks.* Cambridge, Mass.: MIT Press.

HARVEY, D. (1989). *The Condition of Postmodernity.* Oxford: Blackwell.

HILTZ, S. R., & TUROFF, M. (1978). *The Network Nation: Human Communication via Computer.* Reading, Mass.: Addison-Wesley.

JENSEN, J. (1990). *Redeeming Modernity.* Newbury Park, Cal.: Sage.

LAIRD, A. (1993). Computerscape with Letters. Unpublished manuscript prepared for Media History, Faculty of Communication, University of Tulsa.

LESLIE, J. (1993, November). Kids Connecting. *Wired, 1*(5), 90–3.

LICKLIDER, J. C. R., & TAYLOR, R. W. (1968). The Computer as a Communication Device. *Science & Technology, 76,* 21–31.

MARVIN, C. (1988). *When Old Technologies Were New.* Oxford: Oxford University Press.

MORRIS, M. (1992). The Man in the Mirror: David Harvey's 'Condition' of Postmodernity. *Theory, Culture & Society, 9,* 253–79.

MUMFORD, L. (1934). *Technics and Civilization.* New York: Harcourt, Brace & World.

ONG, W. (1982). *Orality and Literacy.* London: Methuen.

PATTON, P. (1986). *Open Road.* New York: Simon & Schuster.

PECK, M. S. (1987). *The Different Drum: Community-Making and Peace.* New York: Simon & Schuster.

QUARTERMAN, J. S. (1993). The Global Matrix of Minds. In L. M. Harasim (ed.), *Global Networks* (pp. 35–56). Cambridge, Mass.: MIT Press.

RAFAELI, S. (1988). Interactivity: From New Media to Communication. In R. P. Hawkins, J. M. Wiesmann, & S. Pingree (eds.), *Advancing Communication Science: Merging Mass and Interpersonal Processes* (Sage Annual Reviews of Communication Research, Vol. 16, pp. 110–34). Newbury Park, Cal.: Sage.

RHEINGOLD, H. (1993). A Slice of Life in my Virtual Community. In L. M. Harasim (ed.), *Global Networks* (pp. 57–80). Cambridge Mass.: MIT Press.

RICE, R. E. (1984). *The New Media: Communication, Research, and Technology.* Beverly Hills, Cal.: Sage.

—— (1987). Computer-Mediated Communication and Organizational Innovation. *Journal of Communication, 37*(4), 65–94.

Rice, R. E. (1989). Issues and concepts in Research on Computer-Mediated Communication Systems. In J. A. Anderson (ed.), *Communication Yearbook* (Vol. 12, pp. 436–76). Newbury Park, Cal.: Sage.

—— & Love, G. (1987). Electronic Emotion: Socioemotional Content in a Computer-Mediated Communication Network. *Communication Research, 14*, 85–108.

—— & McDaniel, B. (1987). *Managing Organizational Innovation: The Evolution from Word Processing to Office Information Systems*. New York: Columbia University Press.

Ross, A. (1990). Hacking Away at the Counterculture. *Postmodern Culture, 1*(1), 1–43.

Schudson, M. (1978). The Ideal of Conversation in the Study of Mass Media. *Communication Research, 12*(5), 320–9.

Soja, E. (1989). *Postmodern Geographies: The Reassertion of Space in Critical Social Theory*. London: Verso.

Sproull, L., & Kiesler, S. (1991, September). Computers, networks and work. *Scientific American*, pp. 116–23.

Stacey, M. (1974). The Myth of Community Studies. In C. Bell & H. Newby (eds.), *The Sociology of Community* (pp. 13–26). London: Frank Cass & Company, Ltd.

Stone, A. R. (1991). Will the Real Body Please Stand Up? Boundary Stories about Virtual Cultures. In M. Benedikt (ed.), *Cyberspace* (pp. 81–118). Cambridge, Mass.: MIT Press.

Taylor, C. (1992). *The Ethics of Authenticity*. Cambridge, Mass.: Harvard University Press.

Tonnies, F. (1967). *Community and Society*. Lansing: Michigan State University Press.

Virtual reality: A New Medium and a New Culture. (1992, November). *Communique*, p. 6.

Walls, J. (1993). Global Networking for Local Development: Task Focus and Relationship Focus in Cross-Cultural Communication. In L. M. Harasim (ed.), *Global Networks* (pp. 153–66). Cambridge, Mass.: MIT Press.

Warner, L. (1963). *Yankee City*. New Haven, Conn.: Yale University Press.

14

Posting in a Different Voice: Gender and Ethics in Computer-Mediated Communication

Susan Herring

In this article Susan Herring probes moral and political dimensions of norms governing on-line behaviour, as well as the mechanism by which these are established. Herring's analysis of postings to electronic fora leads her to conclude that women and men appeal to different, partially incompatible systems of values with respect to their own behaviour on-line and their understanding of the on-line behaviour of others. Herring's investigation is based on observation, survey, and content analysis of 'netiquette' statements. Her analysis leads her to conclude that there are gender differences in public discourse on the Internet. Herring's detailed analysis of gendered media underscores the pervasive normative nature of language-use as behaviour, and that CMC includes, despite the rhetoric of equalization, heavily gendered discourses.

Introduction[1]

MUCH OF THE discussion of ethical issues associated with computer-mediated communication (CMC) has been concerned with the use (or abuse) of CMC in the service of other, essentially CMC-external goals—for example, using computer networks to advertise one's commercial services or products, striking up electronic contact with women (and, in some cases, children) for the purpose of establishing sexual liaisons, or making improper use of computer-mediated information by violating copyright or the privacy of the sender (Dunlop and Kling 1991; Johnson and Snapper 1985; Shea 1994). As yet, however, little work has addressed the ethics of computer-mediated interaction itself, by which I mean the conflicts of interest and potential harm to others which can result from the manner and the extent to which computer-mediated messages are

From Charles Ess (ed.), *Philosophical Perspectives on Computer-Mediated Communication* (Albany, NY: State University of New York Press, 1996), 115–45.

1 The research reported here was partially supported by National Endowment for the Humanities grant no. FT-40112. The author wishes to thank Charles Ess and Robin Lakoff for writing letters of support for the grant application. Thanks also to Robin Lombard and Jim Thomas for commenting on an earlier version of this paper and to Brett Benham for assistance in producing the bell curves.

posted in public places. Although posting behavior falls partially under the rubric of netiquette (as network etiquette is called), more than manners is involved. Netiquette norms have both a moral and a political dimension, in that they are founded on systems of values and judgments which may vary according to different groups of users. Yet it is typically the most powerful or dominant group whose values take on a normative status.

Such is the case with regard to gender and computer-mediated communication. In this essay, I claim that women and men appeal to different—and partially incompatible—systems of values both as the rational foundation of their posting behavior and in interpreting and evaluating the behavior of others online. These values correspond to differences in posting style, and are evident as well in official netiquette guidelines, where the general bias in favor of values preferred by men has practical consequences for how comfortable women feel in mainstream electronic forums.

These claims run counter to two popular beliefs, one about gender and the other about CMC. First, any claim that women and men are different in other than a relatively trivial physiological sense is considered politically incorrect by many feminists, regardless of its intent. Consider, for example, the response generated by the work of psychologist Carol Gilligan.[2] Gilligan (1977, 1982; Gilligan and Attanucci 1988) interviewed adolescents and adults about their responses to moral dilemmas and observed that her female subjects regularly evoked different ethical priorities than did male subjects. Gilligan's concern was that women's 'different voice' is traditionally assessed as deviant or defective relative to a male norm; she presents evidence instead for a mature and internally coherent female moral orientation which she terms an 'ethic of care,' as compared with the 'ethic of justice' preferentially evoked by men. Feminist critics such as Martha Mednick (1989), Katha Pollitt (1992), and Linda Steiner (1989), however, consider such claims dangerous, in that they resemble traditional stereotypes and thus are all too readily embraced by conservative and antifeminist elements as proof that gender inequality—especially the division of labor between highly rewarded male activity in the public domain and devalued female domestic activity—is part of the preordained natural order and should not be changed.[3] Indeed, it is wrong, according to some critics, even to *describe* the differences: 'Descriptions/prescriptions of a female ethic wrongly imply that women are locked into a female experience which is self-authenticating and self-validating' (Grimshaw 1986, 17, cited in Steiner 1989, 161).

The claim that there are gender differences in CMC is also problematic from the perspective of the dominant discourse about computer-mediated communications technology. Part of the idealism surrounding the technology in the early decades of its development, and which still persists in many circles, was the belief that computer networks would neutralize gender and other status-related differences and empower traditionally underrepresented groups (Hiltz and Turoff 1993; Kiesler, Siegal, and McGuire

2 The work of other 'difference feminists' (Pollitt 1992) has provoked similar popular response and similar criticism; notable in this category are Chodorow 1978; Ruddick 1989; and Tannen 1990 (criticized by Troemel-Ploetz 1991).

3 In the case of CMC, the danger is presumably that gender differences could be cited to justify excluding women from influential computer-mediated forums or from policy decisions regarding CMC.

1984; Graddol and Swann 1989; Rheingold 1993). The reasoning was deductive: Because of the 'mediated' nature of the medium, messages posted to others are decontextualized and potentially anonymous, free from physical cues to the sender's sex, age, race, able-bodiedness, attractiveness, and so forth. Never mind that users overwhelmingly choose to forgo the anonymity option by signing their messages. Never mind that similar claims could be made about letter writing, which is hardly gender-neutral. People wanted to believe in the potential of the new technology for equalizing social relations, and thus the assumption of gender neutrality initially was not questioned.

In principle, however, the accuracy of claims of gender differences—in CMC or elsewhere—is independent of their 'naturalness,' their political consequences, or the idealism that accompanies the introduction of a new technology. Moreover, describing gender differences need not be incompatible with feminist or egalitarian ideals. Quite to the contrary, differences that reproduce patterns of dominance must be named and understood, lest inequality be perpetuated and recreated through the uncritical acting out of familiar scripts. It is in this spirit that the present essay was written—with the goal of revealing gender differences (and gender inequalities) in cyberspace that some readers may well find disconcerting, but hopefully will no longer be able to ignore.

The Investigation

The claims advanced in this paper are based on an empirical investigation of gender, ethics, and etiquette on the Internet carried out (with the exception of the first part) during the spring of 1994. The investigation is comprised of three parts:

Behavior: I conducted ethnographic observation ranging from periods of two weeks to three years of daily exchanges in nine computer-mediated discussion lists with varying concentrations of female subscribers (from 11% to 88%),[4] and analyzed the discourse of selected discussions from the lists in terms of amount and style of participation, controlling for gender.

Values: I prepared an anonymous survey that was distributed on eight computer-mediated discussion lists;[5] the survey included three open-ended questions about what Net users most appreciate, dislike, and would like to change about the behavior of others online. I also analyzed the content of metadiscourse about what constitutes appropriate and inappropriate behavior in the nine lists from the 'behavior' part of the investigation.

Netiquette guidelines: A content analysis was performed of explicit netiquette statements from the introductory messages sent out to new subscribers on seven discussion lists and from two general collections of

---

4 The nine lists are, in order of increasing percentage of female subscribers: PHILOSOP (11%), POLITICS (17%), PAGLIA (discussion of the writings of antifeminist feminist Camille Paglia; 34%), LINGUIST (36%), MBU (discussion of computers and writing; 42%), TESL (Teaching English as a Second Language; 56%), SWIP (Society for Women in Philosophy; 80%), WMSPRT (Women's Spirituality and Feminist-Oriented Religions; 81%), and WMST (Women's Studies; 88%). At the time they were sampled, all were active lists generating 20–100 messages per week.

5 The eight lists surveyed are CuD (Computer Underground Digest, a weekly electronic newsletter whose readership includes many computing professionals), PHILCOMM (Philosophy of Communication), PHILOSOP, LINGUIST, SWIP, TESL, WMSPRT, and WMST.

recommended network etiquette.[6] The content of the netiquette guidelines was then compared with the behaviors and values identified in the first two parts of the investigation.

The results of the investigation reveal that not only do many women and men use recognizably gendered posting styles, but they also appeal to different systems of values in rationalizing their posting behavior and in interpreting and judging the behavior of others. Women preferentially evoke an ethic of politeness and consideration for the wants of others, especially their desire to be ratified and liked, while men evoke an ethic of agonistic debate and freedom from rules or imposition. The male ethic predominates in official netiquette guidelines and in discourse about the Internet in general, with the result that women with a politeness ethic must create and defend women-centered spaces online in order to carry out the kind of discourse they value. Although the observed differences do not describe all male and female net users, they are important in that they affect norms of interpretation and evaluation in cyberspace more generally.

The Evidence for Difference

Contrary to the claim that CMC neutralizes gender distinctions, recent empirical studies of computer-mediated interaction suggest that gender differences online reproduce and even exaggerate gender differences found in face-to-face interaction (Hall, forthcoming; Herring 1992, 1993a; Herring, Johnson, and DiBenedetto 1992; Herring and Lombard 1995; Kramarae and Taylor 1993; Selfe and Meyer 1991; Sutton 1994). In what ways do men and women differ in their computer-mediated communication?

In this section, I discuss differences in two domains: public posting to Internet discussion groups and values associated with posting behavior. Since I have already presented considerable evidence for the former in other publications (see especially Herring 1993a), after summarizing this evidence, I will devote most of my attention to making a case for the latter. The third part of this section presents evidence for gender bias in netiquette guidelines.

Different Posting Styles

There is a recognizable style of posting found in most, if not all, public forums on the Internet which, in its most extreme form, manifests itself as 'flaming,' or personal put-downs, and which is generally characterized by a challenging, adversarial, or superior stance vis à vis the intended addressee(s). This style is often, although not always, accompanied by a tendency to post lengthy and/or frequent messages and to participate disproportionately more than others in a given discussion. In forum after electronic forum, the overwhelming majority of participants exhibiting this style are male. Examples of the Adversarial style are given below.[7]

---

6 Netiquette statements were analyzed from the introductory messages of CuD, PHILOSOP, POLITICS, LINGUIST, SWIP, TESL, WMST; the general collections analyzed are 'Rules for Posting to Usenet' (Horton and Spafford 1993), 'What is Usenet?' (Salzenberg and Spafford 1993), and *Toward an Ethics and Etiquette for Electronic Mail* (Shapiro and Anderson 1985).

7 All examples given in this section are from messages posted to public-accessible discussion groups on the Internet. To protect the anonymity of individual participants, names and electronic addresses that appear in the messages have been changed.

1. [PHILOSOP] While I do not especially care how this gets settled, I am surprised by the continuing absurdity of the discussion. [distancing stance, presupposed put-down ('this discussion is absurd')]

2. [LINGUIST] [Jean Linguiste's] proposals towards a more transparent morphology in French are exactly what he calls them: a farce. Nobody could ever take them seriously—unless we want to look as well at pairs such as *père-mère*, *coq-poule* and defigure the French language in the process. [strong assertions, put-down ('JL's proposals are a farce'; implied: 'JL wants to defigure the French language')]

3. [POLITICS] In article <[message number]> [address (Ed [Lastname])] writes:
   >No, but I shall emphasize that should the news admins take it upon
   >themselves to decide the truth of your claim—a remote possibility
   >indeed—we surely would not weight most highly your word on the

   Who the hell are 'we,' 'edo boy'. I was unaware that a net-clown was required to agree on the US Constitution. Well anyway, enough entertainment for a self-exposed 'wieneramus'. The criminal acts of the x-Soviet Armenian Government come directly under the scope of the Convention on Genocide adopted by the General Assembly of the United Nations on December 8, 1948, containing the following provisions: [continues another 8 screens] [name-calling ('edo boy,' 'net-clown,' 'wieneramus'), profanity ('who the hell')]

There exists an equally distinct style, although less widespread in its distribution, that is characterized by expressions of support and appreciation, and in which views are presented in a hedged fashion, often with appeals for ratification from the group. This style is exhibited almost exclusively by women and is the discursive norm in many women-only and women-centered lists. The following examples illustrate the Supportive/ Attenuated style.

4. [WOMEN]
   >Aileen,
   >I just wanted to let you know that I have really enjoyed all your posts about
   >Women's herstory. They have been extremely informative and I've learned alot
   >about the women's movement. Thank you!
   >-Erika

   DITTO!!!! They are wonderful! Did anyone else catch the first part of a Century of Women? I really enjoyed it. Of course, I didn't agree with everything they said. . . . but it was really informative. Roberta
   ~~~~~~~ [appreciates, thanks, agrees, appeals to group]

5. [WMST] Well, enough of my ranting. I am very interested in this subject. My area is experimental social psychology. I am also very excited about the book you mentioned. It is a very worthwhile project. If I can help in any way, typing, whatever, I would love to help. Please let

    me know if there is anything I can do. [apologizes, appreciates, offers help]

6. [TESL] [. . .] I hope this makes sense. This is kind of what I had in mind when I realized I couldn't give a real definitive answer. Of course, maybe I'm just getting into the nuances of the language when it would be easier to just give the simple answer. Any response? [hedges, expresses doubt (supplies counterargument to own position), appeals to group]

In what sense can these two styles be generalized to represent gender differences in posting behavior? Certainly, not all men who post on the Internet are adversarial; indeed, discourse in mixed-sex lists is typically dominated by a small male minority which posts a lot (Selfe and Meyer 1991; Herring 1993a) and accounts for the majority of adversarial behaviors (Herring 1993a, 1993b), while many men are relatively neutral and informative and others are supportive or attenuated in their posting style, especially on women-centered lists. Similarly, not all women are supportive and attenuated; many also adopt a neutral, informative style, and some can be adversarial, especially on male-dominated lists where adversariality is the discursive norm. Nevertheless, the two styles are gendered in that the extremes of each are manifested almost exclusively by one gender and not the other. Moreover, men tend toward adversariality and women toward support/attenuation even in the area of overlap between the two extremes. The distribution of the styles in relation to gender can be represented schematically as two bell-shaped curves that overlap but are out of phase, as shown in Figure 1.

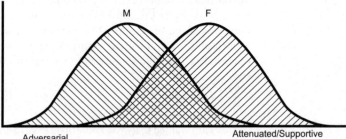

Fig. 1.
Distribution of adversarial and attenuated/supportive posting styles by gender

Figure 1 illustrates two points. First, male and female behaviors are not disjunctive; that is, men and women online are not separate species (cf. Holmstrom 1982). Many posts fall into a middle category that includes mixing male-and female-gendered features or the absence of either.[8] Second,

---

8 This distributional model generalizes across variation based on local list-serve norms and topics of discussion. All other things being equal, normative posting style for both genders tends to shift in the adversarial direction in male-predominant lists such as PAGLIA and LINGUIST and in the attenuated/supportive direction in female-predominant lists such as WMST and TESL, although differences in degree still characterize prototypical 'male' and 'female' contributions. The effect of dominant list usage on gender style is documented in Herring (1996) and Herring and Lombard (1995).

despite the large area of overlap, two distinct populations are involved—in other words, behaviors at the extremes are not randomly distributed between males and females, but are virtually male exclusive (for extreme forms of adversariality) and female exclusive (for extreme forms of appreciation and support). It is this distribution that I seek to explain.

Why focus on the extremes, rather than on the area of overlap where women and men exhibit similar kinds of variation? The existence of gendered styles must be explicitly demonstrated in order to put to rest the myth that gender is invisible on computer networks. This myth not only misrepresents the reality of gender on-line, but further perpetuates the uncritical tolerance of practices (such as flaming) which discourage women from using computer networks (Herring 1992, 1993a). Such practices affect large numbers of users even when only a minority of men are responsible, and thus it behooves those concerned with gender equality in cyberspace to understand them well.

Further, there is evidence that the extreme gendered posting styles illustrated above are psychologically and socially real for net users; that is, they have a *symbolic* status over and above their actual distribution. Thus participants in electronic discussions regularly infer the gender of message posters on the basis of the presence of features of one or the other of these styles. Cases where the self-identified gender of the poster is in question are especially revealing in this regard. Consider the following situations, the first involving a male posing as a female, and the second, a (suspected) female posing as a male.

(i) A male subscriber on SWIP-L posted a message disagreeing with the general consensus that discourse on SWIP should be nonagonistic, commenting, 'There's nothing like a healthy denunciation by one's colleagues every once in a while to get one's blood flowing, and spur one to greater subtlety and exactness of thought.' He signed his message with a female pseudonym, however, causing another (female) subscriber to comment later, 'I must confess to looking for the name of the male who wrote the posting that [Suzi] sent originally and was surprised to find a female name at the end of it.' The female subscriber had (accurately) inferred that anyone actively advocating 'denunciation by one's colleagues' was probably male.

(ii) At a time when another male subscriber had been posting frequent messages to the WOMEN list, a subscriber professing to be a man posted a message inquiring what the list's policy was toward men participating on the list, admitting, 'I sometimes feel guilty for taking up bandwidth.' The message, in addition to showing consideration for the concerns of others on the list, was very attenuated in style and explicitly appreciative of the list: 'I really enjoy this list (actually, it's the best one I'm on).' This prompted another (female) subscriber to respond, 'now that you've posed the question . . . how's one to know you're not a woman posing this question as a man?' Her suspicion indicates that on some level she recognized that anyone posting a message expressing appreciation and consideration for the desires of others was likely to be female.

The existence of gendered prototypes is also supported by cases where males and females are miscast as members of the opposite gender because they do not conform to the expected gender pattern. Hall (forthcoming) cites a case on a women-only list of a poster, 'J.,' suspected of being male on the basis of 'her' offensive, adversarial postings. Discussion ensued on the list of how to handle the case, until someone reported they had met 'J.' in real life in Southern California: 'While they had found her offensive too, they had met her and she was a woman' (155). This shows how probabilistic inferences (based on the empirical tendency for men to be more adversarial than women online) can take on symbolic and even political signification: In order not to be suspected of being male, women must express themselves on this women-only list in an appropriately 'female' style.[9]

These styles and their association with gender are of both practical and theoretical significance. They are of practical significance in that they determine how successfully one is able to 'pass' as a member of a different gender on the Net. They are of theoretical significance in that the existence of different styles and the forms they take are facts requiring further explanation.

Different Values   Why do many Net users post in ways that signal their gender? Why, specifically, do men specialize in flaming and women in supporting others? Flaming is generally considered hostile and rude. Yet the phenomenon is too widespread to be explained away as the crank behavior of a few sociopathic individuals. Indeed, many male-predominant groups, including stuffy academic ones, are adversarial in tone to a degree that, in my female-biased perception, borders on the uncivil. Could it be that men and women have different assessments of what is 'polite' and 'rude' in online communication?

In order to test this hypothesis, I prepared and disseminated an anonymous electronic questionnaire on netiquette. In addition to background questions about respondents' sex, age, ethnicity, professional status, and years of networking, the questionnaire included three open-ended questions asking respondents what online behaviors bother them most, what they most appreciate, and what changes they would like to see in Net interaction in an ideal world.

The questionnaire generated considerable interest: I received nearly 300 usable responses, 60% from men and 40% from women. Immediately I noticed a pattern relating to gender in the responses: Male respondents were more likely than female respondents to 'flame' me about the questionnaire itself.[10] Compare, for example, the following complaints about the length of the questionnaire sent to me by two individuals who elected not to answer it, the first female, the second male.[11]

> [F:]   I hope this doesn't sound terribly rude, but a survey is one of the last things I want to see in my mailbox. And I suspect I'm not alone. This is not to say that you shouldn't have posted it. Rather,

---

9 Interestingly, even gay and lesbian lists are not free of traditionally gendered styles. Hall (forthcoming) reports that men on GAYNET often display an adversarial style, driving some women off the list, while women on SAPPHO display a supportive and attenuated style.

10 Two aspects of the survey generated criticism: its length (about two and a half printed pages), and the fact that respondents were asked to indicate their ethnicity.

11 In keeping with my promise to respondents, all comments quoted in response to the questionnaire are anonymous. For a more detailed description of the survey, see Herring 1994.

please treat your results with caution. They likely will not be representative.

[m:]   What bothers me most are abuses of networking such as yours: unsolicited, lengthy and intrusive postings designed to further others' research by wasting my time.

The female frames her complaint about the survey as a concern for the validity of the investigator's results, while the male expresses concern about the way the survey imposes on him. The female message contains numerous attenuation features, including hedges ('not terribly,' 'I suspect,' 'likely'), an apology, and the use of the politeness marker 'please.' The male message contains no attenuation or politeness features but instead insults the sender of the survey by characterizing the survey in negatively loaded terms such as 'abuse' and 'intrusive' and by intimating that the motives for sending it were selfish and exploitative. While both messages are complaints and thus inherently face-threatening, their style is very different: The first attenuates the threat to the addressee's face, while the second emphasizes it.

Fortunately, many more individuals responded supportively than critically to the survey. However, there were gender differences in the expressions of support as well, as illustrated by the following two comments preceding the completed survey:

[f:]   What an interesting survey! It looks like you've already done at least some informal research into people's 'net peeves'! I'd be very interested to receive a copy of your results at my email address: [address]. Thanks!

[m:]   Here is the response to your survey. Under most circumstances, I would discard the survey due to its length. Kindly, I am replying. I wish you the best of luck in your research!

The female comment compliments the survey (it is interesting) and the sender of the survey (you have done your research), and demonstrates the sincerity of her interest by asking for a copy of the results; the message concludes with an expression of appreciation ('Thanks!'). The male comment criticizes the survey (it is too long) and compliments himself (I am kind for replying);[12] the expression of support comes in the last sentence when he wishes the investigator luck. Both of these messages are friendly and the respondents cooperative, but the first explicitly seeks to make the addressee feel positively valued, while the latter does not.

I reproduce these extraneous comments because they are consistent with the stylistic differences described in the previous section (although the context in which they were produced is quite different) and because they reveal much about the politeness norms of the individuals who wrote them. Politeness can be conceptualized as behavior that addresses two kinds of 'face': positive face, or a person's desire to be ratified and liked, and negative face, or the desire not to be constrained or imposed upon (Brown and Levinson 1987). The comments of the female questionnaire respondents are polite in that they attend to both kinds of face wants in the addressee. The first woman takes

---

12 I assume this was intended ironically, as an attempt at humor.

pains to lessen the imposition ('I hope this doesn't sound terribly rude') and the potential threat to the addressee's positive face ('This is not to say that you shouldn't have posted it') caused by her complaint, and the second woman actively bolsters the addressee's positive face in her appreciative message. In contrast, the men make virtually no concessions to the addressee's positive face (indeed the first man threatens it directly), but do display a concern with their own negative face wants, namely, the desire not to be imposed upon by long surveys. In addition to the apparent contrast between the other-and self-orientation of these concerns, the most striking difference is that only the women appear to be concerned with positive politeness.

Hypothesizing that the difference between the two types of politeness might therefore be significant, I coded each response to the three open-ended questions on the questionnaire in terms of positive and negative politeness. Some examples of common Net behaviors cited in response that illustrate observances (+) and violations (−) of positive (P) and negative (N) politeness are as follows:

Messages support or thank others	(+P; makes others feel valued)
Participants 'flame' or insult others	(−P; makes others feel bad)
Participants post concise messages	(+N; saves others' time)
Messages quote all of the message being responded to	(−N; wastes others' time)

The results of the analysis indicate that women supply politeness-related responses more often than men: 87% of female responses relate to some kind of politeness, as compared with 73% for men. Of politeness-related answers given, women supplied 53% of those related to negative politeness and 61% of those related to positive politeness. A pattern is also evident whereby women evoked *observances* of positive politeness (in response to the questions of what they most like and what changes they would like to see) more often than *violations* (in response to the question of what bothers them most), while for men this pattern is reversed. The distribution of politeness-related responses by gender is summarized for each question and for all questions combined in Table 1.[13]

TABLE 1. *Distribution of responses to open-ended questions by gender and politeness type*

	Bothers		Like		Change		Combined	
	−N	−P	+N	+P	+N	+P	+/−N	+/−P
Male	39	21	16	16	9	2	64	39
	49%	42%	47%	39%	39%	20%	47%	39%
Female	40	29	18	25	14	8	72	62
	51%	58%	53%	61%	61%	80%	53%	61%
Total	79	50	34	41	23	10	136	101
	100%	100%	100%	100%	100%	100%	100%	100%

13 These calculations are based on a subset of survey respondents derived by sampling responses received over time: the first 23 received, then 100–110, 200–210 and all 23 received by nonelectronic means. This produced a sample of 68 respondents, 34 male and 34 female.

Some examples of responses relating to politeness are as follows. When asked what behaviors they most appreciate on the Net, female respondents cited 'thoughtfulness,' 'politeness,' 'short, to the point messages,' 'supportive behaviors,' and 'helpful advice,' and indicated they would like to see 'more please and thank yous,' 'more consideration of others,' and more 'conciseness' in Net interaction. Women report being most bothered by 'overlong, longwinded messages,' 'rude insensitive remarks,' 'unnecessary nastiness,' and 'angry responses or responses designed to provoke.' As one female respondent elaborated:

> The thing that absolutely bothers me the most is when people (in my experience it has always been men) disrupt the list by making provocative and inflammatory remarks designed simply to distress. This only happens on unmoderated lists—but it can be very upsetting.

Rude, nasty, and inflammatory remarks are violations of positive politeness in that they may be taken by the addressee as insulting, and thus threaten her positive face.

Men, in contrast, preferentially mention politeness behaviors associated with the avoidance of imposition. Thus, male respondents complain about 'test messages,' 'cross-posting of messages,' 'advertising,' 'low content and off-topic posts,' 'sending listserv commands to the discussion group,' 'requests by others to do things for them,' 'idiocy and repetitions,' and 'stupid questions,' all of which impose on the receiver's time and resources and threaten negative face. Such abuses are commonly attributed to a lack of knowledge:

> I'd like to see more knowledge out there. Like any public activity, people go on and screw around when they have no idea what they are doing, which wastes a lot of time and energy. People should learn what the net is and how to use it before flooding sixteen groups with the umpteenth repetition [sic] of very simple questions.

While these results would appear to support my initial observations concerning different kinds of politeness, they still leave a basic question unanswered: Why do men violate positive politeness, for example, by engaging in bald criticism, to say nothing of flaming? There is nothing inherent in a desire for freedom from imposition that leads inevitably to an adversarial interactional style. Moreover, despite male concern with freedom from imposition, men are responsible for the majority of violations of negative politeness (my questionnaire notwithstanding) as well: It is men, not women, who post the longest messages, do the most cross-posting, copy the most text from previous messages (and respond, point by point), have the longest signature files, and generally take up the most bandwidth on the net. How can these behaviors be explained?

The questionnaire responses provide the key to this question. Three themes occur repeatedly in male responses to the open-ended questions— themes that are missing almost entirely from female responses. These themes are *freedom from censorship, candor,* and *debate.* Taken together, they make up a coherent and rationally motivated system of values that is separate from and, in some cases, in conflict with politeness values. This system of values, which I call the 'anarchic/agonistic system,' can even be evoked to justify flaming.

Consider, for example, the value accorded *freedom from censorship*. According to this view, the Internet and cyberspace in general is a glorious anarchy, one of the few places in the world in which absolute freedom of speech is possible. Censorship in this view is equated with rules and any form of imposed regulation, with the ultimate threat being take-over and control of the Net by government and/or large corporations. Rather than having imposed rules on the Internet, individual users should self-regulate their behavior to show consideration (i.e., in terms of negative politeness) for others. One male respondent comments as follows in response to the question, In an ideal world, what changes would you like to see in the way people interact on the Net?

> None. Seriously. The net is monitored enough as it is (maybe too much). It should be a forum for free speech and should not be policed by anything but common sense. Though this may seem inconsistent with my answer to (1) above [where he said he was bothered by receiving posts totally unrelated to the topic of a list], just because something bothers me doesn't mean I believe it should be eliminated. In an ideal world people should exercise their rationality more.

Since we do not live in an ideal world, of course, behavior problems on the Net inevitably arise. In keeping with the value placed on individual autonomy, proponents of free speech may advocate harassing offenders until they desist rather than cutting off their access (considered to be 'heavy-handed censorship'). Hauben (1993), writing about the Usenet, expresses this in positive terms as follows:

> When people feel someone is abusing the nature of Usenet News, they let the offender know through e-mail. In this manner . . . people fight to keep it a resource that is helpful to society as a whole.

The ideal of 'fight[ing] to keep [the Net] a resource that is helpful to society as a whole' often translates into action as flaming. One man wrote the following in response to the question, What behaviors bother you most on the Net?

> As much as I am irritated by [incompetent posters], I don't want imposed rules. I would prefer to 'out' such a person and let some public minded citizen fire bomb his house to imposing rules on the net. Letter bombing a [*sic*] annoying individual's feed is usually preferable to building a formal heirarchy [*sic*] of net cops.

Underlying the violent imagery of 'bombing' is the ideal of the 'public minded citizen' who dispenses a rough and ready form of justice in a free and individualistic Net society. A similar ideal underlies the response to the same question by another 'Net vigilante':

> I'd have to say commercial shit. Whenever someone advertises some damn get-rich-quick scheme and plasters it all over the net by crossposting it to every newsgroup, I reach for my 'gatling gun mailer crasher' and fire away at the source address.

Thus an anarchistic value system is constructed: Within this system, by evoking freedom from censorship, flaming and other aggressive behaviors can be interpreted in a prosocial light, as a form of corrective justice. This is not to say that all or even most men who flame have the good of Net society at heart, but rather that the behavior is in principle justifiable for men (and hence tolerable) in ways that it is not for most women.

The second theme evoked by male respondents is *candor*. In this view, honest and frank expression of one's opinions is a desirable attribute in Net interaction: Everything is out in the open, and others know exactly where one stands. One man gave the following response to the question, What Net behaviors do you most appreciate when you encounter them?

> The willingness to respond to just about anything with candor and honesty. There are no positions to hide behind or from on a list.

For many men, candor takes precedence over the positive face wants of the addressee. An extreme expression of this is the response of an African American male citing 'honest bigotry' as what he most appreciates about Net interaction. Expressions of bigotry (e.g., in the form of racial hatred) presumably directly threaten this man's desire to feel ratified and liked, yet for him the advantages of honesty outweigh the threat: 'I'm glad to talk to those who are truly hateful on the net so that I'm prepared for them when I meet them in real life.'

If one disagrees with someone, one should say so directly. It follows from this that failure to disagree openly may be perceived by adherents of this ethic as hypocritical or insincere. Thus a male participant on the SWIP list recently accused feminist philosophers of 'feign[ing] agreement where none exists' when they write 'I wish to *expand* upon so-and-so's thinking,'

> when what's really at issue is the complete rejection of so-and-so. Tamsin Lorraine suggests this is the positive feature of the 'cooperative spirit' of feminist philosophy. But I disagree. I think it's better, when one rejects another feminist's thinking on a matter, simply to say 'I reject so-and-so's approach.' . . . I frankly think [it is] exactly this kind of automatic non-criticism which is partially responsible for feminist philosophy not being taken as seriously as it should by non-feminist philosophers.

Both the poster's critical views (that feminist philosophers 'feign agreement'; that feminist philosophy is not 'taken seriously') and his directly confrontational tone ('But I disagree'; 'I frankly think') are consistent with the value accorded candor by male survey respondents.

More is expressed in this last post than a value on honesty, however; disagreement is also implicitly valued. This leads to the third theme mentioned preferentially by male survey respondents: *debate*. According to this value, confrontational exchanges should be encouraged as a means of arriving at deeper understandings of issues and sharpening one's intellectual skills. As the male participant on the SWIP list (quoted previously) put it, 'There's nothing like a healthy denunciation by one's colleagues every once in a while to get one's blood flowing, and spur one to greater subtlety and exactness of thought.' He goes on, however, to add an important caveat: 'At least if it's constructive denunciation, rather than the mere expression of hostility or misunderstanding.' The distinction between 'constructive denunciation' and 'hostility,' or some version of this distinction, is crucial to many men: Male survey respondents regularly cite 'flaming' as behavior that bothers them online, but exclude from the definition of flaming critical exchanges that are calm and rationally argued, which they characterize instead as 'good debate,' 'balanced argument,' or 'noncombative disagreement.' In other words, there is good adversariality (i.e. agonistic debate) and bad adversariality (i.e. flaming).

In contrast, many—if not most—female Net users do not distinguish between hostile, angry adversariality and calm, rational adversariality, but rather interpret adversariality of any kind (which may include any politeness-threatening act) as unconstructive and hostile in intent. Thus, unlike men, female survey respondents tend to group together all forms of adversariality as 'flaming,' 'rudeness,' or 'provocation,' all 'designed simply to distress.' Further, female participants in online discussions are more likely than men to characterize exchanges as 'flaming' any time baldly face-threatening acts are committed (disagreement, rejection, protest, etc.). This tendency led a male participant in one such discussion to complain recently that 'some members of [this list] perceive aggression where none was intended.'

The problem is not simply one of individual misunderstanding; rather, different sets of values are involved. The strength of the clash in values is evident in the strongly emotive language women use to describe their aversion to adversariality online and off. The following quote was posted by the listowner of the SWIP list to explain why the list follows a nonagonistic practice:

> At the first APA (SWIP) meeting, we discovered we were all offended and disabled by the hierarchies in the profession, by the star system, by the old boy networks. We talked together and shared our feelings about the adversarial method of combat and attack of commentator against presenter, by audience against presenter. We found it ugly, harmful, and counterproductive.[14]

Or, as a female respondent commented about an adversarial discussion in which participants baldly criticized one another's views on the LINGUIST list,[15]

> That is precisely the kind of human interaction I committedly avoid.... I am dismayed that human beings treat each other this way. It makes the world a dangerous place to be.

The choice of evaluative terms such as 'ugly,' 'harmful,' and 'dangerous' to characterize agonistic behaviors and 'offended,' 'disabled,' and 'dismayed' to characterize the women's response reveals the extent to which some women are alienated by behaviors that are positively valued by men.

The set of values cited preferentially by female survey respondents I will call henceforth the 'positive politeness ethic,' in that it is concerned with

14 From a panel presentation given by Kathy Pyne Addelson at the Eastern Division American Philosophical Association meeting, Atlanta, 30 December 1993. The title of the panel was 'Feminist Philosophy after Twenty Years.'

15 See Herring 1992 for a more extensive analysis of the gender dynamics in this discussion.

attending to and protecting participants' positive face or desire to be accepted, supported, and liked. The set of values referred to almost exclusively by male survey respondents I will refer to as the 'anarchic/agonistic ethic,' in that it is concerned with promoting freedom of expression and vigorous exchange of conflicting views. According to the positive politeness ethic, right interaction involves supporting, helping, and generally being considerate of others. As a woman on the WOMEN list posted recently:

> If we take responsibility for developing our own sensitivities to others and controlling our actions to minimize damage—we will each be doing [good deeds] for the whole world constantly.

In contrast, right interaction according to the anarchic/agonistic ethic, is that which permits the development of the individual, in service of which it is desirable to be maximally free to speak and act in the pursuit of one's self-interest. The connection between free speech and self-interest is made explicit by a male survey respondent who quoted American Revolutionary author Thomas Paine:[16]

> He that would make his own liberty secure must guard even his enemy from oppression; for if he violates this duty he establishes a precedent that will reach to himself.

Thus, self-interest leads one to extend concern to others in a principled way.

As with gendered discursive styles, the generalizations I have made here regarding gendered values do not apply universally. The distribution of male and female responses to the combined open-ended questions in terms of the values described above are represented schematically in Figure 2.

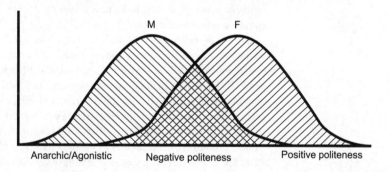

Fig. 2.
Distribution of
politeness-based and
anarchic/agonistic values
by gender

Figure 2 shows that there is a considerable overlap in male and female assessments regarding appropriate behavior on the Net. This area corresponds primarily with dislike of violations of negative politeness. Thus, respondents of both genders cited negative politeness violations such as uninformative subject headers, quoting text, misdirected/inappropriate

---

16 I note, in passing, that Paine is an excellent role model for the CMC anarchic/agonistic ethical standard: He advocated 'the omnipotence of reason when there is freedom to debate all questions,' and claimed he sought to write 'simply, candidly, and clearly; to be bold and forthright in order to shock readers into attention, partly by sharp contrasts; [and] to use wit and satire in order to bring opposing ideas into ridicule' (Encyclopedia Britannica 1971, 17: 65).

messages, messages with little content, and long messages as behaviors that bother them in Net interaction. There was also some agreement on dislike of violations of positive politeness—especially of flaming and egotism, although more women than men said they disliked these behaviors (in the case of flaming, twice as many women as men). Men and women agreed much less about what they like and would like to see more of, however, with women preferentially citing helpful and supportive (positive politeness) behaviors and men citing anarchic and agonistic behaviors. Note, however, that there is a fundamental tension between the values represented by these gendered extremes: Uncensored agonistic expression threatens positive face, and protecting positive face at any cost (e.g., by prohibiting adversariality) threatens freedom of expression.

These results show that when male and female Net users are asked open-ended questions about what they like and dislike, they provide qualitatively different answers. Moreover, the answers cluster and pattern in ways that reflect patterns in posting styles: Expressions of support and appreciation are natural manifestations of positive politeness, and attenuation follows from negative politeness, while adversariality and even flaming can be seen to derive from (and be rationally justified by) anarchic and agonistic ideals.

Netiquette
Guidelines

Having established distributional tendencies for different male and female value systems that correspond to different posting styles, we turn now to netiquette guidelines—publicly available statements of recommended posting and Net use practices. Whose values inform the content of netiquette guidelines? In particular, how do netiquette guidelines resolve the tension inherent between positive politeness values on the one hand and anarchic/ agonistic values on the other?

For this part of the study, I analyzed the content of nine sets of netiquette statements: seven from introductory messages to discussion lists and two global sets of guidelines (one for Usenet and the other for electronic mail in general).[17] The data include two women-centered lists, WMST and SWIP, and one list, TESL, which has a slight majority of female subscribers and represents a feminized field; all three have female listowners. It was hypothesized that netiquette statements for these lists would incorporate positive politeness values. In contrast, while no lists in the data self-identify as 'male-centered,' POLITICS and the Computer Underground Digest (CuD) represent masculinized areas of interest, and PHILOSOP is 90% male; these lists are also owned by men. I hypothesized, therefore, that netiquette statements for these lists would incorporate anarchic/agonistic values. Finally, the global Usenet and e-mail netiquette guidelines are intended to apply to users of either sex, and thus in principle should reflect the values of each (or neither) group.

Each normative statement found in the documents was categorized in terms of positive and negative politeness, if applicable. These statements are of two types: avoid violating N/P (abbreviated Avoid –N/–P), and observe

---

17 See note 6.

N/P (abbreviated +N/+P). An example of each type of statement is given below.

Avoid –N: Avoid irrelevancies. Given the limited phosphor window we have onto this electronic universe, succinctness and relevance become prized attributes. The message that makes its point and fits on one screen does its job best, and you will be well regarded. (Shapiro and Anderson 1985)

+N: Please include a meaningful subject header, so that people will know whether your message deals with a topic of interest to them. (WMST)

Avoid –P: There may be no flames of a personal nature on this list. (POLITICS)

+P: We are strongly committed to maintaining an uncensored list; but to do this, it is important that members respect in their postings the attitudes and sensibilities of all other members. (TESL)

In addition, statements communicating agonistic and anarchic values (abbreviated A/A) were coded. An example of this type is the following:

A/A

those who have never tried electronic communication may not be aware of what a 'social skill' really is. One social skill that must be learned, is that other people have points of view that are not only different, but *threatening*, to your own. In turn, your opinions may be threatening to others. There is nothing wrong with this [emphasis added—SH]. Your beliefs need not be hidden behind a facade, as happens with face-to-face conversation. Not everybody in the world is a bosom buddy, but you can still have a meaningful conversation with them. The person who cannot do this lacks in social skills. (Nick Szabo, quoted in Salzenberg and Spafford 1993)

The distribution of statements of each type by source is summarized in Table 2. (An asterisk after list name indicates that messages sent to that list are screened by the listowner(s) before being posted; i.e., the list is moderated).

Table 2 shows that the guidelines for all of the electronic forums include prescriptive statements about negative politeness. Three, in fact, mention *only* negative politeness; I will call this the 'conservative type.' This type is conservative in that it does not address potentially controversial behaviors such as flaming or supporting others, but, rather, is concerned solely with the avoidance of imposition, a concern that male and female users share. It is noteworthy that the three lists whose guidelines illustrate this pattern—LINGUIST, PHILOSOP, and WMST—are all academic lists that restrict their focus to exchange of information and discussion of academic issues. Possibly, the listowners who prepared these netiquette guidelines consider the sorts of behaviors that lead to strong disagreement or supportive interaction as outside the scope of the lists, and thus did not think it necessary to provide for such eventualities. In any event, the academic nature of these lists appears to take precedence over gender make-up, as there is no correlation between the conservative pattern and gender of subscribers or listowner.

TABLE 2. *Distribution of netiquette statements by source and type*

	Gender of listowner	Percentage of female subscribers[18]	A/A	Avoid –N	+N	Avoid –P	–P
CuD*	M	5	x	x	x	(x)	
PHILOSOP	M	11		x	x		
POLITICS	M	17	x	x	x	(x)	
LINGUIST*	M & F	36		x	x		
TESL	F	56		x	x	x	x
SWIP*	F	80		x		x	x
WMST	F	88		x	x		
Usenet	n.a.	?	x	x	x		
e-mail	n.a.	?	x	x	x	(x)	

Beyond this, however, the distribution of values across lists supports the hypotheses advanced above with regard to gender. Male-centered lists are more likely than female-centered lists to evoke agonistic/anarchic values; of the three male-centered lists—CuD, PHILOSOP, and POLITICS—two contain statements of this type, as compared with none of the female-centered lists. Conversely, female-centered lists are more likely to recommend observations of positive politeness (+P); of the three female-centered lists—SWIP, TESL, and WMST—two contain statements of this type, as compared with none of the male-centered lists. It is possible to observe in this distribution a pattern of partial overlap similar to that found in posting styles and posting ethics, with A/A values on the 'male' end, +/–N values in the area of overlap in the middle, and +P values on the 'female' end. Thus, it is not only individuals who are gendered in their evaluation of Net behaviors but electronic forums as well.

Further support for this conclusion is found in the various lists' recommendations involving avoiding violations of positive politeness (Avoid –P). A different attitude is evident toward adversariality and flaming in the guidelines for the female- and the male-centered lists. SWIP and TESL make it clear that such behavior is not welcome on the lists in any form; SWIP makes it a matter of policy to 'be respectful and constructive rather than agonistic in our discussions,' and the TESL guidelines state: 'If you find something posted on the net objectionable, you have every right to voice your objections . . . but not in public.' In contrast, POLITICS, CuD, and the e-mail guidelines all proscribe flaming in ways that explicitly or implicitly authorize public disagreement. Thus POLITICS prohibits 'flames of a personal nature,' but presumably allows for flames of a nonpersonal nature (e.g., of another

---

18 These percentages are rough estimates calculated from counting unambiguously female and male names on publicly available lists of subscribers to each discussion list. Gender-ambiguous names, organizations, and distribution lists (which typically comprise 10–15% of subscribers to any given list) are then excluded, and the percentages of women and men calculated out of 100%. Thus, if a list has 17% female subscribers, 83% of the subscribers are male. Since subscription is not necessary to read Usenet newsgroups or to send e-mail, comparable figures are not available for the two sets of global guidelines.

participant's views), and explicitly advocates 'argument.' Similarly, Shapiro and Anderson's e-mail guidelines decry 'insult[ing] or criticiz[ing] third parties without giving them a chance to respond,' although if one gives them a chance to respond—which in most electronic forums is automatic if the criticized party reads the forum—insults and criticism are presumably acceptable(!). Finally, CuD discourages 'ad hominem attacks or personal squabbles,' but describes itself as 'a forum for opposing points of view' and stresses 'reasoned debate.' These distinctions are consistent with the distinction made by male survey respondents between 'hostile' adversariality and 'rational' adversariality: The former is to be avoided, while the latter is held up as the ideal for Net interaction.

What, then, of the global guidelines, those that supposedly apply to all three million users and four thousand-plus newsgroups of the Usenet, and those that apply to sending electronic mail in general? The Usenet guidelines (Horton and Spafford 1993; Salzenberg and Spafford 1993) are compatible with a male rather than a female or conservative interactional ethic: They value anarchy as desirable and conflict as inevitable, as can be seen in the statement about 'social skill' given as an example of A/A norms above. They also include, under the heading 'Words to live by,' the following statement:

Anarchy means having to put up with things that really piss you off.
(Salzenberg and Spafford 1993)

The interactional norm assumed in these statements is one of threat, conflict, and control of one's hostile or violent reactions (defined as 'social skill'). While this may represent the reality of online interaction for many men, it is not a comfortable scenario for those whose value system emphasizes harmonious and supportive interaction, and no doubt accounts for why participation on Usenet is overwhelmingly male.[19]

Finally, as if this were not potentially alienating enough to female users, the Usenet guidelines also actively discourage appreciative and supportive postings in the name of reducing message volume:

In aggregate, small savings in disk or CPU add up to a great deal. For instance, messages offering thanks, jibes, or congratulations will only need to be seen by the interested parties—send these by mail rather than posting them. The same goes for simple questions, and especially for any form of 'me too' posting. (Horton and Spafford 1993)

It is not hard to imagine that users with a supportive interactional style could feel uncomfortable participating in forums where exclusively supportive posts are not only not valued but are defined as violations of netiquette.

Shapiro and Anderson's print pamphlet, *Toward an Ethics and Etiquette for Electronic Mail* (1985), also gives an androcentric view. In addition to authorizing insults and criticisms (provided one gives the other party a chance to respond), the guidelines stress the undesirability of emotion in responding to e-mail ('avoid responding while emotional'; 'if a message generates emotion,

19 For a telling example of male domination even in a female-centered newsgroup, see Sutton 1994. According to one estimate, 95% of postings to the Net overall are from men (Sproull, cited in Ebben and Kramarae 1993); this percentage may be higher on the Usenet.

look again'), advocating instead 'self-control.' Consistent with other sets of guidelines with a male bias, there is no mention of appreciative, supportive, or relationship-building behaviors. It is important to recall that what I have characterized (for the sake of balancing my corpus) as 'male-centered' lists are ostensibly ungendered and open to all.[20] When we add to this the masculine orientation of global Net guidelines, the picture that emerges is one in which masculine norms of interaction constitute the default, the exception being in a few women-centered groups. These results not only support the claim that there are different value systems preferentially associated with male and female users, but further reveal gender bias in netiquette guidelines.

This bias is not limited to the particular sets of guidelines included in the present analysis, but can be found in the 'etiquette' section of almost any popular guide to using the Internet. Moreover, it is well on its way to becoming the unquestioned norm for cyberspace as a whole. Thus, a brand-new, attractively packaged paperback volume on netiquette (Shea 1994) advertises itself as 'the first and only book to offer the guidance that all users need to be perfectly polite online.' It has the following to say about flaming:

> Does Netiquette forbid flaming? Not at all. Flaming is a longstanding network tradition (and Netiquette never messes with tradition). Flames can be lots of fun, both to write and to read. And the recipients of flames sometimes deserve the heat. . . . Netiquette doesn't require you to stand idly by while other people spout offensive nonsense. (43, 78)

What Netiquette does forbid, according to Shea, is extended flame wars, which are 'an unfair monopolization of bandwidth.' In other words, agonism is more highly valued than positive face (it's fun; other people deserve it) and only becomes a problem if extended to the point that it violates negative face (monopolizes bandwidth). But what if the person flamed did not 'deserve' it? What if they merely expressed a view that someone else did not like, a feminist view, for example, in response to which they were treated to offensive sexist remarks? And what if, further, that person happens to operate from within an ethical system in which flaming is the ultimate online insult? In that case, according to the new guidelines, 'if you're a sensitive person, it may be best to avoid the many hang-outs of the politically incorrect' (78). Avoidance is, of course, one solution, but as one of the sources quoted in the book itself observes, '*Every* discussion list of which I have been a part—no matter what its subject—has fallen victim to such ills—a few have gone down in e-flames. The pattern is absolutely consistent' (73). Should people with a positive politeness-based communication ethic avoid all discussion lists then? When we consider that the positive politeness ethic is associated predominantly with women, the adverse implications for women's use of the Net become uncomfortably clear: As one contributor to CuD put it, 'if you can't stand the heat, ladies, then get out of the kitchen' (quoted in Taylor and Kramarae, forthcoming, 4). In effect, a proflaming netiquette implicitly sanctions the domination of Net discourse by a minority of men.

---

20 We do not have, for example, a list for the Society for Men in Philosophy (SMIP) corresponding to the SWIP list; the men's list is simply called PHILOSOP (Philosophy).

Discussion   In this paper, I have argued that, contrary to the assumption that CMC neutralizes indications of gender, there are gender differences in public discourse on the Internet. Moreover, these differences are not randomly distributed across individuals, but rather display a systematic pattern of distribution with male users as a group tending toward more adversarial behavior and female users as a group tending toward more attenuated and supportive behaviors. I further submit that these systematic behaviors correspond to two distinctive systems of values each of which can be characterized in positive terms: One considers individual freedom to be the highest good, and the other idealizes harmonious interpersonal interaction.

As with all ideologies, however, these value systems also serve to rationalize less noble behaviors. Thus, adversarial participants justify intimidation of others and excessive use of bandwidth with rhetoric about freedom, openness, and intellectual vigor, and attenuated participants justify flattery, indirectness, and deference to others (and perhaps silence) in terms of ideals of care and consideration. Given that members of the former population are mostly men and members of the latter population mostly women (and, in some cases, male students), the value systems can be seen to reproduce male dominance and female (and other less powerful individuals') submission. They provide a mechanism by which these behaviors can be understood in a favorable, face-saving light by those who engage in them, and thereby facilitate their unquestioned continuation. This arrangement, in which both genders are complicit, is in one sense highly adaptive: It allows people to continue to operate within an oppressive power arrangement that might otherwise make them feel intolerably guilty or angry, depending on the role they play. But from a standpoint that affirms gender equality, a standpoint implicit in proponents' original claim that computer networks would neutralize gender differences, dominance and submission patterns on the Net are disadvantageous to women (as well as to nonadversarial men), and therefore it is important that they be recognized and questioned.

Gendered arrangements of values perpetuate dominance even in cases where no intimidation is intended. The same behavior—for example, directly criticizing another participant—is susceptible to different interpretations under an anarchic/agonistic system, as opposed to a politeness system. As a consequence, cyberspace may be perceived as more hostile and less hospitable by women than by men, thus discouraging female participation. There is no simple solution to this problem, since to require women to understand adversariality differently is to place all the burden for change on the less powerful group, and to prohibit direct criticism, or to require that criticism be attenuated, is to impose what would be seen from the anarchic perspective as unreasonable restrictions on freedom of speech. Nevertheless, this is an issue that must be addressed if the dominant adversarial culture in cyberspace is not to marginalize women by rendering them largely silent in mixed-sex forums or by limiting their active participation to women-centered groups, as is currently the case.

Even women-centered groups are not free from adversarial incursion. Some men are resentful of the existence of women-only groups and attempt to infiltrate their ranks by presenting themselves as women. One male

contributor to CuD offers the following tips to 'she-males,' men who imper-
sonate women to gain access to women-only forums:

> The lesbian channels are hilarious, where the women ask you questions
> that the men 'couldn't possibly' know the answers to, like the small print
> on a packet of tampons. Also you have to string off a list of very right-on
> lesbian-friendly music that you're supposed to like . . . They seem to
> think this will keep the she-males out. Bwahahaha!

Even when gender imposters are exposed, however, it is difficult to exclude
them, since they can always present themselves again from a different account under a different name. Partly for this reason, women-centered lists
such as WOMEN and SWIP do not restrict membership on the basis of gender but rather allow men to participate who are friendly to the purposes of
the list. Inevitably, however, there arise incidents of adversariality involving
men, some of whom are perhaps initially well-intentioned, while others
clearly aim to be disruptive. Thus, within the past several months, SWIP
adopted a moderated format and TESL is contemplating switching to a moderated format because of repeated contentious posts from a few men and the
effects these had on the overall quality of the discourse.[21] Similarly, the GEN-
DER hotline on COMSERVE was shut down in 1992 and reopened as a moderated forum after being taken over by several men who bombarded the list
with misogynistic messages, until only a few hardcore subscribers remained.
In each case, the female listowner who made the decision to restrict access became the target of angry messages from the offending men accusing her of
'heavy-handed tactics,' 'censorship,' and 'authoritarian expressions of
power.' These cases illustrate that freedom of speech when combined with
adversariality may effectively translate into freedom of speech only for the
adversarial; some restrictions on free speech were necessary in these cases in
order to preserve the common good.

In contrast, the anarchic solution of harassing (or ignoring) the offender
until he desists requires a tolerance for adversariality—perhaps even extreme
forms of adversariality—that may be anathema to participants who are offended by adversariality in the first place. This solution has also been spectacularly unsuccessful in two of the worst cases of recent abuse in cyberspace:
the repeated, lengthy, cross-posted flames by several individuals on
Turkish–Armenian hostilities, and the repeated 'spamming' of the Usenet
with advertisements from a small law firm in Phoenix. The individuals responsible for these behaviors have been warned, flamed, and, by feats of technological adversariality, had their messages zapped by 'kill files' and intercepted

---

21 As of this writing, the TESL list is attempting to avoid shifting to a moderated format, but has
instigated several new guidelines. Notable among these are limits on frequency of posting ('no more
than 2 postings per day, 10 per week, per netter') and a proscription against 'baiting, goading,
demeaning messages' and 'complaints about postings, the net, the way the net is run, etc.' As the
listowner, Anthea Tillyer, explained in a recent post to the list (13 July 1994):

> No one is suggesting or advocating a humorlessly rigid and doctrinaire application of inflexible
> rules; the goal is to keep TESL-L on focus and to return it to its previous state of pleasant and co-
> operative collegiality. There will always be netters who enjoy a more abrasive and wide-ranging set
> of debates than we wish to see on TESL-L; and for those netters, we will continue to post news of
> other lists and netnews groups that suit other kinds of discourse. We hope that in this way we can
> serve all our members and at the same time keep TESL-L true to its stated focus and to the pleasant
> atmosphere that has characterized the list for most of its existence.

by electronic 'patriot missiles' before reaching their destination (Elmer-Dewitt 1994; Lewis 1994). Yet still they persist (fueled, no doubt, to new heights of determination by the challenge of holding out against their multiple adversaries). These are cases of anarchy taken to the extreme, anarchy that cannot be stopped by anarchic means. It is interesting in this regard to note that while male Usenet administrators continue to propose ever more violent forms of harassment in the law firm case, a female administrator, less encumbered by anarchic scruples, recently proposed partitioning the net in such a way that incidents of this sort would be impossible.[22] Whether or not such a solution is feasible is irrelevant here; the point is that it is a different kind of solution, one in the spirit of the actions of the women-centered list owners who limited the speech of a troublemaking minority in order to insure that the majority would still have a place to speak.

Conclusion

We have seen that the existence of gender differences in cyberspace has implications for the norms, demographics, and distribution of power on the Internet. I hope to have demonstrated that it is in the interests of those concerned with actualizing egalitarian ideals of CMC to recognize these differences—and their practical implications—for what they are. In particular, I hope to have pointed out that there are problems with an uncritical acceptance of the dominant anarchic/agonistic model as the ideal for CMC: Not only does it incorporate a male bias that marginalizes women, but it authorizes abuse that more generally threatens the common good.

That said, the description of gender differences presented here should not be taken as a prescription for difference, or a glorification of female ways of communicating and valuing to the exclusion of those of men. Both of the gendered extremes described here are just that: extremes. Ideally, citizens of cyberspace would cooperate in minimizing intimidation and abuses of others' resources; failing self-enforcement of this ideal, limits on extreme abuses would be imposed to preserve the 'virtual commons' as a resource for all (Kollock and Smith, forthcoming). Most interaction would fall ideally into a vast middle ground of self-regulated behavior, where free speech would be tempered by consideration for others and where politeness would not preclude the honest exchange of differing views. Ritual adversariality and ritual agreement would be replaced by mature, respectful, and dynamic joint exploration of ideas, leading to the creation of a Net society greater and wiser than the sum of its parts.

Whether such a Net society can in fact be achieved depends in part on our ability to set aside narrow self-interest in the pursuit of shared goals. It also depends on educating a critical mass of the Net population to recognize limiting gender stereotypes in all their manifestations; the present work is intended as a contribution toward this end. Finally, it requires exposing systems of rationalization that mask dominance and opportunistic abuse. At a minimum, freedom from blatant intimidation must be ensured if the

---

22 I am indebted to Arthur Hyun (personal communication) for this information, which is based on recent discussions on the Usenet group <news.admin.misc>.

majority of users are to have meaningful access to the communicative potential of the Internet, irrespective of gender.

References   BROWN, PENELOPE, and STEPHEN C. LEVINSON. 1987. *Politeness: Some Universals in Language Usage.* Cambridge: Cambridge University Press.

CHODOROW, NANCY. 1978. *The Reproduction of Mothering: Psychoanalysis and the Sociology of Gender.* Berkeley: University of California Press.

DUNLOP, CHARLES, and ROB KLING, eds. 1991. *Computerization and Controversy.* New York: Academic Press.

EBBEN, MAUREEN, and CHERIS KRAMARAE. 1993. Women and Information Technologies: Creating a Cyberspace of Our Own. In *Women, Information Technology, and Scholarship*, ed. H. Jeannie Taylor, Cheris Kramarae, and Maureen Ebben, 15–27. Urbana, Ill.: Center for Advanced Study.

ELMER-DEWITT, PHILIP. 1994. Battle for the Soul of the Internet. *Time*, 25 July, 50–6.

GILLIGAN, CAROL. 1977. Concepts of the Self and of Morality. *Harvard Educational Review* 47(4): 481–517.

—— 1982. *In a Different Voice.* Cambridge, Mass.: Harvard University Press.

—— and JANE ATTANUCCI. 1988. Two Moral Orientations. In *Mapping the Moral Domain*, ed. Carol Gilligan, Janie Victoria Ward, and Jill McLean Taylor, 73–86. Cambridge, Mass.: Harvard University Press.

GRADDOL, DAVID, and JOAN SWANN. 1989. *Gender Voices.* London: Blackwell.

GRIMSHAW, JEAN. 1986. *Feminist Philosophers.* Sussex: Wheatsheaf Books.

HALL, KIRA. Forthcoming. Cyberfeminism. In *Computer Mediated Communication*, ed. Susan Herring. Amsterdam: John Benjamins.

HAUBEN, MICHAEL. 1993. The Social Forces behind the Development of Usenet News. [Electronic document, available by ftp from weber.ucsd.edu, directory /pub/ usenet.hist.]

HERRING, SUSAN. 1992. Gender and Participation in Computer-Mediated Linguistic Discourse. ERIC document (ED345552).

—— 1993a. Gender and Democracy in Computer-Mediated Communication. *Electronic Journal of Communication* 3(2), special issue on Computer-Mediated Communication, ed. T. Benson. Reprinted in *Computerization and Controversy*, 2nd edition, ed. Rob Kling. New York: Academic Press, forthcoming.

—— 1993b. Men's Language: A Study of the Discourse of the LINGUIST List. In *Les langues menacées: actes du XVe congrès international des linguistes, Vol. 3*, ed. André Crochetière, Jean-Claude Boulanger, and Conrad Ouellon, 347–50. Sainte-Foy, Québec: Les Presses de l'Université Laval.

—— 1994. Politeness in Computer Culture: Why Women Thank and Men Flame. In *Communicating in, through, and across Cultures: Proceedings of the Third Berkeley Women and Language Conference*, ed. Mary Bucholtz, Anita Liang, and Laurel Sutton. Berkeley, Cal.: Berkeley Women and Language Group.

—— 1996. Two Variants of an Electronic Message Schema. In *Computer Mediated Communication*, ed. Susan Herring. Amsterdam: John Benjamins.

—— DEBORAH JOHNSON, and TAMRA DiBENEDETTO. 1992. Participation in Electronic Discourse in a 'Feminist' Field. In *Locating Power: Proceedings of the Second Berkeley Women and Language Conference*, ed. Mary Bucholtz, Kira Hall, and Birch Moonwomon, 250–62. Berkeley, Cal: Berkeley Women and Language Group.

—— and ROBIN LOMBARD. 1995. Negotiating Gendered Faces: Requests and Disagreements Among Computer Professionals on the Internet. Paper presented at the Georgetown University Round Table on Languages and Linguistics presession on Computer-Mediated Discourse Analysis. Georgetown University, March 8, 1995.

HILTZ, STARR ROXANNE, and MURRAY TUROFF. 1993. *The Network Nation: Human Communication via Computer*, 2d ed. Cambridge Mass.: MIT Press. [1st ed., 1978, Addison-Wesley.]

HOLMSTROM, NANCY. 1982. Do Women Have a Distinctive Nature? *Philosophical Forum* 14(1): 22–42.

HORTON, MARK, and GENE SPAFFORD. 1993. Rules for posting to Usenet. [Electronic document available by ftp from: rtfm.mit.edu, directory /pub/usenet/news.announce.newusers.]

JOHNSON, DEBORAH G., and JOHN W. SNAPPER, eds. 1985. *Ethical Issues in the Use of Computers*. Belmont, CA: Wadsworth.

KIESLER, SARA, JANE SIEGEL, and TIMOTHY W. McGUIRE. 1984. Social Psychological Aspects of Computer-Mediated Communication. *American Psychologist* 39: 1123–34.

KOLLOCK, PETER, and MARC SMITH. Forthcoming. Managing the Virtual Commons: Cooperation and Conflict in Computer Communities. In *Computer-Mediated Communication*, ed. Susan Herring. Amsterdam: John Benjamins.

KRAMARAE, CHERIS, and H. JEANNIE TAYLOR. 1993. Women and Men on Electronic Networks: A Conversation or a Monologue? In *Women, Information Technology, and Scholarship*, ed. H. Jeannie Taylor, Cheris Kramarae, and Maureen Ebben, 52–61. Urbana, Ill.: Center for Advanced Study.

LEWIS, PETER H. 1994. Censorship Growing on Networks of Cyberspace. *Dallas Morning News*, 29 June, 2D.

MEDNICK, MARTHA T. 1989. On the Politics of Psychological Constructs: Stop the Bandwagon, I Want to Get Off. *American Psychologist* 44(8): 1118–23.

POLLITT, KATHA. 1992. Are Women Morally Superior to Men? *The Nation*, 28 December, 799–807.

RHEINGOLD, HOWARD. 1993. *The Virtual Community: Homesteading on the Electronic Frontier*. Reading, Mass.: Addison-Wesley.

RUDDICK, SARA. 1989. *Maternal Thinking: Toward a Politics of Peace*. Boston: Beacon Press.

SALZENBERG, CHIP, and GENE SPAFFORD. 1993. What Is Usenet? [Electronic document available by ftp from: rtfm.mit.edu, directory /pub/usenet/news.announce.newusers.]

SELFE, CYNTHIA L., and PAUL R. MEYER. 1991. Testing Claims for On-line Conferences. *Written Communication* 8(2): 163–92.

SHAPIRO, NORMAN Z., and ROBERT H. ANDERSON. 1985. *Toward an Ethics and Etiquette for Electronic Mail*. The Rand Corporation.

SHEA, VIRGINIA. 1994. *Netiquette*. San Francisco: Albion Books.

STEINER, LINDA. 1989. Feminist Theorizing and Communication Ethics. *Communication* 12: 157–173.

SUTTON, LAUREL. 1994. Gender, Power, and Silencing in Electronic Discourse on USENET. *Proceedings of the 20th Berkeley Linguistics Society*. University of California, Berkeley.

TANNEN, DEBORAH. 1990. *You Just Don't Understand*. New York: Ballantine.

TAYLOR, JEANNIE H., and CHERIS KRAMARAE. Forthcoming. Creating Cybertrust in the Margins. In *The Cultures of Computing*, ed. Susan Leigh Star. Oxford: Basil Blackwell.

TROEMEL-PLOETZ, SENTA. 1991. Selling the Apolitical: Review of Deborah Tannen's *You Just Don't Understand*. *Discourse and Society* 2(4): 489–502.

15

Will the Real Body Please Stand Up? Boundary Stories about Virtual Cultures

Allucquere Rosanne Stone

In this article Allucquere Rosanne Stone offers insights into the nature of on-line communities and a personal perspective upon their cultural significance. With her point of departure in the relationship between nature, society, and technology, Stone describes a range of features of on-line social forms with particular focus on the representation and mediation of the body. Tracing the development of the idea of virtual community in four epochs and discussing a number of specific systems that helped spawn on-line culture, she gives insight into the nature of this new integration of humans and technology. Building upon this discussion, Stone continues with a subtle analysis of the teleology of technology, and thereby furthers understanding about the significance of the representation of embodiment on-line.

The Machines Are Restless Tonight

AFTER DONNA HARAWAY'S 'Promises of Monsters' and Bruno Latour's papers on actor networks and artifacts that speak, I find it hard to think of any artifact as being devoid of agency. Accordingly, when the dryer begins to beep complainingly from the laundry room while I am at dinner with friends, we raise eyebrows at each other and say simultaneously, 'The machines are restless tonight . . .'

It's not the phrase, I don't think, that I find intriguing. Even after Haraway 1991 and Latour 1988, the phrase is hard to appreciate in an intuitive way. It's the ellipsis I notice. You can hear those three dots. What comes after them?

From Michael Benedikt (ed.), *Cyberspace: First Steps* (London: MIT Press, 1991), 81–118.

Thanks to Mischa Adams, Gloria Anzaldúa, Laura Chernaik, Heinz von Foerster, Thyrza Goodeve, John Hartigan, Barbara Joans, Victor Kytasty, Roddey Reid, Chela Sandoval, Susan Leigh Star, and Sharon Traweek for their many suggestions; to Bandit (Seagate), Ron Cain (Borland), Carl Tollander (Autodesk), Ted Kaehler (Sun), Jane T. Lear (Intel), Marc Lentczner, Robert Orr (Amdahl), Jon Singer (soulmate), Brenda Laurel (Telepresence Research and all-around Wonderful Person); Joshua Susser, the Advanced Technology Group of Apple Computer, Inc., Tene Tachyon, Jon Shemitz, John James, and my many respondents in the virtual world of online BBSs. I am grateful to Michael Benedikt and friends and to the University of Texas School of Architecture for making part of the research possible, and to the participants in The First Conference on Cyberspace for their ideas as well as their collaboration in constituting yet another virtual community. In particular I thank Donna Haraway, whose work and encouragement have been invaluable.

The fact that the phrase—obviously a send-up of a vaguely anthropological chestnut—seems funny to us, already says a great deal about the way we think of our complex and frequently uneasy imbrications with the unliving. I, for one, spend more time interacting with Saint-John Perse, my affectionate name for my Macintosh computer, than I do with my friends. I appreciate its foibles, and it gripes to me about mine. That someone comes into the room and reminds me that Perse is merely a 'passage point' for the work practices of a circle of my friends over in Silicon Valley changes my sense of facing a vague but palpable sentience squatting on my desk not one whit. The people I study are deeply imbricated in a complex social network mediated by little technologies to which they have delegated significant amounts of their time and agency, not to mention their humor. I say to myself: Who am I studying? A group of people? Their machines? A group of people and or in their machines? Or something else?

When I study these groups, I try to pay attention to all of their interactions. And as soon as I allow myself to see that most of the interactions of the people I am studying involve vague but palpable sentiences squatting on their desks, I have to start thinking about watching the machines just as attentively as I watch the people, because, for them, the machines are not merely passage points. Haraway and other workers who observe the traffic across the boundaries between 'nature,' 'society,' and 'technology' tend to see nature as lively, unpredictable, and, in some sense, actively resisting interpretations. If nature and technology seem to be collapsing into each other, as Haraway and others claim, then the unhumans can be lively too.

One symptom of this is that the flux of information that passes back and forth across the vanishing divides between nature and technology has become extremely dense. Cyborgs with a vengeance, one of the groups I study, is already talking about colonizing a social space in which the divide between nature and technology has become thoroughly unrecognizable, while one of the individuals I study is busy trying to sort out how the many people who seem to inhabit the social space of her body are colonizing her. When I listen to the voices in these new social spaces I hear a multiplicity of voices, some recognizably human and some quite different, all clamoring at once, frequently saying things whose meanings are tantalizingly familiar but which have subtly changed.

My interest in cyberspace is primarily about communities and how they work. Because I believe that technology and culture constitute each other, studying the actors and actants that make up our lively, troubling, and productive technologies tells me about the actors and actants that make up our culture. Since so much of a culture's knowledge is passed on by means of stories, I will begin by retelling a few boundary stories about virtual cultures.

Schizophrenia as Commodity Fetish

Let us begin with a person I will call Julie, on a computer conference in New York in 1985. Julie was a totally disabled older woman, but she could push the keys of a computer with her headstick. The personality she projected into the 'net'—the vast electronic web that links computers all over the world— was huge. On the net, Julie's disability was invisible and irrelevant. Her standard greeting was a big, expansive 'HI!!!!!!' Her heart was as big as her greeting, and in the intimate electronic companionships that can develop during on-line conferencing between people who may never physically meet, Julie's women friends shared their deepest troubles, and she offered them advice—advice that changed their lives. Trapped inside her ruined body, Julie herself was sharp and perceptive, thoughtful and caring.

After several years, something happened that shook the conference to the core. 'Julie' did not exist. 'She' was, it turned out, a middle-aged male psychiatrist. Logging onto the conference for the first time, this man had accidentally begun a discussion with a woman who mistook him for another woman. 'I was stunned,' he said later, 'at the conversational mode. I hadn't known that women talked among themselves that way. There was so much more vulnerability, so much more depth and complexity. Men's conversations on the nets were much more guarded and superficial, even among intimates. It was fascinating, and I wanted more.' He had spent weeks developing the right persona. A totally disabled, single older woman was perfect. He felt that such a person wouldn't be expected to have a social life. Consequently her existence only as a net persona would seem natural. It worked for years, until one of Julie's devoted admirers, bent on finally meeting her in person, tracked her down.

The news reverberated through the net. Reactions varied from humorous resignation to blind rage. Most deeply affected were the women who had shared their innermost feelings with Julie. 'I felt raped,' one said. 'I felt that my deepest secrets had been violated.' Several went so far as to repudiate the genuine gains they had made in their personal and emotional lives. They felt those gains were predicated on deceit and trickery.

The computer engineers, the people who wrote the programs by means of which the nets exist, just smiled tiredly. They had understood from the beginning the radical changes in social conventions that the nets implied. Young enough in the first days of the net to react and adjust quickly, they had long ago taken for granted that many of the old assumptions about the nature of identity had quietly vanished under the new electronic dispensation. Electronic networks in their myriad kinds, and the mode of interpersonal interaction that they foster, are a new manifestation of a social space that has been better known in its older and more familiar forms in conference calls, communities of letters, and FDR's fireside chats. It can be characterized as 'virtual' space—an imaginary locus of interaction created by communal agreement. In its most recent form, concepts like distance, inside/outside, and even the physical body take on new and frequently disturbing meanings.

Now, one of the more interesting aspects of virtual space is 'computer crossdressing.' Julie was an early manifestation. On the nets, where *warranting*, or grounding, a persona in a physical body, is meaningless, men routinely use female personae whenever they choose, and vice versa. This wholesale appropriation of the other has spawned new modes of interaction. Ethics, trust, and risk still continue, but in different ways. Gendered modes of communication themselves have remained relatively stable, but who uses which of the two socially recognized modes has become more plastic. A woman who has appropriated a male conversational style may be simply assumed to be male at that place and time, so that her/his on-line persona takes on a kind of quasi life of its own, separate from the person's embodied life in the 'real' world.

Sometimes a person's on-line persona becomes so finely developed that it begins to take over their life *off* the net. In studying virtual systems, I will call both the space of interaction that is the net and the space of interaction that we call the 'real' world *consensual loci*. Each consensual locus has its own 'reality,' determined by local conditions. However, not all realities are equal. A whack on the head in the 'real' world can kill you, whereas a whack in one of the virtual worlds will not (although a legal issue currently being debated by futurist attorneys is what liability the whacker has if the fright caused by a virtual whack gives the whackee a 'real' heart attack).

Some conferencees talk of a time when they will be able to abandon war-ranting personae in even more complex ways, when the first 'virtual reality' environments come on line. VR, one of a class of interactive spaces that are coming to be known by the general term *cyberspace*, is a three-dimensional consensual locus or, in the terms of science fiction author William Gibson, a 'consensual hallucination' in which data may be visualized, heard, and even felt. The 'data' in some of these virtual environments are people—3-D repre-sentations of individuals in the cyberspace. While high-resolution images of the human body in cyberspace are years away, when they arrive they will take 'computer crossdressing' even further. In this version of VR a man may be seen, and perhaps touched, as a woman and vice versa—or as anything else. There is talk of renting prepackaged body forms complete with voice and touch . . . multiple personality as commodity fetish!

It is interesting that at just about the time the last of the untouched 'real-world' anthropological field sites are disappearing, a new and unexpected kind of 'field' is opening up—incontrovertibly social spaces in which people still meet face-to-face, but under new definitions of both 'meet' and 'face.' These new spaces instantiate the collapse of the boundaries between the social and technological, biology and machine, natural and artificial that are part of the postmodern imaginary. They are part of the growing imbrication of humans and machines in new social forms that I call *virtual systems*.

A Virtual Systems Origin Myth

Cyberspace, without its high-tech glitz, is partially the idea of virtual com-munity. The earliest cyberspaces may have been virtual communities, pas-sage points for collections of common beliefs and practices that united people who were physically separated. Virtual communities sustain them-selves by constantly circulating those practices. To give some examples of how this works, I'm going to tell an origin story of virtual systems.

There are four epochs in this story. The beginning of each is signaled by a marked change in the character of human communication. Over the years, human communication is increasingly mediated by technology. Because the rate of change in technological innovation increases with time, the more re-cent epochs are shorter, but roughly the same quantity of information is ex-changed in each. Since the basis of virtual communities is communication, this seems like a reasonable way to divide up the field.

Epoch One: Texts. [From the mid-1600s]
Epoch Two: Electronic communication and entertainment media. [1900+]
Epoch Three: Information technology. [1960+]
Epoch Four: Virtual reality and cyberspace. [1984+]

Epoch One   This period of early textual virtual communities starts, for the sake of this discussion, in 1669 when Robert Boyle engaged an apparatus of literary technology to 'dramatize the social relations proper to a community of philosophers.' As Steven Shapin and Simon Shapiro point out in their study of the debate between Boyle and the philosopher Thomas Hobbes, *Leviathan and the Air-Pump*, we probably owe the invention of the boring academic paper to Boyle. Boyle developed a method of compelling assent that Shapin and Shaffer described as *virtual witnessing*. He created what he called a 'community of like-minded gentlemen' to validate his scientific experiments, and he correctly surmised that the 'gentlemen' for whom he was writing believed that boring, detailed writing implied painstaking experimental work. Consequently it came to pass that boring writing was likely to indicate scientific truth. By means of such writing, a group of people were able to 'witness' an experiment without being physically present. Boyle's production of the detailed academic paper was so successful that it is still the exemplar of scholarship.

The document around which community forms might also be a novel, a work of fiction. Arguably the first texts to reach beyond class, gender, and ideological differences were the eighteenth-century sentimental novels, exemplified by the publication of Bernardin de Saint-Pierre's short novel *Paul and Virginia* (1788), which Roddey Reid, in his study 'Tears For Fears,' identifies as one of the early textual productions that 'dismantled the absolutist public sphere and constructed a bourgeois public sphere through fictions of national community.' Reid claims that *Paul and Virginia* was a passage point for a circulating cluster of concepts about the nature of social identity that transformed French society. Reid suggests that an entire social class—the French bourgeoisie—crystallized around the complex of emotional responses that the novel produced. Thus in the first epoch texts became ways of creating, and later of controlling, new kinds of communities.

Epoch Two   The period of the early electronic virtual communities began in the twentieth century with invention of the telegraph and continued with musical communities, previously constituted in the physical public space of the concert hall, shifting and translating to a new kind of virtual communal space around the phonograph. The apex of this period was Franklin Delano Roosevelt's radio 'fireside chats,' creating a community by means of readily available technology.

Once communities grew too big for everyone to know everyone else, which is to say very early on, government had to proceed through delegates who represented absent groups. FDR's use of radio was a way to bypass the need for delegates. Instead of talking to a few hundred representatives, Roosevelt used the radio as a machine for fitting listeners into his living room. The radio was one-way communication, but because of it people were able to begin to think of presence in a different way. Because of radio and of the apparatus for the production of community that it implied and facilitated, it was now possible for millions of people to be 'present' in the same space—seated across from Roosevelt in his living room.

This view implies a new, different, and complex way of experiencing the relationship between the physical human body and the 'I' that inhabits it. FDR did not physically enter listeners' living rooms. He invited listeners into his. In a sense, the listener was in two places at once—the body at home, but the delegate, the 'I' that belonged to the body, in an imaginal space with another person. This space was enabled and constructed with the assistance of a particular technology. In the case of FDR the technology was a device that mediated between physical loci and incommensurable realities—in other words, an interface. In virtual systems *an interface is that which mediates between the human body (or bodies) and an associated 'I' (or 'I's')*. This double view of 'where' the 'person' is, and the corresponding trouble it may cause with thinking about 'who' we are talking about when we discuss such a problematic 'person,' underlies the structure of more recent virtual communities.

During the same period thousands of children, mostly boys, listened avidly to adventure serials, and sent in their coupons to receive the decoder rings and signaling devices that had immense significance within the community of a particular show. Away from the radio, they recognized each other by displaying the community's tokens, an example of communities of consumers organized for marketing purposes.

The motion picture, and later, television, also mobilized a similar power to organize sentimental social groups. Arguably one of the best examples of a virtual community in the late twentieth century is the Trekkies, a huge, heterogenous group partially based on commerce but mostly on a set of ideas. The fictive community of 'Star Trek' and the fantasy Trekkie community interrelate and mutually constitute each other in complex ways across the boundaries of texts, films, and video interfaces.

Epoch Two ended in the mid-1970s with the advent of the first computer, terminal-based, bulletin board systems (BBSs).

Epoch Three   This period began with the era of information technology. The first virtual communities based on information technology were the on-line bulletin board services (BBS) of the middle 1970s. These were not dependent upon the widespread ownership of computers, merely of terminals. But because even a used terminal cost several hundred dollars, access to the first BBSs was mainly limited to electronics experimenters, ham-radio operators, and the early hardy computer builders.

BBSs were named after their perceived function—virtual places, conceived to be just like physical bulletin boards, where people could post notes for general reading. The first successful BBS programs were primitive, usually allowing the user to search for messages alphabetically, or simply to read messages in the order in which they were posted. These programs were sold by their authors for very little, or given away as 'shareware'—part of the early visionary ethic of electronic virtual communities. The idea of shareware, as enunciated by the many programmers who wrote shareware programs, was that the computer was a passage point for circulating concepts of community. The important thing about shareware, rather than making an immediate profit for the producer, was to nourish the community in expectation that such nourishment would 'come around' to the nourisher.

CommuniTree   Within a few months of the first BBS's appearance, a San Francisco group headed by John James, a programmer and visionary thinker, had developed the idea that the BBS was a virtual community, a community that promised radical transformation of existing society and the emergence of new social forms. The CommuniTree Group, as they called themselves, saw the BBS in McLuhanesque terms as transformative because of the ontological structure it presupposed and simultaneously created—the mode of tree-structured discourse and the community that spoke it—and because it was another order of 'extension,' a kind of prosthesis in McLuhan's sense. The BBS that the CommuniTree Group envisioned was an extension of the participant's instrumentality into a virtual social space.

The CommuniTree Group quite correctly foresaw that the BBS in its original form was extremely limited in its usefulness. Their reasoning was simple. The physical bulletin board for which the BBS was the metaphor had the advantage of being quickly scannable. By its nature, the physical bulletin board was small and manageable in size. There was not much need for bulletin boards to be organized by topic. But the on-line BBS could not be scanned in any intuitively satisfactory way. There were primitive search protocols in the early BBSs, but they were usually restricted to alphabetical searches or searches by keywords. The CommuniTree Group proposed a new kind of BBS that they called a tree-structured conference, employing as a working metaphor both the binary tree protocols in computer science and also the organic qualities of trees as such appropriate to the 1970s. Each branch of the tree was to be a separate conference that grew naturally out of its root message by virtue of each subsequent message that was attached to it. Conferences that lacked participation would cease to grow, but would remain on-line as archives of failed discourse and as potential sources of inspiration for other, more flourishing conferences.

With each version of the BBS system, The CommuniTree Group supplied a massive, detailed instruction manual—which was nothing less than a set of directions for constructing a new kind of virtual community. They couched the manual in radical seventies language, giving chapters such titles as 'Downscale, please, Buddha' and 'If you meet the electronic avatar on the road, laserblast hir!' This rich intermingling of spiritual and technological imagery took place in the context of George Lucas's *Star Wars*, a film that embodied the themes of the technological transformativists, from the all-pervading Force to what Vivian Sobchack (1987) called 'the outcome of infinite human and technological progress.' It was around *Star Wars* in particular that the technological and radically spiritual virtual communities of the early BBSs coalesced. *Star Wars* represented a future in which the good guys won out over vastly superior adversaries—with the help of a mystical Force that 'surrounds us and penetrates us . . . it binds the galaxy together' and which the hero can access by learning to 'trust your feelings'—a quintessential injunction of the early seventies.

CommuniTree #1 went on-line in May 1978 in the San Francisco Bay area of northern California, one year after the introduction of the Apple II computer and its first typewritten and hand-drawn operating manual. CommuniTree #2 followed quickly. The opening sentence of the prospectus for the first conference was 'We are as gods and might as well get good at it.' This technospiritual bumptiousness, full of the promise of the redemptive power of technology mixed with the easy, catch-all Eastern mysticism popular in upscale northern California, characterized the early conferences. As might be gathered from the tone of the prospectus, the first conference, entitled 'Origins,' was about successor religions.

The conferencees saw themselves not primarily as readers of bulletin boards or participants in a novel discourse but as agents of a new kind of social experiment. They saw the terminal or personal computer as a tool for social transformation by the ways it refigured social interaction. BBS conversations were time-aliased, like a kind of public letter writing or the posting of broadsides. They were meant to be read and replied to some time later than they were posted. But their participants saw them as conversations nonetheless, as social acts. When asked how sitting alone at a terminal was a social act, they explained that they saw the terminal as a window into a social space. When describing the act of communication, many moved their hands expressively as though typing, emphasizing the gestural quality and essential tactility of the virtual mode. Also present in their descriptions was a propensity to reduce other expressive modalities to the tactile. It seemed clear that, from the beginning, the electronic virtual mode possessed the power to overcome its character of single-mode transmission and limited bandwidth.

By 1982 Apple Computer had entered into the first of a series of agreements with the federal government in which the corporation was permitted to give away computers to public schools in lieu of Apple's paying a substantial portion of its federal taxes. In terms of market strategy, this action dramatically increased Apple's presence in the school system and set the pace for Apple's domination in the education market. Within a fairly brief time there were significant numbers of personal computers accessible to students of grammar school and high school age. Some of those computers had modems.

The students, at first mostly boys and with the linguistic proclivities of pubescent males, discovered the Tree's phone number and wasted no time in logging onto the conferences. They appeared uninspired by the relatively intellectual and spiritual air of the ongoing debates, and proceeded to express their dissatisfaction in ways appropriate to their age, sex, and language abilities. Within a short time the Tree was jammed with obscene and scatalogical messages. There was no way to monitor them as they arrived, and no easy way to remove them once they were in the system. This meant that the entire system had to be purged—a process taking hours—every day or two. In addition, young hackers enjoyed the sport of attempting to 'crash' the system by discovering bugs in the system commands. Because of the provisions of the system that made observing incoming messages impossible, the hackers were free to experiment with impunity, and there was no way for the system operator to know what was taking place until the system crashed. At that time it was generally too late to save the existing disks. The system operator would be obliged to reconstitute ongoing conferences from earlier backup versions.

Within a few months, the Tree had expired, choked to death with what one participant called 'the consequences of freedom of expression.' During the years of its operation, however, several young participants took the lessons and implications of such a community away with them, and proceeded to write their own systems. Within a few years there was a proliferation of on-line virtual communities of somewhat less visionary character but vastly superior message-handling capability—systems that allowed monitoring and disconnection of 'troublesome' participants (hackers attempting to crash the system), and easy removal of messages that did not further the purposes of the system operators. The age of surveillance and social control had arrived for the electronic virtual community.

The visionary character of CommuniTree's electronic ontology proved an obstacle to the Tree's survival. Ensuring privacy in all aspects of the Tree's structure and enabling unlimited access to all conferences did not work in a context of increasing availability of terminals to young men who did not necessarily share the Tree gods' ideas of what counted as community. As one Tree veteran put it, 'The barbarian hordes mowed us down.' Thus, in practice, surveillance and control proved necessary adjuncts to maintaining order in the virtual community.

It is tempting to speculate about what might have happened if the introduction of CommuniTree had not coincided with the first wave of 'computerjugen.' Perhaps the future of electronic virtual communities would have been quite different.

SIMNET   Besides the BBSs, there were more graphic, interactive systems under construction. Their interfaces were similar to arcade games or flight simulators—(relatively) high-resolution, animated graphics. The first example of this type of cyberspace was a military simulation called SIMNET. SIMNET was conducted by a consortium of military interests, primarily represented by DARPA, and a task group from the Institute for Simulation and Training, located at the University of Central Florida. SIMNET came about because DARPA was beginning to worry about whether the Army could continue to stage large-scale military practice exercises in Germany. With the rapid and unpredictable changes that were taking place in Europe in the late 1980s, the army wanted to have a backup—some other place where they could stage practice maneuvers without posing difficult political questions. As one of the developers of SIMNET put it, 'World War III in Central Europe is at the moment an unfashionable anxiety.' In view of the price of land and fuel, and of the escalating cost of staging practice maneuvers, the armed forces felt that if a large-scale consensual simulation could be made practical they could realize an immediate and useful financial advantage. Therefore, DARPA committed significant resources—money, time, and computer power—to funding some research laboratory to generate a 200-tank cyberspace simulation. DARPA put out requests for proposals, and a group at the University of Central Florida won.

The Florida group designed and built the simulator units with old technology, along the lines of conventional aircraft cockpit simulators. Each tank simulator was equipped to carry a crew of four, so the SIMNET environment is an 800-person virtual community.

SIMNET is a two-dimensional cyberspace. The system can be linked up over a very large area geographically; without much difficulty, in fact, to anywhere in the world. A typical SIMNET node is an M-1 tank simulator. Four crew stations contain a total of eight vision blocks, or video screens, visible through the tank's ports. Most of these are 320 × 138 pixels in size, with a 15 Hertz update rate. This means that the image resolution is not very good, but the simulation can be generated with readily available technology no more complex than conventional video games. From inside the 'tank' the crew looks out the viewports, which are the video screens. These display the computer-generated terrain over which the tanks will maneuver (which happens to be the landscape near Fort Knox, Kentucky). Besides hills and fields, the crew can see vehicles, aircraft, and up to 30 other tanks at one time. They can hear and see the vehicles and planes shooting at each other and at them.

By today's standards, SIMNET's video images are low-resolution and hardly convincing. There is no mistaking the view out the ports for real terrain. But the simulation is astonishingly effective, and participants become thoroughly caught up in it. SIMNET's designers believe that it may be the lack of resolution itself that is responsible, since it requires the participants to actively engage their own imaginations to fill the holes in the illusion! McLuhan redux. That it works is unquestionable. When experimenters opened the door to one of the simulators during a test run to photograph the interior, the participants were so caught up in the action that they didn't notice the bulky camera poking at them.

Habitat
Habitat, designed by Chip Morningstar and Randall Farmer, is a large-scale social experiment that is accessible through such common telephone-line computer networks as Tymnet. Habitat was designed for LucasFilm, and has been on-line for about a year and a half. It is a completely decentralized, connectionist system. The technology at the user interface was intended to be simple, this in order to minimize the costs of getting on-line. Habitat is designed to run on a Commodore 64 computer, a piece of very old technology in computer terms (in other words, at least ten years old), but Morningstar and Farmer have milked an amazing amount of effective bandwidth out of the machine. The Commodore 64 is very inexpensive and readily available. Almost anyone can buy one if, as one Habitat participant said, 'they don't already happen to have one sitting around being used as a doorstop.' Commodore 64s cost $100 at such outlets as Toys R Us.

Habitat existed first as a 35-foot mural located in a building in Sausalito, California, but, on-line, each area of the mural represents an entirely expandable area in the cyberspace, be it a forest, a plain, or a city. Habitat is inhabitable in that, when the user signs on, he or she has a window into the ongoing social life of the cyberspace—the community 'inside' the computer. The social space itself is represented by a cartoonlike frame. The virtual person who is the user's delegated agency is represented by a cartoon figure that may be customized from a menu of body parts. When the user wishes his/her character to speak, s/he types out the words on the Commodore's keyboard, and these appear in a speech balloon over the head of the user's character. The speech balloon is visible to any other user nearby in the virtual space.[1] The user sees whatever other people are in the immediate vicinity in the form of other figures.

Habitat is a two-dimensional example of what William Gibson called a 'consensual hallucination.' First, according to Morningstar and Farmer, it has well-known protocols for encoding and exchanging information. By generally accepted usage among cyberspace engineers, this means it is consensual. The simulation software uses agents that can transform information to simulate environment. This means it is an hallucination.

Habitat has proved to be incontrovertibly social in character. During Habitat's beta test, several social institutions sprang up spontaneously. As Randall Farmer points out in his report on the initial test run, there were marriages and divorces, a church (complete with a real-world Greek Orthodox minister), a loose guild of thieves, an elected sheriff (to combat the thieves), a newspaper with a rather eccentric editor, and before long two lawyers hung up their shingles to sort out claims. And this was with only 150 people. My vision (of Habitat) encompasses tens of thousands of simultaneous participants.

Lessons of the Third Epoch

In the third epoch the participants of electronic communities seem to be acquiring skills that are useful for the virtual social environments developing in late twentieth-century technologized nations. Their participants have learned to delegate their agency to body-representatives that exist in an imaginal space contiguously with representatives of other individuals. They have become accustomed to what might be called lucid dreaming in an awake state—to a constellation of activities much like reading, but an active and interactive reading, a participatory social practice in which the actions of the reader have consequences in the world of the dream or the book. In the third epoch the older metaphor of reading is undergoing a transformation in a textual space that is consensual, interactive, and haptic, and that is constituted through inscription practices—the production of microprocessor code. Social spaces are beginning to appear that are simultaneously natural, artificial, and constituted by inscription. The boundaries between the social and the natural and between biology and technology are beginning to take on the generous permeability that characterizes communal space in the fourth epoch.

Epoch Four

Arguably the single most significant event for the development of fourth-stage virtual communities was the publication of William Gibson's science fiction novel *Neuromancer*. *Neuromancer* represents the dividing line between the third and fourth epochs not because it signaled any technological development, but because it crystallized a new community, just as Boyle's scientific papers and *Paul and Virginia* did in an earlier age.

Neuromancer reached the hackers who had been radicalized by George

---

1 'Nearby' is idiosyncratic and local in cyberspace. In the case of Habitat, it means that two puppets (body representatives) occupy that which is visible on both screens simultaneously. In practice this means that each participant navigates his or her screen 'window' to view the same area in the cyberspace. Because Habitat is consensual, the space looks the same to different viewers. Due to processor limitations only nine puppets can occupy the same window at the same time, although there can be more in the neighborhood (just offscreen).

Lucas's powerful cinematic evocation of humanity and technology infinitely extended, and it reached the technologically literate and socially disaffected who were searching for social forms that could transform the fragmented anomie that characterized life in Silicon Valley and all electronic industrial ghettos. In a single stroke, Gibson's powerful vision provided for them the imaginal public sphere and refigured discursive community that established the grounding for the possibility of a new kind of social interaction. As with *Paul and Virginia* in the time of Napoleon and Dupont de Nemours, *Neuromancer* in the time of Reagan and DARPA is a massive intertextual presence not only in other literary productions of the 1980s, but in technical publications, conference topics, hardware design, and scientific and technological discourses in the large.

The three-dimensional inhabitable cyberspace described in *Neuromancer* does not yet exist, but the groundwork for it can be found in a series of experiments in both the military and private sectors.

Many VR engineers concur that the tribal elders of 3-D virtual systems are Scott Fisher and Ivan Sutherland, formerly at MIT, and Tom Furness, with the Air Force. In 1967–68, Sutherland built a see-through helmet at the MIT Draper Lab in Cambridge. This system used television screens and half-silvered mirrors, so that the environment was visible through the TV displays. It was not designed to provide a surround environment. In 1969–70 Sutherland went to the University of Utah, where he continued this work, doing things with vector-generated computer graphics and maps, still see-through technology. In his lab were Jim Clark, who went on to start Silicon Graphics, and Don Vickers.

Tom Furness had been working on VR systems for 15 years or more—he started in the mid-seventies at Wright-Patterson Air Force Base. His systems were also see-through, rather than enclosing. He pushed the technology forward, particularly by adopting the use of high-resolution CRTs. Furness's system, designed for the USAF, was an elaborate flight simulation cyberspace employing a helmet with two large CRT devices, so large and cumbersome that it was dubbed the 'Darth Vader helmet.' He left Wright-Patterson in 1988–89 to start the Human Interface Technology Lab at the University of Washington.

Scott Fisher started at MIT in the machine architecture group. The MA group worked on developing stereo displays and crude helmets to contain them, and received a small proportion of their funding from DARPA. When the group terminated the project, they gave the stereo displays to another group at UNC (University of North Carolina), which was developing a display device called the Pixel Planes Machine. In the UNC lab were Henry Fuchs and Fred Brooks, who had been working on force feedback with systems previously developed at Argonne and Oak Ridge National labs. The UNC group worked on large projected stereo displays, but was aware of Sutherland's and Furness's work with helmets, and experimented with putting a miniature display system into a helmet of their own. Their specialties were medical modeling, molecular modeling, and architectural walkthrough. The new Computer Science building at UNC was designed partially with their system. Using their software and 3-D computer imaging equipment, the architects could 'walk through' the full-sized virtual building and examine its structure. The actual walk-through was accomplished with a treadmill and bicycle handlebars. The experiment was so successful that during the walk-through one of the architects discovered a misplaced wall that would have cost hundreds of thousands of dollars to fix once the actual structure had been built.

In 1982, Fisher went to work for Atari. Alan Kay's style at Atari was to pick self-motivated people and then turn them loose, on anything from flight simulation to personal interactive systems. The lab's philosophy was at the extreme end of visionary. According to Kay, the job of the group was to develop products not for next year or even for five years away, but for no less than 15 to 20 years in the future. In the corporate climate of the 1980s, and in particular in Silicon Valley, where product life and corporate futures are calculated in terms of months, this approach was not merely radical but stratospheric. For the young computer jocks, the lure of Silicon Valley and of pushing the limits of computer imaging into the far future was irresistible, and a group of Cambridge engineers, each outstanding in their way, made the trek out to the coast. Eric Gullichsen arrived first, then Scott Fisher and Susan Brennan, followed a year later by Ann Marion. Michael Naimark was already there, as was Brenda Laurel. Steve Gans was the last to arrive.

As it turned out, this was not a good moment to arrive at Atari. When the Atari lab closed, Ann Marion and Alan Kay went to Apple (followed by a drove of other Atari expatriates), where they started the Vivarium project and continued their research. Susan Brennan went first to the Stanford Psychology Department and also Hewlett-Packard, which she left in 1990 to teach at CUNY Stony Brook. Michael Naimark became an independent producer and designer of interactive video and multimedia art. William Bricken and Eric Gullichsen took jobs at Autodesk, the largest manufacturer of CAD software, where they started a research group called Cyberia.

Scott Fisher went to work for Dave Nagel, head of the NASA-Ames View Lab. To go with their helmet, the Ames lab had developed a primitive sensor to provide the computer with information about the position of the user's hand. The early device used a simple glove with strain gauges wired to two fingers. They contracted with VPL, Inc. to develop it further, using software written in collaboration with Scott. The Ames group referred to the software as 'gesture editors.' The contract started in 1985, and VPL delivered the first glove in March 1986. The Ames group intended to apply the glove and software to such ideas as surgical simulation, 3-D virtual surgery for medical students. In 1988, Dave Nagel left the Ames laboratory to become director of the Advanced Technology Group (ATG) at Apple.

Lusting for images, such organizations as SIGGRAPH gobbled up information about the new medium and spread it out through its swarm of networks and publications. The audience, made up largely of young, talented, computer-literate people in both computer science and art, and working in such fields as advertising, media, and the fine arts, had mastered the current state of the art in computers and was hungry for the next thing. LucasFilm (later LucasArts) in Marin, now doing the bulk of all computerized special effects for the film industry, and Douglas Trumbull's EEG in Hollywood, fresh from their spectacular work on *Blade Runner*, had made the production of spectacular visual imaginaries an everyday fact. They weren't afraid to say that they had solved all of the remaining problems with making artificial images, under particular circumstances, indistinguishable from 'real' ones—a moment that Stewart Brand called '(t)he end of photography as evidence for anything.' Now the artists and engineers who worked with the most powerful imaging systems, like Lucas's Pixar, were ready for more. They wanted to be able to get inside their own fantasies, to experientially inhabit the worlds they designed and built but could never enter. VR touched the same nerve that *Star Wars* had, the englobing specular fantasy made real.

Under Eric Gullichsen and William Bricken, the Autodesk Cyberspace Project quickly acquired the nickname Cyberia. John Walker, president of Autodesk, had seen the UNC architectural system and foresaw a huge market for virtual CAD—3-D drawings that the designers could enter. But after a year or so, Autodesk shrank the Cyberia project. Eric Gullichsen left to start Sense8, a manufacturer of low-end VR systems. William Bricken (and later his wife Meredith) left the company to take up residence at the University of Washington, where Tom Furness and his associates had started the Human Interface Technology Laboratory. Although there were already academic-based research organizations in existence at that time (Florida, North Carolina), and some of them (Florida) were financed at least in part by DOD, the HIT lab became the first academic organization to secure serious research funding from private industry.

During this period, when *Neuromancer* was published, 'virtual reality' acquired a new name and a suddenly prominent social identity as 'cyberspace.' The critical importance of Gibson's book was partly due to the way that it triggered a conceptual revolution among the scattered workers who had been doing virtual reality research for years: As task groups coalesced and dissolved, as the fortunes of companies and projects and laboratories rose and fell, the existence of Gibson's novel and the technological and social imaginary that it articulated enabled the researchers in virtual reality—or, under the new dispensation, cyberspace—to recognize and organize themselves as a community.

By this time private industry, represented by such firms as American Express, PacBell, IBM, MCC, Texas Instruments, and NYNEX, were beginning to explore the possibilities and commercial impact of cyberspace systems. That is not to say that people were rushing out to purchase tickets for a cyberspace vacation! The major thrust of the industrial and institutional commitment to cyberspace research was still focused on data manipulation—just as Gibson's *zaibatsu* did in *Neuromancer*. Gibson's cowboys were outlaws in a military-industrial fairyland dominated by supercomputers, artificial intelligence devices, and data banks. Humans were present, but their effect was minimal. There is no reason to believe that the cyberspaces being designed at NASA or Florida will be any different. However, this knowledge does not seem to daunt the 'real' cyberspace workers. Outside of their attention to the realities of the marketplace and workplace, the young, feisty engineers who do the bulk of the work on VR systems continue their discussions and arguments surrounding the nature and context of virtual environments. That these discussions already take place in a virtual environment—the great, sprawling international complex of commercial, government, military, and academic computers known as Usenet—is in itself suggestive.

Decoupling the Body and the Subject

The illusion will be so powerful you won't be able to tell what's real and what's not.

(*Steve Williams*)

In her complex and provocative 1984 study *The Tremulous Private Body*, Frances Barker suggests that, because of the effects of the Restoration on the social and political imaginary in Britain (1660 and on), the human body gradually ceased to be perceived as public spectacle, as had previously been the case, and became privatized in new ways. In Barker's model of the post-Jacobean citizen, the social economy of the body became rearranged in such a way as to interpose several layers between the individual and public space. Concomitant with this removal of the body from a largely public social economy, Barker argues that the subject, the 'I' or perceiving self that Descartes had recently pried loose from its former unity with the body, reorganized, or was reorganized, in a new economy of its own. In particular, the subject, as did the body, ceased to constitute itself as public spectacle and instead fled from the public sphere and constituted itself in *text*—such as Samuel Pepys' diary (1668).

Such changes in the social economy of both the body and the subject, Barker suggests, very smoothly serve the purposes of capital accumulation. The product of a privatized body and of a subject removed from the public sphere is a social monad more suited to manipulation by virtue of being more isolated. Barker also makes a case that the energies of the individual, which were previously absorbed in a complex public social economy and which regularly returned to nourish the sender, started backing up instead, and needing to find fresh outlets. The machineries of capitalism handily provided a new channel for productive energy. Without this damming of creative energies, Barker suggests, the industrial age, with its vast hunger for productive labor and the consequent creation of surplus value, would have been impossible.

In Barker's account, beginning in the 1600s in England, the body became progressively more hidden, first because of changing conventions of dress, later by conventions of spatial privacy. Concomitantly, the self, Barker's 'subject,' retreated even further inward, until much of its means of expression was through texts. Where social communication had been direct and personal, a warrant was developing for social communication to be indirect and delegated through communication technologies—first pen and paper, and later the technologies and market economics of print. The body (and the subject, although he doesn't lump them together in this way) became 'the site of an operation of power, of an exercise of meaning . . . a transition, effected over a long period of time, from a socially visible object to one which can no longer be seen' (Barker 1984: 13).

While the subject in Barker's account became, in her words, 'raging, solitary, productive,' what it produced was text. On the other hand, it was the newly hidden Victorian body that became physically productive and that later provided the motor for the industrial revolution; it was most useful as a brute body, for which the creative spark was an impediment. In sum, the body became more physical, while the subject became more textual, which is to say nonphysical.

If the information age is an extension of the industrial age, with the passage of time the split between the body and the subject should grow more pronounced still. But in the fourth epoch the split is simultaneously growing and disappearing. The socioepistemic mechanism by which bodies mean is undergoing a deep restructuring in the latter part of the twentieth century, finally fulfilling the furthest extent of the isolation of those bodies through which its domination is authorized and secured.

I don't think it is accidental that one of the earliest, textual, virtual communities—the community of gentlemen assembled by Robert Boyle during his debates with Hobbes—came into existence at the moment about which Barker is writing. The debate between Boyle and Hobbes and the production of Pepys' diary are virtually contemporaneous. In the late twentieth century, Gibson's *Neuromancer* is simultaneously a perverse evocation of the Restoration subject and its annihilation in an implosion of meaning from which arises a new economy of signification.

Barker's work resonates in useful ways with two other accounts of the evolution of the body and the subject through the interventions of late twentieth-century technologies: Donna Haraway's 'A Manifesto for Cyborgs' and 'The Biopolitics of Postmodern Bodies' (1985, 1988). Both these accounts are about the collapse of categories and of the boundaries of the body. (Shortly after being introduced to Haraway's work I wrote a very short paper called 'Sex And Death among the Cyborgs.' The thesis of 'Sex And Death' was similar to Haraway's.) The boundaries between the subject, if not the body, and the 'rest of the world' are undergoing a radical refiguration, brought about in part through the mediation of technology. Further, as Baudrillard and others have pointed out, the boundaries between technology and nature are themselves in the midst of a deep restructuring. This means that many of the usual analytical categories have become unreliable for making the useful distinctions between the biological and the technological, the natural and artificial, the human and mechanical, to which we have become accustomed.

François Dagognet suggests that the recent debates about whether nature is becoming irremediably technologized are based on a false dichotomy: namely that there exists, here and now, a category 'nature' which is 'over here,' and a category 'technology' (or, for those following other debates, 'culture') which is 'over there.' Dagognet argues on the contrary that the category 'nature' has not existed for thousands of years . . . not since the first humans deliberately planted gardens or discovered slash-and-burn farming. I would argue further that 'Nature,' instead of representing some pristine category or originary state of being, has taken on an entirely different function in late twentieth-century economies of meaning. Not only has the character of nature as yet another coconstruct of culture become more patent, but it has become nothing more (or less) than an ordering factor—a construct by means of which we attempt to *keep technology visible* as something separate from our 'natural' selves and our everyday lives. In other words, the category 'nature,' rather than referring to any object or category in the world, is a *strategy* for maintaining boundaries for political and economic ends, and thus a way of making meaning. (In this sense, the project of reifying a 'natural' state over and against a technologized 'fallen' one is not only one of the industries of postmodern nostalgia, but also part of a binary, oppositional cognitive style that some maintain is part of our society's pervasively male epistemology.)

These arguments imply as a corollary that 'technology,' as we customarily think of it, does not exist either; that we must begin to rethink the category of technology as also one that exists only because of its imagined binary opposition to another category upon which it operates and in relation to which it is constituted. In a recent paper Paul Rabinow asks what kind of being might thrive in a world in which nature is becoming increasingly technologized. What about a being who has learned to live in a world in which, rather than nature becoming technologized, technology *is* nature—in which the boundaries between subject and environment have collapsed?

Phone sex workers and VR engineers

I have recently been conducting a study of two groups who seemed to instantiate productive aspects of this implosion of boundaries. One is phone sex workers. The other is computer scientists and engineers working on VR systems that involve making humans visible in the virtual space. I was interested in the ways in which these groups, which seem quite different, are similar. For the work of both is about representing the human body through limited communication channels, and both groups do this by coding cultural expectations as tokens of meaning.

Computer engineers seem fascinated by VR because you not only program a world, but in a real sense inhabit it. Because cyberspace worlds can be inhabited by communities, in the process of articulating a cyberspace system, engineers must model cognition and community; and because communities are inhabited by bodies, they must model bodies as well. While cheap and practical systems are years away, many workers are already hotly debating the form and character of the communities they believe will spring up in their quasi-imaginary cyberspaces. In doing so, they are articulating their own assumptions about bodies and sociality and projecting them onto the codes that define cyberspace systems. Since, for example, programmers create the codes by which VR is generated in interaction with workers in widely diverse fields, how these heterogenous co-working groups understand cognition, community, and bodies will determine the nature of cognition, community, and bodies in VR.

Both the engineers and the sex workers are in the business of constructing tokens that are recognized as objects of desire. Phone sex is the process of provoking, satisfying, *constructing* desire through a single mode of communication, the telephone. In the process, participants draw on a repertoire of cultural codes to construct a scenario that compresses large amounts of information into a very small space. The worker verbally codes for gesture, appearance, and proclivity, and expresses these as tokens, sometimes in no more than a word. The client uncompresses the tokens and constructs a dense, complex interactional image. In these interactions desire appears as a product of the tension between embodied reality and the emptiness of the token, in the forces that maintain the preexisting codes by which the token is constituted. The client mobilizes expectations and preexisting codes for body in the modalities that are not expressed in the token; that is, tokens in phone sex are purely verbal, and the client uses cues in the verbal token to construct a multimodal object of desire with attributes of shape, tactility, odor, etc. This act is thoroughly individual and interpretive; out of a highly compressed token of desire the client constitutes meaning that is dense, locally situated, and socially particular.

Bodies in cyberspace are also constituted by descriptive codes that 'embody' expectations of appearance. Many of the engineers currently debating the form and nature of cyberspace are the young turks of computer engineering, men in their late teens and twenties, and they are preoccupied with the things with which postpubescent men have always been preoccupied. This rather steamy group will generate the codes and descriptors by which bodies in cyberspace are represented. Because of practical limitations, a certain amount of their discussion is concerned with data compression and tokenization. As with phone sex, cyberspace is a relatively narrow-bandwidth representational medium, visual and aural instead of purely aural to be sure, but how bodies are represented will involve how *recognition* works.

One of the most active sites for speculation about how *recognition* might work in cyberspace is the work of computer game developers, in particular the area known as interactive fantasy (IF). Since Gibson's first book burst onto the hackers' scene, interactive fantasy programmers (in particular, Laurel and others) have been taking their most durable stock-in-trade and speculating about how it will be deployed in virtual reality scenarios. For example, how, if they do, will people make love in cyberspace—a space in which everything, including bodies, exists as something close to a metaphor. Fortunately or unfortunately, however, everyone is still preorgasmic in virtual reality.

When I began the short history of virtual systems, I said that I wanted to use accounts of virtual communities as an entry point into a search for two things: an apparatus for the production of community and an apparatus for the production of body. Keeping in mind that this chapter is necessarily brief, let me look at the data so far:

- Members of electronic virtual communities act as if the community met in a physical public space. The number of times that on-line conferencees refer to the conference as an architectural place and to the mode of interaction in that place as being social is overwhelmingly high in proportion to those who do not. They say things like 'This is a nice place to get together' or 'This is a convenient place to meet.'

- The virtual space is most frequently visualized as Cartesian. On-line conferencees tend to visualize the conference system as a three-dimensional space that can be mapped in terms of Cartesian coordinates, so that some branches of the conference are 'higher up' and others 'lower down.' (One of the commands on the Stuart II conference moved the user 'sideways.') Gibson's own visualization of cyberspace was Cartesian. In consideration of the imagination I sometimes see being brought to bear on virtual spaces, this odd fact invites further investigation.

- Conferencees act as if the virtual space were inhabited by bodies. Conferencees construct bodies on-line by describing them, either spontaneously or in response to questions, and articulate their discourses around this assumption.

- Bodies in virtual space have complex erotic components. Conferencees may flirt with each other. Some may engage in 'netsex,' constructing elaborate erotic mutual fantasies. Erotic possibilities for the virtual body are a significant part of the discussions of some of the groups designing cyberspace systems. The consequences of virtual bodies are considerable in the local frame, in that conferencees mobilize significant erotic tension in relation to their virtual bodies. In contrast to the conferences, the bandwidth for physicalities in phone sex is quite limited. (One worker said ironically, '(o)n the phone, every female sex worker is white, five feet four, and has red hair.')

- The meaning of locality and privacy is not settled. The field is rife with debates about the legal status of communications within the networks. One such, for example, is about the meaning of inside and outside. Traditionally, when sending a letter one preserves privacy by enclosing it in an envelope. But in electronic mail, for example, the address is part of the message. The distinction between inside and outside has been erased, and along with it the possibility of privacy. Secure encryption systems are needed.[2]

- Names are local labels. 'Conferencees' seem to have no difficulty addressing, befriending, and developing fairly complex relationships with the delegated puppets—agents—of other conferencees. Such relationships remain stable as long as the provisional name ('handle') attached to the puppet does not change, but an unexpected observation was that relationships remain stable when the conferencee decides to change handles, as long as fair notice is given. Occasionally a conferencee will have several handles on the same conference, and a constructed identity for each. Other conferencees may or may not be aware of this. Conferencees treat others' puppets as if they were embodied people meeting in a public space nonetheless.

Private Body, Public Body, and Cyborg Envy

Partly, my interest in VR engineers stems from observations that suggest that they while are surely engaged in saving the project of late-twentieth-century capitalism, they are also inverting and disrupting its consequences for the body as object of power relationships. They manage both to preserve the privatized sphere of the individual—which Barker characterizes as 'raging, solitary, productive'—as well as to escape to a position that is of the spectacle and incontrovertibly public. But this occurs under a new definition of public and private: one in which warrantability is irrelevant, spectacle is plastic and negotiated, and desire no longer grounds itself in physicality. Under these

2 Although no one has actually given up on encryption systems, the probable reason that international standards for encryption have not proceeded much faster has been the United States Government's opposition to encryption key standards that are reasonably secure. Such standards would prevent such agencies as the CIA from gaining access to communications traffic. The United States' diminishing role as a superpower may change this. Computer industries in other nations have overtaken the United States' lead in electronics and are beginning to produce secure encryption equipment as well. A side effect of this will be to enable those engaged in electronic communication to reinstate the inside-outside dichotomy, and with it the notion of privacy in the virtual social space.

conditions, one might ask, will the future inhabitants of cyberspace 'catch' the engineers' societal imperative to construct desire in gendered, binary terms—coded into the virtual body descriptors—or will they find more appealing the possibilities of difference unconstrained by relationships of dominance and submission? Partly this will depend upon how 'cyberspaceians' engage with the virtual body.

Vivian Sobchack, in her 1987 discussion of cinematic space excludes the space of the video and computer screen from participation in the production of an 'apparatus of engagement.' Sobchack describes engagement with cinematic space as producing a thickening of the present . . . a 'temporal simultaneity (that) also extends presence spatially—transforming the 'thin' abstracted space of the machine into a thickened and concrete world.' Contrasted with video, which is to say with the electronic space of the CRT screen and with its small, low-resolution, and serial mode of display, the viewer of cinema engages with the apparatus of cinematic production in a way that produces 'a space that is deep and textural, that can be materially inhabited . . . a specific and mobile engagement of embodied and enworlded subjects/objects whose visual/visible activity prospects and articulates a shifting field of vision from a world that always exceeds it.' Sobchack speaks of electronic space as 'a phenomenological structure of sensual and psychological experience that seems to belong to no-body.' Sobchack sees the computer screen as 'spatially decentered, weakly temporalized and quasi-disembodied.'

This seems to be true, as long as the mode of engagement remains that of spectator. But it is the quality of direct physical and kinesthetic engagement, the enrolling of hapticity in the service of both the drama and the dramatic, which is not part of the cinematic mode. The cinematic mode of engagement, like that of conventional theater, is mediated by two modalities; the viewer experiences the presentation through sight and hearing. The electronic screen is 'flat,' so long as we consider it in the same bimodal way. But it is the potential for interaction that is one of the things that distinguishes the computer from the cinematic mode, and that transforms the small, low-resolution, and frequently monochromatic electronic screen from a novelty to a powerfully gripping force. Interaction is the physical concretization of a desire to escape the flatness and merge into the created system. It is the sense in which the 'spectator' is more than a participant, but becomes both participant in and creator of the simulation. In brief, it is the sense of unlimited power which the dis/embodied simulation produces, and the different ways in which socialization has led those always-embodied participants confronted with the sign of unlimited power to respond.

In quite different terms from the cinematic, then, cyberspace 'thickens' the present, producing a space that is deep and textural, and one that, in Sobchack's terms, can be materially inhabited. David Tomas, in his article 'The Technophilic Body' (1989), describes cyberspace as 'a purely spectacular, kinesthetically exciting, and often dizzying sense of bodily freedom.' I read this in the additional sense of freedom *from* the body, and in particular perhaps, freedom from the sense of loss of control that accompanies adolescent male embodiment. Cyberspace is surely also a concretization of the psychoanalytically framed desire of the male to achieve the 'kinesthetically exciting, dizzying sense' of freedom.

Some fiction has been written about multimodal, experiential cinema. But the fictional apparatus surrounding imaginary cybernetic spaces seems to have proliferated and pushed experiential cinema into the background. This is because cyberspace is part of, not simply the medium for, the action. Sobchack, on the other hand, argues that cinematic space possesses a power of engagement that the electronic space cannot match:

> Semiotically engaged as subjective and intentional, as presenting representation of the objective world . . . The spectator(s) can share (and thereby to a degree interpretively alter) a film's presentation and representation of embodied experience. (Forthcoming)

Sobchack's argument for the viewer's intentional engagement of cinematic space, slightly modified, however, works equally well for the cybernetic space of the computer. That is, one might say that the console cowboy is also '. . . semiotically engaged as subjective and intentional, as presenting representation of a *subj*ective world . . . the spectator can share (and thereby to a high degree interpretively alter) a simulation's presentation and representation of experience which may be, through cybernetic/semiotic operators not yet existent but present and active in fiction (the cyberspace deck), mapped back upon the physical body.'

In psychoanalytic terms, for the young male, unlimited power first suggests the mother. The experience of unlimited power is both gendered, and, for the male, fraught with the need for control, producing an unresolvable need for reconciliation with an always absent structure of personality. An 'absent structure of personality' is also another way of describing the peculiarly seductive character of the computer that Turkle characterizes as the 'second self.' Danger, the sense of threat as well as seductiveness that the computer can evoke, comes from both within and without. It derives from the complex interrelationships between human and computer, and thus partially within the human; and it exists quasi-autonomously within the simulation. It constitutes simultaneously the senses of erotic pleasure and of loss of control over the body. Both also constitute a constellation of responses to the simulation that deeply engage fear, desire, pleasure, and the need for domination, subjugation, and control.

It seems to be the engagement of the adolescent male within humans of both sexes that is responsible for the seductiveness of the cybernetic mode. There is also a protean quality about cybernetic interaction, a sense of physical as well as conceptual mutability that is implied in the sense of exciting, dizzying physical movement within purely conceptual space. I find that reality hackers experience a sense of longing for an embodied conceptual space like that which cyberspace suggests. This sense, which seems to accompany the desire to cross the human/machine boundary, to penetrate and merge, which is part of the evocation of cyberspace, and which shares certain conceptual and affective characteristics with numerous fictional evocations of the inarticulate longing of the male for the female, I characterize as *cyborg envy*.

Smoothness implies a seductive tactile quality that expresses one of the characteristics of cyborg envy: In the case of the computer, a desire literally to enter into such a discourse, to penetrate the smooth and relatively affectless surface of the electronic screen and enter the deep, complex, and tactile (individual) cybernetic space or (consensual) cyberspace within and beyond. Penetrating the screen involves a state change from the physical, biological space of the embodied viewer to the symbolic, metaphorical 'consensual hallucination' of cyberspace; a space that is a locus of intense desire for refigured embodiment.

The act of programming a computer invokes a set of reading practices both in the literary and cultural sense. 'Console cowboys' such as the cyberspace warriors of William Gibson's cyberpunk novels proliferate and capture the imagination of large groups of readers. Programming itself involves constant creation, interpretation, and reinterpretation of languages. To enter the discursive space of the program is to enter the space of a set of variables and operators to which the programmer assigns names. To enact naming is simultaneously to possess the power of, and to render harmless, the complex of desire and fear that charge the signifiers in such a discourse; to enact naming within the highly charged world of surfaces that is cyberspace is to appropriate the surfaces, to incorporate the surfaces into one's own. Penetration translates into envelopment. In other words, to enter cyberspace is to physically *put on* cyberspace. To become the cyborg, to put on the seductive and dangerous cybernetic space like a garment, is to put on the *female*. Thus cyberspace both *dis*embodies, in Sobchack's terms, but also *re*embodies in the polychrome, hypersurfaced cyborg character of the console cowboy. As the charged, multigendered, hallucinatory space collapses onto the personal physicality of the console cowboy, the intense tactility associated with such a reconceived and refigured body constitutes the seductive quality of what one might call the *cybernetic act*.

In all, the unitary, bounded, safely warranted body constituted within the frame of bourgeois modernity is undergoing a gradual process of translation to the refigured and reinscribed embodiments of the cyberspace community. Sex in the age of the coding metaphor—absent bodies, absent reproduction, perhaps related to desire, but desire itself refigured in terms of bandwidth and internal difference—may mean something quite unexpected. Dying in the age of the coding metaphor—in selectably inhabitable structures of signification, absent warrantability—gives new and disturbing meaning to the title of Steven Levine's book about the process, *Who Dies?*

Cyberspace, Sociotechnics, and Other Neologisms

Part of the problem of 'going on in much the same way,' as Harry Collins put it, is in knowing what the same way is. At the close of the twentieth century, I would argue that two of the problems are, first, as in Paul Virilio's analysis, *speed,* and second, tightly coupled to speed, what happens as human physical evolution falls further and further out of synchronization with human cultural evolution. The product of this growing tension between nature and culture is stress.

Stress management is a major concern of industrial corporations. Donna Haraway points out that

> (t)he threat of intolerable rates of change and of evolutionary and
> ideological obsolescence are the framework that structure much of late

twentieth-century medical, social and technological thought. Stress is part of a complex web of technological discourses in which the organism becomes a particular kind of communications system, strongly analogous to the cybernetic machines that emerged from the war to reorganize ideological discourse and significant sectors of state, industrial, and military practice. . . . Utilization of information at boundaries and transitions, biological or mechanical, is a critical capacity of systems potentially subject to stress, because failure to correctly apprehend and negotiate rapid change could result in communication breakdown—a problem which engages the attention of a broad spectrum of military, governmental, industrial and institutional interests. (1990: 186–230 passim)

The development of cyberspace systems—which I will refer to as part of a new *technics*—may be one of a widely distributed constellation of responses to stress, and secondly as a way of continuing the process of collapsing the categories of nature and culture that Paul Rabinow sees as the outcome of the new genetics. Cyberspace can be viewed as a toolkit for refiguring consciousness in order to permit things to go on in much the same way. Rabinow suggests that nature will be modeled on culture; it will be known and remade through technique. Nature will finally become artificial, just as culture becomes natural.

Haraway (1985) puts this in a slightly different way: 'The certainty of what counts as nature,' she says, '(that is, as) a source of insight, a subject for knowledge, and a promise of innocence—is undermined, perhaps fatally.' The change in the permeability of the boundaries between nature and technics that these accounts suggest does not simply mean that nature and technics mix—but that, seen from the technical side, technics become natural, just as, from Rabinow's anthropological perspective on the culture side, culture becomes artificial. In technosociality, the social world of virtual culture, technics is nature. When exploration, rationalization, remaking, and control mean the same thing, then nature, technics, and the structure of meaning have become indistinguishable. The technosocial subject is able successfully to navigate through this treacherous new world. S/he is constituted as part of the evolution of communications technology and of the human organism, in a time in which technology and organism are collapsing, imploding, into each other.

Electronic virtual communities represent flexible, lively, and practical adaptations to the real circumstances that confront persons seeking community in what Haraway (1987) refers to as 'the mythic time called the late twentieth century.' They are part of a range of innovative solutions to the drive for sociality—a drive that can be frequently thwarted by the geographical and cultural realities of cities increasingly structured according to the needs of powerful economic interests rather than in ways that encourage and facilitate habitation and social interaction in the urban context. In this context, electronic virtual communities are complex and ingenious strategies for *survival*. Whether the seemingly inherent seductiveness of the medium distorts the aims of those strategies, as television has done for literacy and personal interaction, remains to be seen.

So Much for Community. What about the Body?

No matter how virtual the subject may become, there is always a body attached. It may be off somewhere else—and that 'somewhere else' may be a privileged point of view—but consciousness remains firmly rooted in the physical. Historically, body, technology, and community constitute each other.

In her 1990 book *Gender Trouble*, Judith Butler introduces the useful concept of the 'culturally intelligible body,' or the criteria and the textual productions (including writing on or in the body itself) that each society uses to produce physical bodies that it recognizes as members. It is useful to argue that most cultural production of intelligibility is about reading or writing and takes place through the mediation of texts. If we can apply textual analysis to the narrow-bandwidth modes of computers and telephones, then we can examine the production of gendered bodies in cyberspace also as a set of tokens that code difference within a field of ideal types. I refer to this process as the production of the *legible* body.

The opposite production, of course, is of the *illegible* body, the 'boundary-subject' that theorist Gloria Anzaldúa calls the *Mestiza*, one who lives in the borderlands and is only partially recognized by each abutting society. Anzaldúa describes the Mestiza by means of a multiplicity of frequently conflicting accounts. There is no position, she shows, outside of the abutting societies themselves from which an omniscient overview could capture the essence of the Mestiza's predicament, nor is there any single account from within a societal framework that constitutes an adequate description.

If the Mestiza is an illegible subject, existing quantumlike in multiple states, then participants in the electronic virtual communities of cyberspace live in the borderlands of both physical and virtual culture, like the Mestiza. Their social system includes other people, quasi people or delegated agencies that represent specific individuals, and quasi agents that represent 'intelligent' machines, clusters of people, or both. Their ancestors, lower on the chain of evolution, are network conferencers, communities organized around texts such as Boyle's 'community of gentlemen' and the religious traditions based in holy scripture, communities organized around broadcasts, and communities of music such as the Deadheads. What separates the cyberspace communities from their ancestors is that many of the cyberspace communities interact in real time. Agents meet face-to-face, though as I noted before, under a redefinition of both 'meet' and 'face.'

I might have been able to make my point regarding illegible subjects without invoking the Mestiza as an example. But I make an example of a specific kind of person as a way of keeping the discussion grounded in individual bodies: in Paul Churchland's words, in the 'situated biological creatures' that we each are. The work of science is *about* bodies—not in an abstract sense, but in the complex and protean ways that we daily manifest ourselves as physical social beings, vulnerable to the powerful knowledges that surround us, and to the effects upon us of the transformative discourses of science and technology that we both enable and enact.

I am particularly conscious of this because much of the work of cyberspace researchers, reinforced and perhaps created by the soaring imagery of William Gibson's novels, assumes that the human body is 'meat'—obsolete, as soon as consciousness itself can be uploaded into the network. The discourse of visionary virtual world builders is rife with images of imaginal bodies, freed from the constraints that flesh imposes. Cyberspace developers foresee a time when they will be able to forget about the body. But it is important to remember that virtual community originates in, and must return to, the physical. No refigured virtual body, no matter how beautiful, will slow the death of a cyberpunk with AIDS. Even in the age of the technosocial subject, life is lived through bodies.

Forgetting about the body is an old Cartesian trick, one that has unpleasant consequences for those bodies whose speech is silenced by the act of our forgetting; that is to say, those upon whose labor the act of forgetting the body is founded—usually women and minorities. On the other hand, as Haraway points out, forgetting can be a powerful strategy; through forgetting, that which is already built becomes that which can be discovered. But like any powerful and productive strategy, this one has its dangers. Remembering—discovering—that bodies and communities constitute each other surely suggests a set of questions and debates for the burgeoning virtual electronic community. I hope to observe the outcome.

References   ALLAN, FRANCIS, 'The End of Intimacy.' *Human Rights*, Winter 1984: 55.

ANZALDÚA, GLORIA, *Borderlands/La Frontera: The New Mestiza* (San Francisco: Spinsters/Aunt Lute, 1987).

BARKER, FRANCIS, *The Tremulous Private Body: Essays in Subjection* (London: Methuen, 1984).

BAUDRILLARD, JEAN, *The Ecstasy of Communication*, trans. Bernard and Caroline Schutze, Sylvere Lotringer (New York: Semiotext(e), 1987).

BUTLER, JUDITH, *Gender Trouble: Feminism and the Subversion of Identity* (New York: Routledge, 1990).

CAMPBELL, JOSEPH, *The Masks of God: Primitive Mythology* (New York: Viking, 1959).

COHN, CAROL, 'Sex and Death in the Rational World of Defense Intellectuals. *Signs: Journal of Woman in Culture and Society*, 1987, 12: 4.

DE CERTEAU, MICHEL, 'The Arts of Dying: Celibatory Machines.' In *Heterologies*, translated by Brian Massumi (Minneapolis: University of Minnesota Press, 1985).

DEWEY, JOHN, 'The Reflex Arc Concept in Psychology' [1896]. In J. J. McDermott (ed.), *The Philosophy of John Dewey* (Chicago: University of Chicago Press, 1981), pp. 36–148.

EDWARDS, PAUL N., 'Artificial Intelligence and High Technology War: The Perspective of the Formal Machine.' Silicon Valley Research Group Working Paper No. 6, 1986.

GIBSON, WILLIAM, *Neuromancer* (New York: Ace, 1984).

HABERMAS, J., *Communication and the Evolution of Society* (Boston: Beacon Press, 1979).

HARAWAY, DONNA, 'A Manifesto for Cyborgs: Science, Technology and Socialist Feminism in the 1980s,' *Socialist Review*, 1985, 80: 65–107.

—— 'Donna Haraway Reads National Geographic' (Paper Tiger, 1987) Video.

—— 'The Biopolitics of Postmodern Bodies: Determinations of Self and Other in Immune System Discourse,' *Wenner Gren Foundation Conference on Medical Anthropology*, Lisbon, Portugal, 1988.

—— 'Washburn and the New Physical Anthropology.' In *Primate Visions: Gender, Race, and Nature in the World of Modern Science* (New York: Routledge, 1990).

—— 'The Promises of Monsters: A Regenerative Politics for Inappropriate/d Others.' In Treichler, P. and Nelson, G. (eds.), *Cultural Studies Now and in the Future.'* Forthcoming.

HAYLES, N. KATHERINE, 'Text Out Of Context: Situating Postmodernism Within an Information Society,' *Discourse*, 1987, 9: 24–36.

—— 'Denaturalizing Experience: Postmodern Literature and Science.' Abstract from Conference on Literature and Science as Modes of Expression, sponsored by the Society for Literature and Science, Worcester Polytechnic Institute, October 8–11, 1987.

HEAD, HENRY, *Studies in Neurology* (Oxford: Oxford University Press, 1920).

—— *Aphasia and Kindred Disorders of Speech* (Cambridge: Cambridge University Press, 1926).

HEWITT, CARL, 'Viewing Control Structures as Patterns of Passing Messages,' *Artificial Intelligence*, 1977, 8: 323–364.

—— 'The Challenge of Open Systems,' *Byte*, vol. 10 (April 1977).

HUYSSEN, ANDREAS, *After The Great Divide: Modernism, Mass Culture, Postmodernism* (Bloomington: Indiana University Press, 1986).

JAMESON, FREDRIC, 'On Interpretation: Literature as a Socially Symbolic Act.' In *The Political Unconscious* (Ithaca: Cornell University Press, 1981).

LACAN, JACQUES, *The Language of the Self: The Function of Language in Psychoanalysis*, trans. Anthony Wilden (New York: Dell, 1968).

—— *The Four Fundamental Concepts of Psychoanalysis*, trans. Alain Sheridan, ed. Jacques-Alain Miller (London: Hogarth, 1977).

LAPORTE, T. R. (ed.), *Organized Social Complexity: Challenge to Politics and Policy* (New Jersey: Princeton University Press, 1975).

LATOUR, BRUNO, *The Pasteurization of France*, trans. Alan Sheridan and John Law. (Cambridge, Mass.: Harvard University Press, 1988).

LAUREL, BRENDA, 'Interface as Mimesis.' In D. A. Norman, and S. Draper (eds.), *User Centered System Design: New Perspectives on Human-Computer Interaction* (Hillsdale, NJ: Lawrence Erlbaum Associates, 1986).

—— 'Reassessing Interactivity,' *Journal of Computer Game Design*, 1987, 1: 3.

—— 'Culture Hacking,' *Journal of Computer Game Design*, 1988, 1: 8.

—— 'Dramatic Action and Virtual Reality.' In Proceedings of the 1989 NCGA Interactive Arts Conference, 1989a.

—— 'New Interfaces for Entertainment,' *Journal of Computer Game Design*, 1989b, 2: 5.

—— 'A Taxonomy of Interactive Movies,' *New Media News* (The Boston Computer Society), 1989c, 3: 1.

LEHMAN-WILZIG, SAM, 'Frankenstein Unbound: Toward a Legal Definition of Artificial Intelligence,' *Futures*, December 1981, 447.

LEVINE, STEVEN, *Who Dies? An Investigation of Conscious Living and Conscious Dying* (Bath: Gateway Press, 1988).

MERLEAU-PONTY, MAURICE, *Phenomenology of Perception*, trans. Colin Smith (New York: Humanities Press, 1962).

—— *Sense and Non-Sense*, trans. Hubert L. Dreyfus and Patricia Allen Dreyfus (Chicago: Northwestern University Press, 1964a).

—— *Signs*, trans. Richard McCleary (Chicago: Northwestern University Press, 1964b).

MITCHELL, SILAS WEIR, GEORGE READ MOREHOUSE, and WILLIAM WILLIAMS KEEN, 'Gunshot Wounds and Other Injuries of Nerves.' Reprinted with biographical introductions by Ira M. Rutkow, *American Civil War Surgery Series*, vol. 3 (San Francisco: Norman, 1989 [1864]).

MITCHELL, SILAS WEIR, *Injuries of Nerves and Their Consequences*, with a new introduction by Lawrence C. McHenry, Jr., *American Academy of Neurology Reprint series*, vol. 2 (New York: Dover, 1965 [1872]).

NODDINGS, NEL, *Caring: A Feminine Approach to Ethics and Moral Education* (Berkeley: University of California Press, 1984).

REID, RODDEY, 'Tears For Fears: Paul et Virginie, 'Family' and the Politics of the Sentimental Body in pre-revolutionary France.' Forthcoming.

RENTMEISTER, CACILIA, 'Beruftsverbot fur Musen,' *Aesthetik und Kommunikation*, 25 (September 1976), 92–112.

ROHEIM, GEZA, 'Early Stages of the Oedipus Complex,' *International Journal of Psycho-analysis*, vol. 9, 1928.

—— 'Dream Analysis and Field Work.' In *Anthropology, Psychoanalysis and the Social Sciences* (New York: International Universities Press, 1947).

SHAPIN, STEVEN, and SCHAFFER, SIMON, *Leviathan and the Air-Pump: Hobbes, Boyle, and the Experimental Life* (Princeton: Princeton University Press, 1985).

SOBCHACK, VIVIAN, 'The Address of the Eye: A Semiotic Phenomenology of Cinematic Embodiment.' Forthcoming.

—— 'The Scene Of The Screen: Toward a Phenomenology of Cinematic and Electronic "Presence."' In H. V. Gumbrecht and L. K. Pfeiffer (eds.), *Materialitat des Kommunikation* (GDR: Suhrkarp-Verlag, 1988).

—— *Screening Space: The American Science Fiction Film* (New York: Ungar, 1987).

STONE, ALLUCQUERE ROSANNE, 1988. 'So That's What Those Two Robots Were Doing In The Park . . . I Thought They Were Repairing Each Other! The Discourse of Gender, Pornography, and Artificial Intelligence.' Presented at Conference of the Feminist Studies Focused Research Activity, University of California, Santa Cruz, Cal., October 1988.

—— 'How Robots Grew Gonads: A Cautionary Tale.' Presented at *Contact V: Cultures of the Imagination*, Phoenix, Ariz., March 28, 1989. Forthcoming in Funaro and Joans (eds.), *Collected Proceedings of the Contact Conferences*.

—— 'Sex and Death Among the Cyborgs: How to Construct Gender and Boundary in Distributed Systems,' *Contact VI: Cultures of the Imagination* (Phoenix, Ariz., 1990a).

—— 'Sex and Death among the Disembodied: How to Provide Counseling for the Virtually Preorgasmic.' In M. Benedikt (ed.), *Collected Abstracts of The First Cyberspace Conference* (The University of Texas at Austin, School of Architecture, 1990b).

—— 'Aliens, Freaks, Monsters: The Politics of Virtual Sexuality.' For the panel Gender and Cultural Bias in Computer Games, Computer Game Developers' Conference, San Jose, 1990c.

—— 'Ecriture Artifactuelle: Boundary Discourse, Distributed Negotiation, and the Structure of Meaning in Virtual Systems,' forthcoming at the *1991 Conference on Interactive Computer Graphics*.

STONE, CHRISTOPHER D., *Should Trees Have Standing?—Toward Legal Rights for Natural Objects* (New York: William A. Kaufman, 1974).

THEWELEIT, KLAUS, *Male Fantasies*, vol. 1 (Frankfurt am Main: Verlag Roter Stern, 1977).

TOMAS, DAVID, 'The Technophilic Body: On Technicity in William Gibson's Cyborg Culture,' *New Formations*, 8, Spring, 1989.

TURKLE, SHERRY, *The Second Self: Computers and the Human Spirit* (New York: Simon and Schuster, 1984).

VON FOERSTER, HEINZ (ed.), *Transactions of the Conference on Cybernetics* (New York: Josiah Macy, Jr. Foundation, 1951).

WEINER, NORBERT, *The Human Use of Human Beings* (New York: Avon, 1950).

WILDEN, ANTHONY, *System and Structure: Essays in Communication and Exchange*, 2nd edn. (New York: Tavistock, 1980).

WINOGRAD, T., and FLORES, C. F., *Understanding Computers and Cognition: A New Foundation for Design* (Norwood, NJ: Ablex, 1986).

WOLKOMIR, RICHARD, 'High-tech Hokum is Changing the Way Movies are Made,' *Smithsonian* 10/90: 124, 1990.

16

Topographic Writing: Hypertext and the Electronic Writing Space[1]

Jay David Bolter

In this article Jay David Bolter offers a succinct analysis of the act and implications of authorship via forms of computer media. In a graphic illustration of the implications of the shift to non-linear systems of representing knowledge furthered by computer media, Bolter elaborates a metaphor for relations of information based on tree structures in electronic space. In so doing, he addresses a range of theoretical and practical issues related to hypertext and hypermedia.

TED NELSON, WHO coined the term, has defined 'hypertext' as 'non-sequential writing with reader-controlled links.'[2] Good as this succinct definition is, it omits an aspect of hypertext that I wish to emphasize: hypertext as a method for exploring the visual and conceptual writing space presented to us by computer technology. Writing is always spatial, and each technology in the history of writing (e.g. the clay tablet, the papyrus roll, the codex, the printed book) has presented writers and readers with a different space to exploit. The computer is our newest technology of writing, and we are still learning how to use its space. Different computer programs have given us different geometries with which to structure this new writing space. We began with word processing, which is almost strictly linear, and then moved to outline processing, which allows us to create two-dimensional hierarchies of text. Now we are facing the ultimate freedom offered by the hypertextual network. Hypertext forces us to redefine text both as a structure of visible elements on the screen and as a structure of signs in the minds of writers and their readers. The *computer as hypertext* invites us

From Paul Delany and George P. Landow (eds.), *Hypermedia and Literary Studies* (London: MIT Press, 1991), 105–18.

1 True to the spirit of hypertext, portions of this paper have appeared in other places: principally *Writing Space: The Computer, Hypertext and the History of Writing* (Hillsdale, NJ: Lawrence Erlbaum, 1990). Reprinted with permission. Portions appeared earlier in (and are reprinted with permission from) 'Beyond Word Processing: The Computer as a New Writing Space,' *Language and Communication* 9 (1989): 129–42.

2 This definition was offered in the course of his talk 'Hyperworld: One for All and All for One,' delivered on November 14, 1987 at HyperText'87, a conference held at the University of North Carolina at Chapel Hill.

to write with signs that have both an intrinsic and extrinsic significance. That is, the signs have a meaning that may be explained in words, but they also have meaning as elements in a larger structure of verbal and visual gestures. Both words and structures are visible and manipulable in the electronic space.

Writing Places

With or without the computer, whenever we write, we write topically. We conceive of our text as a set of verbal gestures, large and small. To write is to do things with topics—to add, delete, and arrange them. The computer changes the nature of writing simply by giving visual expression to our acts of conceiving and manipulating topics. A writer working with a word processor spends much of the time entering words letter by letter, just as he or she does at a typewriter. Revising is a different matter. With most word processors, writers can delete or replace an entire word; they can highlight phrases, sentences, or paragraphs. They can erase a sentence with a single keystroke; they can select a paragraph, cut it from its current location, and insert it elsewhere, even into another document. In using these facilities, the writer is thinking and writing in terms of verbal units or topics, whose meaning transcends their constituent words. The Greek word *topos* meant literally a place, and ancient rhetoric used the word to refer to commonplaces, conventional units or methods of thought. In the Renaissance, topics became headings that could be used to organize any field of knowledge, and these headings were often set out in elaborate diagrams.[3] Our English word *topic* is appropriate for the computer because its etymology suggests the spatial character of electronic writing: topics exist in a writing space that is not only a visual surface but also a data structure in the computer. The programmers who designed word processors recognized the importance of topical writing, when they gave us operations for adding or deleting sentences and paragraphs as units. They did not, however, take the further step of allowing a writer to associate a name or a visual symbol with such topical units. This important step lends the unit a conceptual identity. The unit symbol becomes an abiding element in the writer's thinking and expression, because its constituent words or phrases can be put out of sight.

On a printed or typed page, we indent and separate paragraphs to indicate the topical structure. Within each paragraph, however, we have only punctuation, occurring in the stream of words, to mark finer structure. A better representation of topical writing is the conventional outline, in which major topics are designated by Roman numerals, subtopics by capital letters, sub-subtopics by Arabic numerals, and so on. Each point of an outline serves to organize and situate the topics subordinate to it, and the outline as a whole is a static representation, a snapshot, of the textual organization. The conventions of outlining turn the writing surface into a tiered space in which the numbering and indentation of lines represent the hierarchy of the author's ideas. A paragraphed text is the flattening or linearization of an outline.

3 See Walter J. Ong, *Ramus, Method, and the Decay of Dialogue: From the Art of Discourse to the Art of Reason* (Cambridge, Mass.: Harvard University Press, 1958), 104–30.

The word processor, which imitates the layout of the typed page, also flattens the text. It offers the writer little help in conceiving the evolving structure of the text. Although the word processor allows the writer to define a verbal unit in order to move or delete it, the definition lasts only until the operation is complete. Whereas the word processor offers the writer only temporary access to his or her structure, another class of programs called *outline processors* makes structure a permanent feature of the text. An outline processor sets the traditional written outline in motion. A writer can add points to an electronic outline in any order while the computer continually renumbers to reflect additions or deletions. The writer can promote minor points to major ones, and the computer will again renumber. The writer can collapse the outline in order to see only those points above a certain level, an action that gives an overview of the evolving text. In short the writer can think globally about the text: one can treat topics as unitary symbols and write with those symbols, just as in a word processor one writes with words.

Writing in topics is not a replacement for writing with words; the writer must eventually attend to the details of his or her prose. The outline processor contains within it a conventional word processor, so that the writer can attach text to each of the points in the outline. But in using an outline processor, writers are not aware of a rigid distinction between outlining and prose writing: they move easily back and forth between structure and prose. What is new is that the points of the outline become functional elements in the text, because when the points move the words move with them. In this way the computer makes visible and almost palpable what writers have always known: that the identifying and arranging of topics is itself an act of writing. Outline processing is writing at a different granularity, a replication on a higher level of the conventional act of writing by choosing and arranging words. The symbols of this higher writing are simply longer and more complicated 'words,' verbal gestures that may be whole sentences or paragraphs.

In an outline processor, then, the prose remains, but it is encased in a formally operative structure. With a pen or typewriter, writing meant literally to form letters on a page, figuratively to create verbal structures. In an electronic writing system, the figurative process becomes a literal act. By defining topical symbols, the writer can, like the programmer or the mathematician, abstract himself or herself temporarily from the details of the prose, and the value of this abstraction lies in seeing more clearly the structural skeleton of the text. It is not possible or desirable that the prose writer should become a mathematician or that human language should be reduced to a system of logical symbols. The result of giving language wholeheartedly over to formalism would simply be the impoverishment of language. On the other hand, the electronic medium can permit us to play creatively with formal structures in our writing without abandoning the richness of natural language.

Electronic Trees

It is no accident that the computer can serve as an outline processor. The machine is designed to create and track such formal structures, which are important for all its various uses. The computer's memory and central processing unit are intricate hierarchies of electronic components. Layers of software in turn transform the machine's physical space of electronic circuits into a space of symbolic information, and it is in this space that a new kind of writing can be located. Like the space of the modern physicist, the space of the computer is shaped by the objects that occupy it. The computer programmer forms his or her space by filling it with symbolic elements and then by connecting these elements as the program requires. Any symbol in the space can refer to another symbol by using its numerical address. Pointers hold together the structure of computer programs, and programming itself may be defined as the art of building symbolic structures in the space that the computer provides—a definition that makes programming a species of writing.

One such programming structure, which represents hierarchy, is called a *tree*. Trees (and their relatives such as *lists, stacks*, and *networks*) are ubiquitous in programs that must record and track large bodies of information or of information subject to frequent change. Tree diagrams, in which elements are connected by branches as in a genealogical tree, have a long history in writing as well. They date back at least to the early Middle Ages and are not uncommon in medieval and Renaissance books, where they were used for the spatial arrangement of topics.[4] The traditional outline is a strict hierarchy that can just as easily be represented by a tree diagram.

Both the tree and the outline give us a better reading of structure than does ordinary paragraphing, because they mold the visual space of the text in a way that reflects its structure. A printed page of paragraphs is by comparison a flat and uninteresting space, as is the window of a word processor. A writer can use a word processor to type an outline, and, if the word processor permits graphics, the writer can insert a tree diagram into the text. But the outline or diagram will then be stored as a picture, a sequence of bits to be shown on the screen; the picture will not be treated as a data structure and will not inform the space in which the writer is working. The writer will not be able to change the structure by manipulating the outline, as he or she can in an outline processor, and that ability is necessary for true electronic writing. In using an outline processor, the writer can intervene at any level of the evolving structure. And if the writer gives the reader a diskette rather than a printed version, then the reader too gains immediate access to that structure. All this is possible, because the writing space itself has become a tree, a hierarchy of topical elements.

The electronic writing space is extremely malleable. It can be fashioned into one tree or into a forest of hierarchical trees. In any printed or written text, one hierarchical order always precludes others. The static medium of print demands that the writer settle on one order of topics, although the writer may find that the topics could be arranged equally well in, say, three orders corresponding to three electronic outlines. Unlike the space of the printed book, the computer's writing space can represent any relationships that can be defined as the interplay of pointers and elements. Multiple relationships pose no special problem. A writer could therefore maintain three outlines, each of which deployed the same topics in a different order. These outlines may all reside in the computer's memory at the same time, each

---

4 Ong, *Ramus*, 74–83, 199–202, and 314–18.

activated at the writer's request. The writer may choose to examine topics from any of the three vantage points and then switch to another; he or she may alter one outline while leaving the others intact; he or she may alter any of the outlines themselves without revising the text in any one of the topics. The structure of an electronic text is in this sense abstracted from its verbal expression.

This multiplicity and abstraction already render the electronic writing space more flexible than its predecessors. And if all writing were only hierarchical, then the outline processor itself would be revolutionary in its freeing of writing from the frozen structure of the printed page. But there is one further step to be taken in liberating the text.

Hypertext   The goal of conventional writing is to create a perfect hierarchy, but it is not always easy to maintain the discipline of such a structure. All writers have had the experience of being overwhelmed with ideas as they write. The act of writing itself releases a flood of thoughts—one idea suggesting another and then another, as the writer struggles to get them down in some form before they slip from his conscious grasp. 'I only wish I could write with both hands,' noted Saint Teresa, 'so as not to forget one thing while I am saying another.'[5] Romantics like Carlyle founded their psychology of literature upon this experience. The experience is not limited to saints and sages: many, perhaps most, writers begin their work with a jumble of verbal ideas and only a vague sense of how these ideas will fit together. The writer may start by laying out topics in an arrangement less formal than an outline: he or she may organize by association rather than strict subordination. Teachers of writing often encourage their students to begin by sketching out topics and connecting them through lines of association, and they call this activity 'prewriting.' What students create in prewriting is a network of elements—exactly what computer programmers mean by the data structure they call a network. The computer can maintain such a network of topics, which reflects the writer's progress as he or she trims the network by removing connections and establishing subordination until there is a strict hierarchy. In the world of print, at least in nonfiction, associative writing is considered only a preliminary stage.

Association is not really prior to writing, as the term 'prewriting' suggests. Association is always present in any text: one word echoes another; one sentence or paragraph recalls others earlier in the text and looks forward to still others. A writer cannot help but write associatively: even if he or she begins with an outline and remains faithful to it, the result is always a network of verbal elements. The hierarchy (in the form of paragraphs, sections, and chapters) is an attempt to impose order on verbal ideas that are always prone to subvert that order. The associative relationships define alternative organizations that lie beneath the order of pages and chapters that a printed text presents to the world. These alternatives constitute subversive texts-behind-the-text.

---

5 See *Complete Works of St Teresa of Jesus*, trans. E. Allison Peers (London: Sheed and Ward, 1972), ii. 88.

Previous technologies of writing, which could not easily accommodate such alternatives, tended to ignore them. The ancient papyrus roll was strongly linear in its presentation of text. The codex, especially in the later Middle Ages, and then the printed book have made better efforts to accommodate association as well as hierarchy. In a modern book the table of contents (listing chapters and sometimes sections) defines the hierarchy, while the indices record associative lines of thought that permeate the text. An index permits the reader to locate passages that share the same word, phrase, or subject and so associates passages that may be widely separated in the pagination of the book. In one sense the index defines other books that could be constructed from the materials at hand, other themes that the author could have formed into an analytical narrative, and so invites the reader to read the book in alternative ways. An index transforms a book from a tree into a network, offering multiplicity in place of a single order of paragraphs and pages.

There need not be any privileged element in a network, as there always is in a tree, no single topic that dominates all others. Instead of strict subordination, we have paths that weave their way through the textual space. A full-fledged hypertext can only be represented by the network, as in Figure. 1. If all texts are ultimately networks of verbal elements, the computer is the first medium that can record and present these networks to writers and readers. Just as the outline processor treats text as a hierarchy, other computer programs can fashion the text into a general network or hypertext.

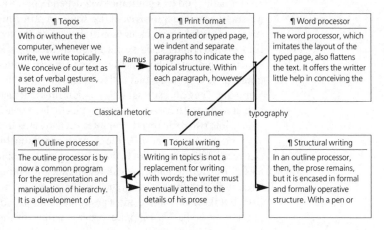

Fig. 1.
A hypertext is a network of textual elements and connections.

¶ Topos
With or without the computer, whenever we write, we write topically. We conceive of our text as a set of verbal gestures, large and small

¶ Print format
On a printed or typed page, we indent and separate paragraphs to indicate the topical structure. Within each paragraph, however

¶ Word processor
The word processor, which imitates the layout of the typed page, also flattens the text. It offers the writter little help in conceiving the

Ramus

Classical rhetoric   forerunner   typography

¶ Outline processor
The outline processor is by now a common program for the representation and manipulation of hierarchy. It is a development of

¶ Topical writing
Writing in topics is not a replacement for writing with words; the writer must eventually attend to the details of his prose

¶ Structural writing
In an outline processor, then, the prose remains, but it is encased in formal and formally operative structure. With a pen or

A hypertext consists of topics and their connections, where again the topics may be paragraphs, sentences, individual words, or indeed digitized graphics. A hypertext is like a printed book that the author has attacked with a pair of scissors and cut into convenient verbal sizes. Electronic hypertext does not simply dissolve into a disordered bundle of slips, as the printed book must, for the author also defines a scheme of electronic connections to indicate relationships among the slips. In fashioning a hypertext, a writer might begin with a passage of continuous prose and then add notes or glosses on important words in the passage. The glosses themselves could contain glosses, leading the reader to further texts. A hypertextual network can extend indefinitely, as a printed text cannot.

A computer hypertext might serve, for example, to collect scholars' notes on complex texts such as Joyce's *Ulysses* and *Finnegans Wake*. The computer can record and update the collective work of many scholars who continue today adding to, refining, and revising the glosses; it can connect notes to other notes as appropriate. Such exegesis, currently recorded in books and journals, would be both easier to use and more appropriate as a hypertext, because *Ulysses* and particularly *Finnegans Wake* are themselves hypertexts that have been flattened out to fit on the printed page. But an author does not have to be as experimental as Joyce to profit from hypertext. A historian might choose to write an essay in which each paragraph or section is a topic in a hypertextual network. The connections would indicate possible orders in which topics could be assembled and read, and each order of reading might produce a different literary and analytic result. A mathematician might choose to write a hypertextbook that could tailor itself to different students with differing degrees of mathematical proficiency. Hypertext can serve for all sorts of more popular materials as well: directories, catalogues, how-to manuals—wherever the reader wishes to move through the text in a variety of orders. In fact thousands of such hypertexts are already available, written for display by HyperCard, a program for the Apple Macintosh computer.

In general, the connections of a hypertext are organized into paths that make operational sense to author and reader. Each topic may participate in several paths, and its significance will depend upon which paths the reader has travelled in order to arrive at that topic. In print, only a few paths can be suggested or followed. In an electronic version the texture of the text becomes thicker, and its paths can serve many functions. Paths can, as in a tree structure, indicate subordination. They can also remind the writer of relationships among topics that had to be sacrificed for the sake of an eventual hierarchy. They can express cyclic relationships among topics that can never be hierarchical. They can categorize topics for later revision: the writer might wish to join two paths together or intersect two paths and preserve only those elements common to both. In the electronic medium, hierarchical and associative thinking may coexist in the structure of a text, since the computer can take care of the mechanics of maintaining and presenting both networks and trees. In the medium of print, the writer may use an index to show alternatives, but these alternatives must always contend with the fixed order of the pages of the book. The canonical order is defined by the book's pagination, and all other suggested orders remain subordinate. A hypertext has no canonical order. Every path defines an equally convincing and appropriate reading, and in that simple fact the reader's relationship to the text changes radically. A text as a network has no univocal sense; it is a multiplicity without the imposition of a principle of domination.

In place of hierarchy, we have a writing that is not only topical: we might also call it 'topographic.' The word 'topography' originally meant a written description of a place, such as an ancient geographer might give. Only later did the word come to refer to mapping or charting—that is, to a visual and mathematical rather than verbal description. Electronic writing is both a visual and verbal description. It is not the writing of a place, but rather a writing *with* places, with spatially realized topics. Topographic writing challenges the idea that writing should be merely the servant of spoken language. The writer and reader can create and examine signs and structures on the computer screen that have no easy equivalent in speech. The point is obvious when the text is a collection of images stored on a video disk, but it is equally true for a purely verbal text that has been fashioned as a tree or a network of topics and connections.

Topographic writing as a mode is not even limited to the computer medium. It is possible to write topographically for print or even in manuscript. Whenever we divide our text into unitary topics and organize those units into a connected structure and whenever we conceive of this textual structure spatially as well as verbally, we are writing topographically. As we shall see in a later chapter, many literary artists in the twentieth century have adopted this mode of writing. Although the computer is not necessary for topographic writing, it is only in the computer that the mode becomes a natural, and therefore also a conventional, way to write.

Hypermedia Some word processors already permit the writer to insert diagrams and pictures directly into his text. But in word processing the graphic image is not really part of the text; it is merely allowed to coexist with the verbal text. We have seen in Figure 1 above that the computer has the capacity to integrate word and image more subtly, to make text itself graphic by representing its structure graphically to the writer and the reader. The computer can even dissolve the distinction between the standardized letter forms and symbols of the writer's own making. True electronic writing is not limited to verbal text: the writeable elements may be words, images, sounds, or even actions that the computer is directed to perform. The writer could use his or her network to organize pictures on videodisk or music and voices on an audio playback device. Instead of moving from paragraph to paragraph in a verbal text, the reader might be shown videotaped scenes of a play in a variety of orders.[6] The reader might move through an aural landscape created by various recorded sounds or walk through a city by viewing photographs of various buildings.[7] Any combination of these elements is possible. The same computer screen might display verbal text below or beside a video image; it might combine sound and verbal writing. These combinations have come to be called *hypermedia* and are already quite sophisticated. Hypermedia shows even more clearly than verbal hypertext how the computer can expand the traditional writing space of the written or printed page.

The introduction of video images might seem to turn electronic writing into mere television. Television itself often displays words on the screen, but it robs the displayed words of their cognitive value. Text on television is mere ornamentation; words appear most often to reinforce the spoken message or to decorate the packages of products being advertised. In fact, hypermedia is

---

6 See Larry Friedlander, 'The Shakespeare Project,' in Paul Delany and George P. London (eds.), *Hypermedia and Literary Studies* (London, MIT Press, 1991).

7 Such was the Aspen project. See Stewart Brand, *The Media Lab: Inventing the Future at M.I.T.* (New York: Penguin Books, 1987), 141–2.

the revenge of text upon television.[8] In television, text is absorbed into the video image, but in hypermedia the televised image becomes part of the text. This incorporation is literally true in MIT's Project Athena, in which the reader can run a videotape in a window on his computer screen. The video image therefore sits among the other textual elements for the reader to examine.[9] The Intermedia system developed at Brown University is another instance of texts and images read and written in the same computer environment.[10]

Once video images and sound are taken into the computer in this fashion, they too become topical elements. Writers can fashion these elements into a structure. They can write with images, because they can direct one topical image to refer to another and join visual and verbal topics in the same network. A journalist might select examples from a library of digitized still pictures and form them into a pictorial essay. An art historian might take images of Renaissance painting and attach explanatory comments. In fact, one can link the comments not only to the whole painting, but also to given areas of the image. The eyes of one portrait may refer to a comment, which may in turn link to eyes of other portrait examples. Other parts of the painting would lead to other comments and other examples. The reader would begin with the first picture and then choose to read the network of examples and explanations in a variety of orders, based on an interest in hands, eyes, or other elements of Renaissance technique. In each case the elements of the pictures have themselves become signs that refer to verbal topics and to other pictures.[11] The image is functioning symbolically within the writer's text.

Such multimedia texts are by no means the death of writing. A hypermedia display is still a text, a weaving together of elements treated symbolically. Hypermedia simply extends the principles of electronic writing into the domain of sound and image. The computer's control of structure promises to create a synaesthesia in which anything that can be seen or heard may contribute to the texture of the text. These synaesthetic texts will have the same qualities as electronic verbal texts. They too will be flexible, dynamic, and interactive; they too will blur the distinction between writer and reader.

The First Collaborative Hypertext

Although experiments have been conducted since the 1960s, workable hypertext systems such as Intermedia are relatively recent. It was not until the advent of personal computers and workstations that hypertext could be made available to a large audience of writers and readers. On the other hand, the principle of hypertext has been implicit in computer programming for

8 Michael Joyce, 'Siren Shapes: Exploratory and Constructive Hypertexts,' *Academic Computing* 3: 4 (1988): 14.

9 For a description of Project Athena, see E. Balkovich, S. Lerman, and R. P. Parmelee, 'Computing in Higher Education: The Athena Project,' *Computer* 18 (1985): 112–25.

10 See Nicole Yankelovich, Bernard J. Haan, Norman K. Meyrowitz, and Steven M. Drucker, 'Intermedia: The Concept and the Construction of a Seamless Information Environment,' *Computer* 21 (1988): 81–96.

11 David Graham, 'The Emblematic Hyperbook,' in Delany and Landow (eds.), *Hypermedia and Literary Studies*.

much longer. Hypertext is the interactive interconnection of a set of symbolic elements, and many kinds of computer programs (databases, simulation programs, even programs for artificial intelligence) are special cases of that principle. Hypertext shows how programming and conventional prose writing can combine in the space provided by the computer. It puts at the disposal of writers data structures (trees and networks) that have been used for decades by programmers. Conversely, it makes us realize that the programmer's data structures are formalized versions of the textual strategies that writers have exploited for centuries.

Important anticipations of hypertext can be found in the computerized communications networks, such as ARPANET or BITNET, put in place in the 1960s and 1970s. Such a network constitutes the physical embodiment of hypertext. Each element or *node* in the network is a computer installation, while the connections among these elements are cables and microwave and satellite links. Each computer node serves dozens or hundreds of individual subscribers, and these subscribers both produce and read messages created by others within their computing facility, around the nation, or around the world. Some messages travel a single path through the communications links until they reach their marked destination, while general messages spread out to all the elements in the net. At any one moment the network holds a vast text of interrelated writings—the intersection of thousands of messages on hundreds of topics. It is a hypertext that no one reader can hope to encompass, one that changes moment by moment as messages are added and deleted.

Subscribers use these networks both for personal mail and to conduct ongoing discussions in so-called 'newsgroups.' When one subscriber in a newsgroup 'publishes' a message, it travels to all the dozens or hundreds of others who belong to that group. The message may elicit responses, which in turn travel back and forth and spawn further responses. The prose of these messages is almost as casual as conversation, precisely because publication in this medium is both easy and almost unrestricted. The transition from reader to writer is completely natural. Readers of one message can with a few keystrokes send off a reply. They may even incorporate part of the original message in the reply, blurring the distinction between their own text and the text to which they are responding. There is also little respect for the conventions of the prior medium of print. Subscribers often type newspaper articles or excerpts from books into their replies without concern for copyright. The notion of copyright seems faintly absurd, since their messages are copied and relayed automatically hundreds of times in a matter of hours.

Writing for such a network is by nature topographical: relatively small units of prose are sent and received. The medium itself encourages brevity, since two correspondents can send and receive several messages in one day. And the addresses of the messages provide a primitive system of links. To reply to a given message is to link your text to the earlier one, and both message and reply may then circulate for days around the network provoking other reponses. No user is bound to read or reply to anything; instead, any message can refer to any other or ignore all previous messages and strike out in a new direction. A communications network is therefore a hypertext in which no one writer or reader has substantial control, and because no one has control, no one has substantial responsibility. The situation is different for hypertext systems for microcomputers, where there is one author and one reader. There the twin issues of control and responsibility are paramount.

Writers and Readers of Hypertext

When we receive a written or typed letter, we hold in our own hands the paper that the sender also has handled. We see and touch the inkmarks that he or she has made. With electronic mail we receive bits of information that correspond to the tapping of keys on the writer's keyboard. We read this information as patches of light on our computer screen, and we touch nothing that the writer has touched. Like all other kinds of writing, electronic writing is an act of postponement or deferral. As writers, we defer our words by setting them down on a writing surface for later reading by ourselves or by others. The reader's task is to reactivate the words on the page and to devise for them a new context, which may be close to or far removed from the author's original context. There is always a gulf between author and reader, a gap that the technique of writing first creates and then mediates. In one sense the computer opens a particularly wide gap because of the abstract nature of electronic technology. On the other hand, the author has a unique opportunity to control the procedure of reading, because he or she can program restrictions into the text itself.

Computer-assisted instruction, for example, is nothing other than a hypertext in which the author has restricted the ways in which the student/reader can proceed. In typical computer-assisted instruction the program poses a question and awaits an answer from the student. If the student gives the correct answer, the program may present another question. If the student gives an incorrect answer, the program may explain the student's error. If the student makes the same error repeatedly, the program may present a review of the point that the student has failed to grasp. In most cases, these questions and explanations are texts that the teacher/programmer has composed and stored in advance. However, good programming can make these simple programs seem uncannily clever in replying to student. In fact such a program takes on a persona created for it by the teacher/programmer, as it transfers the teacher's words into the new context of the student's learning session. In general, the reader of an electronic text is made aware of the author's simultaneous presence in and absence from the text, because the reader constantly confronts structural choices defined by the author. If the program allows the reader to make changes in the text or to add his own connections (as some hypertext systems do), then the game becomes still more complex. As readers we become our own authors, determining the structure of the text for the next reader, or perhaps for ourselves in our next reading.

Electronic text is the first text in which the elements of meaning, of structure, and of visual display are fundamentally unstable. Unlike the printing press or the medieval codex, the computer does not require that any aspect of writing be determined in advance for the whole life of a text. This restlessness is inherent in a technology that records information by collecting for fractions of a second evanescent electrons at tiny junctions of silicon and metal. All information, all data, in the computer world is a kind of controlled movement, and so the natural inclination of computer writing is to change, to grow, and finally to disappear. Nor is it surprising that these constant motions place electronic writing in a kaleidoscope of relationships with the earlier technologies of typewriting, printing, and handwriting.

Eventually, the new dialectic structure of hypertext will compel us, as Derrida put it, to 'reread past writing according to a different organization of space.'[12] Texts that were originally written for print or manuscript can not only be transferred to machine-readable form, but also translated into hypertextual structures. In some cases the translation would restore to these texts their original, conversational tone. Many of the texts of Aristotle, for example, are notes and excerpts from lectures that the philosopher delivered over many years; they were put together either by Aristotle himself or by ancient editors. For decades modern scholars have been trying to sort out the pieces. Printed editions make each text into a single, monumental treatise, but an electronic edition of Aristotle could record and present all the various chronological and thematic orders that scholars have proposed. This might be the best way for readers to approach the carefully interwoven philosophy of Aristotle: following the electronic links would allow readers to sample from various texts and move progressively deeper into the problems that each text poses. This moving back and forth is the way that scholars reread and study Aristotle even now. The computer simply makes explicit the implicit act of deeply informed reading, which unlike casual reading is truly a dialogue with the text.

Rather than eliminating works of the past or making them irrelevant, the electronic writing space gives them a new 'typography.' For hypertext is the typography of the electronic medium. A text always undergoes typographical changes as it moves from one writing space to another. The Greek classics, for example, have moved from the papyrus roll, to codex, and finally the printed book. When we read a paperback edition in English of Plato's dialogues or Sophocles' tragedy, we are aware of the translation from ancient Greek to a modern language. But we should also remember that the original text had no book or scene divisions, no paragraphing, no indices, no punctuation, and even no word division. All these conventions of modern printing make significant organizational intrusions into the original work. They make reading Sophocles easier, but they change the Sophocles that we read. We would find it very difficult to read an English manuscript of the fourteenth century, or even an early printed book, because of the visual conventions. Electronic versions of old texts will not violate their sanctity for the first time: these texts have always been subject to typographic change; they have already been violated.

When it comes to texts written in and for the electronic medium—and a few such texts have already been written—no translation is needed. The new works do not have a single linear order, corresponding to the page of the book or the columns of the papyrus roll, and so there is no order to violate. Precisely this lack of a fixed order and commitment to a linear argument will

---

12 Jacques Derrida, *Of Grammatology*, trans. GayatriSpivak (Baltimore: Johns Hopkins University Press, 1976), 86.

frustrate those used to working with and writing for the medium of print, just as it will liberate those willing to experiment with a new form of dialogue. For writers of the new dialogue, the task will be to build, in place of a single argument, a structure of possibilities. The new dialogue will be, as Plato demanded, interactive: it will provide different answers to each reader and may also in Plato's words from the *Phaedrus* know 'before whom to be silent.'

17

The CD-ROM Novel *Myst* and McLuhan's Fourth Law of Media: *Myst* and Its 'Retrievals'

David Miles

In this article, David Miles provides both an introduction to the multimedia industry and a genre analysis of the CD-ROM novel Myst. *In a fitting application of Marshall McLuhan's fourth law of media, namely their 'retrievals', Miles discusses the literary and art-historical dimensions of* Myst, *arguing that this computer game resurrects literary forms from the Homeric epic to science fiction as well as certain surrealistic paintings. Part of the strength of Miles's analysis rests upon his thesis that multimedia is a form of art that can be analysed in reference to existing pieces and traditions of representation. Miles offers insight into multimedia as commercial products, while at the same time, along with Bolter, clarifying their potential as new, interactive forms of creative expression on a par with literature, painting, photography, and cinema.*

MYST, **THE INTERACTIVE** multimedia novel on CD-ROM, became the digital world's first genuine bestseller during 1994 and 1995. It was celebrated by *Newsweek* as 'an instant classic' (Kantrowitz & King, 1994), the *Wall Street Journal* as the first CD-ROM to 'go platinum' (Syman, 1994), and by *Entertainment Weekly* as 'the 800-pound gorilla of the CD-ROM industry' (Daly, 1994). *Myst* was awarded a gold medal of excellence by *NewMedia* magazine and a Best Entertainment Medal by *CD-ROM World*. It was optioned for $1 million by Hyperion, a publishing subsidiary of Disney, for a trilogy of continuation novels in print form; they began appearing in the fall of 1995. The *New York Times*, hailing it as 'a landmark in the game industry' (Rothstein, 1995), stated that 'its reflective, almost cool aesthetic suggests what is possible: image, sound and narrative woven into a new form of experience.' Amid all this acclaim, *Myst* seems destined for an important place in media history—but precisely what place?

Myst's appeal to adults undoubtedly stems from two major factors: its lack of violence (no kick boxers or shoot-'em-ups) and the measured pacing of its

From *Journal of Communication* 46: 2 (Spring 1996). The original article has been amended for publication in this volume.

narrative. By clicking a mouse, one pages through it in a series of still frames, set to music, that dissolve from one to the next as in a slide show. The measured pace of the narrative is due not only to the plot of the story, but also to the inherent technical slowness of a CD-ROM drive coupled with the Hypercard programming language with which it was written (still frames meticulously computer-modeled using Stratavision 3D software and highly textured, photo-realistic surfaces). As distinguished from the traditional novel, *Myst* actually consists of 25,000 'pages' (100 times the page number of a typical novel), but the reader never sees all these pages when playing the game, even in the multiple 'readings' involved in playing it.

At $15 billion in global sales annually, multimedia CD-ROMs and video games generate a much larger income than feature films, yet we academics say and know little about the industry and the art form. This essay is intended as a first small step toward opening our eyes to a new media and communications phenomenon that is rapidly redefining our traditional view of books, movies, and television. Statistics alone speak to this fact. By the end of 1995, according to *CD-ROM Professional* magazine ('CD-Rom Growth,' 1996), 30 million computer CD-ROM players (computer drives) existed in the United States.

Admittedly, such figures have to be viewed with some caution. For at least three reasons, correct sales totals for the CD-ROM industry are notoriously difficult to come by. First, surveys by market research firms typically inflate the number of units sold, for the obvious reason that it is good for their clients and thus their business. Similarly, such surveys conveniently overlook the fact that one out of four purchasers of a CD-ROM for a PC (unlike for a Macintosh, where they run more smoothly) returns the CD-ROM for a refund. Disney's *Lion King* release on CD-ROM in 1995 was a notorious example of this, with its difficult installation procedure and tendency to crash. Finally, market surveys do not cite the fact that a large portion of CD-ROMs are not sold, but simply bundled with computers ('buy this computer and get $995 worth of free software').

Until *Myst*, the most successful consumer CD-ROMs have largely been child- rather than adult-oriented, either in the form of electronic encyclopedias, as 'edutainment' learning games, or as adventure games loaded with violent chase scenes. For a more realistic view of the actual CD-ROM market and the figures for a bestseller in this new industry, however, we must turn to marketing numbers from smaller electronic publishers such as Voyager. These publishers consider a CD-ROM a bestseller when it sells a minimum of 10,000 to 50,000 copies (excluding bundling and returns). A book, by comparison, must sell millions of copies in order to be considered a bestseller. To give an idea of realistic figures for the CD-ROM market: Voyager's CD-ROM version of the Beatles' *A Hard Day's Night* had sold, by the end of 1995, 100,000 copies. Microsoft's *Encarta* encyclopedia had sold 500,000 copies on CD-ROM (despite Microsoft's attempts to bundle it with every computer in the country). In contrast, *Myst*, by the end of 1995, had sold close to 1,500,000 copies, according to market surveys by Hyperion Press.

What should also be pointed out, amid these statistics, is that by the time you read this article, the CD-ROM market will probably already be giving way to the next-generation platform for multimedia publishing, namely the

Web, and, after that, the digital video disk (DVD). The World Wide Web, the multimedia portion of the Internet, undoubtedly requires little introduction. The digital video disk, promised for consumer release in 1997, is what will slowly replace the VCR, audio CD, and even the multimedia CD-ROM itself, probably sometime after the turn of the century when the medium becomes recordable as well. The reason for this coming shift is that the digital video disk (a sort of souped-up CD-ROM only five inches in diameter) will actually be able to play full-length movies that can play on your computer screen, furnished either from a DVD drive in your computer or from your local cable company through its line and special modems. With DVD, in other words, there will be no more of CD-ROM's herky-jerky movies the size of postage stamps, so reminiscent of Edison's early Kinetoscope with its peepshow-sized movies.

This introduction has served to place the current medium of CD-ROM, as well as *Myst*, in its proper historical and continually evolving technological context. It is also important to recall that new media do not necessarily simply replace old media. The 'strategy guide' print book on *Myst* had, by the end of 1995, sold over 300,000 copies, according to the revised edition of *Myst, the Official Strategy Guide* (Barba & DeMaria, p. x). Finally, the global nature of these media shifts should be emphasized. *Myst*, for example, which cost $600,000 and took two years (1991–3) to produce, was actually an international coproduction between a US and a Japanese company, the Japanese company retaining Japanese distribution rights for its share in the investment.

In what follows, I will suggest the ways in which *Myst* represents both the beginning of a new art form—one that compacts different media together in new combinations—and, equally importantly, retrieves and reinvents earlier art forms long thought obsolete. *Myst* may remind one of 1960s and 1970s maze games such as *Zork* and *Dungeons and Dragons*, or of text-adventure games of the 1980s, but it is equally indebted to Homer's *Odyssey*, Wolfram's *Parsifal*, the Gothic novel, Jules Verne's science fiction, and certain paintings and films by the surrealists.

McLuhan's Laws McLuhan (1988, pp. 98–9, 127–30) suggests that four basic laws apply to any major media shift in history. During the breakup of a previous paradigm, the new medium will operate on older forms in four ways: through acceleration, obsolescence, synthesis, and retrieval. To take a concrete example, the new medium of word-processing operated on previous forms in four ways, (a) accelerating the process of print production; (b) rendering the typewriter obsolete; (c) flipping into a new synthesis that would eventually lead to desktop publishing; and (d) retrieving, by decentralizing print manufacture, the individualized expression of a much earlier, oral age. It is the last law, that of retrieval, that I will explore in *Myst*.

It should perhaps be added, in epistemological good faith, that McLuhan claimed that by adding a fourth law he had fulfilled and completed Hegel's triadic dialectic of thesis, antithesis, and synthesis. Nevertheless, it is quite clear that his tetradic, or fourfold, process actually derived from the brilliant analyses of the role of media by his teacher, Harold Innis, in *Empire and Communication* (1950), as well as from McLuhan's intensive study of James Joyce's *Finnegans Wake* (1939). Joyce openly admitted that his novel was directly inspired by Giambattista Vico's *New Science* (1725), with its hypothesis of the four cyclical stages of history (McLuhan, whose study is tellingly subtitled, 'the new science,' collapses the four stages into a fourfold simultaneous process). This heuristic framework for studying media shifts is a secularization of Vico's schema, with its all-important fourth law of retrieval being a translation of Vico's fourth stage of *ricorso* or 'return' (Marchand, 1989).

Before beginning, however, let us recall the fictional world of *Myst*. Set on half a dozen mysterious and uninhabited islands, *Myst* is the story of a family in conflict. The family members appear in brief video clips, literally framed by and trapped in the pages of different manuscripts. Atrus, the father, is imprisoned in a place called Dunny; his wife Catherine is held hostage elsewhere (we neither see her nor discover where she is during the game); and the two sons, Achenar and Sirrus, suspected by their father of wrongdoing, are trapped still elsewhere. As adventurer through these lands, the player must uncover the background story of Atrus and the two sons, Sirrus and Achenar, and decide who is telling the truth, who is lying, and who should be set free.

Myst and Ancient Epic

Myst's fictional roots lie anchored in an ancient mythic pattern, what Campbell (1949) describes as the triadic journey of the mythical hero: from departure, through initiation, to return. Initially answering the call to adventure, the hero leaves home (departure), then undergoes a series of rites and challenges, often conquering powers of evil (initiation), and finally either joins a special order or returns to his homeland with new knowledge (the mythical return). In the Arthurian epic, for example, the knight Parsifal embarks upon a quest for the Holy Grail, heals the ailing king and his country after a long series of adventures, and ultimately joins the Knights of the Holy Grail. Odysseus, after departing from his home and fighting in the Trojan War, journeys for 10 years among the islands of the Mediterranean gathering knowledge in order to find his way back, and returns to Ithaca just in time to save a kingdom from turmoil and a wife beset by suitors. In each case, the heroic path leads to a higher homecoming.

In *Myst*, this role of the mythical quester hero is assumed by two separate parties, the father Atrus within the story and the player without. At the outset of the game, Atrus, like Odysseus at the beginning of Homer's *The Odyssey*, is imprisoned on an island, and, as in the *Odyssey*, the reader-player is carried on an adventure. The player is instructed, indirectly, to assist the king-like Atrus, and thus must travel from island to island (clicking the mouse to move from scene to scene, object to object), acquiring the knowledge that in the end will permit the release of Atrus. As in *The Odyssey* (Homer, 1967 version, Book XI, p. 171), where the reader is brought 'to the deep-flowing frontiers of the world where fog-bound peoples live in a City of Perpetual Mist,' the player in *Myst* must perform on each island a specific ritual in order to gain access to the knowledge located there. Like Parsifal, who in the end puts the proper question to his king and thereby heals him, the reader-player must eventually hand Atrus a missing page from his book in order to free him.

The precise rituals in *Myst* required to gain access to the secrets of the past are not that distant from those described in *The Odyssey*. Odysseus, in order to access the secrets of the underworld, for instance, must first dig a trench precisely 20 inches deep and 20 inches square, then fill this in order with honey, milk, wine, water, and white barley. At this point the doors to the underworld open. In *Myst*, on virtually every island, the player is asked to manipulate a series of switches, gears, consoles, or sliders, in precise sequence, in order to gain access to the secret underground books with their vital information. *Myst* merely replaces the Homeric, agrarian-based rituals with electro-mechanical ones.

The most important parallel between *Myst* and the ancient epic, however, is the use of the flashback to tell the story. Both *The Iliad* and *The Odyssey* open in the middle of the story and proceed by a process of recollection (miming practices of ancient storytellers) to deliver the back story. *Myst* opens, in fact, not even in the middle, but at the very close of its story, and we, as readers, must uncover all previous events through a series of flashbacks. Only at the very end of the game do we meet Atrus again in the present and have the opportunity to free him by offering the missing page from his book, completing the mythical journey 'back to the future.'

On an Empty Movie Set (You Are a Camera)

Myst, although not a movie itself (it is closer to a slide show, dissolving from slide to slide with each click of the mouse), takes as its central elements inventions from the world of early cinema. From film's silent era it retrieves four art forms and four preoccupations: a dependence on the visual form of the 19th-century novel, a fascination with objects as magical props, a preference for chiaroscuro lighting design (a stark contrast of light and shadows), and a conscious experimentation with subjective camera as embodying cinematic truth.

Myst's dependence on the visual form of the nineteenth-century novel is best suggested by quoting directly from filmmaker Sergei Eisenstein's (1949) well-known essay, 'Dickens, Griffith, and the Film Today.' From Dickens and from the Victorian novel, he writes, 'stem the first shoots of the American film aesthetic, forever linked with the name of D. W. Griffith' (p. 195). He proceeds to quote the opening sentence of Dickens' novel, *The Cricket on the Hearth*: 'The kettle began it' (p. 195). Dickens' novels and individual scenes, as Eisenstein points out, often begin with just such a close-up shot, to establish geography and add atmosphere. 'And this is also pure Griffith,' he continues. 'How often we've seen such a close-up at the beginning of an episode, a sequence, or an entire film by him' (p. 198). Moreover, Eisenstein points out that Griffith's first film was based on Dickens' *The Cricket on the Hearth* and that Griffith defended his parallel-cutting technique (alternating film sequences in order to tell two simultaneous stories at once) by citing its use in Dickens' 'picture-stories' (p. 201), with their frequent use of parallel chapters.

Griffith's greatest films, in fact, incorporated other book elements as well. In *Birth of a Nation* and *Intolerance*, one even finds such on-screen book-driven devices as book covers, page layouts, and even footnotes. The visual world of *Myst*, just like Griffith's films, is partially driven by book devices. Not only is the story itself driven literally by books—by the hand-decorated manuscripts housed in the library on Myst Island—but also by novelistic close-ups of specific objects, such as a kettle or clock, which often open new scenes. The multitude of pathways cutting throughout the islands, each revealing different aspects of the central visual story, ring a creative change on Griffith's parallel-cutting.

The sense that in *Myst* any random object might be magically charged (and thus 'mouse clickable'), harks back to 1920s films by the surrealists. 'Even the most banal image,' observed playwright Antonin Artaud (1927), 'is transformed by the screen; even the smallest detail, the most insignificant object, takes on a meaning and a life which is its alone' (p. 49). Artaud concludes that 'by isolating objects, cinema gives them a life of their own: a leaf, a bottle, and a hand are imbued with a life that begs to be used—raw cinema exudes a trance-like atmosphere' (p. 50).

This magical trance atmosphere of raw cinema is precisely what haunts the beautiful landscapes of *Myst*. Moreover, its eerie and contradictory combinations of elements from reality are painted with a surrealistic attention to photographic detail. On Stoneship Island, for instance, the black umbrella perched atop the crow's nest, high above a land of barren rocks, is straight out of the surrealist paintings of Salvador Dali. Andre Breton, notoriously, defined surrealism as 'the chance meeting—on a dissecting table—of a sewing machine with an umbrella.' *Myst*, with its incongruous conjunctions of a dentist's chair with an astronomical observatory, or a log cabin with a spaceship, approaches this surrealist vision. Moreover, in *Myst* even the most mundane object—a book, a leaf, a door—is clickable, and thus transformable into life. As a result, an almost Zen-like atmosphere pervades the game and the reality of the visible world within it.

Myst is also infatuated with another aspect of early cinema, namely the spell of light and the magic of shadows, what art historians call chiaroscuro. The late afternoon light on the island of Myst falls through the stands of pine trees and casts long shadows on the grass, conjuring up an eerie atmosphere of what might be called California Gothic. Embracing a lush, air-brushed California calendar-art style, it is just as indebted to the darker brush strokes of German Gothic painting at the turn of the century, in such works as Boecklin's *Isle of the Dead* (1880). In terms of cinema we are in the shadowed-and-sunlit world of 1920s German expressionist film, the world of Max Reinhardt, Fritz Lang, and the other designers and directors who believed that the film image must become a graphic art in itself. In fact, the very titles of German expressionist films evoke directly the world of *Myst*: *Warning Shadows, The Stone Rider, The Treasure, Earth Spirit, Waxworks, The Nibelungs,* and *The House on the Moon*. The slanting shadows in *Myst*, cast by its perpetual golden-hour lighting, are a replay of the graphically stylized sunbeams and Nordic forests staged by Fritz Lang in his *Siegfried* of 1923.

Within its movie-in-stills structure, *Myst* makes use of yet a fourth cinematic device: the subjective camera. In his theories of the viewer as an unmediated, surrogate 'Kino-Eye,' revolutionary Russian filmmaker Dziga Vertov (1978) had propounded a cinema of the subjective camera. A boxing match should not be shot, he wrote, 'from the viewpoint of a member of the audience, but rather from that of a participant' (p. 3). In *Myst*, the player-reader also functions as an active participant in the story, as a roving Kino-Eye rather than as a passive audience before a stage.

The Revenge of the Gutenberg Galaxy

From beginning to end, *Myst* is a CD-ROM infatuated with the world of the book. Myst opens with the shot of a book falling through space towards the reader, and closes with Atrus speaking to us about books, from inside a book. In fact, on the rare occasions when we view them in video clips, all three main characters in the story speak to us from inside books, imprisoned there amid the pages. Moreover, the three official hints that accompany the game advise us each time to journey to the library on Myst, to its maps and manuscripts. Without the book—as both content and theme of the game—there would be no *Myst*, the CD-ROM.

Myst's retrieval of the age of linear print reaches deeper than the book-as-prop, however; it reclaims actual forms of the early novel as well. The novel, when it was a 'new medium' in the mid-eighteenth century, consisted largely of adventures recounted in the form of letters, journals, or diaries (e.g., Richardson's *Pamela*, Rousseau's *Julie*). Similarly, the books in the library on *Myst* are journals, diaries, and travel accounts. First-person prose, like the Kino-Eye camera, guarantees reader immediacy and narrative realism.

The literary genre that *Myst* embodies also belongs to the popular beginnings of fiction, that of the Gothic novel, with its romantic quest for secret, even forbidden, knowledge. The principal aim of the Gothic novel was, as in Walpole's *Castle of Otranto*, to save, rescue, or recover someone or some object, and to evoke mystery. Goethe's *Wilhelm Meister*, for instance, which carries strong overtones of Gothic, features a hero whose ultimate destination is a mysterious castle filled with dark passageways, endless chambers and bolted rooms, and a secret tower. Moreover, in its innermost depths, the castle houses a library of manuscripts, handwritten scrolls detailing and revealing the lives of the members of the secret society into which the hero will be initiated. *Myst*'s library, with its mysterious manuscripts and secret passageways, and its shadowy characters with their hints of dark doings, partakes directly of this Gothic world (and its poststructuralist descendants such as Eco's *The Name of the Rose*, with its mysterious castle-like medieval library of endless passageways and secret combinations). We as players step into the novel as the Gothic quester hero himself, aiding the despairing hero Atrus in his quest to unseat 'an even greater foe.'

Victorian Science Fiction: *Myst* and Jules Verne

In tandem with the Gothic novel, *Myst* retrieves the fellow-traveler genre of early science fiction, specifically of Jules Verne's 'extraordinary voyages' (as they were called) of the nineteenth century. *Myst*, in fact, is in one sense a direct remake of Verne in multimedia form, recovering, as it does, Verne's love of deserted islands, moonscapes, electromechanical lore, and a plot uniting the ancient epic quest with the modern scientific expedition. One might say that what Charles Dickens' novels were to D. W. Griffith's early films, Verne's Victorian works are for the multimedia world of *Myst*.

In *Myst* we are asked repeatedly to inventory items, to count things, to measure objects in just the same way that Verne's characters are asked to carry out tasks and to survey their world. 'They were learning this new world by heart,' writes Verne of his characters in *Round the Moon*, 'measuring all angles and diameters' (1870/1983, p. 534). In *From the Earth to the Moon*, 'Barbicane seized his instruments and began to note his position on Stones Hill with extreme exactness: "this spot is situated 1800 feet above the level of the sea, at 27 degrees 7' North latitude, 5 degrees 7' West longitude," he said, concluding, "from here our projectile shall take its flight into the regions of the Solar World" ' (1875/1983, p. 435). When we set the precise directions of the antenna in the main control room on Selenitic Island in *Myst*, we might well be back on a moonscape in a Verne novel, surveying the territory with one of his nineteenth-century surveyor's tools. We remain in the realm of Newtonian science and nineteenth-century mechanics.

Entire plot elements, in fact, are borrowed from Verne by *Myst*. Verne equips his 'mysterious island' with volcanic upheavals and vast underground chasms. A tribe of monkeys and apes, who speak a language of their own, climb rope ladders into the explorers' quarters, and are then tamed by the explorers to help them. In *Myst* there is Selenitic Island (the island's very name likely to have been borrowed from Verne's mention of the Selenites in *Round the Moon*), which houses a vast underground cave system where meteors had set off a period of volcanic activity. There is also Channelwood Island, where a race of tree-dwelling monkey-people live, chattering in their own tongue and climbing up and down rope ladders to reach their dwellings.

There is, finally, the figure of the hero himself. *Myst*'s ultimate rewrite of Verne lies in the character of Atrus. Atrus' brooding temperament, his fascination with drawing maps, making notes, and engineering sketches for nineteenth-century constructs such as fortresses and bridges, strongly suggest that he is a direct descendant of Captain Nemo from *20,000 Leagues Under the Sea* (1870/1983) and *Mysterious Island* (1875/1916; in the latter book Nemo perishes, after recounting his secret past). Atrus shares both Nemo's fear of a foreboding future as well as his dark aura of a mysterious past: Where Nemo had been betrayed by his own people, Atrus has apparently been betrayed by his own two sons.

McLuhan (1967) remarked that each new era assumes as its content the forms of the previous age, romanticizing them in the process. The advent of the railroad, for example, which encircled whole countrysides throughout America, helped inspire the development of the pastoral, romantic style of nineteenth-century writing, from Thoreau onwards. Characteristically, *Myst* romanticizes the forms of nineteenth-century science; levers and switches, gauges and wheels, pumps and generators litter the landscape, transforming it into a vast museum of a bygone mechanical age. The island even boasts a statue erected to the era, a huge gear mounted on a rocky promontory of the island, a giant objet d'art half sunk in the earth. *Myst*'s world of eternal 'button-pushing and lever-pulling,' as the *Wall Street*

Journal (Syman, 1994, p. A10) terms it, is a romantic elegy to nineteenth-century mechanics, as well as to the lost world of Jules Verne.

Interactivity:
Myst and
Borges' Garden
of Forking Paths

Whether by design or not, *Myst* also pays glancing homage to Jorge Luis Borges, the literary godfather of all interactive fiction, as well as of hypertext and hypermedia, and *The Garden of Forking Paths* (1941/1962). The final scene in Borges's story takes place in misty meadows on a western island, with the protagonist headed down a deserted road toward a mysterious house at the end of an avenue of trees. Upon entering the house the patron shows the guest a library filled with books from both East and West, including esoteric manuscripts and the mysterious volume, *The Garden of Forking Paths*.

The library keeper then proceeds to read to the protagonist sample passages from *The Garden of Forking Paths* (the story within the story). To the protagonist's astonishment, the novel turns out to be the story of a symbolic labyrinth, a 'maze of mazes,' a sort of enormous guessing game. The novel-within-the-story concludes with a final scene in which the mysterious forking paths of its plot converge once again, with the following sentence: 'Thus the heroes fought with tranquil heart and bloody sword, resigned to killing and to dying.' We are reminded of the conclusion of *Myst*, where the father Atrus tells the reader-viewer, 'I am fighting a foe much greater than my sons could even imagine.'

Myst, half a century later, delivers a multimedia replica of Borges' *Garden of Forking Paths*, in particular its labyrinthine, multiple pathways, qualities that Borges likened to 'the conjunction of a mirror with an encyclopedia' (Butler, p. 39). Both *Myst* and *The Garden of Forking Paths* follow in the arcane tradition of interactive fiction, whose ultimate patron is Laurence Sterne. In his novel, *Tristram Shandy* (1760), high tricks such as misnumbering pages, tearing out and losing chapters, omitting entire passages, and then turning such omissions into puzzles, or games, provide obstacles for the gentle reader. 'Go back to **** in the last chapter,' the reader is exhorted on several occasions. On another occasion, misplaced manuscript pages are accidentally used by a woman as papers with which to curl her hair, twisting Tristram's remarks beyond all recognition. The larger point of Sterne's novel, of course (all the more precocious because its witty attack on the arbitrarily linear conventions of the novel date from the same period as the birth of the novel), is, as Bolter (1991) puts it, to return the print-based novel to its oral conversational roots (p. 132).

Other novels soon followed Sterne's in this interactive tradition, in particular Brentano's German novel, *Godwi: A Wild Novel* (1805). In a story promoted as 'without a point of view,' the fictional heroine Maria visits the 'real' narrator Godwi in order to set the record straight and collaborate with him on a revised and hence more truthful extension of her story. Toward the end of the book we learn that Maria is doing this, however, not out of a love for truth, but merely to pay doctor's bills for a tongue infection from which she is suffering; she conveniently dies a few pages before the end. The narrator, Godwi, which means 'god-like' or omniscient (something he clearly is not), becomes bored with the story he has been telling and immediately stops the novel right there.

Thus *Godwi*, even more radically than *Tristram Shandy*, launches that antinovel novel tradition, which has subsequently been dubbed the metanovel, supernovel, interactive or polyperspectival novel, or sometimes simply postmodern fiction. Its avatars include Gide's *Counterfeiters* (1926); the French New Novel, including Robbe-Grillet's tellingly entitled novels, *The Erasers* (1953) and *In the Labyrinth* (1959); and Saporta's *Composition No. 1* (1962), with its unnumbered pages. The idea of interactivity has not been confined to the novel, however. Poetry, in its most ironic and self-mocking moods, has practiced this for years (Butler, 1980, p. 41). Nor has theater been immune to interactivity. It can be found in plays ranging from Pirandello's *Six Characters in Search of an Author* (1921) to Brecht's *Threepenny Opera* (1928; a Marxist demolition of the bourgeois illusions of high opera) to Peter Handke's *Offending the Audience* (1965).

What makes *Myst* notable, however, is that, given the advent of the device of the multimedia computer, random access, infinite loops, and multiple-layered, Escher-like constructions have become possible on-screen. Furthermore, they have been enhanced by audio and video. For example, what Michael Joyce had accomplished in 1987 in pure print with his computer-diskette-based, hypertextual short story, 'Afternoon,' is finally realized in full multimedia regalia in *Myst*. As Bolter observes,

> Reading 'Afternoon' several times is like exploring a vast castle. The reader proceeds down the same corridors through familiar rooms but often comes upon a new ballway not previously explored, or a locked door which suddenly gives way, with the reader gradually pushing back the margins of electronic space—much as in a computer game in which the descent down a stairway reveals a whole new level of the dungeon. (1991, p. 125).

Myst, by virtue of its technology and its artistry, pushes this genre even further.

Multimedia: Artwork of the Future

Myst's synthesis of different art forms is remarkable. Yet, as with any ground-breaking work, it is not without flaws. Heckel (1984) remarked that 'movies didn't flourish until the engineers lost control to the artists' (p. 5). *Myst* suffers from the fact that it is still too much in the hands of the programmers and graphic artists, and not yet in the hands of creative storytellers and dramatic scriptwriters.

Much of the writing in *Myst*, in fact, reads like bad Jules Verne, a novel written in the stumbling prose of a teenager who has just discovered the works of Verne.[1] 'His hair,' we read in a book in the library on *Myst*, 'which

---

1 *Myst*'s graphic designer, Robyn Miller, whose older brother, Rand, was lead programmer for the CD-ROM, was actually reading Verne's *The Mysterious Island* at the time he started the project, and recommended the book to his younger brother, Ryan Miller, who wrote the narrative. Ryan at the time was only a senior in high school (Barba, pp. 170–1; Carroll, 1994, p. 71; Milano, p. 43). Selenitic Island in *Myst*, for example, with its giant crystals and moonlike terrain, is undoubtedly a direct lift from Verne's colony of 'Selenites' found in *Round the Moon* ('selenitic' means crystalline or moonlike).

was only on his face and head, was completely grey, almost white, and hung very long around his frail body. His thin head hung limply by an almost grotesque neck that could not hold its head up to look at me.' Critics have pointed to plot deficiencies in the novel as well: The *Wall Street Journal* (Syman, 1994) refers to the 'vague' storyline, *Wired* magazine (Carroll, 1994) to *Myst*'s 'rambling' narratives. Even the *Official Strategy Guide*, painstakingly assembled by Barba and DeMaria (1995), has to wrestle with the plot to make sense of it; even it cannot reconcile some of the contradictions, including that between the beginning of the story and its ending. The fine graphics of *Myst* deserve better scriptwriting and plotting than this.

In fact, *Myst* the narrative game is literally impossible to solve without a guidebook. To take one example: The maze-running sequence on Selenitic Island, in which a player has to proceed sequentially in a multitude of geographical directions in order to pass through a maze unscathed and exit properly, is inherently frustrating, even to a labyrinth-experienced Theseus. Readers should not be driven to a strategy book to find answers on how to navigate a CD-ROM; this constitutes electronic bad faith. A better, epic-based solution would have been to place the guidebook in the hands of a mysterious mentor figure in the story itself.

Furthermore, *Myst's* persistent computer bugs discourage the reader's navigational zeal through the game. For example, the musical keyboard, whose coded melody should launch the reader in a spaceship journey from Myst Island to Selenitic Island, is so buggy that it simply does not work, in the Macintosh version at least. There are several other key navigational elements whose flaws escaped even the bug-testers of the game.

In spite of these flaws, however, *Myst*, with its moody soundtrack and stunning graphics, represents something new in the world of multimedia: 'a sort of novel,' as one critic put it, hidden 'inside a series of paintings—and put to music' (Carroll, 1994, p. 71). Following in the tradition of grand opera, Shakespeare, and Wagner's *Gesamtkunstwerk* (total work of art), *Myst* (even in its small-screen version) presages whole new screen worlds to come. As Wagner (1850) writes, 'when all the arts appear in harmony with one another—drama, epic, opera, pantomime, comedy, and lyric—only then can the artwork of the future arise.' Moreover, in *Myst*, unlike in Wagner, the reader also becomes a quasi-codirector of the work, coacting and coauthoring the novel (in limited fashion, to be sure) from moment to moment. No matter how rudimentary its plotting, no matter how naive its writing, *Myst* remains our first successful electronic example of interactive adult fiction.

In combining genres and media in ways that our university departments still do not recognize and indeed do their best to keep apart (separately budgeting 'departments' of film, literature, art, video, and music, and forcing them to compete for both students and capital equipment), *Myst* presents communication theorists with an interesting new mode of communication, one that must be acknowledged and dealt with. Less related to the world of hard print than to the dynamic and ever-changing world of oral communication, the interactive novel tends to subvert the ideological and epistemological paradigms, namely deconstruction, poststructuralism, or postmodernism, that currently reign on campuses. For each of these methods of discourse still rests on the hypothesis that we harbor unexamined beliefs in rigid constructs, structures, and hierarchies, both in the text and in the world, that the academically adept proceed to dismantle, laying bare the traces in the abyss, the sheer chameleon-like nature of any supposedly solid worldview or preconceived 'text.'

With *Myst*, however, we begin where deconstruction and postmodernism are content to leave off, with the 'chameleon-like nature of the electronic text' (Lanham, 1993, p. 7). No laying bare of preconcealed beliefs in solid 'writing' has to be undertaken here; there is only a continually reconstituted text, which leaves different traces upon the reader. The multimedia novel, with its ever-changing reinvention and retrieval of previous media forms, is changing forever the media landscape in which we live. We should take notice.

References

ARTAUD, A. (1978). Sorcery and the Cinema. In A. Sitney (ed.), *The Avant-Garde Film* (pp. 49–50). New York: New York University Press. (Original work published 1927.)

BARBA, R., & DeMARIA, R. (1995). *Myst, the Official Strategy Guide.* (2nd rev. edn.). Rocklin, Cal.: Prima Publishing.

BOLTER, J. (1991). *Writing Space: The Computer, Hypertext, and the History of Writing.* Hillsdale, NJ: Erlbaum.

BORGES, J. (1962). The Garden of Forking Paths. In J. Borges, *Ficciones* (pp. 89–104). New York: Grove Press. (Original work published 1941.)

BUTLER, C. (1980). *After the Wake: An Essay on the Contemporary Avant-Garde.* Oxford Clarendon Press.

CAMPBELL, J. (1949). *The Hero with a Thousand Faces.* Princeton, NJ: Princeton University Press.

CARROLL, J. (1994, August). Guerrillas in the Myst: From Garage Start-up to the First CD-ROM Superstars. *Wired*, 70–3.

CD-Rom Growth (column). (1996, January), *CD-Rom Professional*, p. 11.

DALY, STEVE. (1994, October 7). The land of 'Myst' opportunity. *Entertainment Weekly*, pp. 16–17.

EISENSTEIN, S. (1949). *Film Form: Essays in Film Theory.* New York: Harcourt, Brace.

HECKEL, P. (1984). *The Elements of Friendly Software Design.* New York: Warner Books.

HOMER. *The Odyssey.* Baltimore: Penguin Books, 1967.

INNIS, HAROLD. *Empire and Communications.* Oxford: Oxford University Press, 1950.

KASTROWITZ, BARBARA, and KING, PATRICIA (1994, December 5). The men behind *Myst. Newsweek*, pp. 84–5.

LANHAM, R. (1993). *The Electronic Word: Democracy, Technology, and the Arts.* Chicago: University of Chicago Press.

LAUREL, B. (1993). *Computers as Theatre.* Reading, Mass.: Addison-Wesley.

MARCHAND, P. (1989). *Marshall McLuhan: The Medium and the Messenger.* New York: Ticknor & Fields.

McLUHAN, M. (1967). *The Medium is the Message.* New York: Bantam Books.

—— and McLuhan, E. (1988). *Laws of Media: The New Science.* Toronto: University of Toronto Press.

MILANO, D. (1995). Case Study: The Making of *Myst*, With an Interview With Robyn Miller. *Interactivity, I*, 37–45.

MILLER, RAND, and MILLER, ROBYN (September 1993). *Myst.* CD-ROM produced by Cyan, Inc. Distributed by Broderbund Software, Spokane, Wash.

REED, SUSAN, and FREE, CATHY (1995, January 16). CD (ROM) of Brotherly Love. *People*, pp. 85–6.

ROTHSTEIN, EDWARD. (1995, December 4). A New Art Form May Arise From the 'Myst.' *New York Times*, p. II/1.

RYMAN, A. (1995). *Myst: Strategies and Secrets*. Alameda, Cal.: Sybex Books.

STEIN, J. (1960; 1973). *Richard Wagner and the Synthesis of the Arts*. Westport, Conn.: Greenwood Press.

SYMAN, S. (1994, August 31). Playing 'Myst': First CD-ROM Bestseller. *Wall Street Journal*, p. A10.

VERNE, J. (1983). *Works of Jules Verne*. New York: Avenel Books: *From the Earth to the Moon* (1865); *Round the Moon* (1870); *20,000 Leagues Under the Sea* (1870).

—— (1916). *The Mysterious Island*. New York: Scribner. (Original work published 1875.)

VERTOV, D. (1978). Resolution of the Council of Three. In A. Sitney (ed.), *The Avant-Garde Film* (pp. 2–7). New York: New York University Press. (Original work published 1923.)

VICO, GIAMBATTISTA. *The New Science of Giambattista Vico*. Ithaca, NY: Cornell University Press, 1970. (Original work published 1725.)

WAGNER, R. (1850). *Saemtliche schriften und dichtungen*, vol. 3, p. 157. Leipzig, Germany: Fischer Verlag.

18

Epilogue
Computer Media Studies:
An Emerging Field

Paul A. Mayer

I N A TYPOLOGY of uses of computers, Terry Winograd proposes three distinct views: The computer as number processor, the computer as data processor, and the computer as knowledge processor.[1] The present volume is especially concerned with the computer as a knowledge processor, with special reference to communication, as expressed in the formulation 'computer media'. By virtue of their fundamental nature as comprehensive systems for processing and exchanging symbols, computer-based media are epochal. More than channels of transmission, computer media extend new possibilities for expression, communication, and interaction in everyday life. In 1977 Alan Kay and Adele Goldberg anticipated this effect in their description of the Dynabook, a prototype of contemporary personal computing, as a *metamedium*.[2] In the 1990s the pace of both technological development and social adoption of new forms of computer media is astounding. By virtue of their functionality and popularity, communication-related applications of computers have a range of significant implications for culture and society. There are a number of good reasons why there is talk about the electronic frontier, cyberspace, and information society. Chief among these is the fact that the use of computer media in diverse forms—from discussion systems to on-line services, from forms of productivity software to game consoles— are effectively altering the conditions of public communication.

Taking their cue from these developments, scholars and writers in many traditions have contributed diverse analyses of forms of computer media, their use, and their manifold consequences. However, the study of computer media as a whole lacks cohesion. Its theoretical discourse and analytical methodologies are often narrow and partial, despite the fact that there are many workers doing excellent research. Correlating their findings is difficult, if not impossible,[3] and identifying areas for further, co-ordinated research has so far most often been an *ad hoc* affair. Thus, if computer media studies can be called a formal field of study, it is a nascent one. It lacks a historical identity, a systematic framework, canonical works, an established tradition

---

1 Winograd (1980), 60 f.

2 Kay and Goldberg (1988); reproduced in this volume as Ch. 6, p. 112. For historical context and further description, see also p. 20, in this volume.

3 December (1995).

of education, and a prospectus for further research. This is despite the common acknowledgement of the imperative need for further research, as well as the recognition of the cultural and social implications of these media forms for government, commerce, education, entertainment, and public communication in general. This suggests there are multiple political and intellectual reasons why scholarly research on computers as media should ask more focused, critical questions about the rigour of its concepts, the validity of its theoretical descriptions, the use and implications of its methodologies, and the relations of specialized discourses to those of other fields.

Notable previous treatments of computer media and their social implications illustrate the complexity of elaborating a systematic approach to these media forms.[4] In terms of the object of study, this complexity can be attributed to at least three sources. First, computers are sign-processing machines *par excellence*. Their capacities for combining and manipulating symbolic representations clearly set them apart from all other machines.[5] Computers change the way we work, access information, and socialize, and as such, they offer us new ways to create meaning and knowledge. Never before has it been possible to navigate and manipulate such vast quantities of diverse information. Secondly, computer-based forms of discourse are historically unique. Computers as media constitute hybrid and new forms that replicate functions of previous media while extending significant new possibilities for communicative exchange and interaction. Most significant, perhaps, is the user's interaction with the device itself. Never before has it been possible to engage in communication with a machine in the way we do with computers. Thirdly, computers, probably more so than other media, are factors in the social construction of knowledge and meaning within what Fred Inglis calls the conventional messiness of culture.[6] Computer media sum up the role of modern media as means of discourse as well as objects constructed in discourse. Taken together, understanding the computer's semantic flexibility, its capacities for simulation and interaction in communication, and its implications for culture and society are central objectives in the study of computer media. With these objectives in mind, a systematic approach to this area of study must provide a framework that relates and clarifies central concepts from diverse traditions in a new synthesis.

Towards developing such a framework, this Epilogue first offers a brief conceptual analysis of computer media that relates these media forms to interdisciplinary issues of meaning, discourse, and culture.[7] Thereafter, the fields of Artificial Intelligence, Human Computer Interaction, and Media Studies are discussed as three significant sources of inspiration for further research on computer media. In discussing the state of computer media studies, this essay describes a broad preliminary framework for further theoretical and empirical research.

---

4 Anderson (1990), Finnemann (1994), Laurel (1993), Turkle (1984)

5 See Ch. 9 in this volume.

6 Inglis (1990), 173.

7 A more complete elaboration is offered in Mayer (1998, b).

Interfaces, Users, and Interactivity

Like other media forms, computer media can be understood as means of representation.[8] However, unlike other media forms, the discourse of computer media is characterized by the user's expressive engagement. The concept of discourse refers to content and processes of communication as both vehicles of meaning and as a form of social action. Constituted via multiple systems of signification, discourse is the means by which meaningful distinctions are created, understanding develops, and communication progresses. Though we can build upon theories and concepts derived from the analysis of other means of representation—from literature to music, from pictorial forms to moving images—the dynamic and open aspects of the discourse of computer media make them unique. The immediacy generated via responsiveness to user meanings represents a leap that demands review and perhaps rethinking of traditional theoretical and conceptual understandings of meaning, discourse, and culture.[9] Evidence for this can be found in the characteristic flexibility in the representation of knowledge, the anticipation of user action, and the quality of interaction often engendered by contemporary computer media forms. An analysis of the unique characteristics of the discourse of computer media can be made via reference to the interlinked concepts of interface, user, and interaction. Highlighting the reception of computer media as a focal point for diverse analytic approaches, these three concepts are also useful for further clarifying and comparing the approaches which different fields of research bring to bear in their analyses of computer media.

Interface

As the means by which the discourse of computer media becomes manifest, it is perhaps best to begin with the concept of interface. In general, an interface is a structured boundary common to two poles of communication, in the present case, between user and computer.[10] The idea of an interface is not exclusive to computers or computer media. The instrumentation and steering devices available to a pilot or an automobile driver are interfaces for the control of a plane or a car. Computer-based discourse arises and proceeds via application interfaces. From the perspective of the user, the operating system and running programs, be they word processors, spreadsheets, games, and so on, are all applications. Therefore, in this discussion *interface discourse* refers to the systems of signification that constitute applications as a means of representation in which user input is a significant element. Interfaces, as specific discursive forms, are particular kinds of semiotic systems.[11] Their role is to structure and convey the basic range of choices available to the user—so that a further exchange of signs may progress. On the one hand they establish constraints by limiting the range of acceptable user input. While on the other they enable interaction by specifying the user's expressive freedom for a given task. As both physical and semantic systems, they contribute both form and content to discourse.

8 See Mayer (1998, b).
9 Bolter (1984).
10 Reisner (1987), 337.
11 Andersen (1990).

In terms of physical systems, the keyboard and mouse are among the expressive devices commonly available to the user, whereas other resources, like the screen, speakers, printer, network resources, and file system, are understood as elements accessed via application interfaces. Control of application resources transpires via explicitly defined sequences of action in which user input is, hopefully, translated into appropriate responses on the part of the system: using the mouse to click on an icon opens a document, requesting a printout results in formatted pages delivered on a printer, inserting a music CD sets it playing, and so forth. On contemporary personal computers, these functions, and a vast repertoire of others, are the result of an integrated system composed of physical hardware, operating system services, and application interfaces. These interfaces specify the particular set of operations available to a user at a given moment, as well as the means by which they may be accessed.

As semantic systems, though their details can be extraordinarily complex,[12] their functions are general: interfaces are central to the discourse of computer media in that they represent contexts for action in which users can participate.[13] Alan Kay explains that, '[t]he user interface was once the last part of a system to be designed. Now it is the first. It is recognized as being primary because, to novices and professionals alike, what is presented to one's senses *is* one's computer.'[14] The famed desktop metaphor is an oft-cited example of this. Seen as a complex of effects, the manner in which it works can be summarized with reference to four interrelated functions:

1. It provides a representational system that contextualizes and differentiates objects like 'documents' and collections of such objects in 'folders'; and the means to create, manipulate, and eliminate both.

2. It provides an environment in which all of the basic functions of the computer as a resource for the user are made available, and specifies the means by which these are to be activated.

3. It creates a parallel between functions and elements of the computer and analogically similar elements from everyday life. This has the possible secondary effect of altering aspects in both contexts over time.

4. It reinforces the 'lifestyle' positioning of the whole device as a medium of expression, communication, and interaction in everyday life, with possible far-reaching effects in a variety of social domains.

As a means of contextualizing the computational resources available in personal computing, by virtue of its popularity, the desktop metaphor has achieved normative status. It has evolved into a cohesive system of representation that suggests how basic resources and interface elements are to be manipulated. Thus, in general, via metaphors, simulations, and environmental qualities, interfaces attempt to orient user understandings and action via thematic symbolic structures. Creating context and relevance for the user while steering the user's exchange with the computer lies at the heart of application interface design.[15] Indeed, Graphic User Interfaces (GUIs),

12 Ibid.

13 Laurel (1993), 1.

14 Kay (1984); reproduced in this volume as Ch. 8, p. 130. (Italics in original.)

15 Durlak (1987).

introduced in the early 1980s, literally created the face of personal computing. With these came a fundamental shift in perception of the computer
itself. Thus, thinking of Kay's observation we might underscore that it is not
only what is presented to one's senses that is primary, but also what one
understands and can *do* as represented via interface discourse. Interfaces are
both the means by which we understand what we can do with computers and
the means through which we act with respect to them.

Users   As discussed, interface discourse includes the user as an active subject. The
user plays both an interpretive *and* expressive part in discursive flow in communicative exchange with an application. The user is conceived here as active
in terms of meaning and interpretation, to which interface discourse is said to
be responsive in a restricted sense. This responsiveness is predicated upon a
communicative exchange in which the actions of the user are narrowly represented, as feedback, by an interface. In terms of user orientations much
meaningful activity with computers can be seen as goal- and task-motivated
even in the most casual of exchanges.[16] This is one reason to speak of 'users'
instead of audiences or readers with respect to these media forms. The user's
interpretive role with respect to interface discourse may be compared to that
of mass media audiences and readers in literary studies; however, the active
context of computer media discourse is a unique element, which invokes the
user's expressive engagement. This 'expressive engagement' can be further
described as a particular configuration of subjectivity, which proceeds from
the degree to which interface discourse addresses the user in a manner that invokes an interest in further 'purposeful action'. In the best outcome, users experience application interfaces as evident, meaningful settings for action. In
their interpretive and expressive acts, users are social actors contextualizing
their uses of computer media in reference to other forms and contexts of discourse. For example, computer game play is an element of a social occasion
for a group that meets to play an adventure game over a network. Here the use
of a form of computer media is an element of a social context in which users
engage in ritual social practices in conjunction with a form of entertainment.
As widespread phenomena, practices which incorporate forms of computer
media may represent new cultural formations—with a number of possible
social, political, and economic implications. Thus, on the one hand, the active user can be understood as a subject engaged by interface discourse. On
the other, the user as a social actor can be understood as an interpretive agent
contextualizing uses of computer media with respect to a variety of other
sources of meaning and domains of action in everyday life.

Interactivity   The communicative exchange that arises between users and interfaces can be
further understood with reference to a qualitative conception of interactivity. Interactivity refers to the responsive quality of exchanges with
application interfaces.[17] As an evaluation, interactivity is dependent on the
subjective experience of such exchanges.

16 It is telling that in their description of the Dynabook as a form of personal media each of Kay and
Goldberg's examples is task related. See Ch. 6 in this volume.

17 For a survey of conceptions of interactivity, see Ch. 10 in this volume.

Communicative exchange between two interpreting subjects with respect to a third object can be differentiated in terms of forms of subjectivity.[18] In *The Social Semiotics of Mass Communication,* Klaus Bruhn Jensen offers two diagrams which help to illustrate this further.[19] Jensen's diagrams for communication and interaction are reproduced here as Figures 1 and 2.

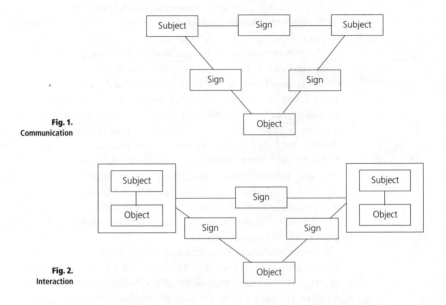

Fig. 1.
Communication

Fig. 2.
Interaction

Both diagrams illustrate *prototypical* relationships between poles of production and reception of meaning that relate, via signs, with reference to an object of common interest. These diagrams reinforce a conception of signs, as the basis of communication, as fulfilling a mediating role in the creation and exchange of meaning. In contrast, the diagrams depict distinctly different configurations of subjectivity, as a result of different forms of communicative action. The prototype of *communication,* as explained by Jensen, is the process of negotiating the status of different signs to arrive at a degree of intersubjectivity about an object. Communication is the ground formation of interaction. The prototype of *interaction* is a form of communicative action in which the negotiation of the status of each subject, sometimes as an object of action, is an added element of the exchange. One of the central distinctions between these two prototypical forms of communicative action is the variety of meaning which they may engender. Gregory Bateson's concept of 'meta-communication' illustrates the potential complexity of meaning in inter-action.[20] Metacommunication is the basis of various forms of bracketing, like irony, sarcasm, and make-believe, where understanding not only pertains to the topic of exchange, but, perhaps more importantly, to the intentions of the speaker. In the diagram of prototypical interaction (Fig. 2), this possibility is illustrated in that each pole of exchange is conceptualized as both

18 This discussion draws upon Mayer (1998a).

19 Jensen (1995), 48 ff.

20 Bateson (1985), 129–44.

subject *and* object in exchange. In the diagram of prototypical communication, subjects' roles and meanings are not interpreted, whereas in interaction their status and meanings as well as those of the common topic of the exchange are negotiated. This prototypical figure of interaction accounts for both mediated and un-mediated forms of communicative exchange, ranging from face-to-face contexts to large-scale institutional and social systems. As such, interaction is a possibility of any one of a number of communicative exchanges through which users, media, and society are related.[21]

The prototype of interaction describes both exchanges with other users via computers and exchanges users' experience with computers. The former are often discussed as kinds of computer mediated communication (CMC). These forms of computer mediated interaction offer the potential reach of broadcast media, the archival aspect of the public record, and a degree of immediacy approaching that of telephony. Like other media they serve to alter the conditions of communication over space and time. However, in that forms of CMC, from E-mail to on-line chat, extend significant, new conditions and contexts for interpersonal interaction, these forms offer new possibilities and challenges for public and private communication.[22] With its focal interest in the uses of on-line facilities and forms of on-line discourse, research on CMC generally places little emphasis on the exchange between users and application interfaces.

Focusing on the quality of interaction users' experience with computers, it is in the user–interface nexus that the term 'interactivity' generally arises in a new regard. The experience of interactivity is dependent on a number of factors. For example, a game, through its interface construction and means of involving the user, might offer an potentially high degree of interactivity, but in actual play on a particular computer, limitations in the capacities of the hardware might yield an unsatisfactory experience. As such, interactivity as an experienced quality is relative—certain application types suggest a greater potential for interactivity than others,[23] and certain implementations of the same application may yield significantly different experiences because of hardware or other specific limitations. Beyond factors relating to technical implementation, interactivity is also a culturally constructed phenomenon. For example, in the early 1960s the quality of interaction offered by the first computer games was deeply inspiring to those who were lucky enough to play them. In the present context, the type of game they played and the way in which it was implemented can only hold the attention of the nostalgic. Now a number of new criteria must be satisfied before applications achieve user interest, anticipated interactivity, and apparent transparency of use.

Achieving this effect is not a trivial problem. Indeed, it lies at the heart of good interface design[24]—yielding what are often considered 'smart features' and 'intelligent applications'. It is important to note that the range of these effects are inherently related to meanings and intentions imparted by

21 Jensen (forthcoming).

22 See Ch. 13 in this volume.

23 Durlak (1987).

24 Negroponte (1995) and Norman (1988) offer accessible and illustrative introductions to thought in this area.

designers. This is significant in that the 'smarts' and 'intelligence' being referred to are not those of a machine. However, for pragmatic reasons we tend to endow computers with intelligent powers, perhaps similar to those of a favorite pet.[25] In terms of the prototype of interaction, 'intelligence' experienced in exchanges with computers arises through a bracketed version of interaction experienced in other contexts. For computer-mediated interactivity to arise, the subjectivity of the user must be organized such that interaction can take place within the semantically limited world of the application. There are various means of achieving this: imperative modes of address, the display and manipulation of on-screen figures or avatars, and the creation of virtual spaces with convincing environmental qualities are three possibilities. Given the current state of the art, in all cases the user must accept the limited discursive premises of an application's interface as well as the static specificity of its functional range. A corollary of this is that users must accept the limited relevance of their own potential range for personal expression.

The effectiveness of successful interface design can be summarized with reference to the principle of the 'user illusion'. Coined at Xerox's Palo Alto Research Center (PARC) in the 1970s, this principle is described by Alan Kay as 'the simplified myth everyone builds to explain (and make guesses about) the [computer] system's actions and what should be done next'.[26] The user illusion is one of understanding, coherence, and control. On the one hand, at the time of production, it refers to the work a designer has done to ensure that an application interface appears consistent, functional, and well matched to relevant contexts of knowledge and domains of action. On the other, at the time of reception, it refers to the cognitive skills and social world of the user, which allows for perception, conceptualization and response relative to an interface as well as to the situated context of the exchange. As discussed below, in the future it is conceivable that applications will be less contingent upon meanings imparted in production, and more flexible with respect to the pragmatics of the contexts of their reception. However, for the time being it is the human intelligence of both designers and users that provides the satisfactory conditions for the dialogic and dramaturgical elements of contemporary application interfaces to be effective, and for interactivity to arise.

Towards a Field of Computer Media Studies

In the preceding discussion, a conceptual analysis of the user–interface nexus identified interactivity as an index of the quality of exchange relative to forms of computer media. Thinking of the increasing relevance of personal computing in daily life and expressions like ease-of-use and 'user-friendliness', the phenomena and implications of computer-based interactivity are also productively described via empirical as well as prognostic analyses. For computer media studies to contribute to the further systematic treatment of

---

25 See Nass and Reeves (1996), and Chs. 7 and 8. For a comment on the philosophical implications of the attribution of intelligence to animals see Fetzer (1990), 8.

26 Kay (1984). See Ch. 8 in this volume.

computers as media in society, it must offer theoretical analyses, and descriptions of the empirical reception of computer media as well as the possible forms of interactivity in future forms. These three varieties of analysis—theoretical, empirical, and prognostic—are integral to the conception of computer media studies advocated here. Towards furthering this programme, the approach presented below draws upon the strengths of existing fields of research, via reference to the concept of interactivity and the user–interface nexus. As a necessary element in the conceptual apparatus of many areas of study related to computer-based communication, the concept of interactivity can be used to illustrate how different fields conceive of relations between users, computers, and society.

Three areas of research, Artificial Intelligence (AI), Human Computer Interaction (HCI), and Media Studies, can be related via reference to the user–interface nexus, insofar as this provides a focal point for overlapping intellectual interests. Therefore, these three fields are examined below as sources for the study of computers as media. Alone none of these approaches offers the intellectual breadth being proposed here for the study of computer media. However, as historically significant sources of computer- and communication-related research, with their own refined theoretical, analytical, and methodological traditions, together they offer inspiration for a significant intellectual undertaking; a field of study that responds to the significance of the computer as knowledge processor for meaning, culture, and society. The remainder of this Epilogue is devoted to describing a conceptual structure for this undertaking.

Artificial Intelligence

Historically AI is a field of research that has focused on the programmability of intelligence.[27] Cybernetics attempted to describe social phenomena in mechanical terms, contributing to behaviouralistic approaches in sociology and psychology; however, the structure of society is rarely an aspect of contemporary AI research, as the analytical orientation focuses on defining intelligent behaviour as such.[28] The definition of intelligence and the procedures by which it should be demonstrated by a programmed system have been the subject of great debate.[29] Nevertheless, AI has contributed to significant advances in the representation of knowledge, the development of expert systems, simulation and modelling of natural behavioural phenomena, and the rapid processing of voluminous data.[30]

One of the original aims of research in AI was to program a system such that it could engage in complex forms of interaction. Alan Turing's description of an intelligent machine that could not be distinguished from a human interlocutor[31] was a primary source of inspiration for this variety of AI research. In the context of that project, as the functionality of the system as

---

27 Dreyfus (1979/1992).

28 However, for a relevant overview of social perspectives and consequences of AI research, see Schoppers (1986).

29 See Dreyfus (1979/1992).

30 Fetzer (1990), p. 20.

31 Turing (1950); reproduced in this volume as Ch. 2.

an intelligent and communicative automaton incorporates the means by which actual exchange is to progress, the concept of an application interface falls away. Further, nor are the specific user and interactivity particularly significant, as questions about how such a system gains independent access to the human world and represents the knowledge found in that world are more significant. However, thinking of the future, complex forms of representation and more encompassing forms of interaction are central, as optimal results in this grain of AI research would be systems capable of forms of discourse in which both contextual and metacommunicational meanings are correctly discerned and understood. Thus far, despite the optimism of early AI research, this goal has proven decidedly difficult to achieve.

Systems for playing professional-level chess can be seen as a significant, though less ambitious pursuit. Turing suggested chess as a means of demonstrating programmed intelligence,[32] and the victory of Deep Blue over Grand Master Garry Kasparov in May 1997 is a landmark for this tradition of development research. Though Deep Blue is not a thinking machine *per se*, it commands the brute capacity for calculating and evaluating combinations of moves in accordance with previously established algorithms. These algorithms represent the applied intelligence and experience of the team of designers and engineers who created the software. The critical argument points out that Deep Blue may win chess games against the best human player, but computers, in their current form, would, of course, never be able to invent the game of chess. That which is missing is the—thus far—exclusively human capacity to generate new symbols and systems for relating them. Though Deep Blue produced moves which chess experts admire for their subtlety, the system is still bound to the conceptual framework of human, programmed interaction described above. Beyond its extraordinary computational power, the meanings engendered by the system are inherently related to the intelligence of its designers.

Another form of research stemming from AI is the development of software agents. This research exemplifies an area that may usefully inform the prognostic dimension of computer media studies. In the mid-1950s John McCarthy and Oliver G. Selfridge at MIT began working on the concept of intelligent agents.[33] These researchers were thinking about systems that, given a goal, would pursue it until they were stuck, whereupon they would ask advice, which would be given by humans. They would learn from these inputs and continue their activity. Such agents may one day become ultimate 'go-fers' in the badlands of immense quantities of information, not only surpassing the organizational and associational capacities of Vannevar Bush's Memex,[34] but also providing means for sophisticated, automatic queries in response to peoples' pragmatic needs. Agent software may be a harbinger of a future computational paradigm, in part, because of the relative independence from the specific knowledge and intentions of the designer and a heightened capacity to respond to the context of use. The range of topical and

---

32 For historical context and further description, see p. 10, in this volume.

33 For further description, see Licklider and Taylor (1968), reproduced in this volume as Ch. 5, and Kay (1984), reproduced in this volume as Ch. 8.

34 Bush (1945); reproduced in this volume as Ch. 1.

interactive possibilities available under the agent model will be significantly less limited than at the present time. The realization of sophisticated, general, agent software will mark a transition towards computing as *automated, pragmatic* knowledge processing. One aspect of agent software, the ability to 'learn', is already exemplified in a number of real-world applications. These include applications of neural networks, like robot motion control systems, software for the recognition of characters, handwriting, and physical features, as well as systems for textual and linguistic analysis. These applications display a form of 'experience' in that they become more 'knowledgeable' through their processing of feedback—responding to data and input encountered in use over time. The representation of experience over time is a fundamental step towards the realization of agent software. Within the prototype of interaction diagrammed in Figure 2 above, such 'soft robots' may be able to carry out a limited form of self-objectifying discourse. In contemporary interface discourse, a self-objectifying element can only be attributed to the trace of remote designers' intelligence represented via fixed structures of meaning and action available to the user in reception. The model of an interactive agent—insofar as it is able to 'realize' that it is 'stuck', and formulate intelligent questions, seek advice, and 'learn' from the responses it receives—implies a capacity to objectify itself in a significant degree, as well as to understand the individual interests and idiosyncrasies of a human (or non-human) interlocutor.[35] In the future, with such agent software, users may come to interact with 'knowledgeable' and 'interested' systems designed to display a degree of pragmatic understanding in communicative exchange.[36] As can be imagined, a limited ability automatically to appreciate the needs of users will represent a significantly greater degree of interactivity than that we experience today. In this regard, the field of AI is one that draws the development of new possibilities of interactivity forward, as it contributes significant technical and conceptual knowledge for advancing the sophistication of computers as knowledge processors.

HCI   With a specific relevance to the current state of popular computing, Human Computer Interaction is a field concerned with the optimization of interface semantics and physical methods of input and output. Much HCI research is focused on modelling and developing systems of interface discourse optimized for the perceptual, cognitive, and responsive capacities of human operators. Research in HCI is often concerned with the performative limits of the human organism and human intelligence. Mission critical systems or computer-controlled systems in which public safety is at significant risk, such as those used in aircraft and nuclear power plant control, are examples of applications addressed in this research. HCI is also concerned with a range of other, less critical application forms; however, the tendency towards engineering solutions and quantitative analyses has been consistent.

In terms of its concept of the user, perceptive and cognitive processes of reception have the been the subject of research in cognitive engineering and

---

35 For a more specific elaboration, see Mayer (1998a).

36 For illustrative, speculative examples of personal uses for such resources, see Licklider and Taylor (1968), reproduced in this volume as Ch. 5, and Negroponte (1995).

cognitive modelling.[37] The prevailing approach to interaction in cognitive HCI research is succinctly summarized by Phyllis Reisner: 'the area of study in the field of human-computer interaction . . . is not the *interaction* of humans and computers. The name is misleading. We already know what the computer will do. It will do whatever it has been programmed to do. The behavior of the human is our chief concern.'[38] In this conception, the user is the element in a system that introduces uncertainty. This research strives to reduce the apparent randomness of this human element. Thus, interfaces are systems to be optimized to the physical and cognitive capacities of human operators.

Certain forms of research in HCI that are more focused on group and organizational activity have been particularly inspired by Douglas Engelbart's program for Augmentation Research.[39] Augmentation Research played a key role in developing prototypical forms of computer media during the 1960s and the 1970s.[40] Since Augmentation Research is focused on extending the capacities of the human intellect and the experience of computing, its approach was centred on the contextual and social uses of knowledge and communication. The purpose of this research was the development of features and applications that extend the capacities of people to create, think, and communicate with and via computers.[41] This research tradition stands in contrast to forms of HCI research that focus on cognitive analyses. Augmentation Research aimed to develop more-effective means for people to work with and create new knowledge. One of the basic theses of this research is that matching the tools with which we work with knowledge of how we work represents a significant advance in our intellectual capacities with respect to computers.[42] Parallel to the epochal consequences of the invention of the Gutenberg press, a corollary of this is that if such tools become widespread, then new systems of working with knowledge effectively alter cultural formations and society as a whole. As development research, this tradition contributed a number of initial versions of the 'user-friendly' features of contemporary personal computers, like the mouse pointing device, the Graphic User Interface (GUI), and composite documents, as well as the forerunners of a number of standard application types like text, data, and graphics editors.[43] Research that has followed in this vein has contributed to a wide range of concepts and techniques, including systems of interface metaphors, forms of direct manipulation, GUI elements, systems of standards for interface graphics and handling features, task analysis, development tools, groupware, multimedia, and research on room-sized and immersive interfaces, to name a few areas.[44] In effect, researchers in this tradition began the process of

---

37 Card (1983), Norman (1986), Norman (1987), Carroll (1987), Booth (1989).

38 Reisner (1987), 337. (Italics in original.)

39 Baecker (1995), 41.

40 For historical context and further description, see pp. 16–17, in this volume as well as Engelbart (1963), reproduced in this volume as Ch. 4.

41 Ibid.

42 Ibid.

43 Engelbart (1988).

44 Baecker (1995), Dix (1993), Laurel (1990), Preece (1994).

conceptual refinement and technical development that underlie the technologies and techniques of contemporary computer media. HCI, and Augmentation Research before it, are areas of computer science explicitly concerned with the user–interface nexus. Their analyses of 'usability' and the user's experience and performance with respect to the computer have played a central role in developing the applications and devices known and used today. As forms of applied science, they have made direct contributions to the development of forms of interactivity experienced now.

Media Studies   Though HCI provides insights into specific concepts and technologies which underlie the 'personal computer revolution', it does not offer the level of social and cultural analysis which Media Studies brings to bear. As a multidisciplinary field that draws upon the humanities as well as the social sciences, Media Studies offers an integrative theoretical framework for the study of discourses, practices, and institutions, through which to study the reception and interpretation of computer media in analyses of these media forms as significant social phenomena. Media, communication, and mass society theory, as well as theories of meaning, culture, and ideology are all areas of particular concern for Media Studies. This research is primarily centred on the study of public communication, including the press, film, television, and radio, as well as forms of popular culture, like theatre, printed serials, music, comics, posters, and signage. In that Media Studies draws theoretical and methodological inspiration from anthropology, cultural studies, ethnography, history, linguistics, literary studies, philosophy, psychology, and sociology, research in this tradition is explicitly concerned with culture and society. In general, Media theory helps us understand the historical nature of forms of public communication as well as elements of the social construction of meaning in everyday contexts. On the one hand, it is a generalist, historical theory of consciousness vis-à-vis means of representation.[45] On the other hand it is a specifically political theory that pursues the ideological relationship between knowledge, power, and economic resources in society.[46] From the perspective of Media Studies, the production and reproduction of meaning, discourse, and culture are inherent, central purposes of communicative exchanges in face-to-face contexts as well as in mediated, often diffuse, forms of interaction. Interaction, from this point of view, relates users, media, and society, as analytical categories, in a diverse array of exchanges in daily life.

Media Studies, as a tradition of research concerned with the nature of communication in society, is also significant for computer media studies. Its discursive conception of meaning and culture,[47] its tradition of audience research, its stratified model of the levels of communication in society,[48] as well as its empirical methods all offer possibilities for formalizing understandings of the means by which computer media impact upon the circulation of

45 McLuhan (1964), McLuhan and McLuhan (1988), Ong (1982), Watzlawick (1976).

46 Innis (1972), Fiske (1987), McLuhan (1962), Williams (1974).

47 Barthes (1957 / 1972), Fiske (1987).

48 McQuail (1994).

meaning in society.[49] Furthermore, as a field of humanistic research, it offers possibilities for historical analyses of these forms that may help correlate new forms of representation and cultural change.[50] In addition, reception analytical and ethnographic methods developed in relation to the study of mediated communication in other contexts[51] may also be applied to the production and reception of computer media forms.[52] And, with respect to existing media forms, media practices, and media institutions, including sources of content and policy,[53] Media Studies offers possibilities for analysing the impact of existing and new forms of computer media on traditional configurations. Both contextualizing the user–interface nexus in analysis and referring beyond it, with its focal centre on the social construction of meaning, Media Studies offers significant resources for the analysis of computer media as discursive social phenomena.

Conclusion   In his conclusion to *Turing's Man*, Jay David Bolter suggests that in our further development of computers we pursue 'synthetic intelligence' and 'tools for the creative interaction of humans and computers'.[54] The framework for the further study of computer media suggested here responds to these goals. The possibilities of future forms of computer media are, in principle, quite open. We see this in the rapid proliferation of new forms, as well as the malleability of these forms demonstrated in the general trend towards integration in technologies, content, and institutional constellations, for which the expression 'convergence' is a common label. Research on computer media has a prognostic role to play in this regard. Developing theoretical descriptions and empirical analyses of computer media-related phenomena is the task which scholars and writers face in developing this role and furthering the development of this emerging field. With respect to the integration of theories, concepts, and analyses from AI, HCI, and Media Studies, the user–interface nexus can be seen as a conceptual bridge in computer media studies. On the one hand, research and concepts from HCI and AI inscribe a world of development research that focuses upon both the production of products reflecting contemporary standards of interactivity and ideas and concepts for future advances. On the other hand, Media Studies provides a theoretical framework for the analysis of the discursive social and cultural world within which our understandings and practices with respect to these media forms are contextualized. The conception of Computer Media Studies offered here proposes that the domains of research inscribed by HCI, AI, and Media Studies be correlated through systematic theoretical, empirical, and prognostic analyses that contribute to our understanding of these media

---

49 For examples, see Jensen (1993) and Jones (1995), reproduced in this volume as Chs. 11 and 13 respectively.

50 McLuhan (1964). Also, see Finnemann (1997), reproduced as Ch. 9 in this volume.

51 Ang (1991), Lull (1990), Morley (1980).

52 Mayer (1996 and 1998, b).

53 Innis (1972).

54 Bolter (1984), 238.

forms, their cultural and social implications, and expectations for their
further development.

References IEN ANG, *Desperately Seeking the Audience* (London: Routledge, 1991).

PETER BØGH ANDERSEN, *A Theory of Computer Semiotics* (Cambridge: Cambridge
University Press, 1990).

RONALD M. BAECKER, *et al.*, eds., *Readings in Human-Computer Interaction: Toward the
Year 2000* (San Francisco: Morgan Kaufmann Publishers, Inc., 1995).

ROLAND BARTHES, *Mythologies* (New York: Noonday Press, 1957 / 1972).

GREGORY BATESON, 'A Theory of Play and Fantasy', in *Semiotics: An Introductory
Anthology*, ed. Robert E. Innis, Advances in Semiotics (Bloomington, Ind.: Indiana
University Press, 1985), 129–144.

JAY DAVID BOLTER, *Turing's Man: Western Culture in the Computer Age* (Chapel Hill:
University of North Carolina Press, 1984).

PAUL A. BOOTH, 'Cognitive Models in Human Computer Interaction,' in *An
Introduction to Human-Computer Interaction*, ed. Paul A. Booth (Hillsdale, NJ:
Lawrence Erlbaum Associates, Publishers, 1989).

VANNEVAR BUSH, 'As We May Think,' *Atlantic Monthly*, no. 176 (1945), 101–8.

STUART K. CARD, THOMAS P MORAN, and ALLEN NEWELL, *The Psychology of Human-
Computer Interaction* (Hillsdale, NJ: Lawrence Erlbaum Associates, 1983).

JOHN M. CARROLL, ed., *Interfacing Thought: Cognitive Aspects of Human-Computer
Interaction* (Cambridge, Mass.: MIT Press, 1987).

JOHN DECEMBER, 'Units of Analysis for Internet Communication,' *Journal of Computer
Mediated Communication*, 1, no. 4 (1995), 14–38.

ALAN DIX, *et al.*, *Human-Computer Interaction* (London: Prentice Hall, 1993).

HUBERT L. DREYFUS, *What Computers Still Can't Do: A Critique of Artificial Reason*
(Cambridge, Mass.: MIT Press, 1979 / 1992).

JEROME T. DURLAK, 'A Typology for Interactive Media,' in *Communication Yearbook
10*, ed. Margaret L. McLaughlin (London: Sage Publications, 1987), 743–57.

DOUGLAS C. ENGELBART, 'A Conceptual Framework for the Augmentation of Man's
Intellect', in *The Augmentation of Man's Intellect by Machine*, eds. Howerton and
Weeks. Vistas in Information, Vol. 1 Handling (Washington, DC: Spartan Books,
1963), 1–27.

—— 'The Augmented Knowledge Workshop', in *A History of Personal Workstations*,
ed. Adele Goldberg. ACM Press History Series (New York: ACM Press, 1988),
187–232.

JAMES H. FETZER, *Artificial Intelligence: It's Scope and Limits*, Studies in Cognitive
Systems, ed. James H. Fetzer (London: Kluwer Academic Publishers, 1990).

NIELS OLE FINNEMANN, *Tanke, Sprog og Maskine: En Teoretisk Analyse af Computerens
Symbolske Egenskaber [Thought, Language and Machine: A Theoretical Analysis of the
Computer's Symbolic Properties]* (Copenhagen: Akademisk Forlag, 1994).

—— 'Modernity Modernised—The Cultural Impact of Computerisation', Center for
Cultural Research—University of Aarhus, Aarhus, Denmark, 50–97, 1997.

JOHN FISKE, *Television Culture* (London: Routledge, 1987).

FRED INGLIS, *Media Theory: An Introduction* (Oxford: Basil Blackwell, 1990).

HAROLD INNIS, *Empire and Communications* (Toronto: University of Toronto Press,
1972).

KLAUS BRUHN JENSEN, 'One Person, One Computer: The Social Construction of the
Personal Computer', in *The Computer as Medium*, eds. Peter Bøgh Andersen, Berit
Homqvist, and Jens F. Jensen. Learning in Doing: Social, Cognitive, and

Computational Perspectives (Cambridge: Cambridge University Press, 1993), 337–60.

—— *The Social Semiotics of Mass Communication* (London: Sage Publications, 1995).

—— 'From Interactivity, through Interaction, to Action: Constituents of a Model of Computer-Mediated Communication', in *Visual Media: History, Aesthetics and Reception*, ed. Ib Bondebjerg (London: Routledge, forthcoming).

STEVEN G. JONES, 'Understanding Community in the Information Age', in *CyberSociety: Computer Mediated Communication and Community*, ed. Steven G. Jones (London: Sage, 1995), 10–35.

ALAN KAY, 'Computer Software,' *Scientific American*, 251, no. 3 (1984), 41–7.

ALAN KAY and ADELE GOLDBERG, 'Personal Dynamic Media', in *A History of Personal Workstations*, ed. Adele Goldberg, ACM Press History Series (New York: ACM Press, 1988), 254–63.

BRENDA K. LAUREL, *The Art of Human Interface Design*, ed. B. Laurel (Reading, Mass.: Addison-Wesley, 1990).

—— *Computers as Theatre* (New York: Addison-Wesley, 1993).

JOHN C. R. LICKLIDER and ROBERT W. TAYLOR, 'The Computer as a Communication Device', *International Science and Technology* (April 1968), 21–31.

JAMES LULL, *Inside Family Viewing: Ethnographic Research on Television's Audiences* (London: Routledge, 1990).

PAUL A. MAYER, 'Representation and Action in the Reception of Myst: A Social Semiotic Approach to Computer Media,' *The Nordicom Review*, 1 (1996), 237–54.

—— 'Computer Mediated Interactivity: A Social Semiotic Perspective,' *Convergence*, 4, no. 3 (1998a), 40–58.

—— 'A Social Semiotic Approach to the Reception of Computer Media', Doctoral Dissertation, Department of Film and Media Studies, University of Copenhagen, (1998b).

MARSHALL MCLUHAN, *The Gutenberg Galaxy* (Toronto: University of Toronto Press, 1962).

—— *Understanding Media: The Extensions of Man*, 2nd edn. (New York: New American Library, 1964).

—— and ERIC MCLUHAN, *Laws of Media: The New Science* (London: University of Toronto, 1988).

DENIS MCQUAIL, *Mass Communication Theory: An Introduction*, 3rd edn. (London: Sage Publications, 1994).

DAVID MORLEY, *The 'Nationwide' Audience* (London: British Film Institute, 1980).

NICHOLAS NEGROPONTE, *Being Digital* (New York: Alfred A. Knopf, 1995).

DONALD. A. NORMAN, 'Cognitive Engineering', in *User Centered System Design: New Perspectives on Human-Computer Interaction*, eds. Donald A. Norman and Stephen W. Draper (Hillsdale, NJ: Lawrence Erlbaum Associates, 1986), 31–61.

—— 'Cognitive Engineering—Cognitive Science', in *Interfacing Thought: Cognitive Aspects of Human-Computer Interaction*, ed. J. M. Carroll (Cambridge, Mass.: MIT Press, 1987), 325–36.

—— *The Psychology of Everyday Things* (New York: Basic Books Mass., 1988).

WALTER J. ONG, *Orality and Literacy: The Technologizing of the Word* (London: Methuen, 1982).

JENNY PREECE, *et al.*, *Human-Computer Interaction* (Reading, Mass.: Addison-Wesley, 1994).

BYRON REEVES and CLIFFORD NASS, *The Media Equation: How People Treat Computers, Television, and New Media Like Real People and Places* (New York: Cambridge University Press, 1996).

PHYLLIS REISNER, 'Discussion: HCI, What Is It and What Research Is Needed', in *Interfacing Thought: Cognitive Aspects of Human-Computer Interaction*, ed. John M. Carroll (Cambridge, Mass.: MIT Press, 1987), 337–52.

M. J. SCHOPPERS, 'A Perspective on Artificial Intelligence in Society', *Communication*, 9 (1986), 195–227.

SHERRY TURKLE, *The Second Self: Computers and the Human Spirit* (New York: Simon and Schuster, 1984).

ALAN M. TURING, 'Computing Machinery and Intelligence', *Mind*, 59, no. 236 (1950), 433–60.

PAUL WATZLAWICK, *How Real is Real? Confusion, Disinformation, Communication* (New York: Vintage Books, 1976).

RAYMOND WILLIAMS, *Television: Technology and Cultural Form* (London: Fontana, 1974).

TERRY WINOGRAD, 'Toward Convivial Computing', in *The Computer Age: A Twenty-Year View*, eds. Michael L. Dertouzos and J. Moses (Cambridge, Mass.: MIT Press, 1980), 56–72.

Index

1984 194, 201
algorithmic procedure 40, 61, 142,
   156–7
Alto 19–20
   see also Dynabook
Analytic Engine 5–6, 41–2, 130
Apple Computer 192, 194, 196, 203,
   273, 278
   Macintosh 201, 267, 300
archive, the:
   encyclopedia 27, 34–5, 54, 109, 180,
      183
   global 147, 150, 152
   and indexing 32
   and technology 25–8, 65
   see also Memex; World Wide Web;
      Xanadu
ARPA (DARPA, DoD, Advanced
   Research Projects Agency) 106,
   274, 277, 303
   see also Internet
Artificial Intelligence (AI) 11, 13, 60–1,
   175, 321, 328–30, 333
Atari Computer 200, 278
Augmentation Research 11, 13, 16–18,
   72, 331
   capability repertory hierarchy 76–8,
      84–93
   classes of augmentation means 74
   conceptual framework 74–93
   H-LAM/T model 76–81, 80, 83,
      84–93

Babagge, C. 5, 25, 41, 130
   see also Analytic Engine; Difference
      Engine
Bateson, G. 129, 325
Billings, J. S. 6
binary notation 144, 146, 149
   see also information
Boole, G. 5
Bordewijk, J., and van Kaam, B. 162–3
Bulletin Board Systems (BBS's) 271–4
Bush, V. 11–13, 93, 153, 329
   see also Memex

calculating machinery 4, 5–10, 29–30,
   61, 63, 142
Carey, J. 171, 221–3, 226–7
Commodore Computer 275

communication:
   as creative 98
   computer-aided 95, 101–10, 147, 201
   face-to-face vs. telecommunication
      99, 109
   interpersonal 170, 172, 182
   and mental models 15, 98–100, 110,
      132
   as ritual 82–3, 221, 227, 326
   as transmission 97, 103, 221, 227, 325
   see also interaction
communication technology 162–75,
      182–5, 189, 193, 317, 320
   and culture 152–8, 219–27, 241–3,
      267–9, 295–6, 304–6, 313–18,
      320–1, 332–3
   and society 207–17
community, definitions of 228–9
   see also on-line community
computer:
   and aesthetics 209
   and business 200–3
   and children 20, 113, 116, 136–7, 202
   and democracy 201, 209, 216–17, 233
   digital, description of 40–1, 46
   and discrete state machines 42–4
   early visions 29–30
   and education 54–6, 113–17, 126–7,
      136, 202, 203, 209, 273
   facilitating thought 60, 62, 92, 201,
      298–9
   and generality of purpose 5–6, 7–9,
      21, 104, 118, 197, 204
   and home 197, 200–2
   as hypertext 294
   and inference 55–6, 64
   and intelligence 10–11, 37, 327
   as knowledge processor 320
   and language 55–6, 67–8
   as logic machine 8
   as medium xiii, 16, 98, 101, 113–19,
      125, 129–30, 142
   as medium, characteristics of 146–7,
      156–7, 297–8
   and memory 54, 65–6
   as metamedium xiii, 20, 112, 117,
      147, 320
   multi-access 94, 102–4
   as multi-semantic 145–7
   and notebook 54, 112

computer (*cont.*):
  and protean nature of 134–5
  real-time 62, 93
  and symbolic representation 142,
    146–7, 156–7, 296–8, 320–1
  and telecommunications 103, 105,
    107, 108, 193, 209, 223, 272–4
  and text 295–306
  as thinking machine 39
  as universal machine 42–4, 50,
    143–4
  and utopia 204
  see also algorithmic procedure;
    calculating machinery;
    simulation; software
computer games 178, 191, 193, 200,
  204, 274–6, 320
  see also *Myst*
computer literacy 136–7, 198
computer mediated communication
  (CMC) 168, 219–21, 326
  and authenticity 231
  and community 226–7
  and copyright 303
  and democracy 233
  and education 223
  and egalitarian ideals 242–3, 251–3,
    261–2
  and face-to-face interaction 232–5,
    244
  and 'flaming' 244, 247–8, 252, 254,
    256, 260, 262
  and gender imposters 247–8, 262,
    267–8
  and gendered discourse 241–63
  and organizational communication
    235–6
  and space 222, 224–5, 235
  see also on-line community
copyright 241
cyberspace 176, 207, 208, 214, 224–6,
  230, 247, 262, 320
  and body representation 282–7,
    289–90
  see also computer mediated
    communication; Gibson, W.;
    on-line community
Cyborg 267, 281, 286

Difference Engine 5–6
discourse, definition of 322
discourse analysis 193–4, 199, 204–5
  examples of 195–204, 243–63
Dynabook 19–21, 111–19, 320

e-mail 176, 181, 185, 222, 326

Eckert, J. P. Jr. 9
Engelbart, D. 13–14, 100, 109, 331
  see also Augmentation Research
ENIAC 9

General Problem Solver (GPS) 61
genre 152, 189, 317
Gibson, W. 176, 276–7, 279, 281, 283,
  287, 289
Gödels theorem 46
Goldberg, A. 20–1, 320
Graphic User Interface (GUI) 19,
  323–4, 331
  see also user interface design

Hollerith, H. 6–7, 29
Human Computer Interaction (HCI)
  11, 17, 168, 321, 330–3
HyperCard 300
hypermedia 18, 161, 301–2, 315
  see also hypertext; multimedia
hypertext 18, 120, 122–4, 127, 148, 180,
  192, 214, 315
  definition of 294
  reception of 304–6
  as textual form 298–301
  see also hypermedia; multimedia

information flow 163
  definition of 129
  and noise 150
  and notation 129, 142, 144–8, 151
  and society 153, 281–4
information society 189, 192, 198, 204,
  207, 214, 320
information superhighway 216, 219–20
intelligence 38–9, 72–3
  and amplification 79–80
  as embodied 55, 79
  and language 74, 87
  and pattern recognition 74
  see also thought
interaction 97, 110, 165–9
  definition of 325
  and society 332
interactivity 148, 160–2, 324–7
  comparison of media forms 175, 181,
    185–6
  cube model 184–5
  definitions of 165–85, 324
  and interpersonal communication
    170, 172, 233–4
  and responsiveness 174
  and subjectivity 325
interface:
  definitions of 130, 322

see also interface systems; user
   interface design
interface systems:
   audio 113
   direct manipulation 69–70, 74, 130
   display 14, 68–9, 94, 104–7, 113, 125,
      277–8
   font systems 114
   keyboard 30, 34–5, 77, 114
   man-artifact 81, 100
   and mechanics of form 74, 78–81,
      84–6, 95, 136
   mouse 72, 100, 113, 131, 134
   speech recognition 69
   see also virtual reality
International Business Machines (IBM)
   7, 13
   advertising 192, 194, 195–6, 199, 200,
      202, 203
Internet 164, 178, 215, 223, 243
   see also computer mediated
      communication; information
      superhighway; World Wide Web
intersubjectivity 193
intertextuality 190–1, 205

Kay, A. 19–21, 278, 320, 323, 327
   see also Dynabook; Reactive Engine
knowledge, and representation 67, 110,
   111–12, 147–8, 157, 297, 313
   see also archive; intelligence; thought

Lasswell, H. 195
Leibniz, G. W. 4–6, 9, 21, 24
Licklider, J. C. R. 13–16, 18, 93, 94, 103,
   219, 224, 229–30
Lincoln Laboratory, Lexington, Mass.
   68, 106
Lovelace, Lady A. 50, 130

McCarthy, J. 135, 329
McLuhan, M. 11, 152, 190, 224, 234,
   275, 307, 309–10, 314
Man:
   and electrical nervous system 36,
      42, 51
   modeled in Augmentation Research
      76–8
   see also intelligence; thought
man–computer symbiosis 59–61,
   63–4, 93
Marx, K. 155
mass communication 164, 167
   reception of 193
mass media 189
   see also media

Massachusetts Institute of Technology
   (MIT) 13, 70, 94, 104, 113, 135,
   277, 329
Mauchly, J. W. 9
media:
   audio recording 28, 98, 154, 180, 209,
      270
   essence of 112
   film 155, 180, 311–13
   historical development 153–8, 190,
      269–70, 294–6
   and para-social interaction 167,
      270–1
   photographic 25–7, 33, 148, 154, 211
   print 148, 154–5, 178, 180, 192, 295,
      304–5, 313, 331
   speech production 28, 69–70
   telephony 31, 99, 109, 154–5, 170,
      193, 210, 221, 222, 326
   videodisk 173
   see also communication technology;
      computer mediated
      communication; hypertext;
      multimedia; radio; television
media environment 189, 190, 192, 205
media studies 321, 332–3
Memex:
   mechanics of 33–4
   as medium 12–13, 35
   operation of 34–5, 329
   see also Bush, V.
modernity 153–6, 211–13
   and computing 156–8, 213–17
multimedia 161, 176, 302, 307
   industry 307–9
   and interactivity 315–16
   and representation 311–15, 316–18
Mumford, L. 189, 224
Myst 307–18

Nelson, T. H. 13, 18
   see also *Xanadu*
network:
   control of via messaging 105
   store and forward 102, 103, 105
   structure of 303

OLIVER ('on-line interactive vicarious
   expediter and responder') 109
on-line community 15–16, 103–6,
   108–10, 225–9, 270–4, 283–4
   and common interests 108, 110, 230
   historical development 269–80
   and netiquette 242, 256–60
   and representational features 267,
      269, 274, 279

on-line community (*cont.*):
  and society 110, 215, 228, 287–8
  as 'supercommunity' 104
  and utopianism 236–8
  see also computer mediated
    communication; cyberspace
Ong, W. J. 152, 190, 221

Palo Alto Research Center (Xerox
    PARC) 19–20, 111, 130, 134, 327

radio 154–5, 173, 178, 180–1, 210, 223,
    270
Reactive Engine (FLEX machine) 19,
    112
reality, social construction of 191, 221

Scheutz, P. G. 5
Selfridge, O. G. 109, 135, 329
simulation 111, 115–17, 130, 136, 142,
    203, 275
Sketchpad 14
SmallTalk 111, 113–14, 116–19
software:
  agent 135, 225, 329–30; *see also*
    OLIVER
  animation 115, 116, 117
  communication 106, 136
  database 7, 123–5, 134, 136, 202
  graphics, drawing, painting 115; see
    also *Sketchpad*
  and object-oriented design 114, 132;
    see also *SmallTalk*
  outline-processor 296
  and sequential programming 7–9,
    41–3, 66, 132
  spread-sheet 133–4, 136
  word-processor 114, 130, 136, 192,
    193, 197, 200, 202, 296
  see also computer games; e-mail;
    simulation
Sutherland, I. 14, 94, 277
  see also Sketchpad

Taylor, R. 14–16
technology:
  and extension of man's capacities
    11–12, 17, 36, 60
  see also Augmentation Research
television 26, 125, 151, 154–5, 167, 171,
    173, 175, 178, 180–1, 210, 216, 223,
    237, 302
Tesler, L. G. 134
thinking machines 10, 37

criticisms of 44–53
and chess 57, 329
and learning 50, 53–7
see also thought
thought:
  associative nature of 33
  concept and symbol manipulation
    81–4, 136–7
  and conjecture 44
  as integrally human 45
  see also intelligence
Turing, A. M. 7–11, 130, 142, 144,
    328–9
  and 'child-machine' 10, 54–7
  and 'computing machine' 7–9
  description of digital computer
    40–2, 46
  description of universal machine 44
  see also Universal Turing Machine

Universal Turing Machine 7–9, 144–6
user interface design:
  and context 136
  and metaphors 132
  and 'user illusion' 130–1, 327
  see also Graphic User Interface;
    interface systems; WYSIWYG
user-interface nexus 326, 327–8, 332,
    333

virtual body 285
  see also cyberspace, and body
    representation; Cyborg
virtual community 288
  see also on-line community
virtual environment, *see* cyberspace;
    virtual reality
virtual reality (VR) 152, 175, 181, 223,
    224, 227, 237, 269, 277, 279, 282–7
  see also cyberspace
virtual space 268
  see also virtual body
virtual systems 269
von Neumann, J. 7, 9

World Wide Web (WWW) 18, 161,
    164, 180, 183, 309
  see also hypertext; Memex; *Xanadu*
WYSIWYG ('what you *see* is what you
    get') 130, 132
  see also Graphic User Interface; user
    interface design

Xanadu 18–19